13th International Workshop on Tree Adjoining Grammars and Related Formalisms 2017 (TAG+13)

Umea, Sweden
4 – 6 September 2017

ISBN: 978-1-5108-4757-6

TAG+13

The 13th International Workshop on Tree Adjoining Grammars and Related Formalisms

Proceedings

September 4–6, 2017
Umeå, Sweden

Introduction

It is our pleasure to introduce the proceedings of the 13th International Workshop on Tree Adjoining Grammars and Related Formalisms, which will be held at Umeå University from September 4–6, 2017.

This year's meeting is special in at least two ways: it is the first workshop in the series to be held in Sweden, and the first one to be co-located with FSMNLP, the International Conference on Finite State Methods and Natural Language Processing. This co-location, which is manifested through joint tutorials, invited talks, and social events, provides an exciting opportunity for scientific exchange between the two research communities. The TAG+-specific program features 14 papers, which were selected from a pool of 21 submissions after a thorough peer review process.

We are deeply grateful to everybody who has been involved in the organization of this meeting: to our colleagues on the program committee for the time and effort that they put into the reviewing of the submissions; to our tutorial speakers Johanna Björklund, Laura Kallmeyer, Rainer Osswald, and Sylvain Pogodalla; to our invited speakers Ann Copestake and Gregory Kobele; to Min-Yen Kan for his help with the publishing of these proceedings in the ACL Anthology – and most of all to our local host, Frank Drewes, for welcoming us to Umeå and for the tremendous energy and work that he put into this project.

And now, we wish you a fruitful meeting!

Marco Kuhlmann and Tatjana Scheffler
TAG+13 Program Chairs

Program Chairs:

Marco Kuhlmann (Linköping University, Sweden)
Tatjana Scheffler (Potsdam University, Germany)

Local Chair:

Frank Drewes (Umeå University, Sweden)

Program Committee:

Daniel Bauer (Columbia University, USA)
Tilman Becker (DFKI GmbH, Germany)
Rajesh Bhatt (UMass Amherst, USA)
David Chiang (University of Notre Dame, USA)
Stephen Clark (University of Cambridge, UK)
Laurence Danlos (U. Paris 7, France)
Vera Demberg (Saarland University, Germany)
Frank Drewes (Umeå University, Sweden)
Robert Frank (Yale University, USA)
Claire Gardent (CNRS/LORIA Nancy, France)
Thomas Graf (Stony Brook University, USA)
Chung-Hye Han (Simon Fraser University, Canada)
Aravind Joshi (University of Pennsylvania, USA)
Laura Kallmeyer (Heinrich Heine University Düsseldorf, Germany)
Makoto Kanazawa (National Institute of Informatics, Japan)
Adam Lopez (University of Edinburgh, UK)
Andreas Maletti (Leipzig University, Germany)
Mark-Jan Nederhof (University of St Andrews, UK)
Sylvain Pogodalla (LORIA/INRIA Lorraine, France)
Owen Rambow (Columbia University, USA)
Sylvain Salvati (Université de Lille, France)
Matthew Stone (Rutgers, USA)
Dennis Ryan Storoshenko (University of Calgary, Canada)
Heiko Vogler (TU Dresden, Germany)
Luke Zettlemoyer (University of Washington, USA)

Invited Speakers:

Ann Copestake (University of Cambridge, UK)
Gregory Kobele (Leipzig University, Germany)

Tutorial Speakers:

Johanna Björklund (Umeå University, Sweden)
Laura Kallmeyer (Heinrich Heine University Düsseldorf, Germany)
Rainer Osswald (Heinrich Heine University Düsseldorf, Germany)
Sylvain Pogodalla (LORIA/INRIA Lorraine, France)

Table of Contents

A Feature Structure Algebra for FTAG
Alexander Koller 1

Parsing Minimalist Languages with Interpreted Regular Tree Grammars
Meaghan Fowlie and Alexander Koller 11

Depictives in English: An LTAG Approach
Benjamin Burkhardt, Timm Lichte and Laura Kallmeyer 21

Reflexives and Reciprocals in Synchronous Tree Adjoining Grammar
Cristina Aggazzotti and Stuart M. Shieber 31

Coordination in TAG without the Conjoin Operation
Chung-hye Han and Anoop Sarkar 43

Scope, Time, and Predicate Restriction in Blackfoot using MC-STAG
Dennis Ryan Storoshenko 53

Combining Predicate-Argument Structure and Operator Projection: Clause Structure in Role and Reference Grammar
Laura Kallmeyer and Rainer Osswald 61

Parsing with Dynamic Continuized CCG
Michael White, Simon Charlow, Jordan Needle and Dylan Bumford 71

Multiword Expression-Aware A∗ TAG Parsing Revisited
Jakub Waszczuk, Agata Savary and Yannick Parmentier 84

Single-Rooted DAGs in Regular DAG Languages: Parikh Image and Path Languages
Martin Berglund, Henrik Björklund and Frank Drewes 94

Contextual Hyperedge Replacement Grammars for Abstract Meaning Representations
Frank Drewes and Anna Jonsson 102

Transforming Dependency Structures to LTAG Derivation Trees
Caio Corro and Joseph Le Roux 112

Linguistically Rich Vector Representations of Supertags for TAG Parsing
Dan Friedman, Jungo Kasai, R. Thomas McCoy, Robert Frank, Forrest Davis and Owen Rambow . . 122

TAG Parser Evaluation using Textual Entailments
Pauli Xu, Robert Frank, Jungo Kasai and Owen Rambow 132

Program

Monday, September 4

08:30–09:00   Registration and Opening

Tutorials

09:00–10:30   *Minimization Techniques for Automata and Grammars*
Johanna Björklund

10:30–11:00   Coffee Break

11:00–12:30   *Abstract Categorial Grammars as a Model of the Syntax–Semantics Interface for TAG*
Sylvain Pogodalla

12:30–13:30   Lunch Break

13:30–15:00   *Syntax-Driven Semantic Frame Composition in Lexicalized Tree Adjoining Grammars*
Laura Kallmeyer and Rainer Osswald

15:00–15:30   Coffee Break

Paper Session 1

15:30–16:00   *A Feature Structure Algebra for FTAG*
Alexander Koller

16:00–16:30   *Parsing Minimalist Languages with Interpreted Regular Tree Grammars*
Meaghan Fowlie and Alexander Koller

Tuesday, September 5

Invited Talk

09:00–10:00   *Higher Order Structures in Minimalist Derivations*
Gregory Kobele

10:00–10:30   Coffee Break

Paper Session 2

10:30–11:00   *Depictives in English: An LTAG Approach*
Benjamin Burkhardt, Timm Lichte and Laura Kallmeyer

11:00–11:30   *Reflexives and Reciprocals in Synchronous Tree Adjoining Grammar*
Cristina Aggazzotti and Stuart M. Shieber

11:30–12:00   *Coordination in TAG without the Conjoin Operation*
Chung-hye Han and Anoop Sarkar

12:00–13:00   Lunch Break

Paper Session 3

13:00–13:30   *Scope, Time, and Predicate Restriction in Blackfoot using MC-STAG*
Dennis Ryan Storoshenko

13:30–14:00   *Combining Predicate-Argument Structure and Operator Projection: Clause Structure in Role and Reference Grammar*
Laura Kallmeyer and Rainer Osswald

14:00–14:30   *Parsing with Dynamic Continuized CCG*
Michael White, Simon Charlow, Jordan Needle and Dylan Bumford

14:30–15:00   Coffee Break

Paper Session 4

15:00–15:30   *Multiword Expression-Aware A∗ TAG Parsing Revisited*
Jakub Waszczuk, Agata Savary and Yannick Parmentier

15:30–16:00   *Single-Rooted DAGs in Regular DAG Languages: Parikh Image and Path Languages*
Martin Berglund, Henrik Björklund and Frank Drewes

16:00–16:30   *Contextual Hyperedge Replacement Grammars for Abstract Meaning Representations*
Frank Drewes and Anna Jonsson

Wednesday, September 6

    Invited Talk

09:00–10:00   *Dependency Semantics and Composition*
Ann Copestake

10:00–10:30   Coffee Break

    Paper Session 5

10:30–11:00   *Transforming Dependency Structures to LTAG Derivation Trees*
Caio Corro and Joseph Le Roux

11:00–11:30   *Linguistically Rich Vector Representations of Supertags for TAG Parsing*
Dan Friedman, Jungo Kasai, R. Thomas McCoy, Robert Frank, Forrest Davis and Owen Rambow

11:30–12:00   *TAG Parser Evaluation using Textual Entailments*
Pauli Xu, Robert Frank, Jungo Kasai and Owen Rambow

12:00–13:00   Closing and Lunch

A Feature Structure Algebra for FTAG

Alexander Koller
Saarland University
`koller@coli.uni-saarland.de`

Abstract

FTAG, the extension of TAG with feature structures, lags behind other feature-based grammar formalisms in the availability of efficient chart parsers. This is in part because of the complex interaction of adjunction and unification, which makes such parsers inconvenient to implement. We present a novel, simple algebra for feature structures and show how FTAG can be encoded as an Interpreted Regular Tree Grammar using this algebra. This yields a straightforward, efficient chart parsing algorithm for FTAG.

1 Introduction

Like many other grammar formalisms, tree-adjoining grammars (TAG) have been extended with feature structures to model linguistic phenomena such as agreement conveniently. The FTAG formalism of Vijay-Shanker and Joshi (1988) equips each node in each elementary tree with a "top" and "bottom" feature structure. These are unified with each other at the end of the derivation if no auxiliary tree is adjoined at this node; otherwise they are unified with feature structures from the root and foot node of such an auxiliary tree. FTAG has been used successfully in large-scale grammar engineering, such as in the XTAG grammar (XTAG Research Group, 2001).

One aspect in which FTAG has lagged behind other feature grammar formalisms, such as HPSG and LFG, is in parsing. Recent efficient parsers for TAG, such as MICA (Bangalore et al., 2009) and Alto (Koller and Kuhlmann, 2012; Groschwitz et al., 2016), do not support feature structures. The recent TuLiPA parser (Kallmeyer et al., 2010) does support feature structures in FTAG parsing, but can be inefficient in practice because it enumerates all TAG derivation trees and then checks each of them for feature structure violations individually, instead of checking features on the parse chart directly. On the theoretical side, Schmitz and Le Roux (2008) explain FTAG through a feature-based formalism for describing languages of derivation trees, with unclear implications for parsing efficiency. Overall, the sense is that because of the complex interaction of unification and adjunction in FTAG, implementing efficient FTAG parsers is uncomfortable and something that tends to get avoided.

In this paper, we offer a simple and modular approach to efficient parsing with FTAG. We encode an FTAG grammar into an Interpreted Regular Tree Grammar (IRTG, Koller and Kuhlmann (2011)) by extending the TAG-to-IRTG encoding of Koller and Kuhlmann (2012) with an additional interpretation into feature structures. This interpretation maps each derivation tree into a term over a novel algebra of feature structures, in a similar way as c-structures are mapped into f-structures in LFG (Kaplan and Bresnan, 1982). This term can be evaluated to a value in the algebra if and only if all unifications required by the grammar succeed. We then show how known algorithms for IRTG chart parsing – which can be efficient for TAG (Groschwitz et al., 2016) – extend naturally to FTAG parsing.

We offer a view on FTAG which brings it more in line with other feature-based grammar formalisms, in that the distinction between top and bottom feature structures is represented correctly, but requires no special treatment by the parser. This simplifies, for instance, the use of existing unification algorithms. At the same time, we offer a very general and modular approach to checking feature unification on a parse chart; no unpacking of the individual derivation trees is required in our algorithm. This approach generalizes straightfor-

Proceedings of the 13th International Workshop on Tree Adjoining Grammars and Related Formalisms (TAG+13), pages 1–10,
Umeå, Sweden, September 4–6, 2017. © 2017 Association for Computational Linguistics

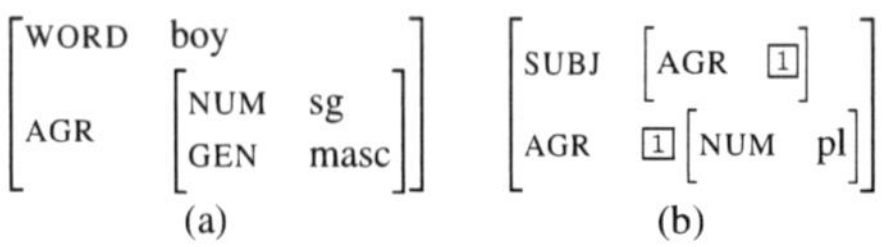

(a)   (b)

Figure 1: Two example feature structures.

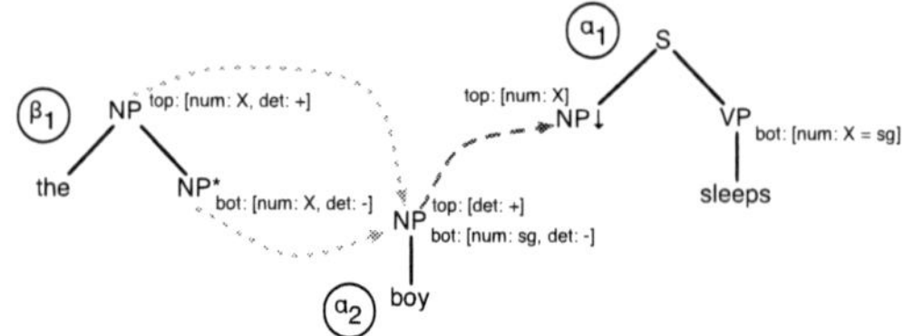

Figure 2: An example FTAG derivation.

wardly to other mechanisms for filtering derivation trees, as long as they can be expressed in terms of finite-state constraints on trees.

Plan of the paper. We will review FTAG in Section 2 and IRTGs and the TAG-to-IRTG encoding in Section 3. We will then define the feature structure algebra and show how it can be used to encode FTAG in Section 4. We show how to do efficient and modular chart parsing for FTAG in Section 5. Section 6 concludes.

2 TAG and feature structures

2.1 Feature structures

Feature structures (Shieber, 1986; Kasper and Rounds, 1986; Carpenter, 1992) are used in many grammar formalisms to represent grammatical information. Intuitively, a feature structure (FS) assigns values to a finite set of features; these values may either be atomic, or they may be feature structures themselves. For instance, the FS in Fig. 1a specifies that the WORD feature has the atomic value 'boy', and the value of the AGR feature is a feature structure with the features NUM and GEN.

Technically, feature structures represent directed, acyclic graphs in which both the top-level FS and all of the FSs it contains are nodes. If F has a feature FT, and the value of this feature in F is G, then there is an edge (with label FT) from the node F to the node G. We define a *feature path* to be a sequence $F_1.F_2. \ldots .F_n$ of features F_i. Then if F is a feature structure, we write $F.f_1.\ldots.f_n$ for feature *selection*, i.e. for the node in F that is reached by the given feature path. We define the *depth* of an FS as the length of the longest defined feature path.

As a special case, it can happen that the same node is reachable via two different feature paths, i.e. we have $F.p_1 = F.p_2$ for feature paths $p_1 \neq p_2$. This is called a *reentrancy* in F. We represent reentrancies in the attribute-value matrix notation of Fig. 1 by marking the endpoints of the reentrant feature paths with the same number. In Fig. 1b, the marker $\boxed{1}$ indicates that F.SUBJ.AGR

and F.AGR are the same node. Thus, we have F.SUBJ.AGR.NUM $=$ pl.

We say that the FS F *subsumes* the FS G if all the information that F specifies, including reentrancies, is also present in G. The *unification* $F \sqcup G$ of F and G is the least informative FS that is subsumed both by F and G. Not all FSs can be unified. For instance, the two example FSs in Fig. 1 cannot be unified because they specify contradictory values for the feature path AGR.NUM, so no feature structure can be subsumed by both.

2.2 Feature TAG

Vijay-Shanker and Joshi (1988) extend TAG with feature structures, obtaining Feature-Based TAG (FTAG). The core point about FTAG is that every node in every elementary tree is decorated with two feature structures (FSs) – one for the "top" half of the node and one for the "bottom" half. If no auxiliary tree is adjoined at a given node u, these two feature structures must be unified with each other. However, if an auxiliary tree β is adjoined, then the top FS of u will be unified with the top FS of the root of β, and the bottom FS of u will be unified with the bottom FS of the foot node. Finally, substitution unifies the top FSs of the substitution node and the root of the initial tree. This makes unification consistent with adjunction, and allows an elegant encoding of obligatory and selective adjunction constraints in terms of FSs.

FTAG assumes that the value of each feature in each top or bottom FS is an atomic value, ensuring that all FSs have depth one. This makes the set of possible FSs finite, and thus the expressive capacity of FTAG is the same as that of TAG without features.

An example derivation of FTAG is shown in Fig. 2. This derivation combines three elementary trees α_1, α_2, β_1 by substituting α_2 into the substitution node of α_1 and then adjoining β_1 into the root of α_2. Every node in these elementary trees is annotated with a top and bottom feature structure; feature structures whose value is $\top$, the trivial feature structure which subsumes all other feature structures, are not shown in the figure. The top and bottom FSs of the root of α_2 cannot be unified with each other because they require different values for the "det" feature; thus a derivation tree in which nothing is adjoined into this node would be ungrammatical. By adjoining β_1 into this node, we instead unify the top FS of α_2's root with the top FS of β_1's root, and the bottom FS of α_2's root with the bottom FS of β_1's foot node. Both unifications succeed.

FTAG requires that multiple occurrences of the same variable (such as X) within the FSs of the same elementary tree must be instantiated with the same value. Thus when the occurrence of X in the bottom FS of β_1's foot node is bound to 'sg', the occurrence of X in the top FS of β_1's root gets the value 'sg' too. Further unifications percolate this value into the occurrence of X in α_1, which is consistent with the requirement defined at α_1's V node. By contrast, an elementary tree for "boys" would assign 'pl' to the "num" feature at its root node, making this unification fail and establishing ungrammaticality of "boys sleeps".

The decision to assign feature structures to nodes (and not elementary trees), and to assign *two* of them to each node, is necessary to make unification consistent with adjunction. However, it makes implementing parsers inconvenient, because we do not even know what FSs need to be unified with each other before we have decided whether and what to adjoin at each node. One way to read this paper is as an illustration that these decisions are not so inextricably linked with each other as it may seem at first glance. Instead, unifications can simply be performed bottom-up at the level of the derivation tree, enabling efficient chart parsing.

We identify the nodes in an elementary tree α through their *node addresses*, i.e. words $\pi \in \mathbb{N}^*$ such that ϵ is the address of the root, and πk is the address of the k-th child of π. Given an elementary tree α in an FTAG grammar, we write $\text{top}_\alpha(\pi)$ for the top FS at the node π and $\text{bot}_\alpha(\pi)$ for the bottom FS. We combine the two into the feature structure

$$\phi_\alpha(\pi) = \begin{bmatrix} \text{TOP} & \text{top}_\alpha(\pi) \\ \text{BOT} & \text{bot}_\alpha(\pi) \end{bmatrix}$$

We drop the subscript α if the elementary tree is clear from the context.

3   Interpreted Regular Tree Grammars

We tackle FTAG parsing below by encoding it as an Interpreted Regular Tree Grammar (IRTG, Koller and Kuhlmann (2011)). IRTG is a grammar formalism in which a language of derivation trees is described using a *regular tree grammar* (RTG, (Comon et al., 2008)) or, equivalently, a *finite tree automaton*, and each derivation tree is then *interpreted* in one or more algebras. Different grammar formalisms can be encoded into IRTG by varying the algebras; for instance, (Koller and Kuhlmann, 2012) encoded TAG into IRTG by introducing two novel algebras for strings and trees.

An IRTG which encodes the TAG grammar underlying the derivation in Fig. 2 is shown in Fig. 3. The first column contains an RTG $\mathcal{G}$ which describes a language $L(\mathcal{G})$ of derivation trees. The RTG contains one rule for each elementary tree α in the TAG grammar, expanding a nonterminal symbol of the form X_S if α is an initial tree with root symbol X, or of the form X_A if α is an auxiliary tree (cf. Schmitz and Le Roux (2008)). Each rule also specifies the substitutions that must and the adjunctions that may take place at this elementary tree. Each of these nonterminals must be expanded by applying another RTG rule, corresponding to performing the respective substitution and adjunction. We can choose not to adjoin an auxiliary tree at a node where an adjunction could take place by expanding the nonterminal X_A with the rule nop_X. One derivation tree $t \in L(\mathcal{G})$ is shown in Fig. 4; note the obvious correspondence to the derivation tree underlying the TAG derivation in Fig. 2.

This derivation tree can now be mapped into a term over an algebra, and evaluated there into an object of this algebra. In general, an *algebra* over the signature Σ of operation symbols is a structure $\mathcal{A} = (A, \mathcal{I})$ consisting of a set A (the *domain* of $\mathcal{A}$) and an *interpretation function* $\mathcal{I}$. This function assigns to each operation symbol $f \in \Sigma$ of arity k a function $\mathcal{I}(f)$ that takes k arguments from A and returns a value in A. Thus, a *term* τ over the signature Σ can be evaluated to a value $[\![\tau]\!]$ recursively by letting $[\![f(\tau_1, \ldots, \tau_k)]\!] = \mathcal{I}(f)([\![\tau_1]\!], \ldots, [\![\tau_k]\!])$.

The second column of Fig. 3 shows how the example IRTG interprets derivation trees into strings. This assumes the TAG string algebra $\mathcal{A}_s = (A_s, \mathcal{I}_s)$ defined by Koller and Kuhlmann (2012). The values A_s of this algebra are all strings and

RTG rule	string homomorphism h_s	FS homomorphism h_F
$S_S \to \alpha_1(NP_S, S_A, VP_A)$	$\mathsf{wrap21}(x_2, \mathsf{conc11}(x_1, \mathsf{wrap21}(x_3, \mathsf{sleeps})))$	$\mathsf{unify}(c_{\alpha_1}, \mathsf{embi}_1(x_1), \mathsf{emba}_\epsilon(x_2), \mathsf{emba}_2(x_3))$
$NP_S \to \alpha_2(NP_A)$	$\mathsf{wrap21}(x_1, \mathsf{boy})$	$\mathsf{unify}(c_{\alpha_2}, \mathsf{emba}_\epsilon(x_1))$
$NP_A \to \beta_1(NP_A)$	$\mathsf{wrap21}(x_1, \mathsf{conc12}(\mathsf{the}, *))$	$\mathsf{unify}(c_{\beta_1}, \mathsf{emba}_\epsilon(x_1))$
$X_A \to \mathsf{nop}_X$	$*$	c_{nop}

Figure 3: The FTAG from Fig. 2, encoded as an IRTG. There is a nop rule for each nonterminal $X \in \{S, VP, NP\}$.

string pairs over a given alphabet; in the example, the alphabet contains the words "sleeps", "boy", and "the". The signature Δ_s contains a constant for each of these words, a constant * denoting the pair (ϵ, ϵ) of empty strings, plus a number of binary operations which combine strings and string pairs. In particular, $\mathcal{I}_s(\mathsf{conc11})$ is a function which takes two strings as arguments and concatenates them; $\mathcal{I}_s(\mathsf{conc12})$ takes a string v and a string pair (w_1, w_2) as arguments and concatenates them into the string pair (vw_1, w_2); and $\mathcal{I}_s(\mathsf{wrap21})$ takes a string pair (v_1, v_2) and a string w as arguments, and then "wraps" the string pair around the string, yielding the string v_1wv_2. Now the IRTG $\mathcal{G}$ has an *interpretation* $(h_s, \mathcal{A}_s)$. A derivation tree t is recursively mapped to a term $h_s(t)$ by the tree homomorphism h_s, and then $h_s(t)$ is evaluated to a value $[\![h_s(t)]\!]$ in $\mathcal{A}_s$. In this way, t describes a string. For instance, for the derivation tree t in Fig. 4, we obtain $[\![h_s(t)]\!] = $ "the boy sleeps".

In general, an IRTG $\mathbb{G} = (\mathcal{G}, (h_1, \mathcal{A}_1), \ldots, (h_n, \mathcal{A}_n))$ consists of an RTG $\mathcal{G}$ and $n \geq 1$ interpretations. It describes the language $L(\mathbb{G}) = \{([\![h_1(t)]\!], \ldots, [\![h_n(t)]\!]) \mid t \in L(\mathcal{G})\}$. Thus, if we consider only the first and second column in the example grammar in Fig. 3, we have a grammar which describes a language of strings, and captures precisely the TAG part of the grammar underlying Fig. 2. The third column is for the feature structure interpretation we define below, and extends the IRTG into an encoding of an FTAG grammar.

4 A feature structure algebra for FTAG

As the grammar in Fig. 3 illustrates, the basic intuition of the TAG-to-IRTG encoding is to traverse the derivation tree bottom-up, calculating an interpretation for each node in the derivation tree. Each rule of the IRTG specifies the function by which the interpretation for the parent is calculated from those of the children; so for instance, the second column of Fig. 3 expresses for each el-

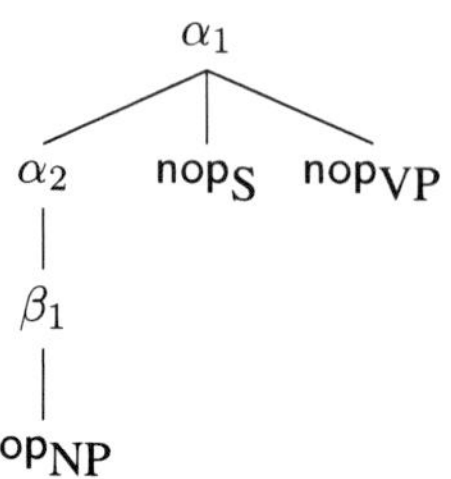

Figure 4: Derivation tree of the IRTG in Fig. 3, representing the (F)TAG derivation of Fig. 2.

ementary tree of the TAG grammar how it combines the strings of its children with each other.

We will follow the same intuition here and specify how the feature structure for a subtree of the derivation tree is computed out of the FSs of its parts. We will first introduce an algebra $\mathbb{F}$ for feature structures, with novel operations that are suitable for FTAG, and then show how an FTAG can be converted into an IRTG over this algebra.

4.1 A feature structure algebra

We define an algebra $\mathbb{F} = (\mathcal{F}, \mathcal{I})$ consisting of a set $\mathcal{F}$ of feature structures and an interpretation function $\mathcal{I}$. We let $\mathcal{F}$ contain all feature structures whose feature paths have the form $\pi\ tb\ f$, where $\pi \in \mathbb{N}^* \cup \{\mathrm{RT}, \mathrm{FT}\}$ is either a node address in an elementary tree or a special feature for the root or foot node, respectively; $tb \in \{\mathrm{TOP}, \mathrm{BOT}\}$; and f is a feature from an FTAG grammar, as in Section 2. The value reached under each feature path is either an atomic value, such as 'sg', or the placeholder $\top$, which unifies with any atomic value. We assume that every feature structure in $\mathcal{F}$ contains a RT feature; it may or may not contain a FT feature as well.

We define $\mathcal{I}$ to provide interpretations for the following four classes of function symbols.

- Any *constant* c is interpreted as a feature structure $\mathcal{I}(c) \in \mathcal{F}$. The construction in Section 4.2 will yield a finite set of feature structures $F \in \mathcal{F}$, one for each elementary tree. We assume that $\mathbb{F}$ has a constant c_F with $\mathcal{I}(c_F) = F$ for each of these.

- For any path $\pi \in \mathbb{N}^*$, we have a function symbol embi_π for *initial-tree embedding*. Given a feature structure $F \in \mathcal{F}$, we let $\mathcal{I}(\mathsf{embi}_\pi) = \mathrm{EI}_\pi$ with $\mathrm{EI}_\pi(F) = [\pi\ F.\mathrm{RT}]$.

- For any path $\pi \in \mathbb{N}^*$, we have a function symbol emba_π for *auxiliary-tree embedding*. Given a feature structure $F \in \mathcal{F}$, we let $\mathcal{I}(\mathsf{emba}_\pi) = \mathrm{EA}_\pi$ with

$$\mathrm{EA}_\pi(F) = \left[\pi \begin{array}{ll} \mathrm{TOP} & F.\mathrm{RT}.\mathrm{TOP} \\ \mathrm{BOT} & F.\mathrm{FT}.\mathrm{BOT} \end{array}\right]$$

- The binary function symbol unify represents unification of two feature structures. For any two arguments $F, G \in \mathcal{F}$, we let $\mathcal{I}(\mathsf{unify})(F, G) = F \sqcup G$ if F and G can be unified; otherwise $\mathcal{I}(\mathsf{unify})(F, G)$ is undefined.

Note that $\mathbb{F}$ is a partial algebra, in that not every term over the algebra has a value. This happens in particular if the unify operation attempts to unify two feature structures which cannot be unified. We say that $[\![t]\!]$ is undefined in such a case.

4.2 Encoding FTAG with the feature structure algebra

We will now use this algebra to encode arbitrary FTAG grammars into IRTGs. We extend the TAG-to-IRTG encoding of Koller and Kuhlmann (2012) with an additional interpretation $(h_F, \mathbb{F})$ into the feature structure algebra (see the third column of Fig. 3). This means that we need to define, for each elementary tree α in the FTAG grammar, an image $h_F(\alpha)$ for the homomorphism into the FS algebra, which specifies how α combines the FSs of its children.

Let us say that the elementary tree α was encoded into an IRTG rule $N \rightarrow \alpha(N_S^{(1)}, \ldots, N_S^{(k)}, N_A^{(k+1)}, \ldots N_A^{(n)})$ by the conversion in Section 3, with k child nonterminals for substitution and $n - k$ for adjunction. The homomorphic image $h_F(\alpha)$ will select the RT and FT entries of the FSs for the child nonterminals and unify them with one large FS $T(\alpha)$ representing the functional behavior of α; we will define $T(\alpha)$ below. Let c_α be the constant with $\mathcal{I}(c_\alpha) = T(\alpha)$

(assumed to exist above). Then we let

$$\begin{aligned} h_F(\alpha) = \quad & \mathsf{unify}(c_\alpha, \\ & \mathsf{embi}_{\pi_1}(X_1), \ldots, \mathsf{embi}_{\pi_k}(X_k), \\ & \mathsf{emba}_{\pi_{k+1}}(X_{k+1}), \ldots, \mathsf{emba}_{\pi_n}(X_n)), \end{aligned}$$

where we abbreviate the $n - 1$ binary unify operations that are needed to combine the arguments by simply writing unify once.

We construct $T(\alpha) = F(\alpha) \sqcup I(\alpha) \sqcup N(\alpha) \sqcup R(\alpha)$ by unifying four smaller feature structures, each of which encodes one specific aspect of α:

1. A feature structure $F(\alpha)$ which captures the top and bottom feature structures at each node of α. For any node π of α, $F(\alpha)$ contains an entry $[\pi\ \phi_\alpha(\pi)]$.

2. A feature structure $I(\alpha)$ which enforces the coindexations for features in α that share variables. If a variable X occurs both at feature f_1 in the tb_1 feature structure of the node π_1 (where $tb_1 \in \{\mathrm{TOP}, \mathrm{BOT}\}$) and at feature f_2 in the tb_2 FS of the node π_2, we let

$$\left[\begin{array}{l} \pi_1 \left[tb_1 \left[f_1 \ \boxed{1}\right]\right] \\ \pi_2 \left[tb_2 \left[f_2 \ \boxed{1}\right]\right] \end{array}\right]$$

subsume $I(\alpha)$.

3. A feature structure $N(\alpha)$ which unifies the top and bottom feature structures at nodes where nothing can be adjoined. This includes all foot nodes, as well as all nodes explicitly marked with a null adjunction constraint. The IRTG rule contains no child nonterminal for adjoining at this node; thus without $N(\alpha)$, the top and bottom FSs at these nodes would not get unified at all. For all such nodes π, we let

$$\left[\pi \begin{array}{ll} \mathrm{TOP} & \boxed{1} \\ \mathrm{BOT} & \boxed{1} \end{array}\right]$$

subsume $N(\alpha)$. Note that substitution nodes do *not* generate entries in $N(\alpha)$, as this would unify the top and bottom FS of the root of an initial tree substituted there.

4. A feature structure $R(\alpha)$ which makes the correct sub-feature-structures accessible under the RT and FT features. If α is an initial

$$\mathcal{I}(c_{\alpha_1}) = T(\alpha_1) \qquad \mathcal{I}(c_{\alpha_2}) = T(\alpha_2) \qquad \mathcal{I}(c_{\beta_1}) = T(\beta_1)$$

$$
\begin{bmatrix}
\epsilon & \boxed{1}\begin{bmatrix}\text{TOP} & \top \\ \text{BOT} & \top\end{bmatrix} \\
1 & \begin{bmatrix}\text{TOP} & [\text{NUM}\ \boxed{2}] \\ \text{BOT} & \top\end{bmatrix} \\
2 & \begin{bmatrix}\text{TOP} & \top \\ \text{BOT} & [\text{NUM}\ \boxed{2}\ \text{sg}]\end{bmatrix} \\
\text{RT} & \boxed{1}
\end{bmatrix}
\qquad
\begin{bmatrix}
\epsilon & \boxed{1}\begin{bmatrix}\text{TOP} & [\text{DET}\ +] \\ \text{BOT} & \begin{bmatrix}\text{NUM} & \text{sg} \\ \text{DET} & -\end{bmatrix}\end{bmatrix} \\
\text{RT} & \boxed{1}
\end{bmatrix}
\qquad
\begin{bmatrix}
\epsilon & \boxed{1}\begin{bmatrix}\text{TOP} & \top \\ \text{BOT} & \begin{bmatrix}\text{DET} & + \\ \text{NUM} & \boxed{2}\end{bmatrix}\end{bmatrix} \\
2 & \boxed{3}\begin{bmatrix}\text{TOP} & \boxed{4}\begin{bmatrix}\text{DET} & - \\ \text{NUM} & \boxed{2}\end{bmatrix} \\ \text{BOT} & \boxed{4}\ \top\end{bmatrix} \\
\text{RT} & \boxed{1} \\
\text{FT} & \boxed{3}
\end{bmatrix}
$$

Figure 5: Feature structure encodings for the elementary trees in Fig. 2.

tree, we let

$$R(\alpha) = \begin{bmatrix}\text{RT} & \boxed{1} \\ \epsilon & \boxed{1}\end{bmatrix}$$

If α is an auxiliary tree with its foot node at address π, we let

$$R(\alpha) = \begin{bmatrix}\text{RT} & \boxed{1} \\ \text{FT} & \boxed{2} \\ \epsilon & \boxed{1} \\ \pi & \boxed{2}\end{bmatrix}$$

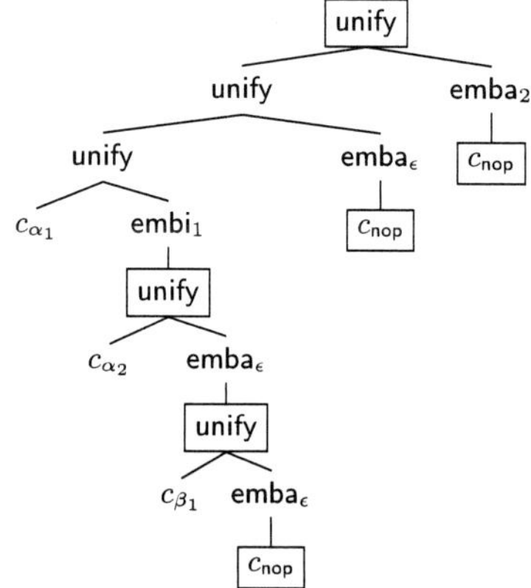

Figure 6: The term $h_F(t)$ over the feature structure algebra for the derivation tree t from Fig. 4.

In addition to rules that encode elementary trees, the IRTG also contains rules $X_A \to \text{nop}_X$ for every nonterminal symbol X. For these symbols, we let $h_F(\text{nop}_N) = c_{\text{nop}}$, with a constant c_{nop} which evaluates to the feature structure

$$\mathcal{I}(c_{\text{nop}}) = F_{\text{nop}} = \begin{bmatrix}\text{RT} & [\text{TOP}\ \boxed{1}] \\ \text{FT} & [\text{BOT}\ \boxed{1}]\end{bmatrix}$$

Thus, whenever we choose not to adjoin an auxiliary tree at a certain node, the IRTG encodes this with a nop operation. When the FS for this nop operation is unified into the parent FS using an emba_π operation, this unifies the top and bottom feature structures of π, as required in FTAG.

4.3 An example

We illustrate this construction with the example FTAG grammar from Fig. 2. The homomorphism h_F is shown in the third column of Fig. 3; it uses constants $c_{\alpha_1}, c_{\alpha_2}, c_{\beta_1}$, whose values are the FSs shown in Fig. 5.

Note first that all three FSs have one feature for each (non-lexical) node in the respective elementary tree, with a TOP and BOT feature nested below, representing the upper and lower feature structure of that node. This part of the feature structure is contributed by $F(\alpha)$. Any two occurrences of the same variable are coindexed through $I(\alpha)$; see e.g. the index $\boxed{2}$ in $T(\alpha_1)$ and the index $\boxed{2}$ in $T(\beta_1)$.

Furthermore, all nodes where no adjunction can take place have had their top and bottom feature structure coindexed by $N(\alpha)$. The index $\boxed{4}$ for the foot node at position 2 in β_1 was introduced like this. Finally, all three FSs have a RT feature, contributed by $R(\alpha)$ and coindexed with the ϵ feature for the root node of the elementary tree. Because β_1 is an auxiliary tree, $T(\beta_1)$ also has a FT feature, coindexed with the foot node at position 2.

Now consider the IRTG derivation tree t in Fig. 4, which encodes the TAG derivation in Fig. 2.

$$T(\alpha_1) \sqcup \left[1 \begin{bmatrix} \text{TOP} & \begin{bmatrix} \text{DET} & + \\ \text{NUM} & \boxed{2} \end{bmatrix} \\ \text{BOT} & \begin{bmatrix} \text{DET} & - \\ \text{NUM} & \boxed{2}\,\text{sg} \end{bmatrix} \end{bmatrix} \right] \sqcup \left[\epsilon \begin{bmatrix} \text{TOP} & \boxed{3} \\ \text{BOT} & \boxed{3} \end{bmatrix} \right] \sqcup \left[2 \begin{bmatrix} \text{TOP} & \boxed{4} \\ \text{BOT} & \boxed{4} \end{bmatrix} \right] = \begin{bmatrix} \epsilon & \boxed{1} \begin{bmatrix} \text{TOP} & \boxed{3} \\ \text{BOT} & \boxed{3} \end{bmatrix} \\[2ex] 1 & \begin{bmatrix} \text{TOP} & \begin{bmatrix} \text{DET} & + \\ \text{NUM} & \boxed{2} \end{bmatrix} \\ \text{BOT} & \begin{bmatrix} \text{DET} & - \\ \text{NUM} & \boxed{2}\,\text{sg} \end{bmatrix} \end{bmatrix} \\[2ex] 2 & \begin{bmatrix} \text{TOP} & \boxed{5} \\ \text{BOT} & \boxed{5}\begin{bmatrix} \text{NUM} & \boxed{2}\,\text{sg} \end{bmatrix} \end{bmatrix} \\[1ex] \text{RT} & \boxed{1} \end{bmatrix}$$

Figure 7: Computing the value $[\![h_F(t)]\!]$ of the term in Fig. 6.

The homomorphism h_F maps t to a term $h_F(t)$ over the FS algebra $\mathbb{F}$, shown in Fig. 6. We have marked with a box the root of each subtree $h_F(t')$ where t' is a subtree of t. Observe that each "block" between two boxed nodes has a consistent shape, in that it unifies c_α with a number of FSs, each of which is obtained by embedding the FS for a subtree into the features of $T(\alpha)$.

The term $h_F(t)$ can then be evaluated to a feature structure $[\![h_F(t)]\!]$ in the algebra $\mathbb{F}$. The last step of computing $[\![h_F(t)]\!]$ for the entire term $h_F(t)$ in Fig. 6 is shown in Fig. 7. We perform three unification operations, with the first argument being $\mathcal{I}(c_{\alpha_1}) = T(\alpha_1)$ and the second being the value of the sub-derivation-tree $\alpha_2(\beta_1(\text{nop}_{\text{NP}}))$, embedded at the substitution node 1. The other two arguments come from the nop nodes, embedded at the appropriate features through emba_π operations. Notice that the top and bottom feature structures at 1 are not coindexed, because we adjoined β_1 into the root of α_2, and the top and bottom features are not coindexed in $T(\beta_1)$.

5 Parsing

We now turn to the issue of FTAG parsing. By encoding an FTAG grammar as an IRTG with an interpretation into the FS algebra, we can apply standard methods from IRTG parsing to FTAG parsing. We will first compute a parse chart for the input string while ignoring the feature structures, and then intersect it with an RTG that carries out the unifications.

The specific parsing problem we solve is as follows: Given an IRTG $\mathbb{G} = (\mathcal{G}, (h_s, \mathcal{A}_s), (h_F, \mathbb{F}))$ and an input string w, find a compact represen-

tation C_w of the set $\text{parses}(w) = \{t \in L(\mathcal{G}) \mid [\![h_s(t)]\!] = w$ and $[\![h_F(t)]\!]$ is defined$\}$ – that is, the derivation t must be grammatical according to $\mathcal{G}$; it must map to the input string under the string interpretation; and all unifications required by the feature structure interpretation succeed. We will represent this *parse chart* C_w as an RTG such that $L(C_w) = \text{parses}(w)$.

5.1 Parsing without feature structures

In a first step, we apply standard methods from IRTG parsing (Koller and Kuhlmann, 2011; Groschwitz et al., 2016) to obtain a parse chart of all grammatical derivation trees that interpret to w. We do this by computing a *decomposition grammar* D_w for w in the TAG string algebra – i.e., an RTG such that $L(D_w)$ is the set of all terms over the TAG string algebra that evaluate to w. We then look at the set $L_I = h_s^{-1}(L(D_w))$ of derivation trees t such that $h_s(t) \in L(D_w)$, i.e. of derivation trees that interpret to w. Because regular tree languages are closed under inverse tree homomorphisms (Comon et al., 2008), we can calculate an RTG I_w such that $L(I_w) = L_I$. Because regular tree languages are also closed under intersection, we can then intersect I_w with $\mathcal{G}$ to obtain an RTG C_w^0 such that $L(C_w^0) = \{t \in L(\mathcal{G}) \mid [\![h_s(t)]\!] = w\}$. We call C_w^0 the *pre-chart* for w.

Consider, by way of example, the pre-chart C_w^0 for the input string $w = $ "the boy sleeps" and our example grammar; see Koller and Kuhlmann (2012) for details. The nonterminals of C_w^0 are pairs of nonterminals of the derivation tree RTG $\mathcal{G}$ and nonterminals of I_w. Nonterminals of I_w of the form $i-k$ can derive terms which evaluate to the substring of w from position i to $k-1$; we write pairs of nonterminals N_s with such nonterminals as $[N_s, i{-}k]$. Nonterminals of I_w can also be of the form $(i{-}j, k{-}l)$, for terms which evaluate to a pair of substrings of w (from position i to $j-1$ and from k to $l-1$ respectively). We write pairs of nonterminals N_A with such nonterminals as $\langle N_a, i{-}j, k{-}l \rangle$. Note that a span $i{-}i$ represents an empty string at position i. Some of the rules in C_w^0 are as follows:

$$
\begin{aligned}
\langle \mathrm{NP}_A, 1{-}1, 3{-}3 \rangle &\rightarrow \mathsf{nop}_{\mathrm{NP}} \\
\langle \mathrm{NP}_A, 2{-}2, 3{-}3 \rangle &\rightarrow \mathsf{nop}_{\mathrm{NP}} \\
\langle \mathrm{NP}_A, 1{-}2, 3{-}3 \rangle &\rightarrow \beta_1(\langle \mathrm{NP}_A, 1{-}1, 3{-}3 \rangle) \\
[\mathrm{NP}_S, 2{-}3] &\rightarrow \alpha_2(\langle \mathrm{NP}_A, 2{-}2, 3{-}3 \rangle) \\
[\mathrm{NP}_S, 1{-}3] &\rightarrow \alpha_2(\langle \mathrm{NP}_A, 1{-}2, 3{-}3 \rangle)
\end{aligned}
$$

Using these rules, we can derive both the sub-derivation-tree $t_1 = \alpha_2(\mathsf{nop}_{\mathrm{NP}})$, which evaluates to the string "boy" (as an NP) on the string interpretation of the IRTG, and the sub-derivation-tree $t_2 = \alpha_2(\beta_1(\mathsf{nop}_{\mathrm{NP}}))$, which evaluates to "the boy". Notice that while both of these subtrees are allowed by the underlying TAG grammar, only $h_F(t_2)$ can be evaluated over the FS algebra. To evaluate $h_F(t_1)$, we would have to unify the top and bottom FS at the root of α_2, which fails.

5.2 Feature structure filtering

In order to exclude t_1 from the language of the chart, while retaining t_2, we can define an RTG FG, which tracks feature structures and filters out trees with unification failures. The nonterminals of FG are symbols $[F]$, where F is any feature structure in $\mathcal{F}$; this is a finite set because we have limited the depth of these feature structures to three. We can then define rules for FG which simply interpret the function symbols of $\mathbb{F}$:

$$
\begin{aligned}
[\mathcal{I}(c)] &\rightarrow c && \text{for constants } c \\
[\mathrm{EI}_\pi(F)] &\rightarrow \mathsf{embi}_\pi([F]) \\
[\mathrm{EA}_\pi(F)] &\rightarrow \mathsf{emba}_\pi([F]) \\
[F \sqcup G] &\rightarrow \mathsf{unify}([F], [G]) && \text{if defined}
\end{aligned}
$$

We add a start symbol S_{FG} and rules $S_{\mathrm{FG}} \rightarrow [F]$ for all feature structures F. Then the language $L(\mathrm{FG})$ consists exactly of all terms τ over $\mathbb{F}$ such that $[\![\tau]\!]$ is defined. As a consequence, we can intersect C_w^0 with $h_F^{-1}(\mathrm{FG})$ to obtain the chart C_w, which describes only derivation trees that can be interpreted in the FS algebra, i.e. where all unifications succeed.

In our example, the intersection C_w of C_w^0 with

FG contains (among others) the following rules:

$$
\begin{aligned}
\langle \mathrm{NP}_A, 1{-}1, 3{-}3, F_{\mathsf{nop}} \rangle &\rightarrow \mathsf{nop}_{\mathrm{N}} \\
\langle \mathrm{NP}_A, 2{-}2, 3{-}3, F_{\mathsf{nop}} \rangle &\rightarrow \mathsf{nop}_{\mathrm{NP}} \\
\langle \mathrm{NP}_A, 1{-}2, 3{-}3, F_1 \rangle &\rightarrow \beta_1(\langle \mathrm{NP}_A, 1{-}1, 3{-}3, F_{\mathsf{nop}} \rangle) \\
[\mathrm{NP}_S, 1{-}3, F_2] &\rightarrow \alpha_2(\langle \mathrm{NP}_A, 1{-}2, 3{-}3, F_1 \rangle) \\
[\mathrm{NP}_S, 1{-}3, S_{\mathrm{FG}}] &\rightarrow [\mathrm{NP}_S, 1{-}3, F_2],
\end{aligned}
$$

where $F_1 = T(\beta_1) \sqcup \mathrm{EA}_\epsilon(F_{\mathsf{nop}})$ and $F_2 = T(\alpha_2) \sqcup \mathrm{EA}_\epsilon(F_1)$; we have already seen F_2 as the second argument of the unification in Fig. 7. One can think of these rules as copies of the rules from C_w^0, each decorated with a feature structure. Observe that the rule for $[\mathrm{NP}_S, 1{-}3]$, corresponding to "the boy", is simply extended with the FS F_2. The chart has further rules (not shown above) which derive the derivation tree t from Fig. 4, which contains t_2 as a subtree, we we find that $t \in L(C_w) = \mathsf{parses}(w)$.

By contrast, C_w does not contain decorated rules for $[\mathrm{NP}_S, 2{-}3]$. This is because $[\![h_F(t_1)]\!]$ is undefined in $\mathbb{F}$, and therefore t_1 is not in $L(\mathrm{FG})$, and the pre-chart rule for $[\mathrm{NP}_S, 2{-}3]$ is filtered out by the intersection algorithm.

5.3 Discussion

Our parsing algorithm computes the full parse chart in two steps: We first parse the input into the pre-chart and then refine the pre-chart into a chart by intersecting it with an RTG which filters out derivation trees that do not unify. The filter grammar FG and the intersection algorithm can be implemented in a way that does not require us to compute all rules of FG beforehand (which would be extremely expensive). Instead, the intersection algorithm can query the rules of FG as it goes along, which essentially amounts to evaluating the operations of $\mathbb{F}$ on the feature structure decorations.

In addition, this algorithm does not require enumerating all derivation trees before the unifications are checked; all unifications are performed on chart items. This is in line with parsers for grammar formalisms such as HPSG and especially LFG, and in contrast to other parsers for FTAG. At the same time, our algorithm avoids the exponential blowup of lexical ambiguity which would result from compiling the FTAG grammar into an ordinary TAG grammar. The filtering method presented here could be used more generally to enforce any well-formedness condition on derivation trees which can be expressed by an RTG, such as well-typedness given a type system.

5.4 Implementation

We have implemented the FS algebra and the filter grammar described above in the context of the Alto IRTG parser (Gontrum et al., 2017). Alto is available open-source from `https://bitbucket.org/tclup/alto`.

Our implementation uses well-known efficient algorithms for unification (Tomabechi, 1991) and subsumption checking (Malouf et al., 2000). Subsumption checking is needed because as the intersection algorithm discovers new candidate rules for C_w, it has to check whether another rule with an equal feature structure already exists; this equality checking is performed by testing whether each FS subsumes the other one. Parsing efficiency could be improved further by replacing this with asymmetric subsumption checks and retaining only the chart rule with the less informative FS (Zhang et al., 2007).

6 Conclusion

We have defined an algebra of feature structures and used it to encode FTAG grammars into IRTG grammars with two interpretations – one over a TAG string algebra and one over the feature structure algebra. We have shown how to do FTAG parsing by intersecting a parse chart with respect to the input string with an RTG which attempts to carry out the unifications required by the FTAG grammar. This yields a clean, LFG-style separation of the derivation process of TAG (including adjunction) from unification, and an efficient parsing algorithm that performs unifications on the chart and not the individual derivation trees.

One advantage of our FS algebra is that it can be combined freely with any other grammar formalism that can be encoded in IRTG. It should, for instance, be straightforward to define feature-based LCFRS by adding variants of $emba_\pi$ for rules of higher fan-out. By adding further interpretations, we can also build feature-based *synchronous* grammars, e.g. for semantic parsing (Peng et al., 2015; Groschwitz et al., 2015). An interesting challenge would be to attempt to encode LFG into IRTG, using a string interpretation for the c-structure and a variant of the FS algebra introduced here for the f-structure. This would require dealing with arbitrarily deep feature structures (as opposed to ones of bounded depth as in FTAG), and encoding LFG's completeness and coherence constraints into a filter grammar.

Acknowledgments. I am grateful to the reviewers for their insightful and constructive comments, and to Jessica Grasso, Jonas Groschwitz, Christoph Teichmann, and Stefan Thater for discussions. I am also indebted to the students in my Grammar Formalisms classes at the University of Potsdam for demanding a faster FTAG parser, and those at Saarland University for being the first users of the system described here.

References

Srinivas Bangalore, Pierre Boullier, Alexis Nasr, Owen Rambow, and Benoit Sagot. 2009. MICA: A probabilistic dependency parser based on Tree Insertion Grammars. In *Proceedings of NAACL HLT 2009: Short Papers*.

Bob Carpenter. 1992. *The logic of typed feature structures*. Cambridge University Press.

Hubert Comon, Max Dauchet, Remi Gilleron, Florent Jacquemard, Denis Lugiez, Christof Lding, Sophie Tison, and Marc Tommasi. 2008. Tree automata techniques and applications. Available on `http://tata.gforge.inria.fr/`.

Johannes Gontrum, Jonas Groschwitz, Alexander Koller, and Christoph Teichmann. 2017. Alto: Rapid prototyping for parsing and translation. In *Proceedings of the 15th Conference of the European Chapter of the Association for Computational Linguistics (EACL): Demo Session*.

Jonas Groschwitz, Alexander Koller, and Mark Johnson. 2016. Efficient techniques for parsing with tree automata. In *Proceedings of the 54th Annual Meeting of the Association for Computational Linguistics (ACL)*.

Jonas Groschwitz, Alexander Koller, and Christoph Teichmann. 2015. Graph parsing with s-graph grammars. In *Proceedings of the 53rd Annual Meeting of the Association for Computational Linguistics (ACL-IJCNLP)*.

Laura Kallmeyer, Wolfgang Maier, Yannick Parmentier, and Johannes Dellert. 2010. TuLiPA – Parsing extensions of TAG with Range Concatenation Grammars. *Bulletin of the Polish Academy of Sciences – Technical Sciences* 58(3):377–391.

Ronald Kaplan and Joan Bresnan. 1982. Lexical-functional grammar: A formal system for grammatical representation. In Joan Bresnan, editor, *The Mental Representation of Grammatical Relations*, MIT Press, Cambridge, MA, pages 173–381.

Robert Kasper and William Rounds. 1986. A logical semantics for feature structures. In *Proceedings of the 24th Annual Meeting of the Association for Computational Linguistics (ACL)*.

Alexander Koller and Marco Kuhlmann. 2011. A generalized view on parsing and translation. In *Proceedings of the 12th International Conference on Parsing Technologies (IWPT)*.

Alexander Koller and Marco Kuhlmann. 2012. Decomposing TAG algorithms using simple algebraizations. In *Proceedings of the 11th TAG+ Workshop*.

Robert Malouf, John Carroll, and Ann Copestake. 2000. Efficient feature structure operations without compilation. *Natural Language Engineering* 6(1):29–46.

Xiaochang Peng, Linfeng Song, and Daniel Gildea. 2015. A synchronous hyperedge replacement grammar based approach for AMR parsing. In *Proceedings of the Nineteenth Conference on Computational Natural Language Learning (CoNLL)*.

Sylvain Schmitz and Joseph Le Roux. 2008. Feature unification in TAG derivation trees. In *Proceedings of the 9th TAG+ Workshop*.

Stuart Shieber. 1986. *An introduction to unification-based approaches to grammar*. CSLI Publications.

Hideto Tomabechi. 1991. Quasi-destructive graph unification. In *Proceedings of the 29th Annual Meeting of the Association for Computational Linguistics (ACL)*.

K. Vijay-Shanker and Aravind Joshi. 1988. Feature structures based tree-adjoining grammar. In *Proceedings of COLING*.

XTAG Research Group. 2001. A lexicalized tree adjoining grammar for english. Technical Report IRCS-01-03, IRCS, University of Pennsylvania. `ftp://ftp.cis.upenn.edu/pub/xtag/release-2.24.2001/tech-report.pdf`.

Yi Zhang, Stephan Oepen, and John Carroll. 2007. Efficiency in unification-based n-best parsing. In *Proceedings of the 10th International Conference on Parsing Technologies (IWPT)*.

Parsing Minimalist Languages with Interpreted Regular Tree Grammars

Meaghan Fowlie
Saarland University
`mfowlie@coli.uni-saarland.de`

Alexander Koller
Saarland University
`koller@coli.uni-saarland.de`

1 Introduction

Minimalist Grammars (MGs) (Stabler, 1997) are a formalisation of Chomsky's minimalist program (Chomsky, 1995), which currently dominates much of mainstream syntax. MGs are simple and intuitive to work with, and are mildly context sensitive (Michaelis, 1998), putting them in the right general class for human language (Joshi, 1985).[1] Minimalist Grammars are known to be more succinct than their Multiple Context-Free equivalents (Stabler, 2013), to have regular derivation tree languages (Kobele et al., 2007), and to be recognisable in polynomial time (Harkema, 2001) with a bottom-up CKY-like parser. However, the polynomial is large, $\mathcal{O}(n^{4k+4})$ where k is a grammar constant. By approaching minimalist grammars from the perspective of Interpreted Regular Tree Grammars, we show that standard chart-based parsing is substantially computationally cheaper than previously thought at $\mathcal{O}(n^{2k+3} \cdot 2^k)$.

1.1 Notation

We treat functions as sets of pairs. For $\langle a, b \rangle \in f$ we write $a \mapsto b$. For a partial function $f : A \rightsquigarrow B$, the domain of f, $Dom(f) = \{a \in A \mid f(a)$ is defined$\}$. The set of all such functions is $[A \rightsquigarrow B]$.

For partial functions $f, g : A \rightsquigarrow B$, let $f \oplus g = f \cup g$ if $Dom(f) \cap Dom(g) = \emptyset$, and undefined otherwise. For $a \in A$, let $f - a = f - \{(a, f(a))\}$

2 Minimalist Grammars

We begin with a brief overview of Minimalist Grammars. Readers familiar with MGs should note that we encode movers with a partial function from licensing features to movers, otherwise

Section 3 should be familiar. Minimalist Grammars are a family of formal grammars in which parts of sentences are put together with operations *merge* and *move*. MGs are feature-driven, which means that lexical items come with a stack of features which determine whether operations apply.

Features encode properties of lexical items, such as syntactic categories (noun, verb, etc), categories of arguments of the word (such as a verb that selects a noun), as well as agreement or displacement, such as person, case, quantifier raising, or wh-movement. For example, lexical item $\langle$Loki, D$\rangle$ has string part *Loki* and feature stack D, meaning it has category D, while $\langle$laughed, =DV$\rangle$ has features =D and V, meaning that it requires something of category D and is itself of category V.

These requirements of the lexical items are fulfilled by applications of Merge and Move operations. For example, *laughed*'s requirement of a D is fulfilled by Merging it with *Loki* or *who*, for example:

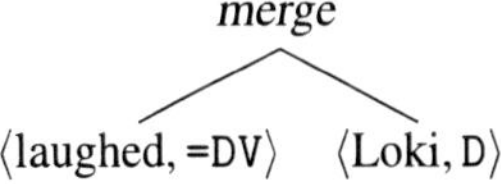

Figure 1: Derivation tree of $\langle$laughed Loki, V$\rangle$

The diagram in 1 above illustrates a ***derivation tree***, a term over $\langle merge^{(2)}, move^{(1)}, Lex^{(0)} \rangle$ which describes the application of *merge* and *move* to expressions.

An operation's applicability is determined by the features on the top of the feature stacks – the ***head features*** – and the application deletes those features; here the =D and D features are deleted, leaving us with V. Notice that deleting D left *Loki* without features; when features remain, something

---

[1]Or slightly below, if unbounded phrasal copying is required: see for example (Kobele, 2006) on Yoruba clefting.

Proceedings of the 13th International Workshop on Tree Adjoining Grammars and Related Formalisms (TAG+13), pages 11–20,
Umeå, Sweden, September 4–6, 2017. © 2017 Association for Computational Linguistics

different happens.

The lexical item $\langle$who, D-wh$\rangle$ has a D like *Loki*, but also has a -wh feature which can ultimately cause it to be pronounced in a different place in the string than it would have if it had had only feature D; this is *movement*. For instance, if instead we applied Merge to *laughed* and *who*, deleting the head features leaves -wh on *who*. This means that although *who* is selected by *laughed* as an argument, its final position in the string will be determined by something else: the operation licensed by its -wh feature. Because the final position is at this point unknown, instead of trying to add it to the string *laughed*, we store it for later insertion.

Our storage mechanism is a partial function from features to moving items. When *laughed* selects *who* and the D features are deleted, $\langle$who, $\epsilon\rangle$ is stored as the image of feature wh, as follows:

Figure 2: Derivation of $\langle\langle$laughed, V$\rangle$, $\{$wh$\mapsto\langle$who, $\epsilon\rangle$ $\}\rangle$

We call the partial function the **storage** and the $\langle$string, feature stack$\rangle$ pair the **workspace**. Together they form an **expression**. Moving items, or **movers**, are taken out of storage when their head feature matches the head feature of the workspace. For example, suppose our expression $\langle\langle$laughed, V$\rangle$, $\{$wh$\mapsto\langle$who,$\epsilon\rangle$ $\}\rangle$ is selected by a silent complementiser that triggers *wh*-movement, $\langle\epsilon$, =V +wh C$\rangle$. The string parts will remain unchanged, and the storage untouched, but the head feature in the workspace becomes +wh.

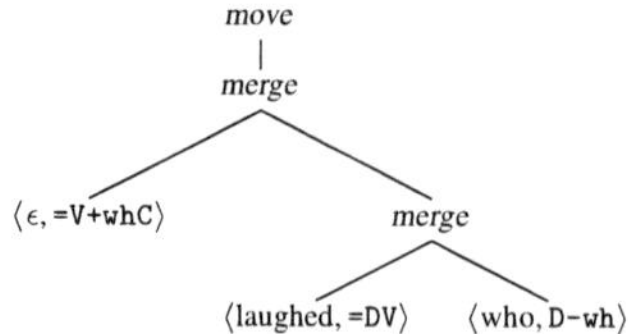

Figure 4: Derivation of $\langle\langle$who laughed, C$\rangle,\emptyset\rangle$

The item $\langle$who, $\epsilon\rangle$ had only its -wh feature left, as represented by its place in storage and the ϵ where its features had been. If it had features left, it would go back into storage after Move, as the image of its new head feature. For example, if *who* also had nominative case — $\langle$who, -nom-wh$\rangle$–, after moving for case it would go back into storage under wh. Such a derivation would also require a locus of case assignment; we add in a silent Tense head, $\langle\epsilon$,=V+nomT$\rangle$. We illustrate this derivation in Figure 5 with a derivation tree annotated by the expression generated at each step.

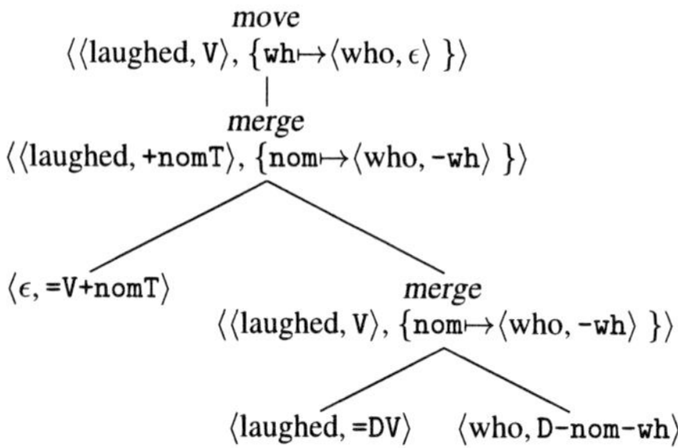

Figure 5: Annotated derivation tree of non-final Move: $\langle$who, -wh$\rangle$ has a feature remaining, so after Move applies it goes back into storage.

Intuitively, it is as though *who* started out beside *laughed* because it is an argument of the verb. But because it needed Case, it moved up to beside the Tense. Next, because it is a *wh*-word, it will move up to the front of the sentence.

2.1 Formal defintion

Formally, following Stabler and Keenan (2003), we define a (string-generating) Minimalist Grammar over expressions, with two finite, disjoint sets of **bare features**. **Selectional features** *sel*, drive Merge, and **licensing features**, *lic* drive Move. Each of *sel* and *lic* has a positive and negative **polarity**. A feature pairs a polarity with a bare feature. Merge and Move apply when head features of two items have the same bare feature,

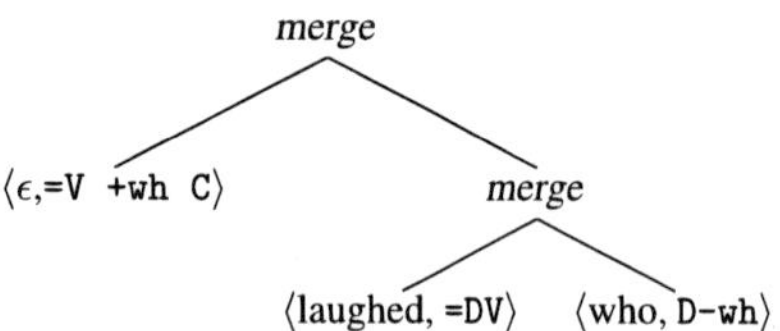

Figure 3: Derivation of $\langle\langle$laughed, +wh C$\rangle$, $\{$wh$\mapsto\langle$who,$\epsilon\rangle$ $\}\rangle$

The +wh feature triggers Move. We look in storage for wh, find $\langle$who, $\epsilon\rangle$, delete the +wh feature, and concatenate *who* with *laughed*:

but with opposite polarities. The *features* are $F=\{$+f,-f,=X,X $\mid$ f$\in$ *lic*, X $\in$ *sel* $\}$. Let Σ be a finite alphabet. The *lexicon Lex* $\subset \Sigma^* \times F^*$ is a finite set of string-feature stack pairs.

An ***expression*** is a string-feature stack pair, paired with a partial function from licensing features to string-feature stack pairs; that is, expressions are Expr $= (\Sigma^* \times F^*) \times [lic \rightsquigarrow \Sigma^* \times F^*]$

MGs have one constraint: for a given negative feature -f, only one pair whose head feature is -f may be in storage. This is the ***shortest move constraint*** (**SMC**), and we implement it by defining storage as a partial function from *lic* to $\langle$string, feature stack$\rangle$ pairs, and by defining storage parts of *merge* and *move* with $\oplus$ as defined in section 1.1 above.

We define four partial functions, $merge_1, merge_2, move_1,$ and $move_2$, as follows.[2] They have $\oplus$ as subfunctions, and are only defined if their subfunctions are defined.

Merge $\quad merge_1, merge_2$: Expr $\times$ Expr $\rightsquigarrow$ Expr
Let $\alpha, \beta \in F^*$, let X$\in$ *sel*, and let f$\in$ *lic*.

$$merge_1(\langle\langle s, \text{=}X\alpha\rangle, S\rangle, \langle\langle t, X\rangle, T\rangle) = \langle\langle st, \alpha\rangle, S\oplus T\rangle$$

$$merge_2(\langle\langle s\text{=}X\alpha\rangle, S_s\rangle, \langle\langle t, X\text{-}f\beta\rangle, S_t\rangle) \quad \cdots \quad =$$
$$\langle\langle s, \alpha\rangle, \{f \mapsto \langle t, \beta\rangle \}\oplus S_s \oplus S_t\rangle$$

Move $\quad\quad\quad move_1, move_2$: Expr $\rightsquigarrow$ Expr
Let $\alpha, \beta, \gamma \in F^*$, let f,g $\in$ *lic*, and suppose $S(f) = \langle t, \beta\rangle$.
$$move_1\langle\langle s, \text{+}f\alpha\rangle, S\rangle = \langle\langle ts, \alpha\rangle, S - f\rangle \quad \text{if } \beta = \epsilon$$
$$move_2(\langle\langle s, \text{+}f\alpha\rangle, S\rangle) =$$
$$\langle\langle s, \alpha\rangle, \{g \mapsto \langle t, \gamma\rangle \}\oplus(S - f)\rangle \quad\quad \text{if } \beta = \text{-}g\gamma$$

For example, in the derivation in Figure 5, the lowest *merge* node is an instance of $merge_2$. *merge* applies because the head feature of *laughed* is =X and that of *who* is D. It is $merge_2$ specifically because, in the language of the definition above, $\beta = $ -nom-wh. The next *merge* node is $merge_1$ because the feature stack of *laughed* is just V. The *move* node is an instance of $move_2$ since $\beta = $ -wh $\neq \epsilon$.

An MG is a 6-tuple

$$g = \langle \Sigma, sel, lic, M, Lex, S\rangle$$

where Σ is a finite alphabet,

$M = \{merge_1, merge_2, move_1, move_2\}$, *Lex* $\subset \Sigma^* \times \{$+f,-f,=X,X $\mid$ f$\in$*lic*,X$\in$*sel*$\}^*$, and $S \subseteq$ *sel* is a designated set of start categories. From our two examples above, we can define an MG g where $\Sigma = \{$Loki, laughed, who$\}$, *sel* $=\{$D,V,T,C$\}$, *lic* $=\{$nom,wh$\}$, *Lex*$=\{\langle$who,D-wh$\rangle$, $\langle$who,D-nom-wh$\rangle$, $\langle$Loki,D$\rangle$, $\langle$laughed,=D V$\rangle$, $\langle\epsilon$,=V +wh C$\rangle$, $\langle\epsilon$,=V +nom T$\rangle$, $\langle\epsilon$,=T +wh C$\rangle \}$, and $S=\{$T,C$\}$.

Let Expr($\langle$s,fs$\rangle$) $= \langle\langle$s,fs$\rangle, \emptyset\rangle$ make an expression with empty storage from a lexical item. $CL(Lex, M)$, the ***closure*** of the lexicon under the operations M, is the closure of Expr(*Lex*) under the operations. Then for a Minimalist Grammar g with lexicon *Lex* and start categories $S \subseteq$ *sel*, the ***language*** generated by g is $L(g) = \{s \mid \langle\langle s, \text{S}\rangle, \emptyset\rangle \in CL(Lex, M)$ and S $\in S\}$; that is, for an expression with empty storage and exactly one feature, where that feature is a start category, the string part of that expression is in the language of g. In our example, $L(g) = \{$who laughed, Loki laughed$\}$.

If *merge* applies because the head feature of the first expression is =X, we say that application of *merge* is ***triggered by*** X. Similarly, if *move* applies because the head feature of the expression is +f, we say the application of *move* is triggered by f. $merge_2$ and $move_2$ always add a mover to storage; if that mover is the image of feature f, then we say it is an f-***storing operation***.

2.2 Expressive capacity

MGs are mildly context sensitive; in particular they are are weakly equivalent to multiple context free grammars (MCFGs) and Linear Context-Free Rewrite Systems (LCFRSs) (Michaelis, 1998), (Michaelis, 2001), and multicomponent tree-adjoining grammars (MC-TAGs), which are more expressive than TAGs. Every MG with k licensing features has a strongly equivalent $(k+1)$-MCFG(2) – an MCFG with at most binary rules and at most $k + 1$-tuples –, where the category names are the features of an expression and the strings behave very much like the string tuple algebra in section 2.3 below.[3] An MG can be exponentially more succinct than its equivalent MCFG (Stabler, 2013); similarly the IRTGs defined here can be ex-

---

[2]The domains of Merge 1 and 2, and those of Move 1 and 2 being disjoint, the operations can alternatively be defined as just Merge and Move with 2 cases each. We choose this variant for parallelism with the minimalist string algebra defined in section 2.3 below.

[3]More preceisely, the licensing features are given an order, and the MCFG category names, rather than having a partial function from licensing features to feature stacks just has the feature stacks in the right order, and similarly for the order of elements in the tuples.

ponentially larger than the MGs they describe.

2.3 Minimalist String Algebra

Kobele et al. (2007) define an algebra of tree tuples, which handles how the Minimalist Grammar builds trees. We define a similar algebra which builds strings, and convert the algebra into our notation of a partial function from licensing features to strings. These functions are just the string parts of the MG operations, separated out from the feature calculus.

The values of the algebra are strings paired with a partial function from *lic* to strings, i.e. $\Sigma^* \times [lic \rightsquigarrow \Sigma^*]$, which we call *minimalist string tuples*. We define $|lic| + 1$ Merge operations and $|lic|^2 + |lic| + 1$ Move operations as follows, $\forall \mathsf{f}, \mathsf{g} \in lic$. $merge_1$ and $move_1$ are for final merge/move, so the string of the merging or moving element concatenates ($\cdot$) with the main string, on the right for Merge and on the left for Move. $merge_{2\mathsf{f}}$ is for f-storing Merge, and $move_{2\mathsf{g}\text{-}\mathsf{f}}$ is for f-storing Move triggered by g.

$$
\begin{aligned}
merge_1(\langle s, \mathsf{S}\rangle, \langle t, \mathsf{T}\rangle) &= \langle s \cdot t, \mathsf{S} \oplus \mathsf{T}\rangle \\
merge_{2\mathsf{f}}(\langle s, \mathsf{S}\rangle, \langle t, \mathsf{T}\rangle) &= \langle s, \mathsf{S} \oplus \mathsf{T} \oplus \{\mathsf{f} \mapsto t\}\rangle \\
move_{1\mathsf{f}}(\langle s, \mathsf{S}\rangle) &= \langle \mathsf{S(f)} \cdot s, \mathsf{S} - \mathsf{f}\rangle \\
move_{2\mathsf{f}\text{-}\mathsf{g}}(\langle s, \mathsf{S}\rangle) &= \langle s, (\mathsf{S} - \mathsf{f}) \\
&\qquad \oplus \{\mathsf{g} \mapsto \mathsf{S(f)}\}\rangle
\end{aligned}
$$

For an MG $\langle \Sigma, sel \cup lic, M, Lex\rangle$, the signature of a tuple-feature algebra includes each element $s^{(0)}$ of the alphabet Σ (evaluates to $\langle s, \emptyset\rangle$), $merge_1^{(2)}$ (evaluates to $merge_1$), $merge_{2\mathsf{f}}^{(2)}$ for each $\mathsf{f} \in lic$ (evaluates to $merge_{2\mathsf{f}}$), $move_{1\mathsf{f}}^{(1)}$ for each $\mathsf{f} \in lic$ (evaluates to $move_{1\mathsf{f}}$), and $move_{2\mathsf{f}\text{-}\mathsf{g}}^{(1)}$ for each pair $\mathsf{f}, \mathsf{g} \in lic$ (evaluates to $move_{2\mathsf{f}\text{-}\mathsf{g}}$).

If $t = m(d_0, \ldots, d_n)$ is a term of the signature of the algebra, t evaluates to the function m evaluates to, applied to what $d_0, \ldots, d_n$ evaluate to. We write $[\![t]\!] = [\![m]\!]([\![d_0]\!], \ldots, [\![d_n]\!])$.

3 Interpreted Regular Tree Grammar

Minimalist Grammars lend themselves readily to so-called "two-step" approaches in which the feature calculus is separated from the algebra of the derived forms (strings, trees, etc). For instance, Kobele et al. (2007) show that for a given MG, the language of valid derivation trees is regular, and that a derived tree can be generated by a multi-bottom up transduction from the derivation tree. Graf (2012) adds MSO-definable constraints on the transduction to constrain movement and define different movement types (sidewards, lowering, covert, etc).

Michaelis et al. (2000), Morawietz (2003), and Mönnich (2006), etc. take a related approach, generating derived trees by Monadic Second-Order (MSO)-definable transduction not from the derivation tree but rather from the equivalent MCGF, translated into a regular tree grammar. (Kobele et al. (2007) note that this second approach can generate transductions that theirs cannot.)

In this tradition, we define an interpreted regular tree grammar for Minimalist Grammars. IRTGs are a generalisation of, among other things, the synchronous grammars of Shieber (1994), 2004, 2006 that form the basis for the tree homomorphisms of Kobele et al. (2007).

3.1 IRTGs

An ***interpreted regular tree grammar (IRTG)*** (Koller and Kuhlmann, 2011) $\mathbb{G} = \langle \mathcal{G}, (h_1, \mathcal{A}_1), \ldots, (h_n, \mathcal{A}_n)\rangle$ derives n-tuples of objects, such as strings or trees from *derivation trees* in $\mathcal{G}$. A given $t \in \mathcal{G}$ is *interpreted* into the n algebras $\mathcal{A}_1, \ldots \mathcal{A}_n$ by means of the n tree homomorphisms $h_1, \ldots, h_n$. For a given $i \leq n$, $h_i(t)$ is a term of the signature of algebra $\mathcal{A}_i$, which is in turn ***evaluated*** ($[\![\cdot]\!]_{\mathcal{A}_i}$) into an object of the algebra. For example, suppose we have a minimalist string algebra $\mathcal{A}$ as defined in Section 2.3, and suppose we have a derivation tree as in the first tree in Table 3, call it t. A tree homomorphism h that includes the rules $\{mv_1 \mapsto merge_{1\text{nom}}, mg_{13} \mapsto merge_1, lex_{11} \mapsto \epsilon, mg_2 \mapsto merge_{2\text{nom}}, lex_9 \mapsto$ laughed, $lex_3 \mapsto$ Loki$\}$ yields the second tree in Table 3, call it u. Then we write $h(t) = u$ and $[\![u]\!]_{\mathcal{A}} = \langle\langle$Loki laughed, $\mathsf{T}\rangle, \emptyset\rangle$. The language of the grammar $L(\mathbb{G})$ is the set of tuples $\{\langle [\![h_1(t)]\!]_{\mathcal{A}_1}, \ldots, [\![h_n(t)]\!]_{\mathcal{A}_n}\rangle \mid t \in L(\mathcal{G})\}$.

An IRTG is *regular* in that $\mathcal{G}$ is a ***regular tree language***, meaning it is a set of trees that can be generated by a finite set of production rules of the form $NT_0 \to t$ or $NT_0 \to t(NT_1, \ldots, NT_n)$ for nonterminals NT_i and terminals t. The terminals are elements of the signature of the tree language. An example is given in Table 3.

3.2 IRTG for Minimalist Grammars

We use the regular tree language of derivation trees defined in Kobele et al. (2007) and define a homomorphism from the derivation trees to terms of the minimalist string algebra (with notation modified to match ours), explicitly defining it as an IRTG. Finally, we calculate the parsing complexity.

For a Minimalist Grammar g with lexicon *Lex*, the production rules of its regular tree grammar, RTG(g), have as their nonterminal symbols the featural configurations of expressions defined by the grammar. Let
$f : [lic \rightsquigarrow \Sigma^* \times F^*] \rightarrow [lic \rightsquigarrow F^*]$ strip away the string parts of a storage function, leaving only the features. Then the nonterminals of RTG(g) are $\{\langle \mathtt{fs}, f(\mathsf{S}) \rangle | \langle \langle \mathtt{s}, \mathtt{fs} \rangle, \mathsf{S} \rangle \in CL(\mathsf{Expr}(Lex))\}$. Since lexical items have finite feature stacks, the SMC limits the size of the storage, and each application of *merge* or *move* deletes features, there are a finite number of nonterminals for a given finite lexicon. Therefore each possible application of *merge* or *move* to expressions of g belong to a finite set of instances; these are the non-lexical rules of the RTG. Each lexical item $\langle \mathtt{s}, \mathtt{fs} \rangle$ has associated with it a rule with left hand side $\langle \mathtt{fs}, \emptyset \rangle$. We give each rule a name from $\{mg_i, mv_i, lex_i \mid i \in \mathbb{N}\}$ by choosing a new $i \in \mathbb{N}$ for each rule: in an IRTG, each rule has its own name. The rules are named according to Table 1. The start categories are $\{\langle \mathsf{S}, \emptyset \rangle \mid \mathsf{S} \in S\}$.

Example 3.1.

Let $sel = \{\mathtt{T}, \mathtt{V}, \mathtt{D}, \mathtt{C}\}$, $lic = \{\mathtt{nom}, \mathtt{wh}\}$. Let $S = \{\mathtt{T}, \mathtt{C}\}$ be the start categories Let *Lex* be defined according to Table 2; for example, $\langle \mathrm{Thor}, \mathtt{D-nom} \rangle \in Lex$.

Table 3 lists the RTG production rules and contains an example tree and its interprtation in the minimalist string algebra defined in section 2.3 above. Rules that are greyed out are rules that can never be used in a complete derivation; the RTG could also be defined to leave them out.

3.3 Interpretation

The derivation trees – the terms over $\{mg_i^{(2)}, mv_i^{(1)}, lex_i^{(0)} \mid i \in \mathbb{N}\}$ – are ***interpreted*** in algebras, meaning for each algebra we want to interpret into, we define a tree homomorphism from derivation trees to terms of the algebra. In our case, we want to interpret into the minimalist string algebra as follows. The examples are from the grammar in Table 3.

Merge 1 Merge of a non-mover is interpreted as merge$_1$. e.g.:
$h(mg_i(t_1, t_2)) = \mathsf{merge}_1(h(t_1), h(t_2))$ for $i \in \{1, 3, 5, 7, 8, 12, 13, 14, 15, 16, 17\}$

Merge 2 f-storing Merge is interpreted as merge$_{2\mathtt{f}}$. e.g.: $h(mg_i(t_1, t_2)) = \mathsf{merge}_{2\mathtt{nom}}(h(t_1), h(t_2))$ for $i \in \{2, 6, 9, 11\}$ or merge$_{2\mathtt{wh}}(h(t_1), h(t_2))$ for $i \in \{4, 10\}$

Move 1 Final move triggered by f is interpreted as move$_{2\mathtt{f}}$. e.g.: $h(mv_i(t)) = \mathsf{move}_{1\mathtt{nom}}(h(t))$ for $i \in \{1, 2\}$

Move 2 g-storing Move triggered by f is interpreted as move$_{2\mathtt{f-g}}$. e.g.: $h(mv_3(t)) = \mathsf{move}_{2\mathtt{nom-wh}}(h(t))$

Lex for a production rule $\langle \mathtt{fs}, \emptyset \rangle \rightarrow lex_i$, each $h(lex_i) = s$ for some $\langle \mathtt{s}, \mathtt{fs} \rangle \in Lex$. e.g.: $h(lex_1) = h(lex_3) = \mathrm{Loki}$

For example, the derivation tree in Table 3 is interpreted by the homomorphism h as a term of the string-feature tuple algebra, which evaluates to the minimalist string tuple $\langle Loki\ laughed, \emptyset \rangle$.

4 IRTG-based parsing for minimalist grammars

Given a minimalist grammar g, we can ask whether a given string w is grammatical according to g, i.e. if $w \in L(g)$. This *parsing problem* has been addressed in a substantial amount of literature (Harkema, 2001), (Stabler, 2013), (Stanojević, 2016). The best known upper bound for a complete parser from this literature is $O(n^{4k+4})$ (Harkema, 2001). This is based on a relatively coarse estimation, by which there are $O(n^{2k+2})$ different parse items, and binary rules such as those for Merge could combine these arbitrarily. Alternatively, by encoding g into an $(k+1)$-MCFG, we can apply standard parsing algorithms for MCFGs, which yields a parsing complexity of $O(n^{3k+3})$ (Seki et al., 1991). The more efficient MCFG parsing algorithm for well-nested MCFGs of Gómez-Rodríguez et al. (2010), which would yield a parsing complexity of $O(n^{2k+4})$, is not applicable because the MCFGs that are produced by the MG-to-MCFG encoding are not well-nested (Boston et al., 2010).

Here we present a parsing algorithm for minimalist grammars that is based on the MG-to-IRTG encoding. This algorithm has a runtime of $O(n^{2k+3})$, a substantial improvement over previously published upper bounds. It is worth noting that we achieve this improved upper bound not through a particularly clever parsing algorithm – indeed, the basic idea of the algorithm presented here is the same as in Harkema (2001) –, but through a more careful analysis of the algorithm's

MG rule application	RTG production rule
$merge_{1|2}(\langle\langle s, \mathtt{fs}\rangle, \mathsf{S}\rangle, \langle\langle t, \mathtt{ft}\rangle, \mathsf{T}\rangle) = \langle\langle s', \mathtt{fs'}\rangle, \mathsf{S'}\rangle$	$\langle\mathtt{fs'}, f(\mathsf{S'})\rangle \rightarrow mg_x(\langle\mathtt{fs}, f(\mathsf{S})\rangle, \langle\mathtt{ft}, f(\mathsf{T})\rangle)$
$move_{1|2}(\langle\langle s, \mathtt{fs}\rangle, \mathsf{S}\rangle) = \langle\langle s', \mathtt{fs'}\rangle, \mathsf{S'}\rangle$	$\langle\mathtt{fs'}, f(\mathsf{S'})\rangle \rightarrow mg_x(\langle\mathtt{fs}, f(\mathsf{S})\rangle)$
$\langle \mathtt{s}, \mathtt{fs}\rangle \in Lex$	$\langle\mathtt{fs}, \emptyset\rangle \rightarrow lex_x$

Table 1: RTG(g) rule template

Types	strings	feature stacks
Nominals	Loki, Thor	D-nom | D
wh-words	who	D-nom-wh | D-wh
Intransitive verbs	laughed, cried	=D V
Transitive verbs	slew, tricked	=D =D V
Tense	ϵ	=V +nom T
Complementiser	ϵ	=T +wh C

Table 2: Sample lexicon

runtime. The primary advantage we obtain from using the standard IRTG parsing algorithm is that it separates the parts that depend on the string length very cleanly from those that depend on the grammar, which makes it a bit easier to see the exact runtime complexity.

We will make a Java implementation of our parsing algorithm available open-source upon publication.

We first sketch the general approach to parsing with IRTGs (Koller and Kuhlmann, 2011). The objective of IRTG parsing is to compute, given an input object w and an IRTG grammar $\mathbb{G} = (\mathcal{G}, (h, \mathcal{A}))$, a compact representation of the language $\mathsf{parses}(w) = \{t \in L(\mathcal{G}) \mid [\![h(t)]\!] = w\}$ – i.e., of those derivation trees that are both grammatically correct and that are interpreted to w. This is done by first computing a *decomposition grammar* D_w, that is, an RTG such that $L(D_w)$ consists of all terms that evaluate to w in the algebra. Then we can exploit closure properties of regular tree languages to compute a *parse chart* – that is, an RTG C such that $L(C) = L(\mathcal{G}) \cap h^{-1}(L(D_w))$ –, by intersecting $\mathcal{G}$ with an RTG that generates all trees which h maps to a term in $L(D_w)$. By construction, we have that $L(C) = \mathsf{parses}(w)$.

Most pieces of this parsing algorithm are completely generic, and do not depend on the algebra that is being used. Thus, when one applies IRTGs to a new algebra, all that is required to obtain a complete parser is to specify how decomposition grammars D_w are computed for arbitrary elements w of the algebra. We now explain how to obtain decomposition grammars for the minimalist string algebra.

Let $w \in \Sigma^*$ be a string that we want to parse with an IRTG $\mathbb{G}$ over the minimalist string algebra. The decomposition grammar D_w will describe a language of terms over this algebra, such as the term in the lower left of Table 3. Let Sp be the set of all *spans* in w, i.e. of all pairs (i, j) of string positions with $1 \le i \le j \le n + 1$. Then the nonterminals of D_w will be pairs $[s, S]$ where $s \in$ Sp and $S : lic \rightsquigarrow$ Sp is a partial function that assigns spans to licensing features. We assume that s and the spans for all features are pairwise disjoint. The start symbol is $[(1, n + 1), \emptyset]$.

Now consider first the constants c of the minimalist string algebra. These derive a span of length one or, if $c = \epsilon$, of length zero. Thus we obtain the following rules for D_w:

$$
\begin{aligned}
[(i, i + 1), \emptyset] &\rightarrow c &&\text{if } w_i = c \in \Sigma \\
[(i, i), \emptyset] &\rightarrow \epsilon &&\text{for all } 1 \le i \le n + 1
\end{aligned}
$$

Furthermore, terms can be combined into larger terms using the merge and move operations. The grammar D_w contains rules which essentially evaluate these operations as defined in Section 2.3, in terms of the spans represented by each substring. Concretely, the rules look as in figure 6.

Rules in which $\oplus$ would yield undefined results (because a feature would appear twice in a partial function) do not exist in the grammar.

4.1 Parsing Complexity

Asymptotic parsing complexity is determined by the time it takes to compute the rules of D_w; the rest of the IRTG parsing algorithm is linear in the size of D_w. The most costly rule of D_w, in terms of parsing complexity, is that for $merge_1$. In this rule there are $O(n^3)$ values for the string positions i, j, p. Within $\mathsf{S} \oplus \mathsf{T}$ there are spans for at most k spans, each of which has $O(n^2)$ possible values. These spans are distributed over the two child nonterminals. This can be done in 2^k different ways. Thus, in total, there are $O(n^{2k+3} \cdot 2^k)$ instances of this rule, which can be enumerated asymptotically in that time.

Lexical	
$\langle \mathrm{D}, \emptyset \rangle$	$\rightarrow$ $lex_1 \mid lex_2$
$\langle \mathrm{D\text{-}nom}, \emptyset \rangle$	$\rightarrow$ $lex_3 \mid lex_4$
$\langle \mathrm{D\text{-}nom\text{-}wh}, \emptyset \rangle$	$\rightarrow$ lex_5
$\langle \mathrm{D\text{-}wh}, \emptyset \rangle$	$\rightarrow$ lex_6
$\langle \mathrm{=D=DV}, \emptyset \rangle$	$\rightarrow$ $lex_7 \mid lex_8$
$\langle \mathrm{=DV}, \emptyset \rangle$	$\rightarrow$ $lex_9 \mid lex_{10}$
$\langle \mathrm{=V+nomT}, \emptyset \rangle$	$\rightarrow$ lex_{11}
$\langle \mathrm{=T+whC}, \emptyset \rangle$	$\rightarrow$ lex_{12}

Derivation tree

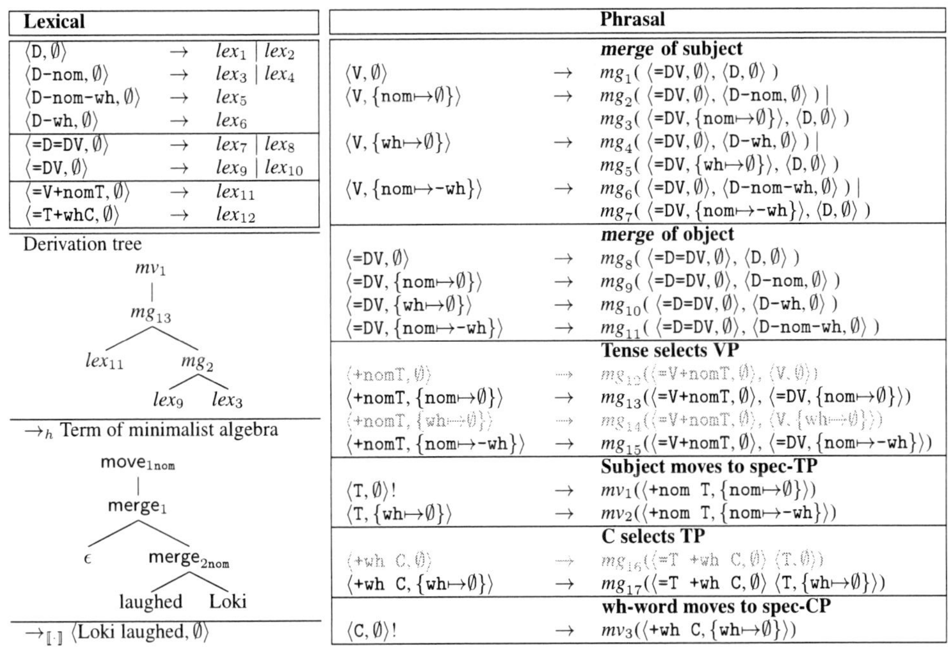

$\rightarrow_h$ Term of minimalist algebra

$\rightarrow_{[\![\cdot]\!]}$ $\langle$Loki laughed$, \emptyset \rangle$

Phrasal

merge of subject

$\langle \mathrm{V}, \emptyset \rangle \rightarrow mg_1(\langle \mathrm{=DV}, \emptyset \rangle, \langle \mathrm{D}, \emptyset \rangle)$

$\langle \mathrm{V}, \{\mathrm{nom} \mapsto \emptyset\} \rangle \rightarrow mg_2(\langle \mathrm{=DV}, \emptyset \rangle, \langle \mathrm{D\text{-}nom}, \emptyset \rangle) \mid mg_3(\langle \mathrm{=DV}, \{\mathrm{nom} \mapsto \emptyset\} \rangle, \langle \mathrm{D}, \emptyset \rangle)$

$\langle \mathrm{V}, \{\mathrm{wh} \mapsto \emptyset\} \rangle \rightarrow mg_4(\langle \mathrm{=DV}, \emptyset \rangle, \langle \mathrm{D\text{-}wh}, \emptyset \rangle) \mid mg_5(\langle \mathrm{=DV}, \{\mathrm{wh} \mapsto \emptyset\} \rangle, \langle \mathrm{D}, \emptyset \rangle)$

$\langle \mathrm{V}, \{\mathrm{nom} \mapsto \mathrm{-wh}\} \rangle \rightarrow mg_6(\langle \mathrm{=DV}, \emptyset \rangle, \langle \mathrm{D\text{-}nom\text{-}wh}, \emptyset \rangle) \mid mg_7(\langle \mathrm{=DV}, \{\mathrm{nom} \mapsto \mathrm{-wh}\} \rangle, \langle \mathrm{D}, \emptyset \rangle)$

merge of object

$\langle \mathrm{=DV}, \emptyset \rangle \rightarrow mg_8(\langle \mathrm{=D=DV}, \emptyset \rangle, \langle \mathrm{D}, \emptyset \rangle)$

$\langle \mathrm{=DV}, \{\mathrm{nom} \mapsto \emptyset\} \rangle \rightarrow mg_9(\langle \mathrm{=D=DV}, \emptyset \rangle, \langle \mathrm{D\text{-}nom}, \emptyset \rangle)$

$\langle \mathrm{=DV}, \{\mathrm{wh} \mapsto \emptyset\} \rangle \rightarrow mg_{10}(\langle \mathrm{=D=DV}, \emptyset \rangle, \langle \mathrm{D\text{-}wh}, \emptyset \rangle)$

$\langle \mathrm{=DV}, \{\mathrm{nom} \mapsto \mathrm{-wh}\} \rangle \rightarrow mg_{11}(\langle \mathrm{=D=DV}, \emptyset \rangle, \langle \mathrm{D\text{-}nom\text{-}wh}, \emptyset \rangle)$

Tense selects VP

$\langle \mathrm{+nomT}, \emptyset \rangle \rightarrow mg_{12}(\langle \mathrm{=V+nomT}, \emptyset \rangle, \langle \mathrm{V}, \emptyset \rangle)$

$\langle \mathrm{+nomT}, \{\mathrm{nom} \mapsto \emptyset\} \rangle \rightarrow mg_{13}(\langle \mathrm{=V+nomT}, \emptyset \rangle, \langle \mathrm{=DV}, \{\mathrm{nom} \mapsto \emptyset\} \rangle)$

$\langle \mathrm{+nomT}, \{\mathrm{wh} \mapsto \emptyset\} \rangle \rightarrow mg_{14}(\langle \mathrm{=V+nomT}, \emptyset \rangle, \langle \mathrm{V}, \{\mathrm{wh} \mapsto \emptyset\} \rangle)$

$\langle \mathrm{+nomT}, \{\mathrm{nom} \mapsto \mathrm{-wh}\} \rangle \rightarrow mg_{15}(\langle \mathrm{=V+nomT}, \emptyset \rangle, \langle \mathrm{=DV}, \{\mathrm{nom} \mapsto \mathrm{-wh}\} \rangle)$

Subject moves to spec-TP

$\langle \mathrm{T}, \emptyset \rangle! \rightarrow mv_1(\langle \mathrm{+nom\ T}, \{\mathrm{nom} \mapsto \emptyset\} \rangle)$

$\langle \mathrm{T}, \{\mathrm{wh} \mapsto \emptyset\} \rangle \rightarrow mv_2(\langle \mathrm{+nom\ T}, \{\mathrm{nom} \mapsto \mathrm{-wh}\} \rangle)$

C selects TP

$\langle \mathrm{+wh\ C}, \emptyset \rangle \rightarrow mg_{16}(\langle \mathrm{=T\ +wh\ C}, \emptyset \rangle \langle \mathrm{T}, \emptyset \rangle)$

$\langle \mathrm{+wh\ C}, \{\mathrm{wh} \mapsto \emptyset\} \rangle \rightarrow mg_{17}(\langle \mathrm{=T\ +wh\ C}, \emptyset \rangle \langle \mathrm{T}, \{\mathrm{wh} \mapsto \emptyset\} \rangle)$

wh-word moves to spec-CP

$\langle \mathrm{C}, \emptyset \rangle! \rightarrow mv_3(\langle \mathrm{+wh\ C}, \{\mathrm{wh} \mapsto \emptyset\} \rangle)$

Table 3: Example IRTG rules and an example derivation of *Loki laughed*

$$
\begin{aligned}
{[(i,p), \mathsf{S} \oplus \mathsf{T}]} &\rightarrow \mathrm{merge}_1([(i,j), \mathsf{S}], [(j,p), \mathsf{T}]) \\
{[(i,j), \mathsf{S} \oplus \mathsf{T} \oplus \{\mathtt{f} \mapsto (p,l)\}]} &\rightarrow \mathrm{merge}_2\mathtt{f}([(i,j), \mathsf{S}], [(p,l), \mathsf{T}]) \\
{[(i,p), \mathsf{S} - \mathtt{f}]} &\rightarrow \mathrm{move}_{1\mathtt{f}}([(j,p), \mathsf{S}]) \qquad \text{if } \mathsf{S}(\mathtt{f}) = (i,j) \\
{[(i,j), (\mathsf{S} - \mathtt{f}) \oplus \{\mathtt{g} \mapsto \mathsf{S}(\mathtt{f})\}]} &\rightarrow \mathrm{move}_{2\mathtt{f}\text{-}\mathtt{g}}([(i,j), \mathsf{S}]),
\end{aligned}
$$

Figure 6: Decomposition rules

5 Comparison with other Mildly Context Sensitive grammars

Mildly context sensitive grammars (Joshi, 1985) frequently come with constants that limit the number of pieces being manipulated by the grammar. In Multiple Context-Free Grammars (MCFGs) (Seki et al., 1991) and Linear Context-Free Rewrite Systems (LCFRSs) (Vijay-Shanker et al., 1987) these are the *rank* – the maximum number of daughters/arguments a rule can have, and the *fanout* – the maximum number of elements in a tuple. In Minimalist Grammars it is the number of licensing features k, which limits the number of movers via the SMC. The maximum number of elements in a minimalist item is therefore $k + 1$ – all possible movers plus the workspace. Transforming an MG into an MCFG yields a grammar with rank 2 and fanout $k + 1$ (Michaelis, 1998). Our $\mathcal{O}(n^{2k+3} \cdot 2^k)$ expressed in terms of fanout $f = k + 1$ is therefore $\mathcal{O}(n^{2f+1} \cdot 2^{f-1})$, which is less than the parsing complexity for an arbitrary binary MCFG with fanout f: $\mathcal{O}(n^{3f})$.

It is difficult to compare parsing complexities across grammars, as moving from one grammar to another can change the fanout. While MGs, MCFGs, and LCFRSs with finite fanout generate the same languages, an arbitrary binary MCFG of fanout f may not have a weakly equivalent MG with $f - 1$ licensing features; indeed Michaelis (2001) shows that an LCFRS with fanout f has a weakly equivalent MG with $3f$ licensing features.

In terms of the string algebra, the difference between an MCFG and an MG is that an MCFG rule is unrestricted in how it concatenates strings; in an MG, only the workspace can be made by concatenation; the movers are simply pooled into one function, never concatenated with one another. In this sense, MG equivalents of MCFGs are a subclass of general MCFGs of the same fanout, one which has a lower parsing complexity. To transform an MG into an MCFG we take as categories the RTG categories, choose an (arbitrary) order on the licensing features, and interpret the mover storage partial function as tuples in the chosen order. We call the class of MCFGs with string concatenation rules restricted to the rules of the Minimalist String Algebra MCFG_{MG}.

Another subclass of MCFGs with lowered parsing complexity is *well-nested* (Kuhlmann, 2007) MCFGs (MCFG_{wn}) in which no rule involves the interleaving of elements from two daughters (no *abab* rules). The parsing complexity of a binary MCFG_{wn} with fanout f is $\mathcal{O}(n^{2f+2})$, due to the fact that there is a normal form in which all deduction rules are either *concatenation* rules or *wrapping* rules, which have complexity $\mathcal{O}(n^{2f+1})$ and $\mathcal{O}(n^{2f+2})$ respectively (Gómez-Rodríguez et al., 2010). In a concatenation rule, we take one element of each tuple and concatenate them, and the rest are kept as they are; in a well-nested MCFG the last element of the first daughter is concatenated with the first element of the second daughter, which maintains the well-nestedness.

Interestingly, although the MCFG equivalent of MGs is not well-nested, the argument for the parsing complexity of $merge_1$ is closely related to that for MCFG_{wn}. The well-nested concatenation rules have the same number of indices as $merge_1$. Therefore the complexity of $merge_1$ ($\mathcal{O}(n^{2f+1} \cdot 2^{f-1})$) and concatenation rules for parsing a MCFG_{wn} ($\mathcal{O}(n^{2f+1})$) have the same polynomial degree, $2f + 1$. This is perhaps counter-intuitive, since well-nested MCFLs are a proper subset of MCFLs/MLs (Gómez-Rodríguez et al., 2010). However, as noted above, transforming between grammars will often change the fanout.

A proper subclass of well-nested MCFGs is monadic-branching MCFGs (MCFG_{mb}), which are binary MCFGs in which only the right daughter may have fanout greater than 1. MGs with the *specifier island condition* (SpIC), in which nothing can move out of a specifier, are weakly equivalent to monadic-branching MCFGs (Kanazawa et al., 2011). These grammars have three kinds of Merge rules: $merge_1$, which merges a lexical item with its complement; $merge_2$, which merges a non-lexical item with its specifier, and $merge_3$, which merges a mover. Move is restricted to prevent a certain kind of movement from within a mover,

and Merge is restricted to prevent movement from within a specifier. The result is grammar that never has to combine mover lists. $merge_1$ can't have movers in the selector, since lexical items never carry movers, and $merge_2$ is constrained by the SpIC not to have movers in the selected item. Our string-tuple analysis of minimalist parsing makes it clear that SpIC-MGs have a parsing complexity of $\mathcal{O}(n^{2k+3})$. The most complex rules are $merge_1$ and $merge_2$, which still have at most 3 indices for the workspace and 2 for each mover. The only difference is that in the standard MG case, the movers could have come from either daughter, but for a SpIC-MG they could only have come from one daughter. For SpIC-MGs the parsing complexity is therefore reduced to $\mathcal{O}(n^{2k+3})$. For our parser the difference is not necessarily huge since 2^k is a constant, but for some, like Stabler (2013)'s top-down beam parser, the SpIC can greatly reduce the search space.

Figure 7 shows the grammars described above.[4] We don't have a linguistic characterization of the "?"-node, which stands for the intersection between the two higher nodes. These would be well-nested MCFGs that only have concatenation in the first element of the tuple. We speculate that this is a linguistically uninteresting class, as the non-well-nestedness of the rules is a reflection of the arbitrarily-chosen order on the licensing features, and has no special linguistic significance.[5]

6 Conclusion

Approaching Minimalist Grammars as interpreted regular tree grammars makes clear the parsing complexity of traditional chart-based parsing, and the options available for interpretation of a derivation as a string. We found that the commonly-cited upper bound of $\mathcal{O}(n^{4k+4})$ was in fact too conservative, and MGs can be parsed in the much smaller polynomial time of $\mathcal{O}(n^{2k+3} \cdot 2^k)$. MGs with the specifier island constraint have a parsing complexity of $\mathcal{O}(n^{2k+3})$.

---

[4]Note that the inclusion refers to the string algebra restrictions in the grammars themselves, and not necessarily to the languages they generate. The left side of the diagram in fact is reflected in the languages – for a given fanout and rank, $\text{MCFL}_{\text{mb}} \subsetneq \text{MCFL}_{\text{wn}} \subsetneq \text{MCFL}$. We don't make any claims about the weak generative capacity on the right side.

[5]Also missing from the lattice is the class of MGs with a looser SpIC where only Move is restricted by the SpIC. This restriction leaves the asymptotic parsing complexity unchanged as Merge is still the most complex rule and is unchanged.

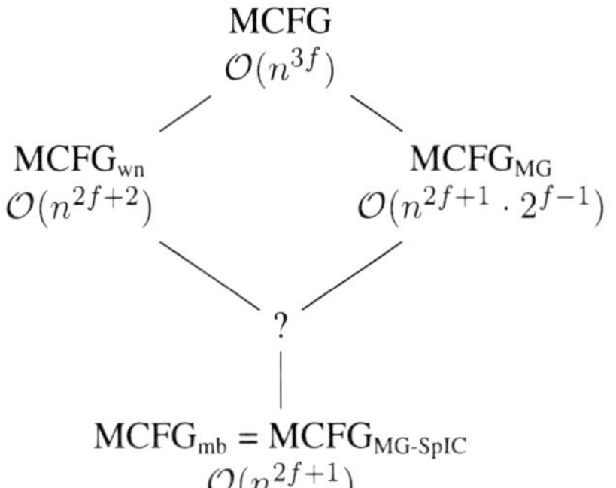

$$\text{MCFG}$$
$$\mathcal{O}(n^{3f})$$

$$\text{MCFG}_{\text{wn}} \qquad \text{MCFG}_{\text{MG}}$$
$$\mathcal{O}(n^{2f+2}) \qquad \mathcal{O}(n^{2f+1} \cdot 2^{f-1})$$

$$?$$

$$\text{MCFG}_{\text{mb}} = \text{MCFG}_{\text{MG-SpIC}}$$
$$\mathcal{O}(n^{2f+1})$$

Figure 7: Subclasses of binary MCFGs with fanout f and their parsing complexities

References

Marisa Ferrara Boston, John Hale, and Marco Kuhlmann. 2010. Dependency structures derived from minimalist grammars. In Christian Ebert, Gerhard Jäger, and Jens Michaelis, editors, *The Mathematics of Language. 10th and 11th Biennial Conference, MOL 10, Revised Selected Papers*. Springer, volume 6149 of *Lecture Notes in Computer Science*, pages 1–12.

Noam Chomsky. 1995. *The Minimalist Program*. MIT Press, Cambridge, MA.

Carlos Gómez-Rodríguez, Marco Kuhlmann, and Giorgio Satta. 2010. Efficient parsing of well-nested linear context-free rewriting systems. In *Human Language Technologies: The 2010 Annual Conference of the North American Chapter of the Association for Computational Linguistics (NAACL 2010)*. Association for Computational Linguistics, pages 276–284. http://www.aclweb.org/anthology/N10-1035.

Thomas Graf. 2012. Movement-generalized minimalist grammars. In Denis Béchet and Alexander J. Dikovsky, editors, *LACL 2012*. volume 7351 of *Lecture Notes in Computer Science*, pages 58–73.

Henk Harkema. 2001. *Parsing minimalist languages*. Ph.D. thesis, University of California Los Angeles.

Aravind Joshi. 1985. How much context-sensitivity is necessary for characterizing structural descriptions. In D. Dowty, L. Karttunen, and A. Zwicky, editors, *Natural Language Processing: Theoretical, Computational and Psychological Perspectives*, Cambridge University Press, New York, pages 206–250.

Makoto Kanazawa, Jens Michaelis, Sylvain Salvati, and Ryo Yoshinaka. 2011. Well-nestedness properly subsumes strict derivational minimalism. In *International Conference on Logical Aspects of Computational Linguistics*. Springer, pages 112–128.

Greg Kobele. 2006. *Generating copies*. Ph.D. thesis, UCLA.

Gregory M. Kobele, Christian Retoré, and Sylvain Salvati. 2007. An automata-theoretic approach to minimalism. In J. Rogers and S. Kepser, editors, *Model Theoretic Syntax at ESSLLI '07*. ESSLLI.

Alexander Koller and Marco Kuhlmann. 2011. A generalized view on parsing and translation. In *Proceedings of the 12th International Conference on Parsing Technologies (IWPT)*. Dublin.

Marco Kuhlmann. 2007. *Dependency Structures and Lexicalized Grammars*. Doctoral Dissertation, Saarland University, Saarbrücken, Germany.

Jens Michaelis. 1998. Derivational minimalism is mildly context-sensitive. In *LACL*. Springer, volume 98, pages 179–198.

Jens Michaelis. 2001. Transforming linear context-free rewriting systems into minimalist grammars. In Philippe de Groote, Glyn Morrill, and Christian Retoré, editors, *Logical Aspects of Computational Linguistics: 4th International Conference, LACL 2001 Le Croisic, France, June 27–29, 2001 Proceedings*, Springer Berlin Heidelberg, Berlin, Heidelberg, pages 228–244. https://doi.org/10.1007/3-540-48199-0_14.

Jens Michaelis, Uwe Mönnich, and Frank Morawietz. 2000. Derivational minimalism in two regular and logical steps. In *Proceedings of the 5th international workshop on tree adjoining grammars and related formalisms (tag+ 5)*.

Uwe Mönnich. 2006. Grammar morphisms. *Ms. University of Tübingen* .

Frank Morawietz. 2003. *Two-Step Approaches to Natural Language Formalism*, volume 64. Walter de Gruyter.

H. Seki, T. Matsumura, M. Fujii, and T. Kasami. 1991. On Multiple Context-Free Grammars. *Theoretical Computer Science* 88(2):191–229.

Stuart Shieber. 2004. Synchronous grammars as tree transducers. In *Proceedings of the Seventh International Workshop on Tree Adjoining Grammar and Related Formalisms (TAG+ 7)*.

Stuart Shieber. 2006. Unifying synchronous tree-adjoining grammars and tree transducers via bimorphisms. In *Proceedings of the 11th Conference of the European Chapter of the Association for Computational Linguistics (EACL-2006)*. Association for Computational Linguistics.

Stuart M Shieber. 1994. Restricting the weak-generative capacity of synchronous tree-adjoining grammars. *Computational Intelligence* 10(4):371–385.

Edward Stabler. 1997. Derivational minimalism. *Logical Aspects of Computational Linguistics* pages 68–95.

Edward P Stabler. 2013. Two models of minimalist, incremental syntactic analysis. *Topics in Cognitive Science* 5(3):611–633.

Edward P Stabler and Edward L Keenan. 2003. Structural similarity within and among languages. *Theoretical Computer Science* 293(2):345–363.

Miloš Stanojević. 2016. Minimalist grammar transition-based parsing. In *Logical Aspects of Computational Linguistics. Celebrating 20 Years of LACL (1996–2016) 9th International Conference, LACL 2016, Nancy, France, December 5-7, 2016, Proceedings 9*. Springer, pages 273–290.

Krishnamurti Vijay-Shanker, David J Weir, and Aravind K Joshi. 1987. Characterizing structural descriptions produced by various grammatical formalisms. In *Proceedings of the 25th annual meeting on Association for Computational Linguistics*. Association for Computational Linguistics, pages 104–111.

Depictives in English: An LTAG Approach

Benjamin Burkhardt and **Timm Lichte** and **Laura Kallmeyer**
CRC 991, Heinrich Heine University Düsseldorf
{burkhardt,lichte,kallmeyer}@phil.hhu.de

Abstract

In this paper, we explore different ways to account for the peculiarities of depictive secondary predication in English, which we think can be characterized as long-distance modification. Other than with resultative secondary predication, the depictive and its target, typically the subject or direct object of a verbal phrase, do not form a contiguous constituent. Instead, the depictive attaches to the verbal domain that also embeds the target phrase. This sibling configuration, together with the constrained flexibility in choosing a target, obviously poses a challenge to the syntax-semantics interface and we therefore compare three general LTAG approaches to deal with this. We eventually favor a rather semantic approach that also allows for a more principled view in terms of Van Valin's ACTOR-UNDERGOER distinction. Our analysis predicts that only the verbal arguments which are the respective lowest and highest entries in the ACTOR-UNDERGOER hierarchy can act as targets for a depictive. To our knowledge, this is the first work that investigates the treatment of secondary predication within the TAG framework.

1 Introduction

The term SECONDARY PREDICATE refers to a typically sentence final, adjectival element that predicates one of the (main) verbal predicate's arguments, which we will refer to as the TARGET (see, e.g., Winkler 1997; Pylkkänen 2002; Müller 2002; Geuder 2004; Simpson 2005). Furthermore, within the set of secondary predicates two kinds are usually distinguished: DEPICTIVES and RE-

SULTATIVES. While resultative secondary predicates characterize states that are brought about by the event that is expressed by the main verb as in (1), depictive secondary predicates, as in (2), express properties that hold for at least some part of the event time, but do not immediately result from the verb event.[1]

(1) Sean stomped the can$_i$ flat$_i$.

(2) a. Kim ate the steak$_i$ raw$_i$.
     b. Kim$_i$ ate the steak hungry$_i$.

In (1), the flatness that is predicated of the can is a result of the stomping it underwent. By contrast, the rawness of the steak or Kim's appetite in (2) are rather peripheral to the overall act of eating – even though they *could* influence the manner of eating. However, we will put event semantic subtleties of this distinction aside for the rest of the paper. What we are interested in is the capability of depictives to target different arguments of the main verb, for instance the object in (2-a) and the subject in (2-b). This is highly relevant to models of the syntax-semantics interface in that it raises the following questions: how can the relation between a depictive and its potential targets be established? And how can the possible choice of constituents that a depictive may target be correctly captured? These are the questions addressed in this paper, taking English as the object language and, for the first time, Lexicalized Tree-Adjoining Grammar (LTAG, Joshi and Schabes 1997; Abeillé and Rambow 2000) as the syntactic framework.

2 Data

In this section, we will give a more detailed overview over syntactic properties of depictives that also pertains to the possible choice of targets.

---

[1] In the examples, we will use coindexation to mark the secondary predicate and its target.

Proceedings of the 13th International Workshop on Tree Adjoining Grammars and Related Formalisms (TAG+13), pages 21–30,
Umeå, Sweden, September 4–6, 2017. © 2017 Association for Computational Linguistics

On this, we will base the discussion of previous analyses in Section 3 as well as our own proposal for an LTAG analysis in Sections 5 and 6.

2.1 Target ambiguity and stacking

In (2), we have seen clear-cut cases where the depictive can target either the subject or the object due to their respective semantic (in)compatibility. Consequently, when semantics does not constrain the possible readings, TARGET AMBIGUITY as in (3) arises.

(3) Kim$_i$ ate the apple$_j$ unwashed$_{i/j}$.

Here, both verbal arguments are viable targets for the depictive element *unwashed*, even though native speakers seem to generally prefer the subject target readings.

Interacting with target ambiguity, depictives can also be stacked as in (4).

(4) a. ? Kim$_i$ ate the steak$_j$ raw$_j$ hungry$_i$.
    b?? Kim$_i$ ate the steak$_j$ hungry$_i$ raw$_j$.
    c?? Kim ate the steak$_j$ raw$_j$ salted$_j$.

While STACKING OF DEPICTIVES generally decreases the acceptability of sentences, such stacks with alternating targets and in the wellnested order as in (4-a), i.e. object depictive followed by subject depictive, seem more acceptable than the illnested order in (4-b), or those in which both depictives have the same target, as in (4-c).

2.2 Depictives and unrealized arguments

Another important property of depictives is that the targeted constituent does not need to be syntactically realized, as the passive constructions in (5) show. In both examples, the depictive element target the unrealized AGENT argument of the verb.

(5) a. The game$_j$ was played barefoot$_{i/*j}$.
    b. The book$_j$ is to be read naked$_{i/*j}$.

The example in (5-a), discussed in Roberts (1987), was originally used to raise the question whether adjectival elements of this kind should actually be treated as such or rather as adverbials that modify the event itself. In any case, assuming a non-metaphorical meaning and sticking with the adjectival use of *barefoot*, we must conclude that the depictive in fact targets the unrealized AGENT argument rather than the THEME constituent. The same is true for *the book* and *naked* in the passive infinitive construction in (5-b). Finally, as (6)

shows, it is also possible for depictives to target unrealized direct objects.

(6) We$_i$ usually bake gluten-free$_{*i/j}$.

2.3 Depictives and oblique arguments

The examples discussed so far were only concerned with depictives targeting either the subject or the verb's direct object. What about "oblique" arguments, that is, indirect objects and PP-objects? Judging by the observations made this far, one could assume that depictives can target either one of the verb's arguments. This does not seem to be the case however, as shown in (7).

(7) a. The cash machine$_i$ gave John$_j$ the money$_k$ hungry$_{*i/*j/*k}$.
    b. Peter crashed into him$_i$ tired$_{*i}$.

As for (7-a), even though the verb's indirect object is the only animate argument, it cannot be targeted by the depictive *hungry*. A similar observation can be made for most verbs that require a prepositional argument. In almost all cases, native speakers dismiss readings in which the nominal constituent inside the PP is targeted, as in (7-b).

However, there are counterexamples like (8).

(8) a. You can't give them$_j$ injections unconscious$_j$.   (Simpson, 2005, (46))
    b. Tom$_i$ talked to Meg$_j$ drunk$_{i/j}$.

For (8-a), the possibility to target the indirect object could be explained with the presence of a light verb construction *give injections*, which doesn't assign argument status to *injections*. Similarly, the targeting of the prepositional object in (8-b) could be ascribed to the reanalysis into a verb-particle construction *talk to*. This needs to be more carefully examined in future work.

2.4 Depictives and non-arguments

Finally, depictives cannot target constituents of complex arguments, such as the genitive noun in (9-a) or the single conjuncts in (9-b), nor modifying constituents like PP-adjuncts as in (9-c).

(9) a. John met Maria's$_i$ father naked$_{*i}$.
    b. [John$_i$ and Paul$_j$]$_k$ met [Maria$_m$ and her boyfriend$_n$]$_o$ naked$_{*i/*j/k/*m/*n/o}$.
    c. John drilled a hole with a power tool$_i$ new$_{*i}$.

Again, single counterexamples like the one in (10)

can be found, where the depictive seems in fact to be able to target the reflexive pronoun inside the complex NP-argument.

(10) If you're an investment banker, don't choose a profile of yourself$_i$ [drunk at a house party]$_i$.[2]

It is yet unclear whether the putative locality violation in (10) could be explained with the involvement of a multi-word expression. One reviewer has noticed that the acceptability of (10) decreases as soon as the PP *at a house party* is left out, which could hint at the presence of a construction different from the depictive one, for example some sort of small clause. A closer inspection of such examples is left to future work.

3 Previous analyses

We will briefly report on two very different proposals from other frameworks that precede our work.

In the framework of Generative Grammar, Geuder (2002, 2004), following Winkler (1997), asserts that depictives always occur in postverbal position and are preceded by resultatives, as shown in (11). This leads him to the assumption that depictives must be right-adjoined.

(11) John$_i$ kicked the door$_j$ open$_j$ tired$_j$.

Furthermore, pointing to earlier work by Roberts (1988), he states that depictives, without discriminating between subject and object depictives, must be adjoined at VP-level and bases this on several constituency tests, i.e. VP fronting, though-movement, and pseudoclefts, as well as on the behavior of depictives under negation. Geuder further strengthens this position through an observation made by Ernst (2001): depictives precede manner adverbs, which themselves cannot adjoin higher than at VP-level (see (12)).

(12) Al$_i$ sits$_j$ clothed$_i$ quietly$_j$ [...].

While the argument is valid in the context of the Generative Grammar framework, LTAG is not necessarily restricted in such a way. That said, the analysis proposed here eventually adopts Geuder's view such that the depictive is adjoined at VP-level as well. The main point in Geuder (2004),

however, is to tease apart the differences of the semantics of depictives in comparison to "normal" adverbial modification and modification by the class of so called transparent adverbs. Furthermore, Geuder (2004) states that target resolution is not driven by syntax, but that the restictions on possible targets of depictives "arise on an interpretational level". This runs contrary to, e.g., Wunderlich (1997) who assumes distinct adjunction sites for subject and object depictives. However, Geuder's analysis remains at a rather informal level compared to what we are aiming at.

In contrast to Geuder (2004), the analysis of depictives in Müller (2008) is based on Head-Driven Phrase Structure Grammar (HPSG) and aims to give a mainly syntax-driven account of depictive targeting phenomena. Following an extensive discussion of both English and German data, he summarizes that *all* verb arguments, including indirect objects, are possible targets of depictives. This contradicts the observations made in section 2 about indirect objects as targets of depictives, e.g. in example (7-a). Additionally, he emphasizes that the target has to precede the depictive itself. In the provided analyses, which largely cover German examples, Müller deviates from Pollard and Sag (1994) by adopting a version of HPSG in which the verb arguments in the SUBCAT list are marked as realized, but are not deleted from it. This assumption is essential for Müller's analysis of English, because depictives are included after the target has been combined with the verbal head. Under standard assumptions, the target would have been removed from the SUBCAT list too early. With the distinction of realized and unrealized items on the SUBCAT list, however, also the stacking of depictives seems to be manageable, even though Müller remains silent on this.

4 Modification in LTAG

Since we want to treat depictive secondary predicates as long-distance modification, the approaches we present in the following section are based on assumptions commonly followed in the TAG literature, namely that, in accordance with valency-driven design principles for elementary trees (Abeillé and Rambow, 2000; Frank, 2002), modifiers (or adjuncts) are attached via adjunction. From this and the shape of the target trees, it immediately follows that it must be possible to adjoin a modifier to its target non-immediately, for

---

[2]From the book *The Short and Great Guide to Online Business Networking* by Michel Semienchuk from 2016.

the simple fact that modifiers are seen as optional material without argument status. As such, they are not uniquely reflected in the elementary tree of the target, for example, by a non-terminal leaf node, which makes them act very differently from arguments. Thus, when modifiers are stacked similarly to the topicalized *yesterday* and *in Paris* in (13), one is not adjoined to the elementary tree of *elected*, but rather to the other modifier:[3]

(13) Yesterday, in Paris, Kim ate the steak.

This can be seen from the analysis sketch in Figure 1. Hence, in LTAG analyses, even rather stan-

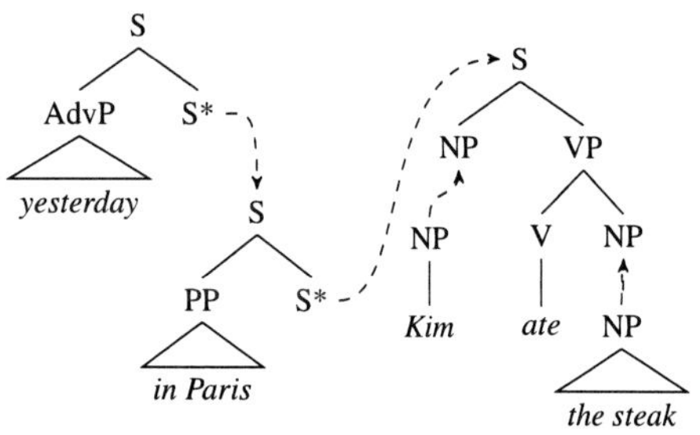

Figure 1: Analysis of topicalized modifier stacking in (13)

dard instances of modification can turn out "long distance".

The situation with depictives is even worse, as will become clear in the next section: (i) the auxiliary tree of the depictive can *never* adjoin immediately to the elementary tree of the target if it is the subject, and (ii) the depictive tree does not add to the lexical projection of the target, namely the NP. We suspect that the connection between a depictive and its target can be more directly established with some sort of MCTAG, but we also see good reasons *not* to use tree sets here. One reason that has been mentioned in Section 2.2 is that the realization of the target can be optional. We will therefore not fully explore this possibility in this work and only provide some general thoughts in Section 7.

5   LTAG approaches to depictives

Staying with LTAG, there are thus two primary challenges when dealing with depictive secondary predicates: firstly, one has to make sure that

the depictive finds its target through the syntax-semantics interface; secondly, one has to cope with the fact that sometimes more than one constituent can be chosen as target at a time. In other words, there is the possibility of target ambiguity. With respect to target ambiguity, one can think of three general approaches, namely treating it either in syntax or in semantics, or in the syntax-semantics interface proper. Let us go through them one by one.

5.1   Syntactic ambiguity approach

With a SYNTACTIC AMBIGUITY APPROACH, subject and object depictives induce different syntactic derivations. Hence, either they anchor different trees, that is, trees that differ in the structure or labeling of the nodes, or they adjoin to different nodes of the verbal tree, or both.

So one effect could be that the target of a depictive is uniquely determined through the syntactic position at which the elementary tree of a depictive is adjoined. Hence, depictives targeting the subject are always adjoined at a different node than depictives that target the object. A rough example analysis of this kind is shown in Figure 2, which models the postverbal stacking of subject and object depictives in (14), repeated from (4-a) above:

(14) Kim$_i$ ate the steak$_j$ raw$_j$ hungry$_i$.

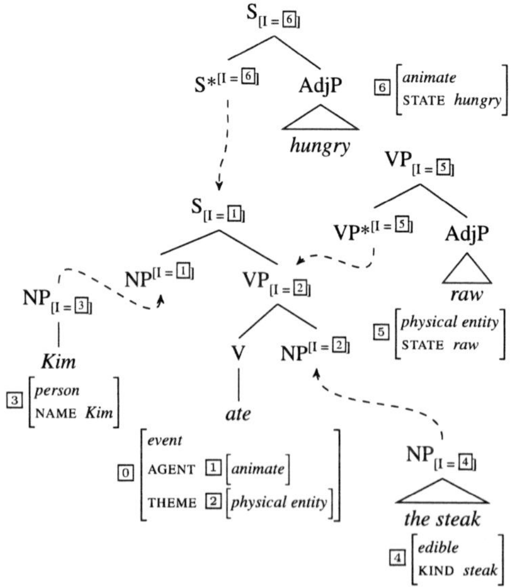

Figure 2: Analysis of (14) with a syntactic ambiguity approach

[3]Yet multiple adjunction (Schabes and Shieber, 1994) would allow for a direct adjunction of both modifiers to the verbal elementary tree.

The analysis we propose employs the syntax-semantics interface of Kallmeyer and Osswald (2013) where syntactic nodes are enriched with interface features and the semantic representations consist of semantic frames. Interface features such as I(NDIVIDUAL) and E(VENT) contribute base labels (i.e. boxed numbers) that also appear in the semantic frames. Upon substitution and adjunction, the unification of interface features triggers the identification of base labels and, consequently, the unification of the linked semantic frames.

The example in Figure 2 is thus to be understood in the following way: when adjoining the elementary tree of the depictive *hungry* to the S-node of the elementary tree of *ate*, the unfication of their I-features triggers the identification of base labels ⓵, which is linked to the semantic content of the subject, and ⓺, which points at the semantic contribution of the depictive. Interface features therefore serve to establish but also limit the visibility of a potential target to specific nodes.

The syntactic ambiguity then emerges from a specific distribution of base labels as values of the I-feature. In Figure 2, the subject is only visible in the S-node (via ⓵) and the object only in the VP-node (via ⓶). Hence, the target of the depictive is determined by whether it is adjoined to S or VP.

Considering coverage and sparseness, this implementation of the syntactic ambiguity approach comes with certain drawbacks, some of which can be overcome easily, and some with more difficulties – if at all. Concerning grammar sparseness, every depictive anchors at least two elementary trees that differ only in their respective root/foot category. Hence, in the grammar, the depictive *hungry* would not only anchor the auxiliary tree with S-root, but also the one with a VP-root in order to be usable as an object depictive. Of course, this duplication can be overcome easily by generally replacing the S-category for the VP-category (and representing the S-category by, e.g., an extra feature). With this change, depictives would only adjoin to VP-nodes. Another challenge is posed by unrealized arguments, e.g. involving passives such as in (5). But here the answer would be to leave the interface unchanged compared to the active alternate. Hence, the subject position of the passive would still be linked to the VP-node, while the S-node would remain linked to the *logical* subject. Lastly, and most severely, the syntactic ambiguity approach forces a certain linear order onto the depictives, depending on which argument they target: in postverbal position, depictives targeting the object can only precede subject depictives since the latter are adjoined at a higher syntactic position. Similarly, the presented syntactic ambiguity approach predicts that only subject depictives may appear in a topicalized position. Both predictions seem to be too strong (see, e.g., (4-b)), but are hardly adjustable when one wants to retain the common verbal phrase structure.

Given these issues, an alternative worth considering seems to be one that assumes specific interface features for the subject and the object. For example, there could be interface features I_{subj} and I_{obj} and they could be made accessible in both S and VP. This would indeed help to relax the mentioned linearization constraints, but it would also necessitate the duplication of entries on the side of depictives, in order to be able to let a depictive target either the subject or the object.

5.2 Interface ambiguity approach

Instead of representing target ambiguity by means of distinct interface features or by assigning different values to the I-feature in distinct syntactic nodes, one could as well trigger target ambiguity with one value of the I-feature only. This is what we want to call an INTERFACE AMBIGUITY APPROACH. It consists of giving a local choice regarding the value of the I-feature, namely that it is linked either to the subject or the object. We formally write this as a disjunctive expression [I = ⓵ ∨ ⓶], using ∨ as the disjunction operator. The sample analysis from above then turns into the one in Figure 3.

The challenge here is to pass the disjunctive value from the foot node to the root of the depictive elementary tree without also projecting the final value of the I-feature, which it receives after top-bottom unification – otherwise only either subject or object depictives could be adjoined to VP. To this end, we include a special variable ⓐ that is valid during substitution and adjunction, but becomes void when top-bottom unification is applied.

Obviously, this sort of disjunction helps to remedy the duplication issue that can arise in the syntactic ambiguity approach. Hence, in the interface ambiguity approach, one can maintain a uniform auxiliary tree for depictives without having to harmonize syntactic categories (but see below). An-

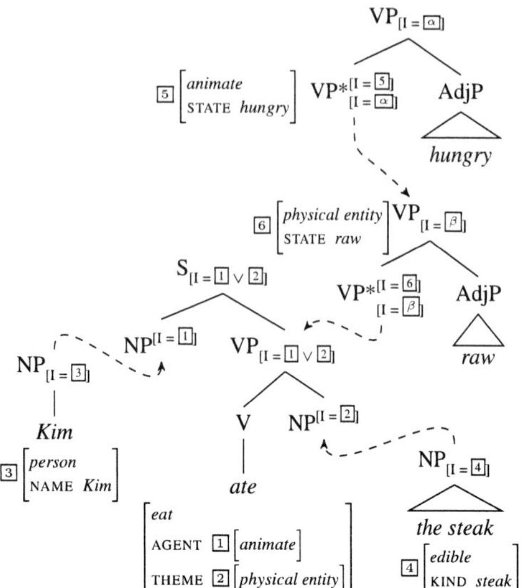

Figure 3: Analysis of (14) with an interface ambiguity approach

other advantage over the syntactic ambiguity approach in Figure 2 is that postverbal linearization is left underspecified and the topicalized position can be occupied by both the subject and the object depictive. However, the critical drawback is that one has to allow for logical operators to be included into elementary trees. This is a big step, formally speaking, because it means to treat the syntactic feature structures in elementary trees as descriptions and to introduce special variables for descriptions such as ⍺ in Figure 3. Otherwise, when first resolving disjunctions such as the one in the I-feature, the duplication issue would return back on the scene, not to mention the narrowing to either subject or object depictives that can adjoin at VP. Having said this, tree and feature structure descriptions are widely used in metagrammars (cf. Crabbé et al., 2013) and certain TAG variants (cf. Rambow et al., 2001). So it is a possible strategy.

Nevertheless, we want to propose yet another type of approach, namely the semantic ambiguity approach, that circumvents this extension and is also more explanatory with respect to the linking aspects of target ambiguity.

5.3 Semantic ambiguity approach

At first glance, the SEMANTIC AMBIGUITY APPROACH differs from the interface ambiguity approach in just one detail: disjunction does not appear in elementary trees (or their descriptions), but in their semantics. Remember that we follow

Kallmeyer and Osswald (2013) in that we use descriptions of semantic frames as semantic representation, and in these descriptions, disjunction is a natural ingredient.

We can thus recast the LTAG analyses from Figures 2 and 3 into the one in Figure 4, which now embeds the disjunction AGENT ∨ THEME in the semantics of the depictive.

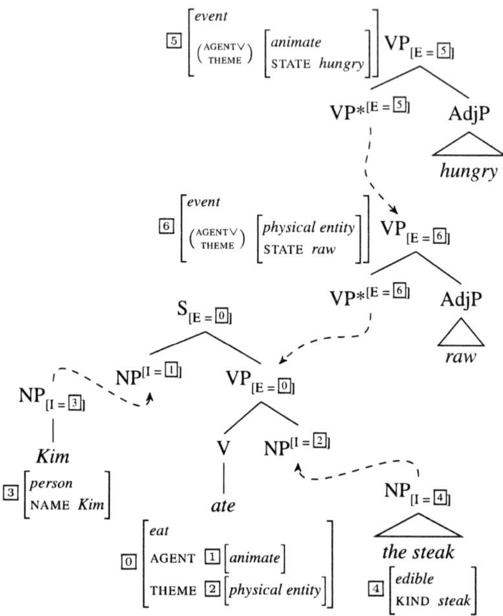

Figure 4: Analysis of (14) with the semantic amibuity approach

This move has far reaching consequences regarding the interface and the semantics of the depictive: instead of accessing the I-feature of the respective target NPs, the depictive now reads off the E-feature, which commonly points to the semantics of the verbal head. The semantics of the depictive has to reflect this, that is, the root type has to be of type *event*, while its actual semantic content, which either contributes to the AGENT role or the THEME role of the event, is more deeply embedded compared to the other two approaches.

As with the interface ambiguity approach, it should be obvious that the semantic ambiguity approach avoids the unwanted proliferation of elementary trees that have to be assumed for a single depictive. Similarly, no post- or preverbial linearization constraints are imposed. But on the other hand, the semantic ambiguity approach improves on the interface ambiguity approach since no additional descriptive means need to be included ad hoc. Furthermore, it does not hinge on making the I-features of subject and object accessible within the whole verbal phrase. Yet one could criticize that this simplification in the syntax puts additional burden on the semantics: the possible targets of depictives are not immediately determined by the syntactic argument structure of the verbal head any more, but entirely follow from the semantic roles that are specified in the frame-semantic event descriptions assigned to the verbal head and the depictive. Going back to Figure 4, this means that semantic roles such as AGENT and THEME and their linking to syntactic argument positions have to be taken into account, for instance, in order to avoid depictive predication on non-arguments. The following section will show, how to achieve this in a principled manner.

6 A semantic approach with actor-undergoer linking

The semantic solution discussed in the previous section simply lists all semantic roles that are potential targets for depictive modification. The question is whether we can generalize this in some way. One abstraction over semantic roles is provided by the MACROROLES actor and undergoer introduced in Van Valin, Jr. (2005) (see also the similar concepts of proto-agent and proto-patient in Dowty, 1991). Van Valin, Jr. (2005) explains how to determine actor and undergoer based on the semantic characterization of an event, more specifically based on the semantic roles of its participants. A constraint-based LTAG implementation of his linking theory within the metagrammar (using XMG) has been proposed in Kallmeyer et al. (2016). With the additional linking constraints in the metagrammar, the frame for *eating* for instance gets enriched with marcorole information, as shown in Figure 5.

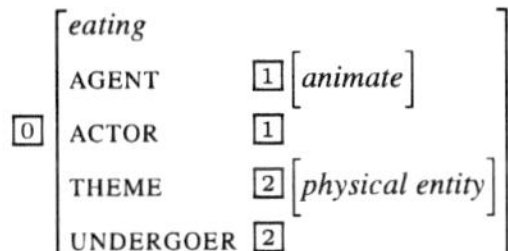

Figure 5: *eating* frame with macroroles

The hypothesis we want to pursue in the following is that depictives target either the actor or the undergoer of the event that they modify (see Figure 6 for the revised elementary tree for *raw*). This hypothesis is not just a generalization over the analysis proposed in Section 5.3 but it comes with the additional claim that non-macroroles cannot be targeted by depictive modifiers or, more precisely, the depictive has to target one of the macroroles.

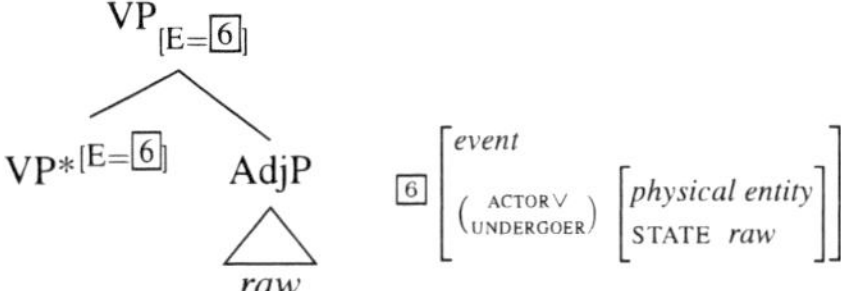

Figure 6: Revised elementary tree for *raw*

This hypothesis clearly holds for the examples in (2). The two arguments of the verb *eat* are the actor and the undergoer and both are possible targets for depictives. The question is whether it also holds that event participants that are neither actor nor undergoer cannot be targeted by a depictive. This seems to be supported by the data in (7-a).

Let us consider further examples involving participants that are neither actor nor undergoer.

(15) $John_i$ ran into the $building_j$ $burning_{i/*j}$.

(16) $John_i$ worried about the $apples_j$ $unwashed_{i/*j}$.

In (15), *the building*, which is neither actor nor undergoer, is actually not available as antecedent for a depicitive. In (16), *John* is the undergoer while *the apples* are neither actor nor undergoer. And in fact, they do not seem to be available for modification by a depictive.

(17) a. $Chris_i$ ate the $apples_j$ with a fork $unwashed_{i/j}$.
   b. $Chris_i$ ate the soup with a $spoon_j$ $unwashed_{i/*j}$.

(17) gives examples where we have an actor and an undergoer and, as a third participant, an instrument. The instrument cannot be targeted by depictive modification.

(15)–(17) suggest that particpants that are realized as PPs are in general not available for modification by depictives. This seems to be the case even for semantic roles that are relatively low on the actor–undergoer hierarchy, as in (18). According to Van Valin, Jr. (2005), arguments that are selected as undergoers are by definition not marked by an oblique case or an adposition. For example, *Chris* is not the undergoer in the sentences in (18). But this is different for (19), where *Chris* becomes the undergoer due to the passivization. And here

Chris is in fact accessible as a target for a depictive.

(18) a. The car crashed into Chris$_i$ unprepared$_{*i}$.
   b. The bewitched machine hammered on Chris$_i$ drunk$_{*i}$.

(19) Chris$_i$ was crashed into unprepared$_i$.

Even though these data indicate that actor and undergoer are more easily accessible for depictive modifiers, we need broader empirical evidence for our hypothesis. Corresponding tests, including a corpus study and acceptability judgment tests, are planned for the very near future.

7 Remaining issues

Considering the still underresearched wealth of depictive secondary predication, the presented analyses are certainly not meant to be conclusive. They are rather supposed to highlight general LTAG-related options when dealing with some critical challenges posed by depictive secondary predication: the non-local relation between the depictive and its target, the rather strict choice of targets, and the flexibility in stacking and linearizing depictives. Therefore, it might be that the proposed analyses have to be revised in the light of more data and more languages. In what follows, we want to mention some of the potential "breaking points".

One challenge to the analysis in Section 6 would be that a depictive can target an argument of the verb that does not bear a macrorole. While English seems to be largely consistent in only allowing macroroles, there seem to be languages that are less strict (e.g. Warlpiri, see Simpson 2005). For these languages, a more syntactic approach might be preferable. A more severe challenge would be if a depictive was able to target a constituent that cannot even be considered an argument of the verb, for instance, a modifying expression or some more deeply embedded part of an argument. While it is hard to find acceptable data where a depictive targets a modifier, there are indeed cases that seem to challenge the locality restriction. If they were possible in general and not just side effects of multi-word expressions as argued in Section 2.4, either the set of interface features would have to be considerably extended in order to make the embedded targets accessible or the semantics of the depictive would have to be more complex in order to access elements embedded below the event participants. On the other hand, restrictions on linearization (and stacking) could be rather easily implemented using purely syntactic features.

Finally, our choice for LTAG as such could be seen as another weakness. As mentioned in Section 4, we deliberately decided against MCTAG, even though we thereby rule out the possibility to establish a more direct derivational relation between the depictive and its target. Within an MC-TAG, depictives could be represented as tree sets consisting of two trees: one tree anchored by the depitive word, namely roughly the auxiliary tree that was used above in the presented LTAG analyses, and one degenerated elementary tree, the scope taking part. The degenerated elementary tree possibly only consists of a single node and is supposed to either adjoin to the root node of the target NP or to substitute into the target NP slot of the verbal tree, yielding again a substitution node. Similar tree sets can be found in works that deal, for example, with reflexives (Ryant and Scheffler, 2006; Kallmeyer and Romero, 2007; Storoshenko et al., 2008; Frank, 2008) and extraposed relative clauses (Kroch and Joshi, 1987; Chen-Main and Joshi, 2014). The approach in Frank (2008) adopts a tree-local solution where reflexives introduce on the syntactic side, in addition to the initial tree of the reflexive, an initial single-node NP tree that substitutes into the antecedent slot. A similar solution might be possible for depicitves. The approach in Chen-Main and Joshi (2014) is interesting because it remains tree-local even for illnested dependency structures, thanks to flexible composition and multiple adjunction. As was shown with (4-b), depictives can give rise to illnested dependencies as well. Even so, the strongest argument against using MCTAG for depictives is that the target does not have to be realized. Consequently, there are cases where the target NP is missing as a landing site for the scope part of the depictive tree set, unless it is made part of the verbal elementary tree for this very reason. Therefore, in place of decorating the verbal elementary tree in such a way, we prefer to remain with LTAG.

8 Conclusion

Depictives challenge the syntax-semantics interface in many ways: as for English, locality is extended, but still restricted to the verbal domain, that is, maximally extending to the syntactic arguments of the verbal head. But as flexible as it might look, within this there is some additional restrictiveness that is hard to capture in only syntactic or semantic terms. Therefore, among the three LTAG approaches we developed in this paper, we favour a semantic approach that is enhanced with Van Valin's argument linking mechanism. The prediction then made is that depictives are restricted to the syntactically and semantically determined macroroles actor and undergoer. While, from what we have seen in this paper, the prediction seems to be empirically valid at least for English, the data survey is still very preliminary. This needs to be tackled in future work while also broadening the scope crosslinguistically. Finally, as one of the reviewers pointed out to us, there are other constructions that also seem to involve long-distance modification, such as absolutes and free adjuncts (examples taken from Stump 1985):

(20) a. His father being a sailor, John knows all about boats.
    b. Walking home, he found a dollar.

The differences and commonalities with constructions of this kind need to be investigated in future work as well.

9 Acknowledgments

We are grateful to Wilhelm Geuder and the two anonymous reviewers for detailed comments and discussion. The work presented in this paper was financed by the Deutsche Forschungsgemeinschaft (DFG) within the CRC 991 "The Structure of Representations in Language, Cognition, and Science".

References

Anne Abeillé and Owen Rambow. 2000. Tree Adjoining Grammar: An overview. In Anne Abeillé and Owen Rambow, editors, *Tree Adjoining Grammars: Formalisms, Linguistic Analyses and Processing*, CSLI Publications, Stanford, CA, number 107 in CSLI Lecture Notes, pages 1–68.

Joan Chen-Main and Aravind K. Joshi. 2014. A dependency perspective on the adequacy of tree local multi-component tree adjoining grammar. *Journal of Logic and Computation* 24(5):989–1022. https://doi.org/10.1093/logcom/exs012.

Benoit Crabbé, Denys Duchier, Claire Gardent, Joseph Le Roux, and Yannick Parmentier. 2013. XMG: eXtensible MetaGrammar. *Computational Linguistics* 39(3):1–66.

David Dowty. 1991. Thematic proto-roles and argument selection. *Language* 67(3):547–619.

Thomas Ernst. 2001. *The syntax of adjuncts*. Number 96 in Cambridge Studies in Linguistics. Cambridge University Press, Cambridge, UK.

Robert Frank. 2002. *Phrase Structure Composition and Syntactic Dependencies*. MIT Press, Cambridge, MA.

Robert Frank. 2008. Reflexives and TAG semantics. In *Proceedings of the Ninth International Workshop on Tree Adjoining Grammar and Related Frameworks (TAG+9)*. Tübingen, Germany, pages 97–104. http://www.aclweb.org/anthology/W08-2313.

Wilhelm Geuder. 2002. *Oriented adverbs: Issues in the lexical semantics of event adverbs*. Doctoral dissertation, University of Tübingen, Tübingen, Germany.

Wilhelm Geuder. 2004. Depictives and transparent adverbs. In Jennifer R. Austin, Stefan Engelberg, and Gisa Rauh, editors, *Adverbials: The interplay between meaning, context, and syntactic structure*, John Benjamins Publishing Company, Amsterdam, pages 131–166. https://doi.org/10.1075/la.70.06geu.

Aravind K. Joshi and Yves Schabes. 1997. Tree-Adjoining Grammars. In Grzegorz Rozenberg and Arto Salomaa, editors, *Handbook of Formal Languages*, Springer, Berlin, volume 3, pages 69–124.

Laura Kallmeyer, Timm Lichte, Rainer Osswald, and Simon Petitjean. 2016. Argument linking in LTAG: A constraint-based implementation with XMG. In *Proceedings of the 12th International Workshop on Tree Adjoining Grammars and Related Formalisms (TAG+12)*. Düsseldorf, Germany, pages 48–57. http://www.aclweb.org/anthology/W16-3305.

Laura Kallmeyer and Rainer Osswald. 2013. Syntax-driven semantic frame composition in Lexicalized Tree Adjoining Grammar. *Journal of Language Modelling* 1:267–330.

Laura Kallmeyer and Maribel Romero. 2007. Reflexives and reciprocals in LTAG. In Jeroen Geertzen, Elias Thijsse, Harry Bunt, and Amanda Schiffrin, editors, *Proceedings of the Seventh International Workshop on Computational Semantics IWCS-7*. Tilburg, pages 271–282.

Anthony S. Kroch and Aravind K. Joshi. 1987. Analyzing extraposition in a tree adjoining grammar. In Geoffrey J. Huck and Almerido E. Ojeda, editors, *Syntax and Semantics: Discontinuous Constituency*, Academic Press, Inc., pages 107–149.

Stefan Müller. 2002. *Complex Predicates. Verbal Complexes, Resultative Constructions, and Particle Verbs in German*. Studies in Constraint-Based Lexicalism. CSLI Publications, Stanford.

Stefan Müller. 2008. Depictive secondary predicates in German and English. In Christoph Schroeder, Gerd Hentschel, and Winfried Boeder, editors, *Secondary Predicates in Eastern European Languages and Beyond*, BIS-Verlag, Oldenburg, number 16 in Studia Slavica Oldenburgensia, pages 255–273. http://hpsg.fu-berlin.de/ stefan/Pub/depiktiv-2006.html.

Carl Pollard and Ivan A. Sag. 1994. *Head-Driven Phrase Structure Grammar*. Studies in Contemporary Linguistics. The University of Chicago Press, Chicago.

Liina Pylkkänen. 2002. *Introducing Arguments*. Ph.D. thesis, Massachusetts Institute of Technology, Cambridge, MA.

Owen Rambow, K. Vijay-Shanker, and David Weir. 2001. D-tree substitution grammars. *Computational Linguistic* 27(1):87–121.

Ian Roberts. 1987. *The Representation of Implicit and Dethematized Subjects*. Number 10 in Linguistic Models. De Gruyter Mouton, Berlin. https://doi.org/10.1515/9783110877304.

Ian Roberts. 1988. Predicative aps. *Linguistic Inquiry* 19(4):703–710.

Neville Ryant and Tatjana Scheffler. 2006. Binding of anaphors in LTAG. In *Proceedings of the Eighth International Workshop on Tree Adjoining Grammar and Related Formalisms*. Sydney, Australia, pages 65–72. http://www.aclweb.org/anthology/W/W06/W06-1509.

Yves Schabes and Stuart M. Shieber. 1994. An Alternative Conception of Tree-Adjoining Derivation. *Computational Linguistics* 20(1):91–124.

Jane Simpson. 2005. Depictives in English and Warlpiri. In Nikolaus P. Himmelmann and Eva Schultze-Berndt, editors, *Secondary Predication and Adverbial Modification: The Typology of Depictives*, Oxford University Press, Oxford, pages 69–106.

Dennis R. Storoshenko, Chung-hye Han, and David Potter. 2008. Reflexivity in English: An STAG analysis. In *Proceedings of the Ninth International Workshop on Tree Adjoining Grammar and Related Frameworks (TAG+9)*. Tübingen, Germany, pages 149–156. http://www.aclweb.org/anthology/W08-2320.

Gregory Stump. 1985. *The semantic variability of absolute constructions*. Number 25 in Synthese language library. D. Reidel Publishing, Dordrecht, The Netherlands.

Robert D. Van Valin, Jr. 2005. *Exploring the Syntax-Semantics Interface*. Cambridge University Press, Cambridge.

Susanne Winkler. 1997. *Focus and Secondary Predication*. Number 43 in Studies in Generative Grammar. Mouton de Gruyter, Berlin.

Dieter Wunderlich. 1997. Argument extension by lexical adjunction. *Journal of Semantics* 14(2):95–142.

Reflexives and Reciprocals in Synchronous Tree Adjoining Grammar

Cristina Aggazzotti
Department of Linguistics
Harvard University
Cambridge, MA 02138
caggazzotti@g.harvard.edu

Stuart M. Shieber
Paulson School of Eng'g. and Applied Sciences
Harvard University
Cambridge, MA 02138
shieber@seas.harvard.edu

Abstract

An attractive feature of the formalism of synchronous tree adjoining grammar (STAG) is its potential to handle linguistic phenomena whose syntactic and semantic derivations seem to diverge. Recent work has aimed at adapting STAG to capture such cases. Anaphors, including both reflexives and reciprocals, have presented a particular challenge due to the locality constraints imposed by the STAG formalism. Previous attempts to model anaphors in STAG have focused specifically on reflexives and have not expanded to incorporate reciprocals. We show how STAG can not only capture the syntactic distribution and semantic representation of both reflexives and reciprocals, but also do so in a unified way.

1 Introduction

In this paper, we present a novel unified analysis of both reflexives and reciprocals in synchronous tree adjoining grammar (STAG). STAG utilizes syntactic-semantic tree pairs that undergo synchronized operations to produce a unified syntactic and semantic analysis of linguistic phenomena. Since anaphors, specifically reflexives (*himself, themselves*) and reciprocals (*each other*), require a referential lexical item, or antecedent, to supply their semantic value, they depend on both syntax, in the form of distributional constraints, and semantics, in the form of specific relations with the antecedent. Thus, STAG has the potential to be an effective way of modeling both reflexives and reciprocals. Yet STAG's tight integration of syntax and semantics places strong constraints on the syntax-semantics interface, making anaphors a challenging and illuminating test case for the formalism.

By way of example, consider the sentences in (1), identical except for the alternation between reflexive and reciprocal.

(1) a. Noah and Emma saw themselves.

    b. Noah and Emma saw each other.

As reciprocals require a plural antecedent, for consistency throughout this paper we use examples with plural antecedents for both reflexives and reciprocals. In the *distributive* reading of the reflexive, the relation (here, *saw*) holds between each atom in the plural antecedent and itself. Similarly, for reciprocals, the core reading (so-called *strong reciprocity*) is one in which the relation holds between each atom in the antecedent and each other distinct atom.[1]

The variant of STAG that we assume, following other recent work on STAG for natural-language semantics, is based on set-local multicomponent TAG (MCTAG). In synchronous set-local MC-TAG (henceforth, simply "STAG"), a lexical item is represented by a set of syntactic and semantic elementary trees, all of which substitute or adjoin at the same time into another tree set (thus "set-locally") (Weir, 1988). This formalism has been shown to handle a range of phenomena at the syntax-semantics interface, including nested quantifiers (Nesson and Shieber, 2006), extraction

---

[1] There are additional readings for reflexives and reciprocals as well. For instance, in a *cumulative* reading of the reflexive, Noah and Emma both see the pair containing both of them (as, perhaps, in a mirror). The relation holds of the entire plurality and itself. Similarly, reciprocals can display weaker readings than strong reciprocity (Langendoen, 1978; Dalrymple et al., 1998). Incorporation of these readings into the present framework is enabled by our abstracting out the meanings of the reflexive and reciprocal into separable relations REFL and RECP below, but is well beyond the scope of this paper.

Proceedings of the 13th International Workshop on Tree Adjoining Grammars and Related Formalisms (TAG+13), pages 31–42,
Umeå, Sweden, September 4–6, 2017. © 2017 Association for Computational Linguistics

phenomena (Nesson and Shieber, 2007), prepositions (Nesson, 2009), it-clefts (Han and Hedberg, 2006), pied-piping in relative clauses (Han, 2006), and clitic climbing (Bleam, 2000).

Previous applications of TAG to anaphors have either appealed to extra facilities, such as recursive semantic features (Kallmeyer and Romero, 2007; Ryant and Scheffler, 2006; Champollion, 2008), or used the more constrained STAG plus adjustments, such as using de Bruijn indices in the semantics (Nesson, 2009), creating multiple reflexive trees (Storoshenko et al., 2008), or operating at multiple links in the derivation (Frank, 2008). No STAG approach to our knowledge has captured both reflexives and reciprocals. Our analysis seeks to fill this void by showing that both kinds of anaphors can be captured uniformly in STAG.

To achieve this, we simplify and generalize one previous analysis of reflexives in STAG, namely that of Frank (2008), so it can apply to reciprocals and a variety of reflexive cases. We simplify Frank's analysis, eliminating the c-command and dominance relations used for proper variable binding by appealing to fundamental syntactic and semantic constraints. We also generalize his analysis to apply to both reflexives and reciprocals. Our full analysis is described in Section 2. We demonstrate the power of this approach in Section 3 using the examples of cataphoric constructions and anaphors as arguments of object control verbs. Analogous derivations capture ditransitive verbs in which the reflexive can be coindexed with the subject or object, though space limitations preclude their inclusion. To handle non-local cases, we avail ourselves of a version of delayed locality, originally proposed by Chiang and Scheffler (2008), and in Section 4 we show how delayed locality accounts for syntactic constructions such as anaphors as arguments of raising verbs and Exceptional Case Marking (ECM) verbs. The analysis also accounts for anaphors in *picture*-DPs and quantificational *picture*-DPs, anaphors in adjuncts, and sentences with multiple anaphors.

1.1 Synchronous tree adjoining grammar

We use set-local feature-structure-based synchronous MCTAG, supplemented with a version of delayed locality for non-local anaphoric cases. Nodes in syntactic trees are notated with syntactic categories and in semantic trees with semantic types, using the notation $\langle \sigma, \tau \rangle$ to express function types from σ to τ, or the abbreviated version $\sigma\tau$ where no ambiguity results. The feature-structure-based synchronous MCTAG framework we use is exemplified in Figure 1. Elementary tree sets for DPs, as in (a) and (b), contain multiple syntactic trees and semantic trees, two of each, independently motivated for handling quantification and topicalization. The syntax has a TP auxiliary tree (allowing for frontings such as topicalization, following Nesson and Shieber (2007)) in addition to the "in situ" DP tree; the synchronous semantics has a t auxiliary tree (used for quantifier scope, following Shieber and Schabes (1990) and Williford (1993)) and an e-rooted reference tree. Non-quantificational DPs like *Noah* have a degenerate scope tree t_* that does not modify the derived tree, so merely serves as a placeholder to maintain structural consistency.

Syntactic nodes have an associated feature structure containing finite feature values. The feature structure must unify with the feature structure of any substituting or adjoining node in order for the operation to take place; if any features conflict, the unification fails (Vijay-Shanker and Joshi, 1988). In particular, we can mark DP substitution nodes in their feature structure with their case requirements (which can be thought of as a manifestation of their being assigned abstract Case (Polinsky and Preminger, 2014)), while lexical item trees rooted at DP that exhibit morphological case will have that case depicted in the root feature structure as well. This built-in feature checking system will play a role in several aspects of our STAG framework, including matching phi-features (number, person, gender) of anaphors and antecedents, making c-command and dominance constraints unnecessary, and accounting for cataphoric constructions. For reasons of readability and succinctness, we do not show feature structures explicitly in subsequent examples.

Reciprocals reciprocate over plural entities. For our purposes, we do not require a sophisticated semantic notion of plurality (such as Scha (1981), van Bentham (1989), or Westerståhl (1989)). We notate the type of sets of entities of type σ as $\overline{\sigma}$ and the plural entity combining a and b as $a + b$; we further optionally identify singular entities a with singleton plural entities $\{a\}$. Plural DPs will sometimes denote plural entities (like *Noah and Emma* of type $\overline{e}$), and certain verbs (of type $\overline{e}t$, like *met*) will require plural entities. Certain quantified

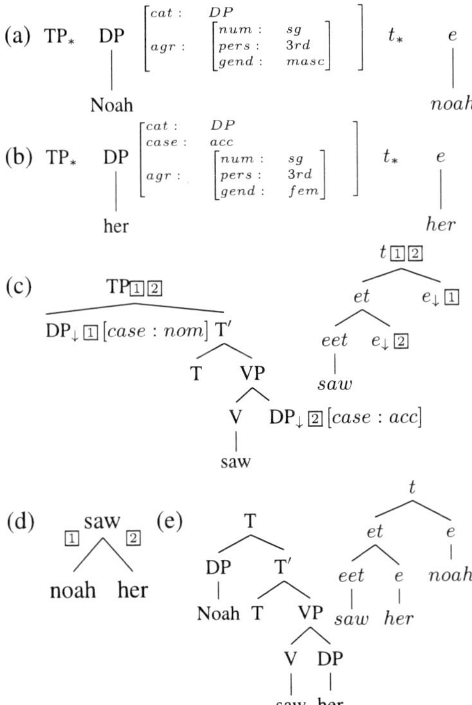

Figure 1: Elementary STAG trees and feature structures for (a) DPs, (b) pronouns, and (c) transitive verbs; (d) is the derivation tree and (e) the derived trees for the simple transitive sentence *Noah saw her.*

DPs (like *everyone*) may involve both interpretations – the quantifier meaning (as in *everyone left*) of type $\langle et, t \rangle$ and the plural interpretation (as in *everyone met*) of type $\bar{e}$.

Nodes that can undergo operations are designated by links, shown in the trees with numbered boxes ($\boxed{1}$), that ensure the syntactic and semantic trees accept synchronous operations at corresponding nodes, as in (c). Multiple boxes marked with the same numbered link specify the sites of operation of a set of trees.

1.2 Previous work on reflexives in TAG

In the literature, there are six main applications of TAG to capture anaphors. Three are non-synchronous, building a semantic representation using recursive feature structures (Ryant and Scheffler, 2006; Kallmeyer and Romero, 2007; Champollion, 2008),[2] which can be more pow-

erful than TAG (indeed Turing-equivalent under some usages), and look at both reflexives and reciprocals. The other three use the more restrictive STAG framework for both the syntax and semantics but only look at reflexives (Nesson, 2009; Storoshenko et al., 2008; Frank, 2008).

For the non-synchronous TAG approaches, Ryant and Scheffler (2006) employ tree-local multicomponent lexicalized TAG (LTAG) with semantic feature structures and a flat compositional semantics for each elementary tree. The multicomponent tree set for reflexives and reciprocals contains two trees: an NP tree with the lexical anaphor that is c-commanded by a degenerate NP tree that composes with its antecedent through flexible composition (FC) (Joshi et al., 2003), an extension of LTAG. This approach captures reflexives and reciprocals but requires extra subject intervention and c-command constraints to prevent overgeneration.

Kallmeyer and Romero (2007) use a similar approach, but replace Ryant and Scheffler's degenerate anaphor NP tree with a degenerate VP tree. This change does not require the FC extension (except for adjuncts) or stronger c-command constraints, but does require a dominance relation between the degenerate VP and the lexical anaphor as well as a procedure for passing antecedent features. Only with both of these additions do the locality and c-command restrictions of classic binding theory (Chomsky, 1981) then follow.

Instead of compositional semantics, Champollion (2008) uses the feature-based LTAG formalism of Vijay-Shanker (1987) extended by the use of lists as values of features, as in HPSG (Pollard and Sag, 1992), and list operations, such as appending lists together. Champollion (2008) improves upon the previous non-synchronous approaches in several ways, such as by capturing ECM verbs, adjuncts, and all conditions in binding theory with no further additions to the framework; however, the analysis does not include reciprocals and requires recursive features.

For the STAG approaches, Nesson (2009) uses MCTAG but extends the lambda calculus notation for semantic representation with de Bruijn indices. The de Bruijn notation uses integer indices – instead of explicitly-named free variables – to indicate how many enclosing λ terms away the variable's binding λ is. Although this approach pro-

---

[2]Steedman (2000) also provides an account for binding but uses a combination of LTAG and combinatory categorical grammar (CCG).

vides more flexibility for locality constraints and can successfully account for a variety of reflexive sentences, it does not allow the differentiation needed for reciprocals because the indices allow specification only of coindexation.

Storoshenko et al. (2008) take a different MC-TAG approach by positing three separate reflexive syntactic trees, whose use depends on the reflexive's binding option as a verbal argument. The semantics relies on dynamically varying what is a function and what is an argument. For a sentence containing a reflexive, the reflexive plays the function role, taking its sister node as its argument; however, if an entity fills that position in the sentence instead of a reflexive, the entity would be an argument and its sister node the function. Although the analysis captures ditransitives, raising verbs, and ECM verbs, why these three reflexive tree sets are the (only) possible options and why each reflexive has its specific semantic type is not well motivated.

It may be possible to extend this analysis to reciprocals: following reflexives, the semantics could be separately defined for each case as needed and agreement could be handled in the syntax through a clever use of features. However, this approach seems to lack a unifying story behind the choice of tree set configuration. We thus turn to the final application of STAG to reflexives, which we show can be extended to both reflexives and reciprocals in a more straightforward way.

1.3 The analysis of Frank (2008)

Frank (2008) uses tree-local MCTAG to capture simple reflexive cases but does not attempt to capture reciprocals and does not definitively extend the analysis to more complicated cases, such as raising and ECM verbs. The analysis is illustrated in Figure 2 for the sentence in (2).[3]

---

[3] We have diverged from Frank's elementary trees (Frank, 2008, Figure 1) slightly, modifying them by clarifying and making explicit two notational issues, according to our understanding. First, we include an explicit t_* tree in the tree set for *John* based on the ☐1 link at the root of the reflexive tree, which we assume indicates the adjunction of a *John* tree at the same time its e-rooted tree substitutes. Second, we removed the ☐2 links on the NP *himself* and on the second semantic x variable tree (see Frank's Figure 1(a)) because they seem to serve as labels, rather than as operable sites like the ☐1 links. We leave the ☐2 link on the root of the semantic verb tree (even though it does not correspond to an explicit adjoining tree) because it may be intended for an extra scope tree in the reflexive tree set; however, it is unclear how that extra scope tree would fit into the included dominance relations so we do not explicitly add it to the reflexive tree set here.

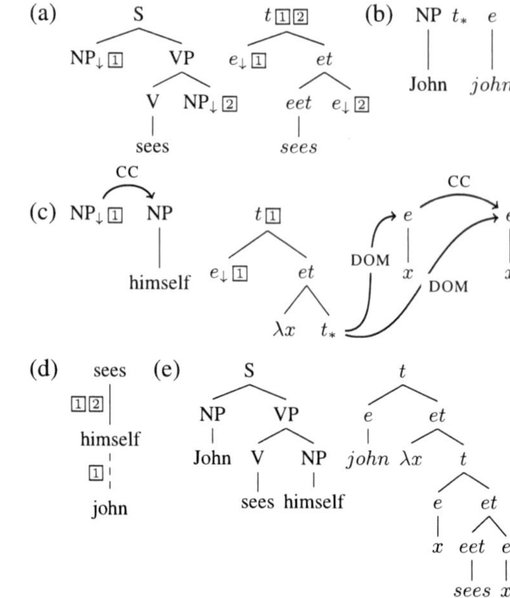

Figure 2: Frank's elementary trees for (a) transitive verbs, (b) type e NPs, and (c) reflexives; (d) is the derivation tree and (e) the derived trees for sentence (2). Extra constraints are indicated with labeled arrows: CC for c-command, DOM for dominance.

(2) John sees himself.

Frank's analysis is novel in two ways: the structure of the derivation and the use of multiple links. First, derivations of reflexive sentences (Figure 2(d)) diverge from derivations of non-reflexive sentences (Figure 1(d)). The derivation tree in Figure 2(d) has the antecedent (subject) first substitute into the reflexive (object), which then as a whole composes into the verb tree at the respective links.[4]

The structure of this derivation is unusual in the TAG literature in not paralleling the non-reflexive derivation tree, in which the subject and object separately substitute directly into the verb tree. However, there may be cross-linguistic evidence for this type of derivation. In languages such as Finnish, which represent reflexivization with a verbal affix that detransitivizes the verb into an intransitive verb, Büring (2005) explains that this verbal reflexive marker is not a syntactic argument

---

[4] Ryant and Scheffler (2006) use a similar derivation tree in that the antecedent composes with the anaphor before both compose into the verb tree, but their use of flexible composition allows composition of trees in either direction, so the derivation tree is not actually equivalent.

or clitic, providing support for a derivation tree in which the verb accepts just one argument, the subject. An analysis of clitics along these lines may be apposite as well.

Second, Frank's analysis crucially relies on allowing a tree set to operate at multiple links. The reflex of this innovation is the multiple links decorating edges in the derivation tree, where in standard STAG, only a single link would appear. In particular, Frank's derivation tree in (d) portrays the reflexive *himself* going into the verb tree at both links ① and ②. Implicitly, Frank is appealing to a novel generalization of MCTAG, in which multiple components of a tree set can apply at multiple links.

Frank's approach accounts for simple reflexive antecedents, quantifier-bound reflexives, reflexives embedded in a *picture*-DP, and reflexives occurring as the argument of a ditransitive predicate. However, the approach does not directly extend to reciprocals.

Unlike reflexives, reciprocals are not simply inherently coindexed with their antecedent since the antecedent must be distributed into its atomic parts. Frank's approach as it stands cannot account for this. The semantic trees contain only one binder of two instantiations of the same variable and are thus inherently detransitivizing. By maintaining separate binders of the two argument positions, our modifications below not only account for both reflexives and reciprocals, but also do so in a unified and simplified way.

2 Our analysis

In this section, we explain how our analysis builds directly on Frank's. We adjust the analysis to be in line with the framework outlined in Section 1.1.

2.1 Frank's analysis revised

As in Frank's analysis, the reflexives will use *both* subject and object links, and thus will be composed of four syntactic and four semantic trees. The tree set follows Frank's approach with only minor changes, as shown in Figure 3(a). In the syntactic tree set are two TP$_*$ placeholder trees, one for each of the DP trees. The first DP tree is degenerate, accepting the antecedent by substitution, and the second contains the reflexive. The semantic tree set contains a t auxiliary scope tree for each of the e-rooted variables. In the first scope tree, a reflexive operator REFL (described shortly)

has been added as another binary branch in the elementary reflexive tree, along with two binding λ terms (instead of just one). The e-rooted variable trees correspondingly contain two distinct variables. As shown in (b), we use the same derivation tree as Frank, also taking advantage of the multi-link extension of MCTAG.

As described in Section 1.1, our framework makes use of case and feature unification for pronouns, which can additionally ensure the correct configuration of lexical substitution of the antecedent and reflexive, thus making the c-command (CC) and dominance (DOM) constraints redundant. Eliminating these extra constraints greatly simplifies the analysis by relying on the inherent features of the formalism instead of on externally-added restrictions.

On the semantics side, the reflexive operator REFL serves as a formalization of the reflexive relation. For the purposes of this paper, in which we focus on the distributive reflexive reading of plural reflexives, the REFL operator is given as in (3). Abstracting out the reflexive operator allows flexibility in its semantic definition and comparison to alternatives (such as the RECP operator we introduce shortly).

(3) $\text{REFL} \equiv \lambda R \, . \, \lambda Z \, . \, \forall x : x \in Z \, .$
$$\forall y : y \in Z \land y = x \, . \, R \, y \, x$$

Informally speaking, the operator holds of a binary relation R and an antecedent set Z just in case every pair x and y in the set Z, where x and y are not distinct, are in the relation R.[5] (The benefit of the apparent redundancy of the two universal quantifiers will become evident shortly.)

The STAG derivation corresponding to sentence (1a) proceeds as in Figure 3. The resulting logical form can be simplified as shown in (4), demonstrating that the distributive reading is appropriately captured.

(4) $\text{REFL} \, (\lambda a \, . \, \lambda b \, . \, saw \, a \, b) \, (n + e)$
$$= (\lambda R \, . \, \lambda Z \, . \, \forall x : x \in Z.$$
$$\forall y : y \in Z \land y = x \, . \, R \, y \, x)$$
$$(\lambda a \, . \, \lambda b \, . \, saw \, a \, b) \, (n + e)$$
$$= \forall x : x \in (n + e).$$
$$\forall y : y \in (n + e) \land y = x \, . \, saw \, y \, x$$
$$= saw \, n \, n \land saw \, e \, e$$

---

[5]This definition of REFL can also account for singular antecedents by interpreting them as singleton plural entities.

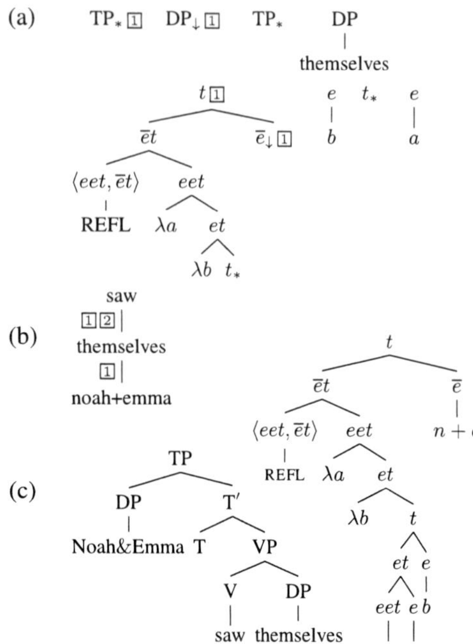

Figure 3: (a) Elementary tree set for a reflexive; (b) is the derivation tree and (c) the derived trees for sentence (1a).

2.2 Comparison of analyses

There are four differences between our reflexive analysis and Frank's.

1. We use extra placeholder trees to maintain a parallel structure among all DPs. The extra trees are necessitated on the syntax side by the DP tree used in the Nesson and Shieber (2007) fronting analysis and on the semantics side by the quantifier scope tree. This modification is not essential to our reflexive analysis as it arises solely from our incorporation of the independent fronting analysis (as described in Section 3.1).

2. We eliminate binding constraints like c-command and dominance, which permits the flexibility needed for cataphora, since these relations are already captured through case checking.

3. We employ two bindings of distinct variables instead of one binding of a single variable twice, as this allows the appropriate grain needed for reciprocals.

4. We abstract away the reflexivity notion from Frank's trees with an operator REFL, which

generalizes to also be compatible with reciprocals using a parallel operator RECP, as described in the next section.

2.3 Adding reciprocals

Using an operator for both reflexives and reciprocals captures their underlying similarities, creating a unified account of both. It seems logical to group reflexives and reciprocals together syntactically, as structurally interchangeable constructions, and distinguish between them semantically, as differing with respect solely to distribution over the antecedent. This is the motivation behind our proposed approach.

In order to incorporate reciprocals into the STAG framework, we simply add the reciprocal counterparts in the same place as reflexives in the multicomponent tree set for reflexives, as in Figure 4. On the syntax side, we replace the lexical item *themselves* with *each other* and on the semantics side, we replace the reflexive operator (REFL) with a reciprocal operator (RECP). We indicate the shared structure by placing corresponding components of reflexives and reciprocals in the same node as interchangeable options.

An attractive property of this analysis is that simply by replacing the $=$ in the semantic representation of REFL with $\neq$, we get the formalization of the reciprocal relation RECP:

$$(5) \quad \text{RECP} \equiv \lambda R \,.\, \lambda Z \,.\, \forall x : x \in Z \,.$$
$$\forall y : y \in Z \wedge y \neq x \,.\, R\,y\,x$$

Similarly to REFL, the RECP operator holds of a binary relation R and an antecedent set Z just in case every pair x and y in the set Z, where x and y *are* distinct, are in the relation R. For the reciprocal version of sentence (1a), in (1b), RECP provides the correct (and only) reading – the strong reciprocity reading – that Noah saw Emma and Emma saw Noah. The reduction proceeds in parallel fashion to that of reflexives. Comparing these trees to Frank's trees in Figure 2, the reader can confirm that the derivation tree is identical and both methods produce the same result (up to the modification in the logical form). With this example as a foundation, we now show the utility of this representation for a range of increasingly complex reflexive and reciprocal phenomena.

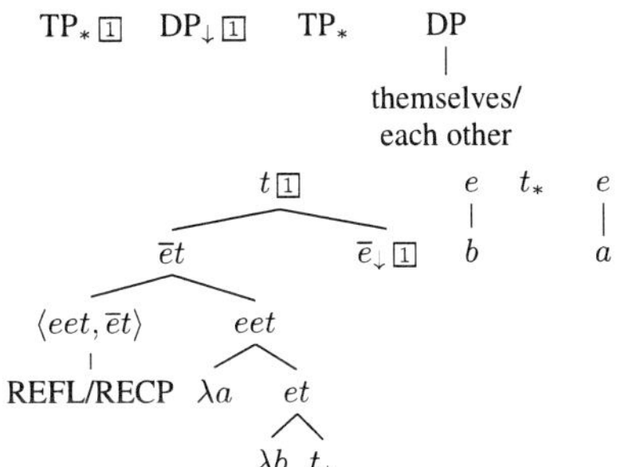

Figure 4: Anaphor elementary tree set for both a reflexive and a reciprocal

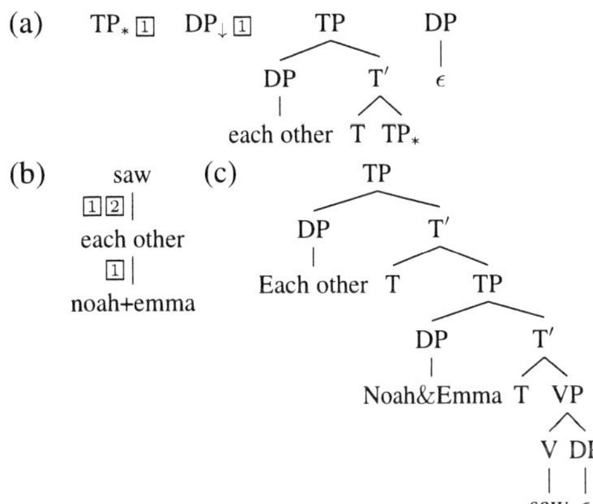

Figure 5: (a) Syntactic elementary trees for a cataphoric (topicalized) reflexive; (b) is the derivation tree and (c) the syntactic derived tree for sentence (6b)

3 Applications

The analysis essentially unchanged accounts for various reflexive and reciprocal phenomena, including cataphora, anaphors with object control verbs, and anaphors as arguments of ditransitive verbs. The analysis also has the potential to apply to reflexives and reciprocals in other languages, but we leave this extension for future work. We show here only the analysis for cataphora and anaphors with object control verbs due to space constraints, but the other applications follow similarly.

3.1 Cataphora

Cataphora, such as in (6a), would appear to present a problem for analyses requiring c-command constraints, as the required c-command relation does not appear to hold overtly in the derived tree. Our approach however is completely consistent with the account of topicalization of Nesson and Shieber (2007), by treating the anaphor as a topicalized item.[6] We illustrate this derivation in Figure 5 for the simplified cataphoric reciprocal sentence in (6b).[7]

(6) a. (Noah and Emma like many people, but) each other, they can't stand.

    b. Each other, Noah and Emma saw.

The syntactic tree set for the reflexive, shown in Figure 5(a), simply reflects topicalization of the

reflexive following directly the topicalization analysis of Nesson and Shieber (2007): the TP auxiliary tree now contains the lexical reflexive and the corresponding DP tree contains the empty string; the semantics side remains unchanged so is not shown. The derivation proceeds as usual.

Using a feature-checking system instead of binding principles provides the flexibility needed for capturing cataphora without additional machinery because the topicalized anaphor, instead of the empty DP, receives accusative case and thus no feature conflicts arise.

3.2 Anaphors with object control verbs

Syntactic constructions with object control verbs, such as *persuade* in (7), follow directly from our analysis as put forth so far.

(7) Noah and Emma persuaded themselves/each other to be happy.

Object control verbs have three arguments: an agent (*Noah and Emma*), a theme (*themselves/each other*), and an open proposition (*to be happy*). This configuration is represented in the elementary object control verb tree set in Figure 6(a). The lower verb cannot have its own subject, so the *persuaded* tree set contains a DP tree in the syntax and a corresponding variable tree in the semantics that substitute into the subject position of the lower verb. The derivation proceeds according to the derivation tree in (c), in which the antecedent composes into the anaphor tree set,

---

[6]In this paper, we focus on the core anaphoric cases, excluding logophoric (point of view or emphatic/focus) anaphors, as discussed in, for instance, Reinhart and Reuland (1993). For cataphora in particular, we only consider examples in which the anaphor stands alone as a topicalized item, and do not address anaphors embedded in topicalized adjuncts or adverbial phrases.

[7]Cataphoric reflexives follow similarly so are not shown.

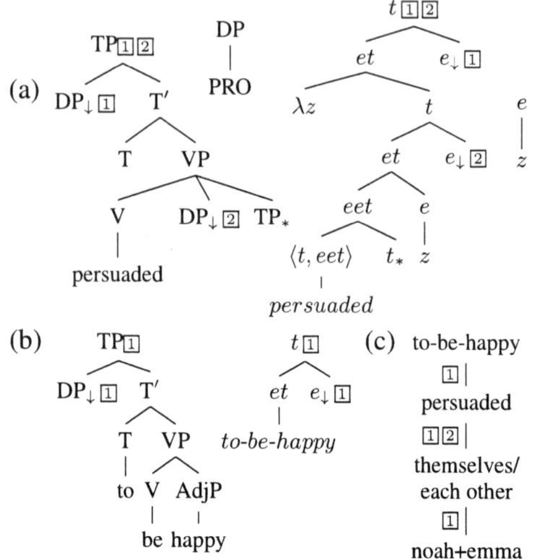

Figure 6: Elementary trees for (a) object control verbs and (b) non-finite predicates with appropriate links; (c) is the derivation tree. The derived tree pair is provided in Figure 8 in the appendix.

which then as a whole composes into the object control tree set in a tree-local fashion. This tree set then composes into the non-finite verb tree.

4 Extensions with delayed locality

Although a wide variety of interactions between anaphors and other constructions are captured by this analysis, there is an entire class of cases that are not expressible under the set-local view of STAG derivation we have been presupposing. In this section, we extend the derivation notion to allow for *delayed locality*, first proposed by Chiang and Scheffler (2008). Delayed locality relaxes the set-locality constraint to allow a delay in composition. Two trees in a multicomponent tree set may compose into (any number of) other trees before eventually composing into the same elementary tree.[8] This differs from the more expressive non-local MCTAG in requiring that the members eventually compose into the same elementary tree (Chiang and Scheffler, 2008). Delayed locality has permitted analyses of non-local right-node raising (Han et al., 2010), bound vari-

___

[8] Storoshenko and Han (2013) propose a slightly different definition of a delay than Chiang and Scheffler (2008); we postpone committing to a particular definition to future work, but recognize that overgeneration is a concern, since without further constraint our analysis could allow, for instance,

(8) * Noah$_i$ thinks that Emma likes himself$_i$.

able pronouns (Storoshenko and Han, 2010), and clitic climbing (Chen-Main et al., 2012).

With this extension, our analysis allows for anaphors in a variety of syntactic constructions, including *picture*-DPs, quantificational *picture*-DPs, adjuncts, raising verbs, ECM verbs, and multiple anaphors in the same sentence, but due to space limitations we again demonstrate only for raising and ECM verbs.

4.1 Anaphors with raising verbs

In contrast to object control verbs, raising verbs, such as *seem* in (9), do not have an inherent subject argument; therefore, the usual representation of *seem* in the TAG literature (with minor variations) does not contain a DP subject node, as shown in Figure 7(b).

(9) Noah and Emma seem to themselves/each other to be happy.

Use of the present anaphor analysis with this configuration violates set-locality because the anaphor would compose into the raising verb tree, but there would not be a position for the antecedent to also compose.[9] However, the relaxation provided by delayed locality allows the lexical anaphor part of the tree set to compose into the raising verb through delay, which then composes into the lower clause verb trees at link ③, while the antecedent part is not delayed and composes directly into the lower clause verb trees, as depicted in Figure 7(c). In order to ensure that all variables are properly bound, the semantic predicate *to-be-happy* tree in Figure 7(a) has the root node split into an upper $t_{①②}$ node and a lower $t_{③}$ node to ensure that the REFL/RECP tree binds the a variable in the raising verb tree.

4.2 Anaphors with ECM verbs

ECM (or "subject-to-object raising") verbs, as in (10), have two arguments: a subject (*Noah and Emma*) and a proposition (*themselves/each other to be happy*). Based on these structural properties, the elementary tree for an ECM verb contains a subject position and adjoins into a predicate to fill its proposition argument, as shown in Figure 7(d).

___

[9] An alternative local derivation would be to simply include a subject position in the elementary raising verb tree. Although this solution solves the locality issue, it has implications for the treatment of raising constructions in general so we do not pursue it here.

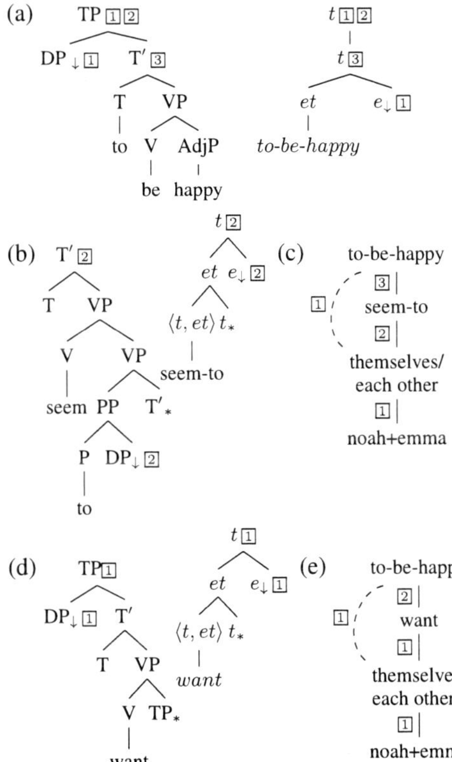

Figure 7: Elementary trees for (a) non-finite predicates with appropriate links and configuration for variable binding and (b) raising verbs with an anaphor object; (c) is the derivation tree with delayed locality for sentence (9); (d) elementary trees for ECM verbs and (e) is the derivation tree with delayed locality for sentence (10).

(10) Noah and Emma want themselves/each other to be happy.

In contrast to the previous example, for ECM verbs the antecedent part of the anaphor tree set is the delayed part, first composing into the ECM verb trees and then composing into the non-finite verb trees at link ②. The derivation tree in (e) reflects this difference through the links shown.

For cases in English with multiple (surface accusative) objects, such as in the ECM construction in (11a), appealing to case is not sufficient to account for the ungrammaticality of (11b). A more nuanced case analysis, in which the equational constraint on case (that the antecedent's case is nominative and the anaphor's case is accusative) is replaced by an inequational constraint over a set of cases ordered by obliqueness (that the an-

tecedent's case is less oblique than the anaphor's case) suffices to cover these as well, predicting the grammaticality of (11a) and ungrammaticality of (11b).

(11)   a. Emma wants him to love himself.

      b. * Emma wants himself to love him.

5 Conclusion

In this paper, we have shown how the formalism of STAG can not only handle both reflexives and reciprocals, but also provide a unified account of both, founded on the idea that these anaphors share a syntactic distribution but differ slightly and uniformly in their semantics. To accomplish this, we provide STAG tree sets for reflexives and reciprocals that differ only in their lexical presentation and their interpretation through operators REFL and RECP that capture the parallel semantic nature of reflexives and reciprocals. It is, to our knowledge, the first STAG analysis to provide for reciprocals as well as reflexives. The analysis is consistent with earlier STAG analyses accounting for such syntactic phenomena as topicalization and semantic phenomena as quantification, while building on the previous STAG account by Frank (2008) of reflexives alone, making anaphoric notions more explicit, eliminating the need for c-command and dominance constraints, and generalizing the analysis to capture reciprocals as well.

Areas for future work include investigating appropriate further limits on delayed locality to prevent overgeneration, expanding our preliminary application of the operators crosslinguistically, and refining the operators' semantic definitions to account for additional anaphoric interpretations.

Acknowledgments

We wish to thank Gennaro Chierchia, Robert Frank, and Jennifer Hu for valuable conversations on the topic of this paper and the anonymous reviewers for their helpful comments.

References

Tonia Bleam. 2000. Clitic climbing and the power of tree adjoining grammar. In Anne Abeillé and Owen Rambow, editors, *Tree Adjoining Grammars: Formalisms, Linguistic Analysis, and Processing*, CSLI Publications, pages 193–219.

Daniel Büring. 2005. *Binding Theory*. Cambridge University Press, UK.

Lucas Champollion. 2008. Binding theory in LTAG. In *Proceedings of the Ninth International Workshop on Tree Adjoining Grammar and Related Formalisms (TAG+9)*. Tübingen, Germany, pages 1–8. http://aclweb.org/anthology/W08-2301.

Joan Chen-Main, Tonia Bleam, and Aravind K. Joshi. 2012. Delayed tree-locality, set-locality, and clitic climbing. In *Proceedings of the 11th International Workshop on Tree Adjoining Grammar and Related Formalisms (TAG+11)*. Paris, France, pages 1–9. http://aclweb.org/anthology/W12-4601.

David Chiang and Tatjana Scheffler. 2008. Flexible composition and delayed tree-locality. In *Proceedings of the Ninth International Workshop on Tree Adjoining Grammars and Related Formalisms (TAG+9)*. Association for Computational Linguistics, Tübingen, Germany, pages 17–24. http://aclweb.org/anthology/W08-2303.

Noam Chomsky. 1981. *Lectures on Government and Binding*. Dordrecht: Foris.

Mary Dalrymple, Makoto Kanazawa, Yookyung Kim, Sam McHombo, and Stanley Peters. 1998. Reciprocal expressions and the concept of reciprocity. *Linguistics and Philosophy* 21(2):159–210. https://doi.org/10.1023/A:1005330227480.

Robert Frank. 2008. Reflexives and TAG semantics. In *Proceedings of the Ninth International Workshop on Tree Adjoining Grammar and Related Formalisms (TAG+9)*. Association for Computational Linguistics, Tübingen, Germany, pages 97–104. http://aclweb.org/anthology/W08-2313.

Chung-hye Han. 2006. Pied-piping in relative clauses: Syntax and compositional semantics based on synchronous tree adjoining grammar. In *Proceedings of the Eighth International Workshop on tree Adjoining Grammars and Related Formalisms (TAG+8)*. Association for Computational Linguistics, Sydney, Australia, pages 41–48. http://aclweb.org/anthology/W06-1506.

Chung-hye Han and Nancy Hedberg. 2006. A tree adjoining grammar analysis of the syntax and semantics of it-clefts. In *Proceedings of the Eighth International Workshop on tree Adjoining Grammars and Related Formalisms (TAG+ 8)*. Association for Computational Linguistics, Sydney, Australia, pages 33–40. http://aclweb.org/anthology/W06-1505.

Chung-hye Han, David Potter, and Dennis Ryan Storoshenko. 2010. Non-local right-node raising: An analysis using delayed tree-local mc-tag. In *Proceedings of the 10th International Workshop on Tree Adjoining Grammars and Related Formalisms (TAG+10)*. Linguistics Department, Yale University, New Haven, Connecticut, pages 9–16. http://aclweb.org/anthology/W10-4402.

Aravind K. Joshi, Laura Kallmeyer, and Maribel Romero. 2003. Flexible composition in LTAG: Quantifier scope and inverse linking. In *Proceedings of the International Workshop on Compositional Semantics*. Tilburg, The Netherlands.

Laura Kallmeyer and Maribel Romero. 2007. Reflexives and reciprocals in LTAG. In Harry Bunt, Jeroen Geertzen, Elias Thijsse, and Amanda Schiffrin, editors, *Proceedings of the Seventh International Workshop on Computational Semantics ICWS-7*. Tilburg, pages 271–282.

D. Terence Langendoen. 1978. The logic of reciprocity. *Linguistic Inquiry* 9(2):177–197. http://www.jstor.org/stable/4178051.

Rebecca Nesson. 2009. *Synchronous and Multicomponent Tree-Adjoining Grammars: Complexity, Algorithms and Linguistic Applications*. Ph.D. thesis, Harvard University.

Rebecca Nesson and Stuart M. Shieber. 2006. Simpler TAG semantics through synchronization. In *Proceedings of the 11th Conference on Formal Grammar*. Malaga, Spain. https://perma.cc/JM6Y-6QBY.

Rebecca Nesson and Stuart M. Shieber. 2007. Extraction phenomena in synchronous TAG syntax and semantics. In *Proceedings of SSST, NAACL-HLT 2007 / AMTA Workshop on Syntax and Structure in Statistical Translation*. Association for Computational Linguistics, pages 9–16. http://aclweb.org/anthology/W07-0402.

Maria Polinsky and Omer Preminger. 2014. Case and grammatical relations. In Andrew Carnie, Dan Siddiqi, and Yosuke Sato, editors, *Routledge Handbook of Syntax*, Routledge, chapter 8.

Carl Pollard and Ivan A. Sag. 1992. *Head-driven Phrase Structure Grammar*. University of Chicago Press.

Tanya Reinhart and Eric Reuland. 1993. Reflexivity. *Linguistic Inquiry* 24(4):657–720. http://www.jstor.org/stable/4178836.

Neville Ryant and Tatjana Scheffler. 2006. Binding of anaphors in LTAG. In *Proceedings of the Eighth International Workshop on Tree Adjoining Grammar and Related Formalisms (TAG+8)*. Association for Computational Linguistics, Sydney, Australia, pages 65–72. http://aclweb.org/anthology/W06-1509.

Remko Scha. 1981. Distributive, collective and cumulative quantification. In J. A. G. Groenendijk, T. M. V. Janssen, and M. B. J. Stokhof, editors, *Formal Methods in the Study of Language, Part 2*, Mathematisch Centrum, Amsterdam, pages 483–512.

Stuart M. Shieber and Yves Schabes. 1990. Synchronous tree-adjoining grammars. In *Proceedings of the 13th International Conference on Computational Linguistics*. Helsinki, Finland, volume 3, pages 253–258. http://aclweb.org/anthology/C90-3045.

Mark Steedman. 2000. Implications of binding for lexicalized grammars. *Tree Adjoining Grammars: Formalisms, Linguistic Analysis, and Processing* pages 283–301.

Dennis R. Storoshenko, Chung-hye Han, and David Potter. 2008. Reflexivity in English: an STAG analysis. In *Proceedings of the Ninth International Workshop on Tree Adjoining Grammars and Related Formalisms (TAG+9)*. Association for Computational Linguistics, Tübingen, Germany, pages 149–156. http://aclweb.org/anthology/W08-2320.

Dennis Ryan Storoshenko and Chung-hye Han. 2010. Binding variables in english: An analysis using delayed tree locality. In *Proceedings of the 10th International Workshop on Tree Adjoining Grammars and Related Formalisms (TAG+10)*. Linguistics Department, Yale University, New Haven, Connecticut, pages 143–150. http://aclweb.org/anthology/W10-4418.

Dennis Ryan Storoshenko and Chung-hye Han. 2013. Using synchronous tree adjoining grammar to model the typology of bound variable pronouns. *Journal of Logic and Computation* 25(2):371–403. https://doi.org/10.1093/logcom/exs064.

Johan van Bentham. 1989. Polyadic quantifiers. *Linguistics and Philosophy* 12(4):437–464. https://doi.org/10.1007/BF00632472.

K. Vijay-Shanker. 1987. *A study of Tree Adjoining Grammars*. Ph.D. thesis, University of Pennsylvania.

K. Vijay-Shanker and Aravind K. Joshi. 1988. Feature structures based tree adjoining grammars. In *Coling Budapest 1988 Volume 2: International Conference on Computational Linguistics*. http://aclweb.org/anthology/C88-2147.

David Jeremy Weir. 1988. *Characterizing mildly context-sensitive grammar formalisms*. Ph.D. thesis, University of Pennsylvania.

Dag Westerståhl. 1989. Quantifiers in formal and natural languages. In D. Gabbay and F. Guenthner, editors, *Handbook of Philosophical Logic: Volume IV: Topics in the Philosophy of Language*, Springer Netherlands, Dordrecht, pages 1–131.

Sean Michael Williford. 1993. *Application of Synchronous Tree-Adjoining Grammar to Quantifier Scoping Phenomena in English*. Bachelor's thesis, Harvard College. http://nrs.harvard.edu/urn-3:HUL.InstRepos:10951941.

A Appendix: Derived trees

The derived trees for the object control example (7) using the elementary trees and derivation of Figure 6 are provided in Figure 8.

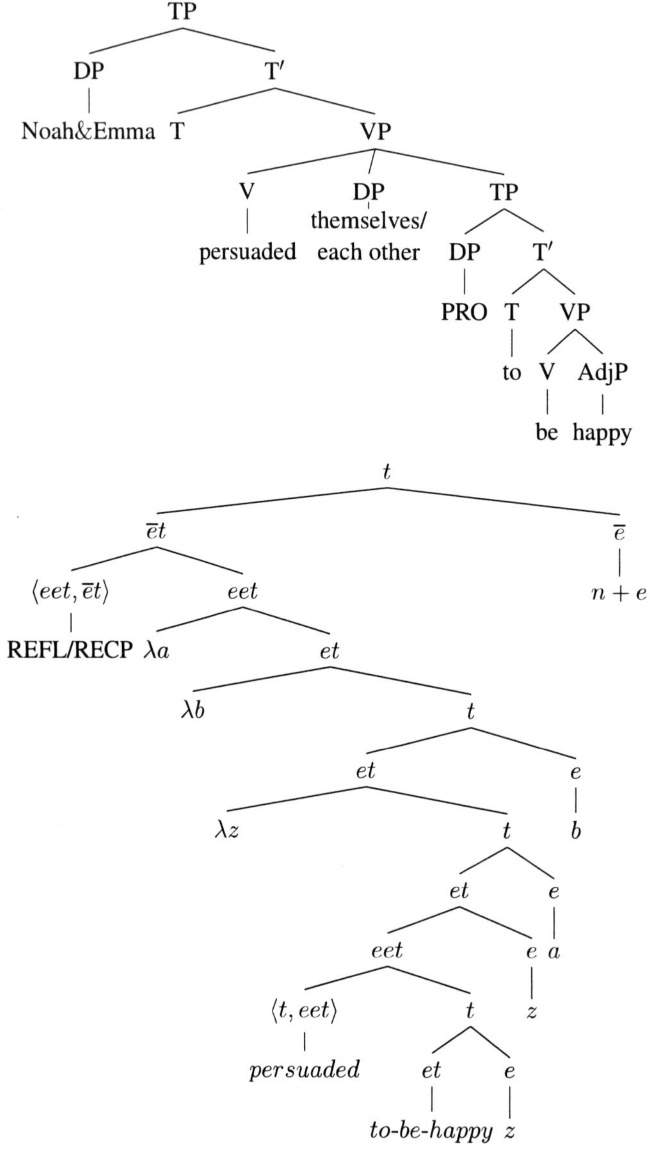

Figure 8: Derived trees for the object control example (7)

Coordination in TAG without the Conjoin Operation

Chung-hye Han
Simon Fraser University
Department of Linguistics
8888 University Drive
Burnaby BC, V5A 1S6, Canada
chunghye@sfu.ca

Anoop Sarkar
Simon Fraser University
School of Computing Science
8888 University Drive
Burnaby BC, V5A 1S6, Canada
anoop@cs.sfu.ca

Abstract

In this paper, we propose an alternative to Sarkar and Joshi's (1996) Conjoin Operation approach to clausal coordination with shared arguments. The Conjoin Operation applies across elementary trees, identifying and merging arguments from each clause, yielding a derivation tree in which the shared arguments are combined with multiple elementary trees, and a derived tree in which the shared arguments are dominated by multiple verbal projections. In contrast, our analysis uses Synchronous Tree Adjoining Grammar in order to pair syntactic elementary trees that participate in the derivation of clausal coordination with semantic elementary trees that use a lambda term to abstract over the shared argument. This allows the sharing of arguments in coordination to be instantiated in semantics, without being represented in syntax in the form of multiple dominance.

1 Introduction

In clausal coordination, one or more arguments can be shared by the verbal predicates of the conjuncts. For example, in (1), an object argument, *Pete*, is shared by *likes* and *hates*, and in (2), a subject argument, *Sue*, is shared by the two verbs.

(1)　Sue likes and Kim hates Pete.

　　a.　likes(Sue,Pete) $\wedge$ hates(Kim,Pete)

(2)　Sue hates Pete and likes Kim.

　　a.　hates(Sue,Pete) $\wedge$ likes(Sue,Kim)

A widely adopted analysis to such coordination, since Ross (1967), is to postulate an across-the-board (ATB) movement of the shared argument, in which multiple underlying copies of the shared material are identified during movement, yielding a single overt copy located outside of the coordinate structure. So, (1) and (2) would be derived from movement of the shared argument from both conjuncts to a position outside of the coordinate structure, as in (3) and (4).

(3)　[Sue likes t_i] and [Kim hates t_i] **Pete**$_i$.

(4)　**Sue**$_i$ [t_i hates Pete] and [t_i likes Kim].

Not to mention the problematic aspects of the exact mechanism where movement somehow identifies two syntactically distinct objects, the ATB movement analysis incorrectly predicts that shared arguments be barred from islands, given that movement dependency is subject to island constraints (Wexler and Culicover, 1980). (5) illustrates that a *wh*-movement dependency cannot be formed across a relative clause, an island. In contrast, in (6), a shared argument can form a putative ATB movement dependency across relative clauses.

(5)　* What did Max denounce [the senator who wrote t_i]]? (Sabbagh, 2014, 14)

(6)　Max publicly denounced [the senator [who wrote t_i]], and Pauline outwardly criticized [the magazine editor [who published t_i]], **[the speech that encouraged the riot]**$_i$. (Sabbagh, 2014, 15)

Combinatory Categorial Grammar (CCG) (Steedman, 1996) places the shared argument outside the coordinating conjuncts without postulating movement. It uses a syntactic combinator $(X \backslash X)/X$ for conjunctions, which combines two constituents of any type (one on the left and the other on the right represented by the slash direction). In semantics, the coordinated constituents provide a predicate lambda term which is then reduced using the shared argument. CCG

Proceedings of the 13th International Workshop on Tree Adjoining Grammars and Related Formalisms (TAG+13), pages 43–52,
Umeå, Sweden, September 4–6, 2017. © 2017 Association for Computational Linguistics

combines type-raising and function composition to handle coordination which leads to a view of constituency that is quite different from traditional phrase structure.

Another prominent analysis, starting with Wexler and Culicover (1980), is to postulate that the appearance of a shared argument is a result of ellipsis of corresponding arguments from other conjuncts. Under the ellipsis analysis, (1) and (2) would be a result of eliding the object argument from the first conjunct (7) and the subject argument from the second conjunct (8), respectively.

(7) [Sue likes ~~Pete~~] and [Kim hates **Pete**].

(8) [**Sue** hates Pete] and [~~Sue~~ likes Kim].

The ellipsis analysis predicts that a clausal coordination with a shared argument and the corresponding non-elided version should have the same meaning. But this is not always the case (Sabbagh, 2007). For instance, while (9) means that the same student read every paper and summarized every book, (10) can mean different students read every paper and summarized every book.

(9) **A student** read every paper and summarized every book.

(10) A student read every paper and a student summarized every book.

This takes us to the multiple dominance analysis, first proposed by McCawley (1982), that postulates that a shared argument is multiply dominated by elements from multiple conjuncts. A version of this approach has been developed in Sarkar and Joshi (1996) within the TAG literature. Sarkar and Joshi (1996) posit that the shared argument is located in the canonical position within each conjunct, and propose an operation, the Conjoin Operation, that applies across elementary trees. This operation identifies and merges the shared argument when two elementary trees combine via coordination, yielding a derived tree in which an argument is multiply dominated by two verbal projections. The Conjoin Operation analysis has been used and extended often in TAG-based linguistic research, including the semantics of clausal coordination and scope (Banik, 2004; Han et al., 2008; Storoshenko and Frank, 2012), and the syntax of Right-Node-Raising (Han et al., 2010).

According to the multiple dominance analysis, as the shared argument is in a dominance relation

within each conjunct, it must be syntactically licensed in each conjunct. However, as observed in Cann et al. (2005), the syntactic requirement of the shared argument must be met by the elements within the conjunct it occurs with, and not by elements in other conjuncts. For instance, the negative polarity item in the shared object, which occurs in the second conjunct on the surface, is licensed by negation in the second conjunct (11), but not by negation in the first conjunct (12).

(11) John has read, but he hasn't understood **any of my books**. (Cann et al., 2005, 1e)

(12) * John hasn't understood, but has read **any of my books**.

In this paper, using Synchronous Tree Adjoining Grammar, we propose an alternative to the TAG analysis of coordination, which does not rely on the Conjoin Operation. In our proposal, the shared argument is syntactically present only in one conjunct, and syntactically missing in other conjuncts. The syntactic elementary trees representing the conjuncts with missing arguments are paired with semantic elementary trees with unsaturated arguments, and the syntactic elementary trees with shared arguments are paired with semantic elementary trees that use lambda terms to abstract over the shared arguments. Composition of these trees via adjoining allows sharing of arguments to be instantiated in semantics, without being represented in syntax in the form of ATB movement, ellipsis or multiple dominance.

The remainder of this paper is organized as follows. In Section 2, we illustrate in more detail how the Conjoin Operation identifies a shared argument. Our STAG analysis where sharing of arguments takes place in semantics, not in syntax, is presented in Section 3. This analysis is extended in Section 4 to account for ATB *wh*-movement, and the interaction of coordination and quantification.

2 Argument Sharing via the Conjoin Operation

Sarkar and Joshi (1996) utilize elementary trees with contraction sets and coordinating auxiliary trees. The elementary trees necessary to derive (1) are given in Figure 1.[1] In each of (αlikes$_{\{DP\}}$)

---

[1] We follow Frank's (2002) Condition on Elementary Tree Minimality (CETM), and adopt the DP Hypothesis and the VP-internal Subject Hypothesis in defining our elementary

and (βand_hates$_{\{DP\}}$), the object DP node is in the contraction set, notated as a subscript in the tree name and marked in the tree with a circle around it, and represents a shared argument. When (βand_hates$_{\{DP\}}$) adjoins to (αlikes$_{\{DP\}}$) via the Conjoin Operation, the two trees undergo contraction, sharing the node in the contraction set. Effectively, this allows the DP tree, (αPete), to simultaneously substitute into the contraction nodes, and in the derived tree, the two nodes are identified, merging into one. The substitution of (αSue) and (αKim) into the subject DP nodes of (αlikes$_{\{DP\}}$) and (βand_hates$_{\{DP\}}$), in addition to the simultaneous substitution of (αPete) into the object DP nodes of the two elementary trees, generates the derived tree (γ1) in Figure 1. The resulting derived tree is a directed graph as a single node is dominated by multiple nodes. The shared argument, *Pete*, is thus represented as a syntactic argument of both the verbs, *likes* and *hates*, capturing the meaning of the sentence that the person that Sue likes and the person that Kim hates are the same individual.

3 Argument Sharing via Semantics using STAG

According to the NPI examples (11)-(12) discussed in section 1, the shared argument seems to be forming syntactic dependencies only with elements in the conjunct in which it appears on the surface, but not with elements in other conjuncts. We capture this intuition with the proposal that the shared argument is syntactically present only in one of the conjuncts, and missing in other conjuncts, resulting in predicates with unsaturated arguments in semantics. We explain our analysis with a shared object argument example in subsection 3.1 and a shared subject argument example in subsection 3.2.

3.1 Object argument sharing

For the analysis of (1), an example of clausal coordination with a shared object argument, we propose elementary tree pairs in (βlikes$_{\{DP\}}$) and (β'likes$_{\{DP\}}$) in Figure 2. (βlikes$_{\{DP\}}$) is an auxiliary TP tree that introduces a coordinator and adjoins to another TP it coordinates with. The object argument of this auxiliary tree is null, directly reflecting the fact that it is absent in the

first conjunct. The content of the null object argument, however, must be resolved in semantics. This requirement is implemented by the semantic elementary tree (β'likes$_{\{DP\}}$), in which the variable corresponding to the object argument (x) has been λ-abstracted over, turning the conjunct into a predicate ($\langle e, t \rangle$). This predicate must adjoin to another predicate whose object argument has been similarly λ-abstracted over. This adjunction requirement is represented in the elementary tree by the *obligatory adjunction* or *oa* constraint (Vijay-Shanker, 1992) on the TP node of (αhates$_{\{DP\}}$). The *oa* constraint should also provide a list of auxiliary trees compatible with this elementary tree in order to satisfy the object sharing requirement in the semantic structure. To save space in the figures, we show the *oa* constraint but we do not explicitly provide a list of trees. In all the subsequent trees we will also provide such an *oa* constraint and since it serves the same purpose in all of them we do not comment on it further. The boxed numeral $\boxed{1}$ in (βlikes$_{\{DP\}}$) and (β'likes$_{\{DP\}}$) indicates a link between the syntactic and semantic tree pairs to ensure the synchronous derivation between the syntax and the semantics: a DP tree substitutes into the subject position marked with $\boxed{1}$ in (βlikes$_{\{DP\}}$), and the semantic tree paired with this DP must substitute into the position marked with $\boxed{1}$ in (β'likes$_{\{DP\}}$).[2]

The TP and the predicate that (βlikes$_{\{DP\}}$) and (β'likes$_{\{DP\}}$) adjoin to are provided by elementary tree pairs in (αhates$_{\{DP\}}$) and (α'hates$_{\{DP\}}$) in Figure 2. (αhates$_{\{DP\}}$) is a typical transitive initial tree in syntax with subject and object substitution sites. (α'hates$_{\{DP\}}$), however, is an atypical transitive elementary tree in semantics in which the object argument has been λ-abstracted over: here, the variable corresponding to the object argument (x) is λ-abstracted over to provide a predicate ($\langle e, t \rangle$).[3] This predicate will combine with the meaning of the object argument to provide a formula (t). Note that the TP node in (αhates$_{\{DP\}}$) and the highest $\langle e, t \rangle$ node in (α'hates$_{\{DP\}}$) are marked with the link $\boxed{3}$. These are the positions onto which (βlikes$_{\{DP\}}$) and (β'likes$_{\{DP\}}$) adjoin in syntax and semantics respectively.

---

trees. Elementary trees such as (βand_hates$_{\{DP\}}$) are in accordance with CETM, as coordinators are functional heads.

[2]For the sake of simplicity, we include only the links that are relevant for the current discussion.

[3]Semantic elementary trees in which λ-operators abstract over argument variables have been proposed and utilized in Frank and Storoshenko (2012) to handle many difficult cases of quantifier scope within tree-local MC-TAG.

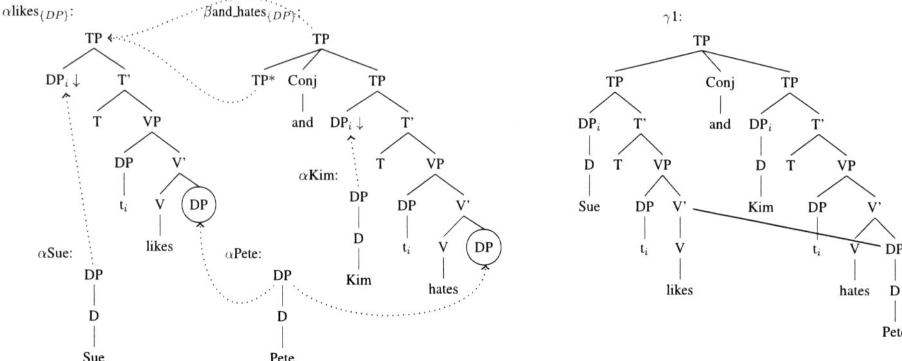

Figure 1: Elementary trees and derived tree for *Sue likes and Kim hates Pete* with the Conjoin Operation

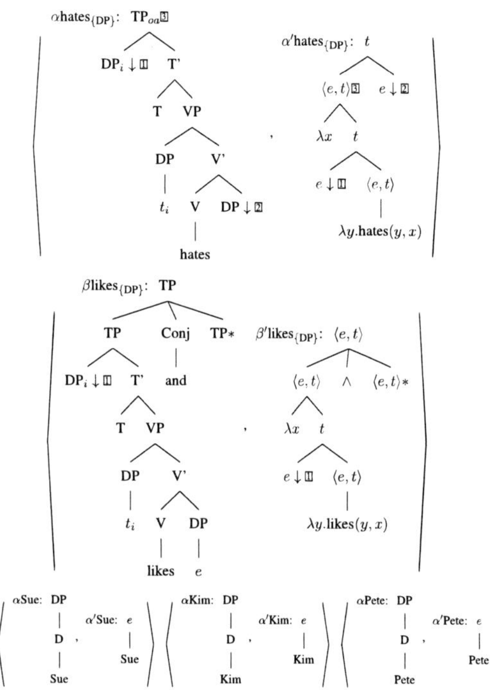

Figure 2: Elementary trees for *Sue likes and Kim hates Pete*

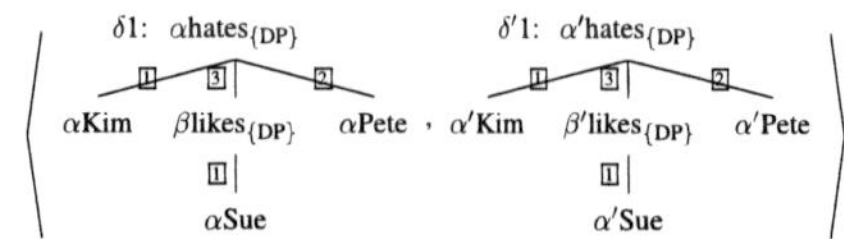

Figure 3: Derivation structures for *Sue likes and Kim hates Pete*

Figure 3 depicts the isomorphic syntactic and semantic derivation structures for (1). Following the convention in Nesson and Shieber (2006; 2007), here we use boxed numerals for links to denote locations in parent elementary trees where the TAG operations took place. The syntactic and the semantic derived trees are given in Figure 4. In contrast to the Conjoin Operation approach, in our analysis, (αPete), the syntactic elementary tree representing the shared argument, composes only with a single predicative elementary tree, (αhates$_{\{DP\}}$). In the syntactic derived tree (γ1), therefore, *Pete* is represented as the object DP of *hates*, but not *likes*. Similarly in semantics, (α'Pete) composes only with (α'hates$_{\{DP\}}$). However, because the object abstracted predicate of (β'likes$_{\{DP\}}$) is adjoining onto the predicate node in the object abstracted (α'hates$_{\{DP\}}$), the correct meaning of (1) is derived, in which the person Sue likes and Kim hates is Pete, as stated in the logical form in (1a). (γ'1) can be reduced to (1a) via λ-conversion following the application of the Generalized Conjunction (GC) Rule (Barwise and Cooper, 1981) defined in (13).

(13) Generalized Conjunction (GC) Rule:
      [Pred1 $\wedge$ Pred2] = λz[Pred1$(z) \wedge$ Pred2(z)]

3.2 Subject argument sharing

Figure 5 contains our proposed elementary trees to derive (2), an example of clausal coordination with a subject shared argument. (βlikes$_{\{DP_i\}}$) introduces a coordinator and its subject argument is null, reflecting the fact that it is absent in the second conjunct. In (β'likes$_{\{DP_i\}}$), the variable cor-

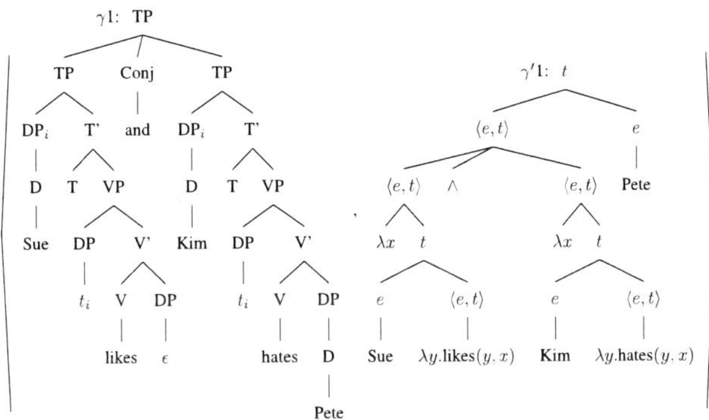

Figure 4: Derived trees for *Sue likes and Kim hates Pete*

responding to the subject argument (x) has been λ-abstracted over, turning the conjunct into a predicate ($\langle e, t \rangle$). This implements the requirement that the subject argument still needs to be saturated. ($\alpha\text{hates}_{\{DP_i\}}$) is a typical transitive initial tree in syntax. In ($\alpha'\text{hates}_{\{DP_i\}}$), however, the variable corresponding to the subject argument (x) has been λ-abstracted over to provide a predicate ($\langle e, t \rangle$) which will combine with the meaning of the subject argument to provide a formula (t).

$\langle \alpha\text{hates}_{\{DP_i\}}, \alpha'\text{hates}_{\{DP_i\}} \rangle$. Therefore, in the syntactic derived tree, *Sue* is represented as the subject DP of *hates*, but not *likes*. In the semantic derived tree, however, the subject abstracted predicate of ($\beta'\text{likes}_{\{DP_i\}}$) adjoins onto the predicate node in the subject abstracted ($\alpha'\text{hates}_{\{DP_i\}}$), and so the correct meaning of (2) is derived via the application of λ-conversion and the GC Rule to ($\gamma'2$), in which the person that hates Pete and likes Kim is Sue, as stated in the local form in (2a).

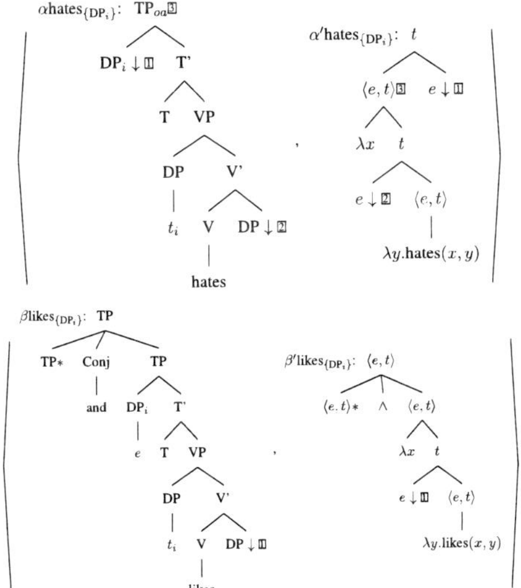

Figure 5: Elementary trees for *Sue hates Pete and likes Kim*

The isomorphic syntactic and semantic derivation structures for (2) are provided in Figure 6 and the derived trees are given in Figure 7. The shared subject argument represented by the elementary tree pair $\langle \alpha\text{Sue}, \alpha'\text{Sue} \rangle$ composes only with the predicative elementary tree pair

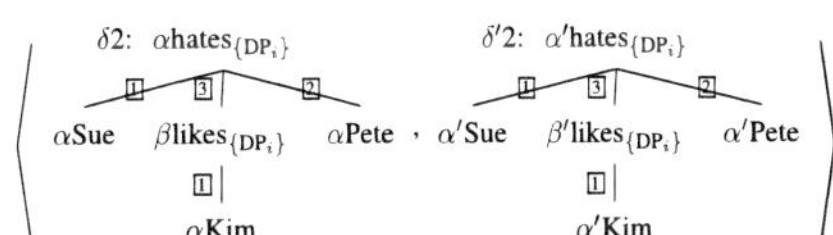

Figure 6: Derivation structures for *Sue hates Pete and likes Kim*

4 Extensions

4.1 ATB wh-movement

According to the Conjoin Operation analysis, instances of ATB *wh*-movement, as in (14), involve a *wh*-movement in each clausal conjunct followed by identification and merging of the *wh*-phrases as the two clauses compose. In our analysis, a *wh*-movement takes place only in one conjunct in syntax, while the function of the *wh*-phrase is captured as a shared argument in semantics.

(14)   Who does Sue like and Kim hate?

    a. $\text{WH}x[\text{person}(x)][\text{likes}(\text{Sue}, x) \wedge \text{hates}(\text{Kim}, x)]$

Additional elementary trees required to derive (14) are given in Figure 8. ($\alpha\text{wh\_hates}_{\{DP_j\}}$) is a typical transitive initial tree with a *wh*-movement of the object argument. ($\alpha'\text{wh\_hates}_{\{DP_j\}}$) is a

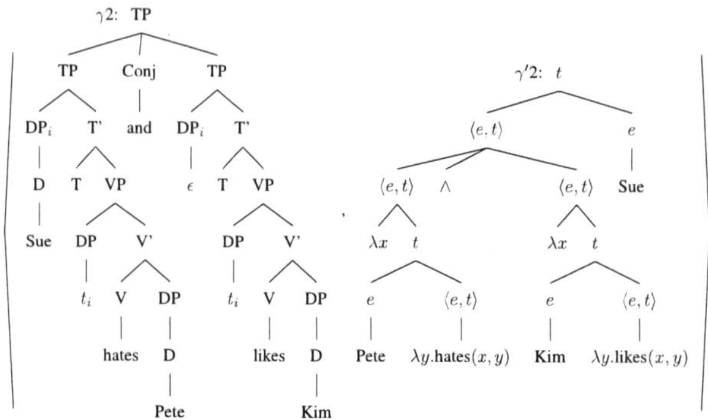

Figure 7: Derived trees for *Sue hates Pete and likes Kim*

corresponding semantics tree with a λ-abstrated object argument. Here, we abstract away from the full semantics of *wh*-questions and simply represent the predicate-argument structure. In representing the semantics of *who*, we follow the tree-local multi-component treatment of quantification (Shieber and Schabes, 1990; Nesson and Shieber, 2006) and implement a generalized quantifier analysis to adopt the model of Han et al. (2008). We thus propose that the semantics of *who* has two components: (α'who) is a variable and substitutes into the argument position e linked with ② in (α'wh_hates$_{\{DP_j\}}$), and (β'who) represents the scope and adjoins onto t again linked with ② in (α'wh_hates$_{\{DP_j\}}$). The coordinating auxiliary tree pairs (βlikes$_{\{DP\}}$) and (β'likes$_{\{DP\}}$) depicted in Figure 2 will each adjoin onto the TP node in (αwh_hates$_{\{DP_j\}}$) and the $\langle e,t \rangle$ node in (α'wh_hates$_{\{DP_j\}}$), both linked with ③. The full derivation structures and derived trees are given in Figure 9 and Figure 10.

In our analysis, the *wh*-movement of the object argument takes place within the predicative initial tree representing the second conjunct, onto which the coordinating auxiliary tree representing the first conjunct adjoins, stretching the distance between the *wh*-moved DP in [Spec,CP] and the trace position within the VP. The application of λ-conversion and the GC Rule to (γ'14) reduces it to the logical form in (14a), which correctly states that the person that Sue likes and Kim hates is the same individual and the question is asking for the identity of this individual.

4.2 Quantification and coordination

In clausal coordination with shared arguments, in general, these shared arguments scope over the

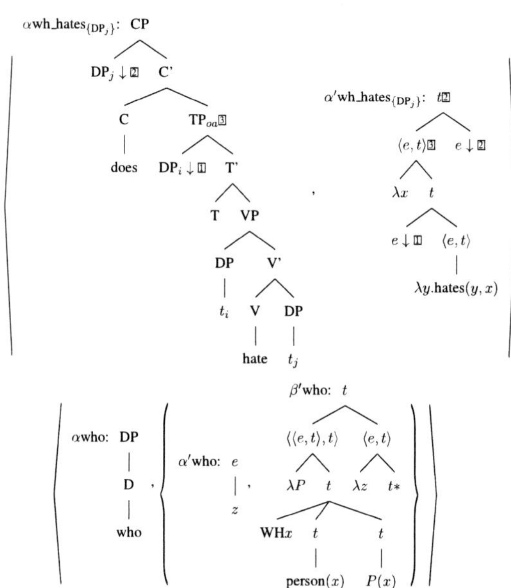

Figure 8: Elementary trees for *Who does Sue like and Kim hate?*

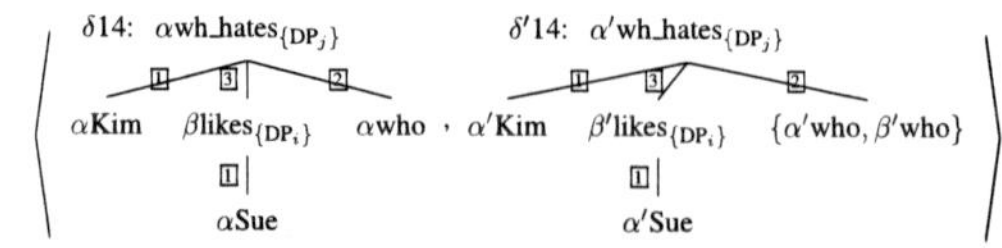

Figure 9: Derivation structures for *Who does Sue like and Kim hate?*

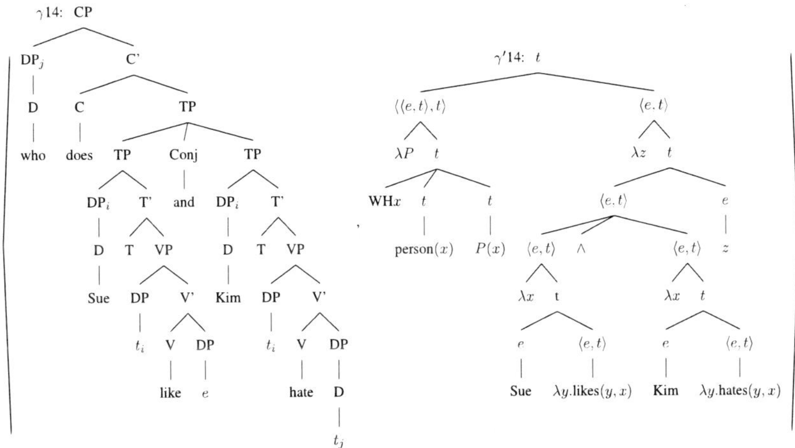

Figure 10: Derived trees for *Who does Sue like and Kim hate?*

coordinator, and the non-shared arguments scope under the coordinator (Banik, 2004; Han et al., 2008). This is illustrated in (15) (repeated from (9)) for a subject shared argument, and (16) for an object shared argument. In addition, clausal coordination with multiple shared arguments, as in (17), exhibits scope ambiguity. All three examples are taken from Han et al. (2008).

(15) A student read every paper and summarized every book. ($\exists > \wedge > \forall$)

    a. $\exists x_1[\text{student}(x_1)][\forall x_2[\text{paper}(x_2)][\text{read}(x_1, x_2)]\wedge \forall x_2[\text{book}(x_2)][\text{summarized}(x_1, x_2)]]$

(16) A student takes and a professor teaches every course. ($\forall > \wedge > \exists$)

    a. $\forall x_2[\text{course}(x_2)][\exists x_1[\text{student}(x_1)][\text{takes}(x_1, x_2)]\wedge \exists x_1[\text{professor}(x_1)][\text{teaches}(x_1, x_2)]]$

(17) A student likes and takes every course. ($\exists > \forall > \wedge, \forall > \exists > \wedge$)

    a. $\exists x_1[\text{student}(x_1)][\forall x_2[\text{course}(x_2)][\text{likes}(x_1, x_2)\wedge \text{takes}(x_1, x_2)]]$

    b. $\forall x_2[\text{course}(x_2)][\exists x_1[\text{student}(x_1)][\text{likes}(x_1, x_2)\wedge \text{takes}(x_1, x_2)]]$

In Han et al. (2008), semantic derivation of examples such as (15)-(17) requires a composition of an initial predicative tree and a coordinating auxiliary tree, each with a contraction node representing the shared argument. These elementary trees both project to t. The wide scope of the shared argument is enforced by stipulating that the scope component of the contraction node is active only in the coordinating auxiliary tree, which adjoins onto the highest t above the coordinator. The

scope information of the contraction node in the initial predicative tree is inherited from the scope component of the contraction node in the coordinating auxiliary tree. In our analysis, the shared argument is present only in one of the conjuncts, and so a single scope component straightforwardly interacts with the coordinator as the coordinating auxiliary tree adjoins below the scope of the shared argument.

We use (16) to illustrate our analysis with a single shared argument and briefly discuss (17) to illustrate how our analysis can be extended to multiple shared arguments. Additional elementary trees needed to derive (16) are given in Figure 11. We represent the semantics of quantified nominal phrases as multi-component sets, as we did for the semantics of *who*. For example, for the semantics of *a student*, (α'a_student) provides the argument variable, and (β'a_student) introduces the existential quantifier and provides the scope of the quantification. In addition to the elementary tree pairs for *a student*, we will utilize similar elementary tree pairs for *a professor* and *every course*, with one difference being that the elementary tree representing the scope component of *every course* will contain a universal quantifier, instead of an existential quantifier. The elementary tree pairs $\langle \alpha\text{teaches}_{\{DP\}}, \alpha'\text{teaches}_{\{DP\}}\rangle$ and $\langle \beta\text{takes}_{\{DP\}}, \beta'\text{takes}_{\{DP\}}\rangle$ are similar to the predicative initial tree and the coordinating auxiliary tree we have seen before in Figure 2. The only difference is that ($\alpha'\text{teaches}_{\{DP\}}$) and ($\beta'\text{takes}_{\{DP\}}$) are now augmented with links to accommodate the scope components of the quan-

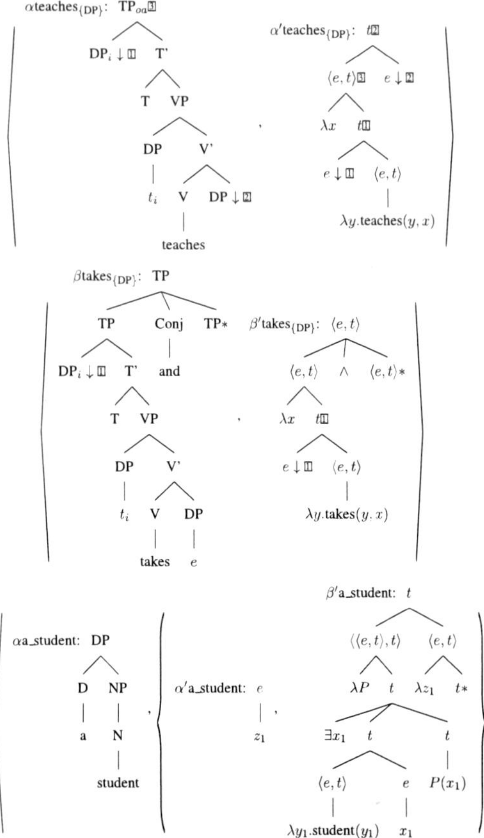

Figure 11: Elementary trees for *A student takes and a professor teaches every course*

tified noun phrases. In (β'takes$_{\{DP\}}$), the link $\boxed{1}$ for the scope component of the subject DP is on t, which is below the coordinator. In (α'teaches$_{\{DP\}}$), the link $\boxed{1}$ for the scope component of the subject DP is on the t below the $\langle e, t\rangle$ node onto which the coordinating auxiliary tree adjoins. Together, the non-shared arguments in each conjunct are guaranteed to scope below the coordinator. Moreover, in (α'teaches$_{\{DP\}}$), the scope component of the object DP, which is the shared argument, is linked to the highest t above the $\langle e, t\rangle$ node onto which the coordinating auxiliary tree adjoins. This then ensures that the shared argument scopes over the coordinator.

The isomorphic syntactic and semantic derivation structures are given in Figure 12 and the derived trees are given in Figure 13. To save space, we have reduced all the generalized quantifier ($\langle\langle e, t\rangle, t\rangle$) nodes in the semantic derived tree, (γ'16). Application of the GC Rule and λ-conversion to (γ'16) further reduces it to the logical form in (16a).

To derive the clausal coordination with subject and object shared arguments in (17), elementary tree pairs for *likes* and *takes* consistent with our proposal are provided in Figure 14. (βlikes$_{\{DP_i, DP\}}$) is a coordinating auxiliary tree with an empty DP position for the object and a DP substitution site for the subject, and is paired with a multi-component set in semantics that includes an auxiliary tree recursive on $\langle e, \langle e, t\rangle\rangle$, an e substitution tree for the subject argument variable, and a t auxiliary tree for the scope component of the subject argument. (αtakes$_{\{DP_i, DP\}}$) is an initial predicative tree with an empty DP position for the subject and a DP substitution site for the object, and is paired with (α'takes$_{\{DP_i, DP\}}$), which has e substitution sites for the subject and the object argument variables. Note that the t node of (α'takes$_{\{DP_i, DP\}}$) has multiple links, $\boxed{1}$ and $\boxed{2}$, for the scope components of the subject and the object DPs. This indicates that the two scope component trees will multiply-adjoin to the t node, as defined in Schabes and Shieber (1994), and predicts scope ambiguity, as the order in which the two trees adjoin is not specified.

5 Conclusion and Future Work

We have outlined a Synchronous TAG analysis of clausal coordination with shared arguments that does not rely on the Conjoin Operation, utilizing only the standard TAG operations, substitution and adjoining. Therefore, we do not require modified parsing algorithms to handle the Conjoin Operation, unrooted trees, or tree nodes with multiple parents as in Sarkar and Joshi (1996). In our analysis, the shared argument is present syntactically only in one conjunct in which it appears on the surface. In semantics, the conjunct with a missing argument is represented as a predicate with an unsaturated argument, and adjoins onto the predicate node that has been λ-abstracted over by the shared argument. The shared argument, thus, does not participate in movement, ellipsis or multiple-dominance in our analysis, eschewing the incorrect predictions made by these approaches.

It remains as future work to extend our analysis to cases where the shared object argument is in an island, as in (6). The phenomenon where a syntactic constituent at the right periphery of a rightmost clause appears to be shared is generally known as

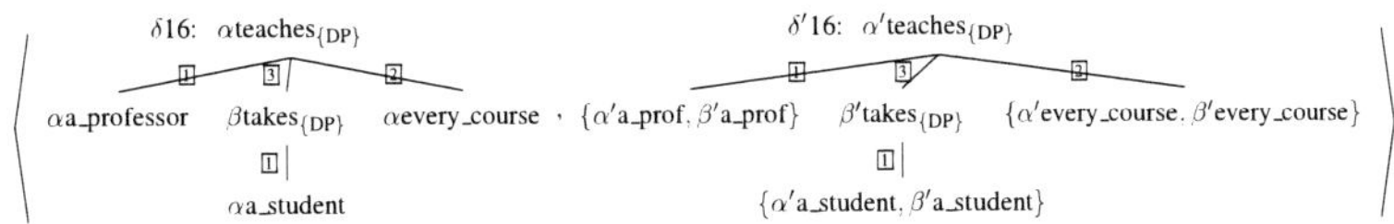

Figure 12: Derivation structures for *A student takes and a professor teaches every course*

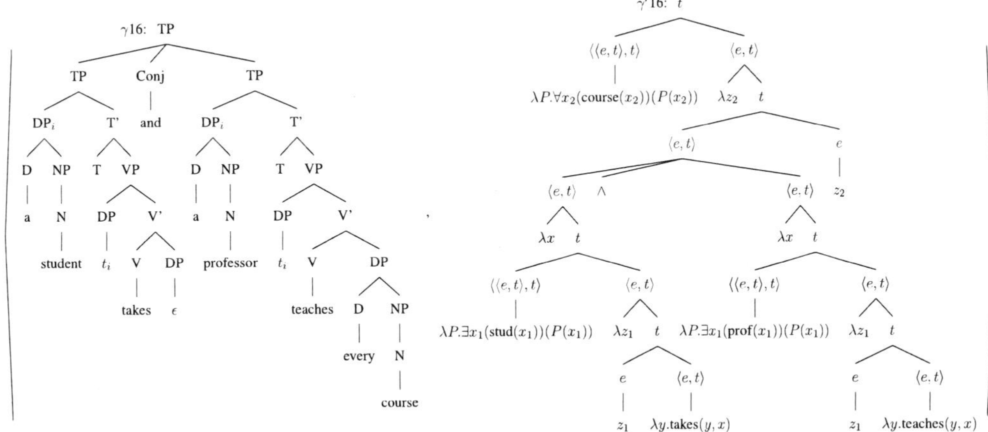

Figure 13: Derived trees for *A student takes and a professor teaches every course*

Figure 14: Elementary trees for *A student likes and takes every course*

Right-Node-Raising (RNR). RNR is not restricted to coordination, as can be seen in (18) (Hudson, 1976; Goodall, 1987; Postal, 1994).

(18) Politicians [who have fought for] may well snub those [who have fought against **animal rights**]. (Postal, 1994)

A question that must be addressed first though is whether all apparent RNR constructions should be given a unified account (Barros and Vicente, 2011). We leave this as future research as well.

Acknowledgments

We thank the three anonymous reviewers of TAG+13 for their insightful comments. This research was partially supported by SSHRC 435-2014-0161 to Han and NSERC RGPIN 262313 and RGPAS 446348 to Sarkar.

References

Eva Banik. 2004. Semantics of VP coordination in LTAG. In *Proceedings of the 7th International Workshop on Tree Adjoining Grammars and Related Formalisms (TAG+7)*. Vancouver, Canada, pages 118–125.

Matthew Barros and Luis Vicente. 2011. Right node raising requires both ellipsis and multidomination.

University of Pennsylvania Working Papers in Linguistics 17(1):Article 2.

Jon Barwise and Robin Cooper. 1981. Generalized quantifiers and natural language. *Linguistics and Philosophy* 4:159–219.

Ronnie Cann, Ruth Kempson, Lutz Marten, and Masayuki Otsuka. 2005. Right node raising, coordination and the dynamics of language processing. *Lingua* 115:503–525.

Robert Frank. 2002. *Phrase Structure Composition and Syntactic Dependencies*. MIT Press, Cambridge, MA.

Robert Frank and Dennis Ryan Storoshenko. 2012. The shape of elementary trees and scope possibilities in STAG. In *Proceedings of the 11th International Workshop on Tree Adjoining Grammars and Related Formalisms (TAG+11)*. Paris, pages 232–240.

Grant Goodall. 1987. *Parallel structures in syntax*. Cambridge University Press.

Chung-hye Han, David Potter, and Dennis Storoshenko. 2008. Compositional semantics of coordination using synchronous tree adjoining grammar. In *Proceedings of the 9th International Workshop on Tree Adjoining Grammars and Related Formalisms (TAG+9)*. Tuebingen, Germany, pages 33–40.

Chung-hye Han, David Potter, and Dennis Storoshenko. 2010. Non-local right node raising: an analysis using delayed tree-local MC-TAG. In *Proceedings of the 10th International Workshop on Tree Adjoining Grammars and Related Formalisms (TAG+10)*. Yale University.

Richard A. Hudson. 1976. Conjunction reduction, gapping, and right-node raising. *Language* 52(3):535–562.

James D. McCawley. 1982. Parentheticals and discontinuous constituent structure. *Linguistic Inquiry* 13:91–106.

Rebecca Nesson and Stuart Shieber. 2007. Extraction phenomena in Synchronous TAG syntax and semantics. In Dekai Wu and David Chiang, editors, *Proceedings of the Workshop on Syntax and Structure in Statistical Translation*. Rochester, New York.

Rebecca Nesson and Stuart M. Shieber. 2006. Simpler TAG Semantics through Synchronization. In *Proceedings of the 11th Conference on Formal Grammar*. CSLI, Malaga, Spain.

Paul Postal. 1994. Parasitic and pseudoparasitic gaps. *Linguistic Inquiry* 25:63–117.

John Robert Ross. 1967. *Constraints on variables in syntax*. Ph.D. thesis, MIT, Cambridge, MA.

Joseph Sabbagh. 2007. Ordering and linearizing rightward movement. *Natural Language and Linguistic Theory* 25:349–401.

Joseph Sabbagh. 2014. Right node raising. *Language and Linguistic Compass* 8/1:24–35.

Anoop Sarkar and Aravind Joshi. 1996. Coordination in Tree Adjoining Grammars: formalization and implementation. In *Proceedings of COLING'96*. Copenhagen, pages 610–615.

Yves Schabes and Stuart M. Shieber. 1994. An Alternative Conception of Tree-Adjoining Derivation. *Computational Linguistics* 20(1):91–124.

Stuart Shieber and Yves Schabes. 1990. Synchronous Tree Adjoining Grammars. In *Proceedings of COLING'90*. Helsinki, Finland.

Mark Steedman. 1996. *Surface Structure and Interpretation*. MIT Press, Cambridge, MA.

Dennis Ryan Storoshenko and Robert Frank. 2012. Deriving syntax-semantics mappings: node linking, type shifting and scope ambiguity. In *Proceedings of the 11th International Workshop on Tree Adjoining Grammars and Related Formalisms (TAG+11)*. Paris, pages 10–18.

K Vijay-Shanker. 1992. Using descriptions of trees in a tree adjoining grammar. *Computational Linguistics* 18(4):481–517.

Ken Wexler and Peter W. Culicover. 1980. *Formal Principles of Language Acquisition*. MIT Press, Cambridge, MA.

Scope, Time, and Predicate Restriction in Blackfoot using MC-STAG

Dennis Ryan Storoshenko
University of Calgary
2500 University Dr. NW
Calgary, AB, Canada, T2R 1H4
`dstorosh@ucalgary.ca`

Abstract

We use STAG to model the interaction between demonstratives and tense found in Blackfoot (Algonquian). In clauses with no tense or aspect marking, past tense can be encoded through a distal demonstrative on either the internal argument (transitives, unaccusatives) or the external argument (unergatives). A fourth class of predicate, semantically transitive but syntactically intransitive with a pseudo-incorporated object, does not allow either argument to mark tense. Using the scope mechanics described in Frank and Storoshenko (2012), we first model the unique scope properties of pseudo-incorporation, following on the Bliss (2013) claim that predicate saturation in these cases derives from the Chung and Ladusaw (2004) operation of predicate restriction, not function application. Modelling the predicate restriction operation within a STAG derivation is shown to correctly predict the scope facts in a way such that the tense facts are also easily captured.

1 Tense and Demonstratives

In this section, we present the basic tense data, and discuss the challenges it presents for a GB/Minimalism-style analysis before moving on to STAG. Blackfoot is an Algonquian language of Southern Alberta and Montana with a largely polysynthetic morphology. While the language has a range of tense and aspect markers, clauses may appear untensed. As described in Lewis (2014), untensed predicates may receive an obligatory temporal interpretation from a demonstrative on one of their arguments:[1]

(1) amo   ninaa ispii
     DEM.PROX man dance
     'This man is dancing/danced.'
     (either tense)

(2) oma   ninaa ispii
     DEM.DIST man dance
     'That man danced.'
     (past only, Lewis 2014 ex19b)

As shown, while the proximal demonstrative does not fix the tense, a distal demonstrative fixes the interpretation in the past. The task of writing a function which could accomplish this is simply a matter of lambda gymnastics:

(3) $\llbracket F \rrbracket = \lambda P \lambda s'.P(s') \wedge DIST(s') \rightarrow s' < s^*$

F, a recursive function of type $\langle\langle s,t\rangle,\langle s,t\rangle\rangle$ on the verbal projection inspects its complement for situation variables in the scope of a DIST function (assuming demonstratives to also carry situation variables, see Elbourne (2008)), dictating that such situations be interpreted as prior to the utterance time s^*. The proposal is not that demonstratives themselves carry any temporal interpretation, rather that is built into the verbal projection (and therefore inherently part of the predicate) which interacts with demonstratives in its scope.

The same pattern of past tense following from distal demonstratives has been shown for unaccusative predicates:

(4) amo   ninaa o'too
     DEM.PROX man arrive
     'This man arrives/arrived.' (either tense)

---

[1] In the interests of space, we will only give the minimal morphemic breakdown necessary to illustrate the facts salient to our discussion. Readers are encouraged to consult the sources cited in this paper to appreciate the complexity of the morphology.

Proceedings of the 13th International Workshop on Tree Adjoining Grammars and Related Formalisms (TAG+13), pages 53–60,
Umeå, Sweden, September 4–6, 2017. © 2017 Association for Computational Linguistics

(5) oma   ninaa o'too
     DEM.DIST man arrive
     'That man arrived.' (past only)

However, in (syntactically) transitive constructions, only the internal argument fixes the tense:

(6) oma   ninaa si'kataa amo
     DEM.DIST man   kick.TR DEM.PROX
     ninaa
     man
     'That man kick/kicked this man'
     (either tense, Lewis 2014 ex20a)

(7) amo   ninaa si'kataa oma
     DEM.PROX man   kick.TR DEM.DIST
     ninaa
     man
     'This man kicked that man.'
     (past only, Lewis 2014 ex20c)

The fact that distal demonstratives do not always
trigger a past interpretation is taken as evidence
that the demonstratives themselves do not inherently carry tense, and that the F operator must be
a part of the predicate, with a narrowly defined
scope. The challenge therefore lies in locating the
position of this F function on the verbal spine. To
account for the transitives and, by extension, unaccusatives, the scope of F must exclude the external
argument (specifier of vP); however the unergative
cases show that the specifier of vP can also be in
the scope of F. An additional complication arises
when considering a fourth construction, known in
the literature as the Animate Intransitive + Object
(AI+O) construction:

(8) amo   ninaa ooyi   mamii
     DEM.PROX man   eat.INTR fish
     'This man is eating/ate fish.'

(9) oma   ninaa ooyi   mamii
     DEM.DIST man   eat.INTR fish
     'That man is eating/ate fish.'

In (8) and (9), the predicates are syntactically intransitive, lacking the morphological marking of
transitives, though they still take two arguments
semantically. According to Bliss (2013), the object (*mamii* in this case) is pseudo-incorporated
into the verbal predicate as an NP, not a full DP.
As shown in our data, the subject of this type of
intransitive does not fix the tense, while the object
by definition has no ability to do so as a bare NP.

Assuming that the relevant function which inspects demonstratives is contributed by some
functional head on the verbal spine, it would need
to be in a flexible position, sometimes above vP
(unergatives) and sometimes below vP (all others). This would also imply that in the case of
a transitive, the function would not even scope
over a fully-saturated predicate, surely an unde-
sirable state of affairs if we want to assume a single operator is responsible for this phenomenon.
To solve this, one could adopt a Kratzer (1996)-
inspired deconstruction of predicates, in which external arguments are introduced to a fully saturated predicate through event identification. Taking this step, and then defining the position of F
as the first opportunity to merge a function of the
semantic type $\langle\langle s,t\rangle,\langle s,t\rangle\rangle$ would again correctly
capture the subjects of unaccusatives, objects of
transitives, and correctly exclude the subject of the
AI+O construction saturated by object incorporation, but would miss the unergatives, as the necessary condition for applying the F function would
be met before event identification ever took place.
The only solution would be to then add a syntactic
constraint in the form of some uninterpretable feature requiring the functional head to have at least
one nominal (NP or DP) in its scope. While such a
move is possible, the necessary syntactic feature is
not a natural one in the framework, and the notion
of merging a functional head as soon as semantically possible in a derivation, regardless of the
syntactic form of the object derived to that point,
goes against most notions of functional cartogra-
phies. However, the clear judgement particularly
in the case of the intransitive subject of AI+O not
triggering a past tense interpretation strongly suggests that there is some interplay with the mechanics of argument saturation underlying this phenomenon, and that it should not be downplayed as
a spatial metaphor residing in the pragmatics. This
paper argues that implementing an STAG analysis of the Blackfoot clause provides a more natural
way to characterize the position of F.

In an STAG context, this means we should be
looking to define a position for F on the semantic side of the derivation rather than the syntactic
one. However, this first requires a semantics for
pseudo-incorporation. In the next section we look
at the scope differences between canonical transitives with animate agents (so-called TA constructions) and the AI+O construction. This will serve

as independent motivation for the STAG account of these predicates which will in turn more easily capture the tense data.

2 Blackfoot Scope

Quantification in Blackfoot can be expressed via a verbal suffix, which is able to associate with either the subject or the object of a transitive predicate:

(10)   nit-ohkana-ohpommatoop-innaan-
        1ST-all-buy.TR-1PL-
        iaawa
        PL.OBJ
        'We all bought them.' or
        'We bought all of them.'
        (Weber & Matthewson 2013 ex10)

Following the Constraint on Elementary Tree Minimality defined in Frank (2002), we treat these quantifiers as being part of the verb's elementary tree. This is shown in Figure 1. The only elements of the morphology we take to be part of the verb's elementary tree here are the quantification and the verb root itself including morphological marking of valence. The argument positions are DP substitution sites, and the additional agreement affixes arise as a result of the arguments which substitute in, both φ-feature valued instances of *pro* in the case of (10). A discussion of how this agreement is manifested in an STAG context is orthogonal to the present discussion. However, it is worth noting that the universal quantification can also combine with full DPs:

(11)   óm-iksi   aakííkoan-iksi
        DEM.DIST-PL girl-PL
        ik-ohkana-issta-yi-aawa...
        DEG-all-want.INTR-3PL-PL.OBJ ...
        'Those girls all want...'
        (Weber & Matthewson 2013 ex13)

So, while these argument positions may be occupied by *pro* or by overt DPs with determiners, they take on a complex meaning incorporating the meaning of the quantifier that originates in the verbal predicate.

Extending further to the Frank and Storoshenko (2012) treatment of scope, wherein the semantic form of a predicate in STAG is broken into a predicate part and a scope part, we place this quantifier in the scope part. Whereas traditional STAG analyses of scope ambiguity make use of an undetermined order of operations leading to two distinct

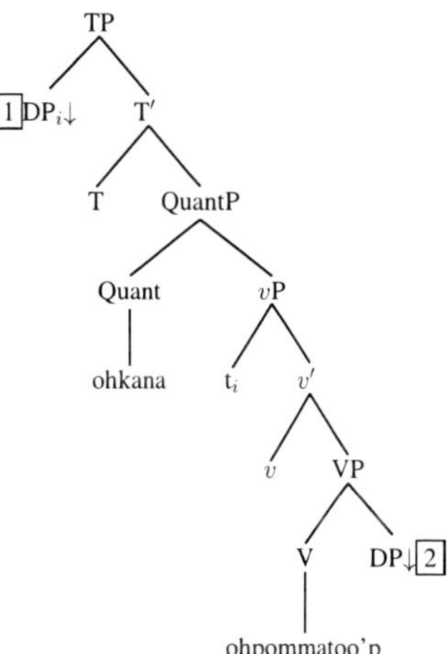

Figure 1: Basic syntactic tree for the predicate in (10)

derivations (Schabes and Shieber, 1994), here we claim that the Blackfoot facts must be captured by two different semantic elementary tree sets for the verbal predicate, shown in Figure 2[2]. Though not strictly necessary for the example in (10) with pronominal arguments, the form presented here is robust enough to accommodate interaction between predicate modifying affixes and DPs with determiners, yielding complex expressions such as *all the men*. For the moment, we assume that definite and demonstrative DPs in this language are of type $\langle e \rangle$, consisting of definite descriptions closed using the iota operator:

(12) $[\![\text{the man}]\!] = \iota x.\text{man}(x)$

We further assume that forms such as (12) are not specified for number; following Link (1983), the unique x variable here may also denote a plurality of entities. Following the quantification presented in Figure 2, the semantic content of the argument DP substitutes into the restrictor of the quantifier, rather than directly into an argument position. This restrictor contains a simple set membership function, in this case defining all entities that belong to the set defined by the plurality which substitutes in.

Having established the basic mechanics of the verbal quantification, we move on to the interac-

---

[2]This may be thought of as the output of two distinct elementary tree building operations. The construction of elementary tree sets in STAG remaining a somewhat unexplored realm, we step back from this issue and simply assert the two tree sets.

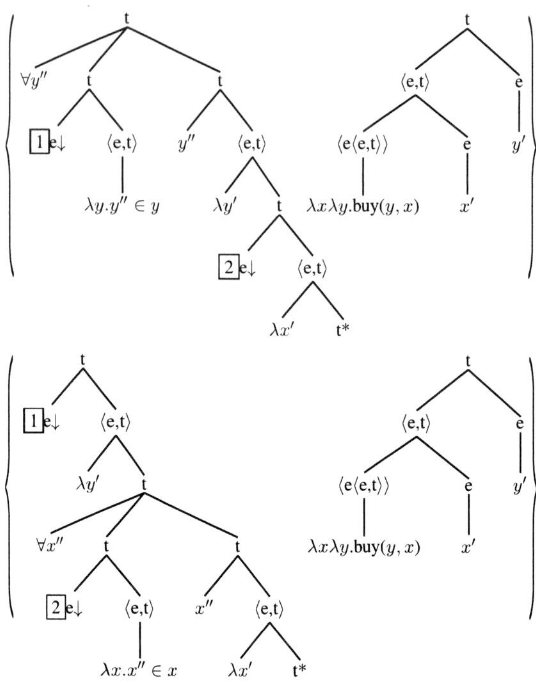

Figure 2: Semantic tree sets for the predicate in (10)

tion with quantified DPs and the AI+O construction. In the following examples, the verbal prefix *iihkana* (a phonological variant of the prefix in (10)) denotes universal quantification, now interacting with another quantified DP in the same clause:

(13)   iihkana-inoyiiya anniskey piita
        all-see.TR   one certain eagle
        'They all saw this one eagle'
        $1 > \forall, \ast\forall > 1$
        (Weber & Matthewson 2013 ex21)

(14)   iihkana-yaapiiya piita
        all-see.INTR   eagle
        'They all saw a different eagle'
        $\ast 1 > \forall, \forall > 1$
        (Weber & Matthewson 2013 ex26)

Weber and Matthewson (2013) note that in examples such as (13), a transitive clause with a quantified object DP, the DP quantifier obligatorily takes wide scope over the verbal prefix quantifier, which in turn associates with the subject. That the objects obligatorily outscope the verb-affixed quantifiers means that in such cases, the affixed quantifier must associate with the subject. In other words, only the upper MCS configuration in Figure 2 is available. We propose that this may be the

result of a semantic well-formedness constraint. While the affixal quantifiers may associate with DPs bearing simple determiners or demonstratives (i.e. objects of type $\langle e \rangle$), the available data show no examples of the affixal quantifier associating with an independently quantified DP. Such quantified DPs, we assume, combine using the typical two-tree semantic multi-component set (MCS) consisting of a type $\langle e \rangle$ variable substituting at the argument site and a $\langle t \rangle$-recursive scope tree which must adjoin high enough to bind the variable. This would be the familiar type of quantificational MCS as in Figure 3. A constraint against "overloading" an argument with two quantifiers, essentially preventing a quantified DP from combining into an argument position already part of a verb's quantifier, would block a derivation for (13) using the lower MCS in Figure 2 and creating a clash between the verbal suffix universal and the DP's specific numeral in this case. From here, we turn to the type-shifting operation defined in Storoshenko and Frank (2012) and applying it to the scope tree in the upper MCS, targeting the root node as the adjoining site for the DP's scope, allowing the specific 'one' to scope wide[3] The sub-

---

[3]Another possibility for blocking the unwanted derivation for (13) may be to invoke a constraint against targeting the

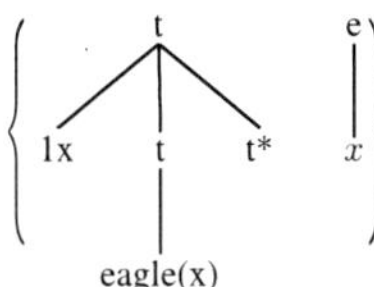

eagle(x)

Figure 3: Semantic tree set for DP quantifier as in (13)

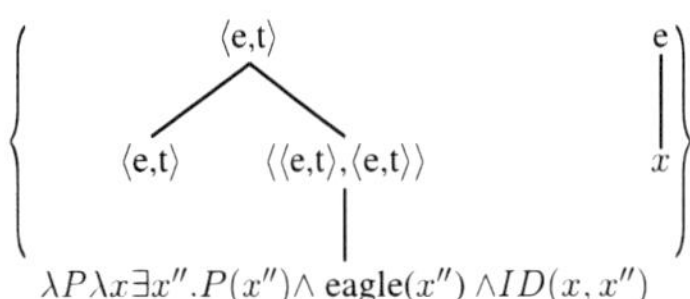

$\lambda P \lambda x \exists x''.P(x'') \wedge \text{eagle}(x'') \wedge ID(x, x'')$

Figure 4: Semantic tree set for incorporated object (first attempt)

ject, again a pronoun, associates with the verbal quantifier by way of set membership. Note this is *contra* Weber and Matthewson who derive the wide scope of the object through a choice function.

In the AI+O case (14), they find that the incorporated singular object obligatorily takes narrow scope, yielding only an interpretation where each person sees a different eagle. Translated into STAG, this means that the object is not composing with the scope tree of the predicate in the same way as a quantified object. Following Bliss (and Weber and Matthewson for this example), the semantic operation is Predicate Restriction (PR). As defined by Chung and Ladusaw (2004), PR is an alternative to Function Application (FA) as a means of saturating the argument position of a given predicate. PR is a two step process: first the argument is taken to be of type $\langle e,t \rangle$, and acts as a restrictor on the targeted argument position inside the predicate. Then, existential closure binds the argument position. In an STAG context, this will of course be a single operation, a composition of the predicate's MCS with the tree set of the incorporated argument. The key distinction will be that such pseudo-incorporated arguments will have unique tree sets, shown in Figure 4. Again, as with a standard GQ, there is a variable portion of type $\langle e \rangle$ which will substitute into the relevant argument position of a predicate's scope tree. The difference here is that the recursive "scope part" of the MCS is not recursive on $\langle t \rangle$, but rather on $\langle e,t \rangle$. The function from $\langle e,t \rangle$ to $\langle e,t \rangle$ within the auxiliary tree accomplishes the operations of restriction and closure in one step. The type $\langle e \rangle$ component is associated with the restricted and existentially-closed variable by way of an identity function. Adjoining the auxiliary tree into the lowest $\langle e,t \rangle$ node of scope tree in the upper (subject universal quantifier) MCS in Figure 2, while substituting the type $\langle e \rangle$ variable into the [2]-linked argument position

yields the form in (15), composed up to the $\langle t \rangle$ node immediately dominating [2] in the scope tree.

(15) $\exists x''.\text{see}(y', x'') \wedge \text{eagle}(x'') \wedge ID(x, x'')$

Though inelegant, and leaving the x variable free but identified with the existentially bound x'', the method in Figure 4 allows us to retain the same basic predicate tree sets regardless of the type of argument (DP or incorporated object), and to easily derive the obligatory narrow scope of the object.

An alternative approach would be to take more seriously the syntactic differences between not just the objects in (13) and (14), but also the predicates, which do have different morphology, and assume that the predicate trees will be different as well. For (13), we assume the object to be a full DP, combining into predicate trees similar to those in Figures 1 and 2. However, a predicate taking a pseudo-incorporated object may have a distinct semantics, mirroring the fact that on the syntax side it combines with a bare NP rather than a DP. This is the scenario sketched in Figure 5. Here, the scope part of the predicate does not contain an abstraction over the object position; instead, the object position [2], which would be an NP substitution site in the syntax, is now linked to the $\langle e,\langle e,t \rangle \rangle$ node in the lower predicate part of the semantic tree.

The gain from this method can be seen in Figure 6, where we present the updated semantic trees for the incorporated argument. Here, the only contribution of the nominal is to act as a function over the semantically transitive predicate, and incorporate the restriction on the object. The existential closure is already built into the root of the predicate's lower tree, which will necessarily be under the scope of the subject combining into the scope tree for the same predicate. Simplification of the resulting expression yields (16) as the final denotation of the lower member of the predicate's MCS after the incorporated object adjoins.

(16) $\exists x'.\text{see}(y', x') \wedge \text{eagle}(x')$

---

[2] node in the lower MCS from type shifting.

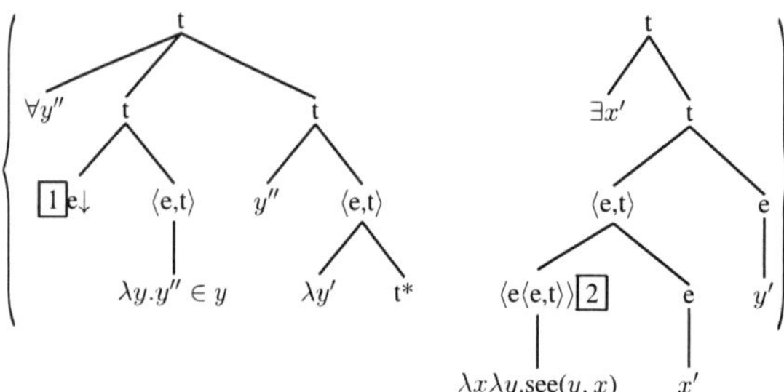

Figure 5: Alternate Predicate for PR (including universal quantifier over subject)

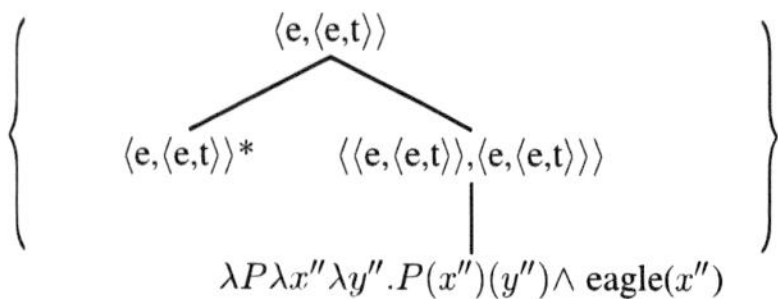

Figure 6: Alternate semantic tree set for incorporated argument

Avoiding the issue of the unbound variable makes this method preferable, and we will adopt it going forward, but it comes at the apparent cost of proposing a different tree set for the predicate. Incidentally, this approach also directly encodes the fact that incorporation is uniquely available for objects but not subjects, which the prior attempt does not. With the basics of handling different types of arguments and quantification settled, we return to the matter of tense in the next section.

3 Accounting for Tense

To get back on track, recall the formula from (1), repeated below as (17):

(17) $[\![F]\!] = \lambda P \lambda s'.P(s') \wedge DIST(s') \rightarrow s' < s^*$

What we need to get the temporal interpretation correct is a function which inspects a predicate of type $\langle s,t \rangle$ from situations to propositions (truth values), and dictates that if the current situation has been taken as the argument of a DISTal function, then the current situation is in the past relative to the present speech time defined as s^*. As noted earlier, this calls upon a treatment of demonstratives described in Elbourne (2008) where situation variables proliferate; one place predicates are of type $\langle \langle s,e \rangle, \langle s,t \rangle \rangle$, arguments normally taken to be type $\langle e \rangle$ are $\langle s,e \rangle$, and so on. Essentially, all entities and propositions are interpreted with respect to situations. Having already motivated a

treatment of demonstratives and definite DPs as type $\langle e \rangle$, the lift to type $\langle s,e \rangle$ is no great stretch. Revised trees, showing only one argument under the universal quantifier for the sake of brevity, are given in Figure 7.

For a definite DP, the update is quite simple:

(18) $[\![\text{the man}]\!] = \lambda s.\iota x.\text{man}(x)$ in s

Combining this form with our updated universal quantification yields the following (abstracting away from tense and the object position for the time being):

(19) $\lambda s \forall y''[y'' \in \iota x.[\text{man}(x)$ in $s]$ in $s]$ $[\text{kick}(y'', x(s))]$

While there is some redundancy, this gives all y'' who, in the given situation, are part of the plurality defined as being men in the given situation.

The next ingredient of our account for tense will be a form for the distal demonstrative. Again, this is accomplished with a minor simplification of Elbourne's form, here conflating temporal and world variables into the single type $\langle s \rangle$ for convenience:

(20) $[\![\text{oma ninaa}]\!] = \lambda s.[[[\iota x.x$ is a man in $s] = z] \wedge DIST(z, a, s)]$

Following Elbourne, the iota operator defines an x as a man, and then associates that x with another variable of the same type (z here). This second variable is passed along as an argument of a second function defined as DIST, here taking three arguments. The first is the associated entity, while the third is the given situation in which x's man-hood is defined. The middle variable a is a contextually-defined indexical, providing the frame of reference for distance. In essence, "z is distant with respect to a in the situation s".

Once this argument has composed into the predicate tree, the function defined in (17) comes into play. The action of this function is to check the

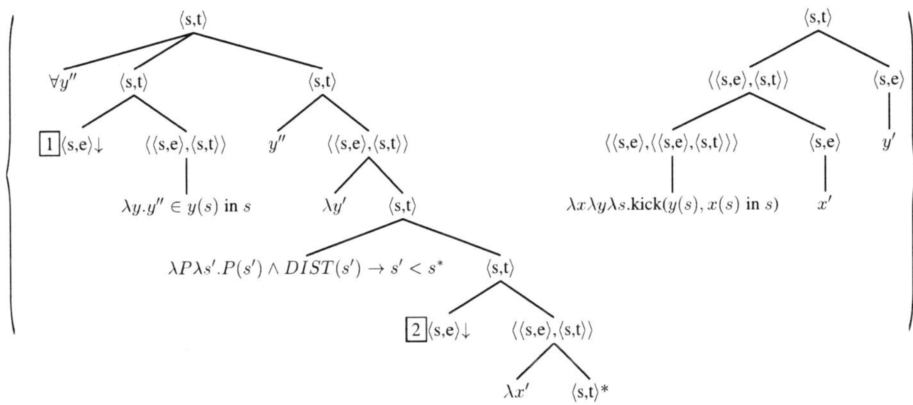

Figure 7: Semantic tree set for the predicate in (10), updated to situations and including F. For (un-quantified) unergatives and unaccusatives, F appears at the root, still immediately above the lowest $\langle s,e \rangle$ substitution site.

object of type $\langle s,t \rangle$ in its scope for any DIST functions taking the given situation as an argument. The presence of such a function triggers an implication that the given situation is in the past relative to the present situation of utterance. Recalling the facts in Section 1, the relevant syntactic positions triggering this implication were the internal argument of transitives, and the sole argument of unergatives and unaccusatives. The latter two are simplest, as while their arguments may have different positions in the syntax, the semantic tree sets for both will have the same basic shape. For these, we need simply to posit that they will have a scope tree similar to that for the AI+O case in Figure 5, and that this function from $\langle s,t \rangle$ to $\langle s,t \rangle$ is generated at the root of the scope tree, being a part of the verb's semantics. For the syntactically transitive case, we must make an uncomfortable stipulation, placing the function immediately above the node marked 2 in Figure 7. This will guarantee scope over the substitution position for the object but not the subject.

The crucial step in the derivation of (7), with the distal demonstrative triggering a past tense interpretation, comes at the stage where F takes its argument. Assuming the object of *kick* to have been *oma ninaa*, the expression would be as in (21):

(21) $\lambda s'.\text{kick}(y'(s'), \iota x.x \text{ is a man in } s' = z \wedge$
$DIST(z, a, s')) \wedge DIST(s') \rightarrow s' <$
$s*$

Crucially, the material implication is calculated immediately, such that in this case the statement that the bound s' is temporally prior to the present

$s*$ is coordinated to the expression for the duration of the final computation. If s' is not the argument of a DIST function at this stage, then F takes no action and is inert for the rest of the interpretation.

Turning to the AI+O cases, we capitalize on the conclusion that the best solution to dealing with PR is to say that the semantic elementary trees of the predicates involved are substantially different. It is then not unreasonable to claim that another consequence of this is that the F function is not a part of the Figure 5 tree set. This allows us to claim that for the rest, F is built into the predicate's scope tree immediately above the lowest $\langle s,e \rangle$ substitution site during the generation of the predicate's elementary tree. Assuming F has a syntactic analogue, the separation of syntax and semantics provided by STAG allows us to define a consistent syntactic position for F which maps to an equally consistent semantic one.

4 Conclusion and Future Work

This paper has dealt with three major challenges arising from an examination of Blackfoot arguments: quantification from the verbal predicate, predicate restriction as a combinatory operation, and the definition of a function for deriving past tense from distal demonstratives. The STAG approach to the first issue is reasonably straightforward, building the quantification into the verbal predicate's scope tree, while having the DP substitute into a position linked to the restrictor inside of a generalized quantifier structure. What is less clear is how the two different elementary tree sets for this quantification are defined. A quantifier on a transitive predicate may bind either the subject or the object; our solution to this has been to stipulate there must be different elementary tree sets for each eventuality. This suggests that there is some room for variability in the mapping between syntax and semantics during the process of elementary tree construction. More work in this area is called for, as the complicated interactions between verbal morphology and argument structure in this language do suggest that a parallel derivational process is also at work before the TAG combinatory operations begin.

This is reinforced by the second issue, that of Predicate Restriction. The ideal solution seems to be to follow the lead of the verb morphology and again assume that there is a fundamentally different semantic tree set for what is essentially the same predicate. Once this leap is made, the implementation of PR is relatively simple, with the two steps split between the two lexical items involved: the verb's semantic MCS provides the existential closure, while the incorporating argument provides the restriction over the argument position by way of a function over the predicate.

The issue of the positioning of the function which determines temporal interpretations from the presence of a demonstrative is where the benefits of the STAG approach to semantics shine though. As discussed above, the expanded scope trees adopted in this paper allow not only for the function to be divorced from a given syntactic position, but they allow for a consistent position above a saturated predicate in the scope trees to be defined. The position unifying the subject of unergatives and unaccusatives, along with the object of transitives is that they are all associated with the lowest λ-abstractor in the scope tree. No such generalization is possible in a mainstream framework. We also now have a principled reason for treating the AI+O cases as distinct. The STAG account may feel somewhat *ad hoc*, but it still seems preferable to conceive of this as a function of syntactic elementary tree building interfacing with a distinct semantic tree than trying to read the semantics off the syntactic tree directly.

Lastly, we must point out that beyond the contributions of derivational morphology to elementary tree building in both the syntax and the semantics, there is a rather intricate agreement system at work in this language which we have made no effort to capture. This remains for future work.

Acknowledgments

Thanks go first to the members of the Blackfoot community for sharing their language; unless otherwise cited, data in this paper are from fieldwork carried out at the University of Calgary with the support of a Faculty Start-Up Grant. This paper has been improved by the detailed comments of the TAG+ reviewers. All errors are my own.

References

Heather Bliss. 2013. *The Blackfoot configurationality conspiracy: Parallels and differences in clausal and nominal structures*. Ph.D. thesis, University of British Columbia.

Sandra Chung and William Ladusaw. 2004. *Restriction and Saturation*. Cambridge, MA: MIT Press.

Paul Elbourne. 2008. Demonstratives as individual concepts. *Linguistics and Philosophy* 31:409–466.

Robert Frank. 2002. *Phrase Structure Composition and Syntactic Dependencies*. Cambridge, MA: MIT Press.

Robert Frank and Dennis Ryan Storoshenko. 2012. The shape of elementary trees and scope possibilities in STAG. In *Proceedings of the 11th International Workshop on Tree Adjoining Grammars and Related Formalisms*.

Angelika Kratzer. 1996. Severing the external argument from its verb. In Johan Rooryck and Laurie Zaring, editors, *Phrase Structure and the Lexicon*, Dordrecht: Kluwer Academic Publishers, pages 109–138.

Blake Lewis. 2014. The syntax and semantics of demonstratives: A DP-external approach. In Laura Teddiman, editor, *Proceedings of the 2014 Annual Conference of the Canadian Linguistics Association*. http://cla-acl.ca/wp-content/uploads/Lewis-2014.pdf.

Godehard Link. 1983. Logical semantics for natural language. *Erkenntnis* 19(1-3):261–283.

Yves Schabes and Stuart M. Shieber. 1994. An alternative conception of tree-adjoining derivation. *Computational Linguistics* 20(1):91–124.

Dennis Ryan Storoshenko and Robert Frank. 2012. Deriving syntax-semantics mappings: node linking, type shifting and scope ambiguity. In *Proceedings of the 11th International Workshop on Tree Adjoining Grammars and Related Formalisms*.

Natalie Weber and Lisa Matthewson. 2013. The semantics of Blackfoot arguments. In *Papers of the 45th Algonquian Conference*.

Combining Predicate-Argument Structure and Operator Projection:
Clause Structure in Role and Reference Grammar

Laura Kallmeyer
Heinrich Heine University
Düsseldorf, Germany
kallmeyer@phil.hhu.de

Rainer Osswald
Heinrich Heine University
Düsseldorf, Germany
osswald@phil.hhu.de

Abstract

This work presented here is motivated by the goal of formalizing the theory of Role and Reference Grammar (RRG; Van Valin and LaPolla 1997; Van Valin 2005). The main contribution of this paper is to show how RRG's rather flat constituent structure and its operator projection, which reflects the scopal properties of functional operators, can be integrated in a single tree. Inspired by Tree Adjoining Grammar (TAG), we model the operator structure by means of feature structures. Furthermore, we develop an architecture that allows us to impose constraints on sister adjunction, which is the mechanism used for adding operators and modifiers, by appropriate edge and node features.

1 Introduction

Role and Reference Grammar (RRG; Van Valin and LaPolla 1997; Van Valin 2005) is a non-transformational linguistic theory whose development has been strongly inspired by typological concerns and in which semantics and pragmatics play significant roles. One of the basic assumptions of RRG is that clauses have a *layered structure* which reflects the distinction between predicates, arguments, and non-arguments. The *core* (CO) layer consists of the *nucleus* (NUC), which specifies the verb, and its arguments. The *clause* (CL) layer contains the core as well as extracted arguments. Each of the layers can have a *periphery* (PERI) for attaching adjuncts. In the following, we refer to the top clause node and its (non-peripheral) clause, core, and nucleus descendants as the *skeleton* of the clause.

Another important aspect of RRG is the representation of *operators*, which are closed-class

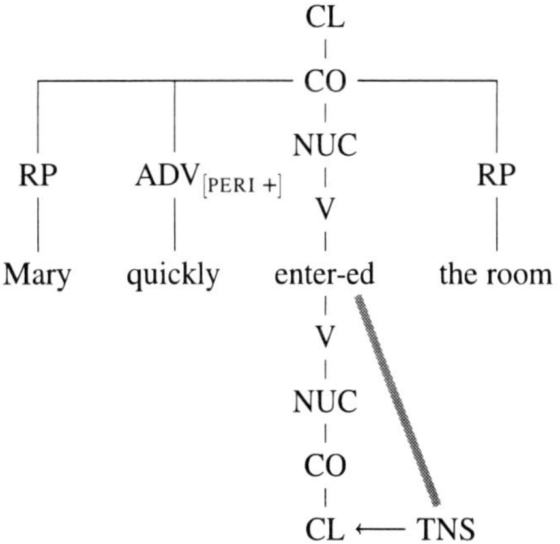

Figure 1: Simplified example of a syntactic representation in RRG with operator projection

grammatical categories such as aspect, modality, and tense. Each type of operator is assumed to attach to a specific layer: tense operators attach to the clause, modality to the core, aspect to the nucleus. Moreover, the surface order of the operators reflects their attachment site in that the higher the layer an operator is attached to, the farther away from the nucleus the operator occurs on the surface.

While the ordering among the operators is thus systematically correlated with the scope given by their attachment site at the clausal skeleton, the surface order of the operators relative to arguments and adjuncts is much less transparent and often requires crossing branches. For this reason, RRG represents the constituent structure and the operator structure as different *projections* of the clause. The syntactic representation in Fig. 1 illustrates this idea: The tense (TNS) operator, which is a clause-level operator, attaches morphosyntactically to the verb. The example also shows that the peripheral pace adverb *quickly* modifies the core.

Proceedings of the 13th International Workshop on Tree Adjoining Grammars and Related Formalisms (TAG+13), pages 61–70,
Umeå, Sweden, September 4–6, 2017. © 2017 Association for Computational Linguistics

('RP' stands for 'referential phrase'.)

Johnson (1987) once proposed a formalization of the projection approach which uses two different context free grammars, one for analyzing the sequence consisting of the verb plus arguments and adjuncts, and one for the sequence consisting of the verb plus operators. The two grammars taken together then constitute a "projection grammar". However, Johnson's proposal is purely surface oriented and does not capture the fact that the two projections share basically the same clausal skeleton.

In the present paper, we propose a new approach that conflates the operator projection with the constituent structure, preserves the scope-related ordering constraints of the operators and avoids crossing branches with other constituents. The basic idea is that operators can attach to the clausal skeleton "in situ" and then project their content upwards (or downwards) to their respective scope layer. For instance, a tense operator, whose scope level is the clause, can be attached by sister adjunction to a nuclear node and thereby avoids crossing branches with argument constituents.

The adjunction of the operators needs to be controlled in the following two respects: (i) The adjunction of an operator is *obligatory* if the information conveyed by the operator is required for a sentence to be complete. (ii) The scope-related *ordering* of the operators must be respected. In our approach, these constraints are implemented with the help of feature structures attached to the edges of the trees.

The rest of the paper is organized as follows: Section 2 briefly introduces a proposal for defining tree composition in a way that leads to the kind of flat syntactic representations postulated by RRG. The two operations, (wrapping) substitution and sister adjunction are intended to capture argument structure constructions, including long distance dependencies, and the flat adjunction of modifier expressions. Section 3 presents the core idea of this paper which is to add feature structures to edges (as well as to nodes) for bookkeeping purposes. The approach is then applied in Section 4 for the seamless alignment of the operator projection of RRG with the constituent projection. Section 5 shows how the proposed representation of the operator projection behaves in the case of complex sentences, in which the structure of the clausal skeleton interacts with the scope-

taking behavior of the operators in intricate ways.

2 Tree composition in Role and Reference Grammar

RRG shares some fundamental properties with Tree Adjoining Grammar (TAG, Joshi and Schabes, 1997; Abeillé and Rambow, 2000), notably its extended domain of locality and certain underlying assumptions about the structure of elementary syntactic building blocks. In particular, RRG assumes that a predicate and its arguments are realized within the same elementary tree (cf. Frank, 2002, for similar assumptions in TAG). Therefore RRG can be formalized as a tree-rewriting grammar in the spirit of TAG, albeit with slightly different operations for combining elementary trees.

Previous work on formalizing tree composition in RRG (Kallmeyer et al., 2013; Osswald and Kallmeyer, in press) has identified two operations that are needed in order to cope with the flat structure of RRG trees: An operation called *(wrapping) substitution* that serves to fill argument slots, i.e., to fill substitution nodes, and an operation called *sister adjunction* used to add so-called periphery elements, i.e., modifiers.

2.1 (Wrapping) substitution for argument composition

Simple substitution, as in TAG, consists of replacing a non-terminal leaf with a new tree of the same category. The idea behind wrapping substitution is that a substitution node (i.e., a non-terminal leaf) in the target tree gets filled by adding a subtree from a new tree. More concretely, this new tree gets split at a point where the lower part has the category of the substitution slot and can be inserted there. The higher part is identified with the root of the target tree. It can add material above that root but also new material to the right or left of all the daughters of that root. Potential sites for splitting a tree are indicated by dominance links. In other words, wrapping such a tree around another one means stretching the dominance link in such a way that its upper node merges with the root while the lower node merges with a substitution node in the target tree. Such a wrapping substitution occurs for instance in the derivation of the long-distance dependency (1), given in Fig. 2 (where the dashed edge indicates a dominance relation). The result is the tree in Fig. 3. ('PrCS' stands for 'pre-core slot'.)

(1) What does John think Bill smashed?

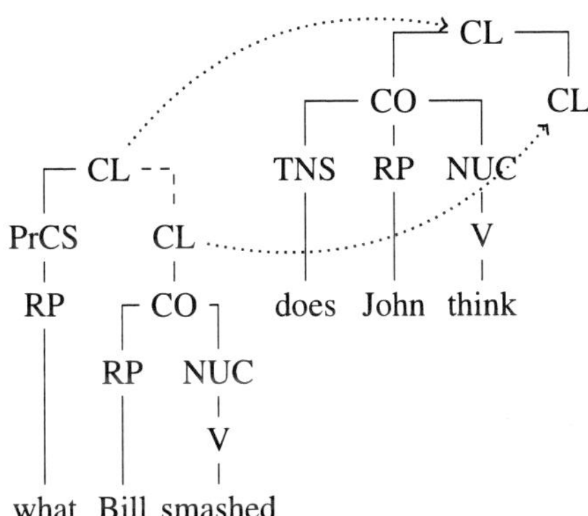

Figure 2: Derivation for (1): wrapping substitution

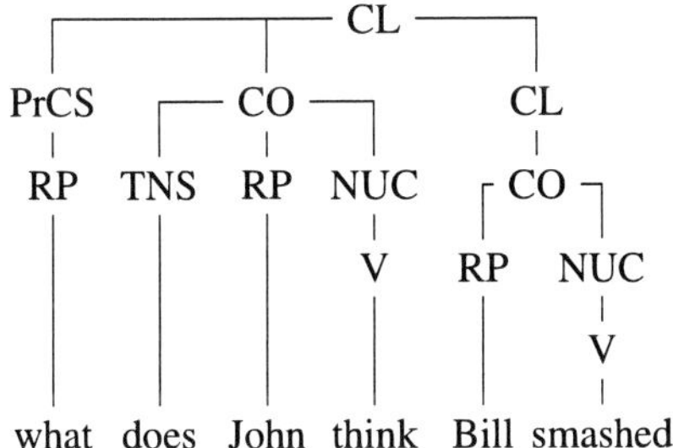

Figure 3: Derived tree for (1)

Note that in a first proposal of how to apply wrapping substitution to tree composition in RRG, Kallmeyer et al. (2013) assumed a more binary structure. The version sketched above goes back to Osswald and Kallmeyer (in press) and is more in line with the flat structures used in RRG. The idea of using wrapping substitution is partly inspired by the operations *subsertion* in D-Tree Grammar (Rambow et al., 1995) and *generalized substitution* in D-Tree Substitution Grammar (Rambow et al., 2001), which, however, are more general. Wrapping substitution shares with subsertion the non-locality: the two nodes targeted by the wrapping substitution (i.e., the substitution node and the root node of the target tree) need not come from the same elementary tree and can be far apart from each other. If the number of wrapping substitutions that stretch across a node in the derived tree is limited by some constant k, it can be shown that an equivalent *simple Context-Free Tree Grammar* (CFTG) (Kanazawa, 2016) of rank k can be constructed, which is in turn equivalent to a

well-nested *Linear Context-Free Rewriting System* (LCFRS) (Vijay-Shanker et al., 1987; Seki et al., 1991; Kanazawa, 2009; Gómez-Rodríguez et al., 2010) of fan-out $k + 1$ (see Kallmeyer, 2016, for more details on this equivalence).

2.2 Sister adjunction for modification

So-called peripheral elements in RRG are added via sister adjunction. An example is the modifier *quickly* in the example in (2). The corresponding derivation is given in Fig. 4. The root of the modifier tree merges with the target node n of the adjunction and the (necessarily unique) daughter is inserted as a new daughter of n. The categories of the root and n have to be the same.

(2) Mary quickly entered the room

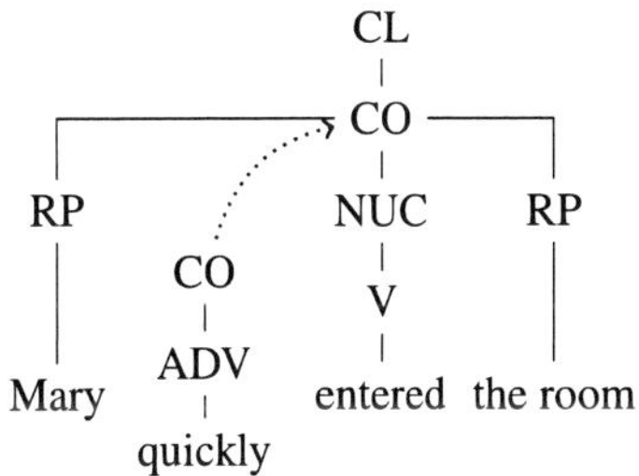

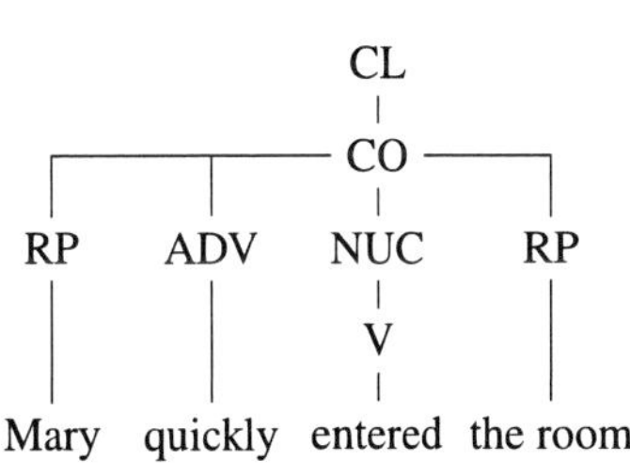

Figure 4: Derivation for (2): modification via sister adjunction

3 Adding feature structures to the syntactic trees

In TAG, internal nodes have top and bottom feature structures. The underlying idea is that the top reflects properties of the node visible from above while the bottom reflects properties of the subtree below the node. These features control the adjunction possibilities at that node. In particular, mismatches between them (i.e., the fact that they do not unify) express an obligatory adjunction constraint.

In RRG, we want to pursue a similar strategy, namely modeling obligatory adjunction via feature mismatches. However, these mismatches cannot be on top and bottom features of the nodes as in TAG. But we can retain the idea that in places where adjunction occurs, two feature structures that are not unifiable get separated. In the case of sister adjunction, we add a new sister between two nodes or, to put it differently, between two edges. Therefore we propose the following for feature-based sister adjunction:

Nodes have just a single feature structure. In contrast, edges have two feature structures, a left one and a right one. In a sister adjunction, the feature structure of the root of the adjoined tree unifies with the feature structure of the node targeted by the adjunction. In the final derived tree, the two feature structures between two neighbouring edges have to unify. (Consequently, if they are not unifiable, this acts as an obligatory adjunction constraint.) Furthermore, features on the leftmost (resp. rightmost) edge percolate upwards, except if there is a substitution node, which blocks feature percolation. More precisely, the following unifications occur in the final derived tree:

1. Whenever there are nodes v, v_1, v_2 with edges $\langle v, v_1 \rangle$ and $\langle v, v_2 \rangle$ such that v_1 immediately precedes v_2, the right feature structure f_{r_1} of $\langle v, v_1 \rangle$ unifies with the left feature structure f_{l_2} of $\langle v, v_2 \rangle$.

$$\Rightarrow f_{r_1} \text{ and } f_{l_2} \text{ are replaced with } f_{r_1} \sqcup f_{l_2}$$

2. Whenever there are nodes v_1, v_2, v_3 with edges $\langle v_1, v_2 \rangle, \langle v_2, v_3 \rangle$ such that v_3 does not have a sister to the left (to the right) and v_2 was not a substitution node, the left (right) feature structure of $\langle v_2, v_3 \rangle$ unifies with the left (right) feature structure of $\langle v_1, v_2 \rangle$.

$$\Rightarrow f_{l_1} \text{ and } f_{l_2} \text{ are both replaced with } f_{l_1} \sqcup f_{l_2} \text{ if } v_2 \text{ was not filled by substitution}$$

For illustration consider the simple example in Fig. 5. The initial tree α carries an obligatory adjunction constraint since the feature structures between the two edges do not unifiy. β can adjoin repeatedly in between and, as a result, we obtain derived trees where the feature structures between neighbouring edges are unifiable.

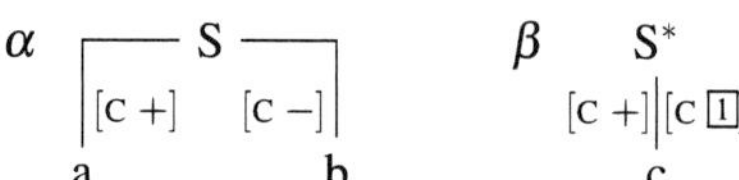

Figure 5: Obligatory sister adjunction

In a substitution, the feature structure at the root of the tree that gets added and the one at the substitution site unify as well. In the more general case of a wrapping substitution with a dominance link from node n_1 to n_2 that gets stretched and a target tree with root n_r and substitution node n_s, the feature structures of n_1 and n_r unify and the ones of n_2 and n_s unify.

The constraint in 2. that v_2 was not a substitution site is motivated by the hypothesis that substitution nodes act as islands concerning operators. An example is (1) where the complement clause is added by wrapping substitution and each of the two clauses requires its own tense operator. This restriction for the feature percolation is a working hypothesis; further examples of (wrapping) substitution need to be examined in order to determine whether this assumption makes the right generalization or whether it is too restrictive.

With the above definition of feature structure unification for edge features, the requirement for a non-finite verbal nucleus to obtain tense from a finite verb can for instance be modeled in a way similar to Fig. 5 via a TNS feature with values $+/-$, as illustrated in Fig. 6. The *sleeping* tree requires that a tense marker adjoins to the core node somewhere to the left of the nucleus, i.e., either preceding or following the subject RP. Besides contributing tense, the finite verb also assigns case to the subject RP and it specifies the agreement features that constrain the subject. This can be modeled via the node features, using features from the XTAG grammar (XTAG Research Group, 2001).

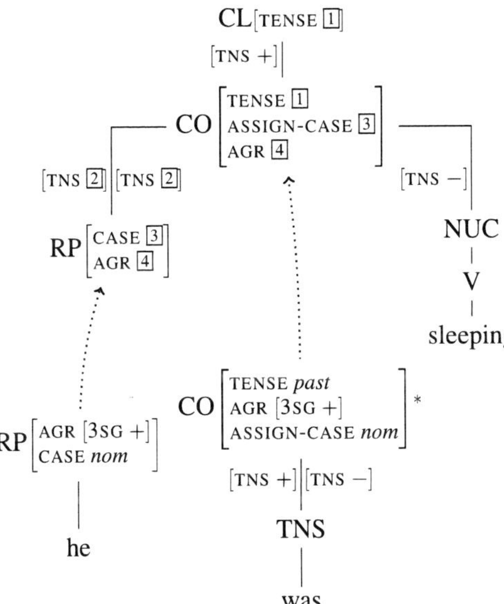

Figure 6: Obligatory adjunction of a tense marker.

4 Modeling the operator projection with features

We have seen that, in line with Van Valin (2005), we treat operators as modifiers that are added by sister adjunction. Moreover, we have illustrated in Fig. 6 how features can be used to enforce the adjunction of certain operators.

What is missing is a modeling of the operator projection of RRG. Each operator belongs to a certain level of the layered structure (see Fig. 7). The mapping from operators to levels of the layered structure explains (i) the scope behavior of operators, since structurally higher operators take scope

Layer	operators
Nucleus	Aspect
	Negation
	Directionals
Core	Directionals
	Event quantification
	Modality
	Negation
Clause	Status
	Tense
	Evidentials
	Illocutionary Force

Figure 7: Operators in the layered structure of the clause (cf. Van Valin, 2005, p. 9)

over lower ones, and (ii) surface order constraints for operators; higher operators are further away from the nucleus of the structure.

The problem is that the constituent and the operator structure are not completely parallel, i.e., one can have structures where an operator belonging to a specific layer is, on the surface structure, surrounded by elements belonging to a lower layer in the constituent structure. Examples are (3) and the Turkish example in (4) (taken from Van Valin, 2005, p.10), where a clause-level tense operator is embedded in the core. In (3), we have the RP *John* and the NUC *sleeping* that form the CO constituent. In between, two operators are added, namely the nucleus-level aspectual operator *been* and the clause-level tense operator *has*. The former can attach at the NUC node, consistent with its operator level. The latter, however, cannot adjoin to the clause node, except if crossing branches are allowed. Within the constituent structure, it is part of the CO constituent while its operator level is higher.

(3) John has$_{TNS}$ been$_{ASP}$ sleeping.

(4) Gel-emi-yebil-ir-im.
    come-ABLE.NEG$_{MOD}$-PSBL$_{STA}$-AOR$_{TNS}$-1SG
    'I may be unable to come'

Similarly, in the Turkish example in (4), the clause-level status and tense operators occur between the verb and the pronominal affix, which is part of the core.

Even though the constituent structure and the operator structure are not fully aligned, they depend on each other. Their hierarchical order is the same and the existence of a layer in the operator projection requires that this layer also exists in the constituent structure. For instance, one can only have clause-level operators if a clause node exists in the constituent structure. In the following we will show that the feature structure-based definition of tree rewriting with sister adjunction proposed above allows us to model the operator projection within the features while attaching the operators at their surface position. In other words, operators sometimes attach lower than their position in the operator structure. The features capture the constraints mentioned above.

Let us illustrate the feature architecture for operators by the analysis of (3) shown in Fig. 8.[1] We

---

[1] To keep things simple, the analysis does not take into ac-

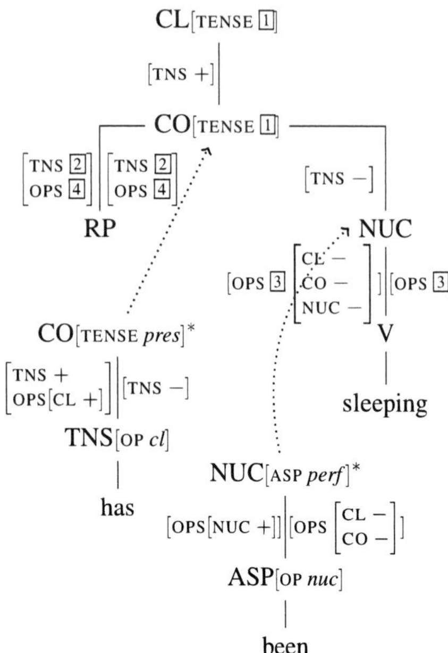

Figure 8: Trees for (3)

assume a feature OPS (for operator structure) used on the edges that specifies which operator projection layer(s) have been reached so far. Its value is a feature structure with features CL, CO and NUC for the three layers, each with possible values + or −. This feature is used in such a way as to guarantee that nuclear, core and clausal operators have to appear in this order when moving outwards in the sentence, starting from the nuclear predicate. For instance, a nuclear operator such as *been* that adjoins to the left of the predicate has a requirement to the right that the levels CL and CO have values −, i.e., are not reached yet. To the left, it just gives the information NUC +. On the other hand, a clausal operator such as the tense operator *has*, when adjoining to the left of the nucleus, does not have any requirement for the operator level that has already been reached (hence there is no OPS feature specified on the right of the top-most edge) but it states to the left of the edge that now CL has value +. In addition to the OPS feature, the preterminal nodes of the operator trees have a feature OP indicating the operator level that the tree targets, which can be different from the root node

category of the tree that specifies the constituency level, i.e., the surface position. For example, *has* is a clause-level operator that adjoins at the core node.

The OPS feature can also be used to make sure that operator levels are licensed by corresponding nodes in the constituent structure of the targeted elementary tree. If, for instance, the core layer is the highest layer of the predicative elementary tree, then the OPS features on the left of the leftmost edge and on the right of the rightmost edge immediately below the core node will have features CL −, which means that clausal operators are not allowed within this core.

Fig. 9 shows the derived tree for sentence (3). The final feature unifications between neighbouring edges and between leftmost/rightmost edges below a node and the left feature structure/right feature structure of the edge to the mother lead to the following: The NUC + information is passed from the NUC–ASP edge to the left of the CO–NUC edge and it gets unified with the feature structure on the right of the CO–TNS edge. Furthermore, the feature structures between CO–RP and CO–TNS unify and the resulting values of TNS and OPS are passed to the left of the CO–RP edge and from there to the left of the CL–CO edge.

Note that the root category of the operator tree (in our example CO in the case of *has* and NUC in the case of *been*) determines the attachment site of the operator in the constituent structure. A possible constraint on these elementary trees, which remains to be verified empirically, is that with respect to RRG's layered structure, the root node label of an operator tree has to be lower or equal to the OP value at the operator node (i.e., at the daughter of that root). This means for instance that there cannot be an operator with [OP *nuc*] and root category CO or CL.[2]

Since the preterminal nodes of the operators specify which operator projection layer the operator belongs to, we can deterministically map a derived tree to the standard RRG structure where the constituent structure and the operator projection are separated. The two structures for our example are given in Fig. 10.

Note that a single lexical item can also contribute more than one operator. The operator *had* in (5), for instance, contributes aspect (nuclear

count the progressive aspect of the present perfect progressive construction in (3). A more thorough analysis would derive *perfect* from the auxiliary choice 'have' and the past participle morphology of 'be', while *progressive* derives from 'be' and the '-ing' form of the main verb.

[2]Such constraints can be implemented in a principled way within a metagrammatical representation using for instance XMG (Crabbé et al., 2013).

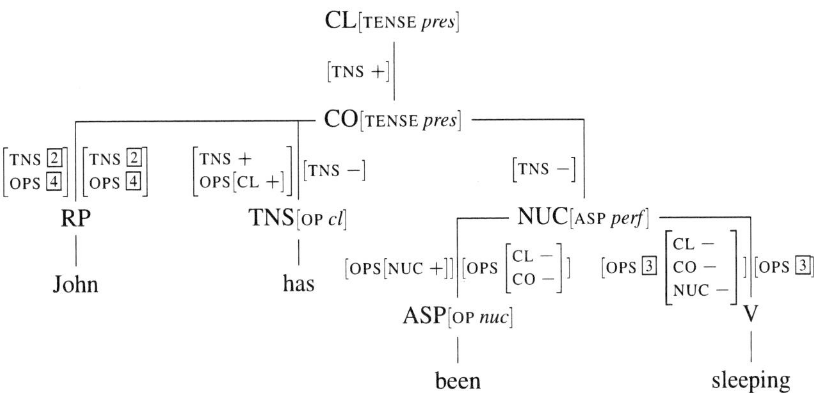

Figure 9: Derived tree for (3) (before final edge feature unification)

level) and tense (clause level).

(5) John had slept.

We therefore modify the representation slightly in that we replace non-terminal operator categories such as TNS, ASP, etc. by a more general category OP, and the single feature OP by a complex feature structure that lists all the features contributed on the different operator layers. In the case of the operator in (5), this would yield the feature structure [NUC [ASP *perf*], CLAUSE [TENSE *past*]]. Likewise, the node label ASP$_{[\text{OP } nuc]}$ in the upper tree of Fig. 10 is to be replaced by the label OP$_{[\text{NUC}[\text{ASP } perf]]}$ under the new convention.

5　Operators in complex sentences

A crucial assumption of RRG concerning the structure of complex sentences is the distinction between embedded and non-embedded dependent structures. Embedded dependent structures correpsond to *subordinations*. By contrast, non-embedded dependent structures, which are referred to as *cosubordination* structures, have basically the form [[ ]$_X$ [ ]$_X$]$_X$. It is characteristic of this type of construction that operators that apply to category X are realized only once but have scope over both constituents. Cosubordination differs from the *coordination* of two independent structures in that the latter type of construction has the form [[ ]$_X$ [ ]$_X$]$_Y$, where Y is a higher-level category than X.

The Turkish sentence in (6) (taken from Van Valin, 2005, p. 201) is an example of a core cosubordination construction (see also Bohnemeyer and Van Valin, 2017, p. 155f). On the surface,

the deontic modal operator *-meli* ('should, ought to') is embedded in the second core, but it takes scope over the entire complex core. ('LM' stands for 'linkage marker'.)

(6) [[Gid-ip]$_{CO}$ [gör-meli-yiz]$_{CO}$]$_{CO}$.
　　 go-LM　　 see-MOD-1PL
　　 'We ought to go and see.'

In the following, we leave aside the question of how to derive cosubordination structures. As a tentative working hypothesis, we may assume that the second embedded core in (6) is not added by substitution but, rather, that the first core is added to the second core by sister adjunction, due to the possible iteration of the construction. The focus of the present paper is on the adjunction of the operator and the construction of the operator projection from the constituent structure. The modal operator in (6) adjoins to the second embedded core node and it carries a feature indicating that it is a core operator. The result is the derived structure in Fig. 11 (cf. Van Valin, 2005, p. 204). In the case of a cosubordination as in Fig. 11, an operator embedded in one part of the complex structure generally takes scope over the larger category. Accordingly, in all elementary trees for cosubordination configurations, the relevant features (here MOD) are shared between the lower and the higher category in question (here the two CO nodes). This is taken to be a general property of cosubordination structures. Corresponding to this, we assume that when mapping our derived structure to the standard RRG structure, the operator targets the highest corresponding node, as long as there is no higher operator level and no substitution node in

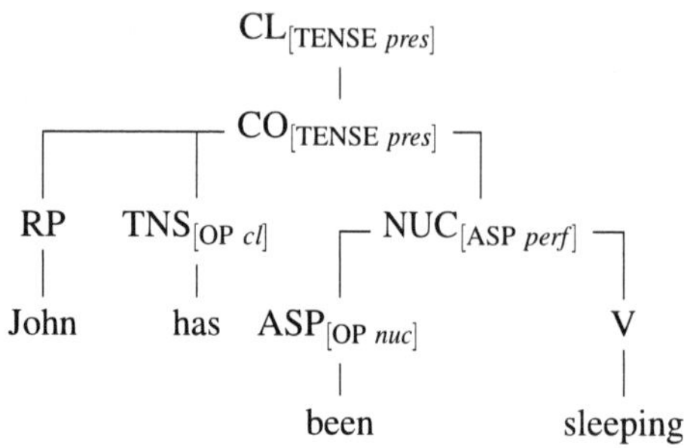

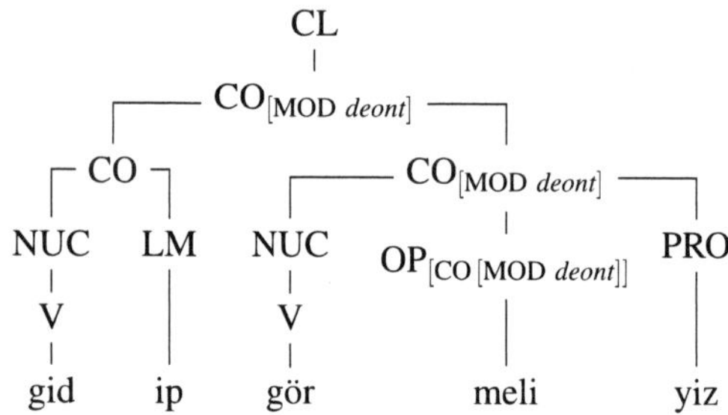

Figure 11: Derived tree for (6)

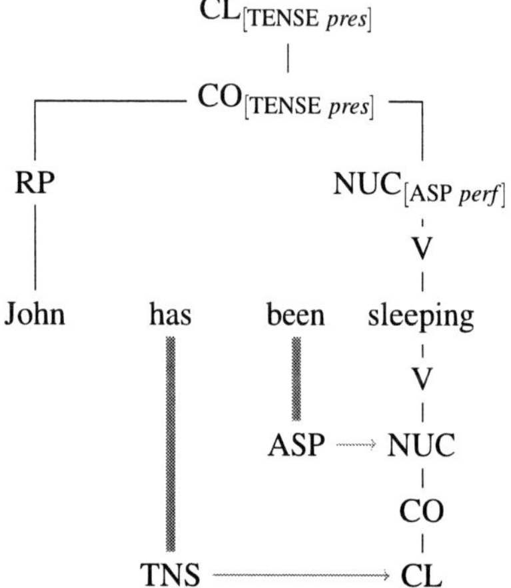

Figure 10: Derived tree for (3) (without edge features) and corresponding RRG structure

ordinate constructions. Another diagnostic is the independent accessibility of the embedded cores by time-positional adverbials, which are analyzed as core-level modifiers (cf. Bohnemeyer and Van Valin, 2017). While (7b) does allow independent time-positional modification, as in *Kim must ask Pat now to wash the car tomorrow*, this is not an option for (7a): Both, *#Kim must go now to try to wash the car tomorrow* and *#Kim must go to try now to wash the car tomorrow* are excluded.

Finally, let us consider a case of subordination in which the same layer category occurs twice on a path in the tree but an embedded operator targets only the lower of the two.

(8) Kim told Pat that she will arrive late.

The example in (8) (adapted from Van Valin, 2005, p. 200) involves substituting a clausal argument into the tree anchored by *told*. This substitution step is shown in Fig. 12.[3] The operator *will* in the embedded clause is a clausal operator that contributes tense. In the resulting tree, it will be dominated by the CL node of the embedded complement clause and, dominating this one, the CL node of the entire sentence. The latter, however, is not available as possible scope of this operator because there is a substitution node between this node and the operator. Consequently, we correctly predict that the tense operator only scopes over the embedded clause. Concering features, this would be reflected in the elementary tree for *told* by the fact that the two CL nodes would *not* share the TENSE feature.

between. In the case of Fig. 11, this is the core of the entire sentence.

A similar example from English is given in (7a) (cf. Van Valin, 2005, p.203) where we have a core consisting of three embedded core constituents where the first contains the modal operator *must*. This operator takes scope over the entire large core. By contrast, in (7b) we have a structure consisting of several cores which constitute a clause. I.e., we have a core coordination and not a core cosubordination. In this case, as correctly predicted by our analysis, the modal embedded in the first core scopes only over this one and not over both cores.

(7) a. [[Kim must*MOD* go]*CO* [to try]*CO* [to wash the car]*CO*]*CO*
    b. [[Kim must*MOD* ask Pat]*CO* [to wash the car]*CO*]*CL*

The shared operator scope in (7a) is a standard criterion for distinguishing cosubordinate from co-

___

[3]Note that even in a long-distance dependency such as *Who did Kim tell John that Mary likes?*, the composition operation is wrapping substitution and not adjunction.

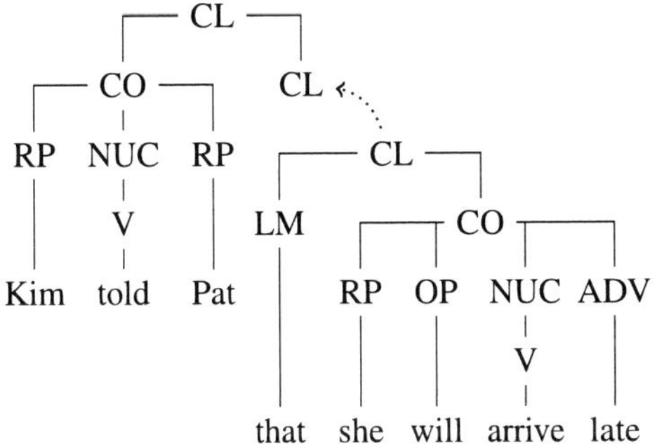

that she will arrive late

Figure 12: Derivation for (8)

6 Conclusion

The work presented in this paper is part of a larger project of formalizing the theory of Role and Reference Grammar (Foley and Van Valin, 1984; Van Valin, 2005). Based on extensive typological research, RRG assumes a rather flat constituent structure that is interleaved with an operator projection which reflects the scopal properties of functional elements. We offered a formalization of this approach that is inspired from Tree Adjoining Grammars (TAG) and that integrates both structures in one tree, modeling the operator structure within appropriate feature structures. Furthermore, due to the flat constituency structure, modifiers are added via sister adjunction and adjunction constraints are modeled via features attached to edges. The resulting architecture shares central assumptions about elementary trees with TAG but adopts a flat structure. Therefore, instead of using the standard TAG top and bottom feature structure of syntactic nodes, we proposed to use left and right features of edges in order to express adjunction constraints. Due to the features, additional projections such as the operator projection, that are not completely parallel to the constituency structure, can be captured as well.

We assume that the scopal structure of periphery modifiers can be modeled in a similar way as the one of the operators. Their scope order also depends on their order with respect to the nuclear predicate: modifiers that are more outwards scope over modifiers that are closer to the nucleus. At the same time, the surface position of a modifier does not always correspond to its scope. For instance, a modifier scoping only over the nucleus of a clause can be separated from the verb by a core constituent. An example is the aspectual adverb *completely* in (9) (Van Valin, 2005, pp. 19f).

(9) Leslie immersed herself completely in the new language.

This leads to a periphery projection that can be modeled via features in a way similar to the treatment of operators proposed in this paper.

One of the next steps towards a complete formalization of RRG will be a detailed analysis of the different types of complex sentences (subordination, cosubordination and coordination at the levels of the different layers) with respect to the composition operations and the elementary trees involved. At that point, our hypothesis that substitution nodes block the feature passing on the edges and act as islands for the operator projection will be tested again.

Another topic to be investigated concerns a binarization of RRG's flat structures. We have argued in the beginning of this paper that the left and right feature structures between edges, which are used in the flat RRG structures to constrain sister adjunction, correspond to the top and bottom feature structures on the nodes in the more binary standard TAG trees. A question is then whether we can actually define a binarization transformation for RRG that turns the features into top and bottom on the nodes and that can be used for instance for feature-based RRG parsing.

Acknowledgments

We thank the anonymous reviewers for their valuable comments. The work presented in this paper has been supported by the Collaborative Research Centre 991 "The Structure of Representations in Language, Cognition, and Science" funded by the German Research Foundation (DFG).

References

Anne Abeillé and Owen Rambow. 2000. Tree Adjoining Grammar: An Overview. In Anne Abeillé and Owen Rambow, editors, *Tree Adjoining Grammars: Formalisms, Linguistic Analysis and Processing*, CSLI, pages 1–68.

Jürgen Bohnemeyer and Robert D. Van Valin, Jr. 2017. The macro-event property and the layered structure of the clause. *Studies in Language* 41(1):142–197.

Benoit Crabbé, Denys Duchier, Claire Gardent, Joseph Le Roux, and Yannick Parmentier. 2013. XMG: eXtensible MetaGrammar. *Computational Linguistics* 39(3):1–66.

William A. Foley and Robert D. Van Valin, Jr. 1984. *Functional syntax and universal grammar*. Cambridge University Press, Cambridge.

Robert Frank. 2002. *Phrase Structure Composition and Syntactic Dependencies*. MIT Press, Cambridge, Mass.

Carlos Gómez-Rodríguez, Marco Kuhlmann, and Giorgio Satta. 2010. Efficient parsing of well-nested linear context-free rewriting systems. In *Human Language Technologies: The 2010 Annual Conference of the North American Chapter of the Association for Computational Linguistics*. Association for Computational Linguistics, Los Angeles, California, pages 276–284. http://www.aclweb.org/anthology/N10-1035.

Mark Johnson. 1987. A new approach to clause structure in Role and Reference Grammar. In *Davis Working Papers in Linguistics 2*, University of California, Davis, CA, pages 55–59.

Aravind K. Joshi and Yves Schabes. 1997. Tree-Adjoning Grammars. In G. Rozenberg and A. Salomaa, editors, *Handbook of Formal Languages*, Springer, Berlin, pages 69–123.

Laura Kallmeyer. 2016. On the mild context-sensitivity of *k*-tree wrapping grammar. In Annie Foret, Glyn Morrill, Reinhard Muskens, Rainer Osswald, and Sylvain Pogodalla, editors, *Formal Grammar. 20th and 21st International Conferences, FG 2015, Barcelona, Spain, August 2015, Revised Selected Papers. FG 2016, Bozen, Italy, August 2016, Proceedings*. Springer, volume 9804 of *Lecture Notes in Computer Science*, pages 77–93.

Laura Kallmeyer, Rainer Osswald, and Robert D. Van Valin, Jr. 2013. Tree wrapping for Role and Reference Grammar. In Glyn Morrill and Mark-Jan Nederhof, editors, *Formal Grammar 2012/2013*. Springer, volume 8036 of *LNCS*, pages 175–190.

Makoto Kanazawa. 2009. The pumping lemma for well-nested Multiple Context-Free Languages. In V. Diekert and D. Nowotka, editors, *DLT 2009*. Springer, Berlin Heidelberg, volume 5583 of *LNCS*, pages 312–325.

Makoto Kanazawa. 2016. Multidimensional trees and a Chomsky-Schützenberger-Weir representation theorem for simple context-free tree grammars. *Journal of Logic and Computation* 26(5):1469–1516.

Rainer Osswald and Laura Kallmeyer. in press. Towards a formalization of Role and Reference Grammar. In R. Kailuweit, E. Staudinger, and L. Künkel, editors, *Applying and Expanding Role and Reference Grammar*.

Owen Rambow, K. Vijay-Shanker, and David Weir. 1995. D-Tree Grammars. In *Proceedings of ACL*.

Owen Rambow, K. Vijay-Shanker, and David Weir. 2001. D-Tree Substitution Grammars. *Computational Linguistics* .

Hiroyuki Seki, Takahashi Matsumura, Mamoru Fujii, and Tadao Kasami. 1991. On multiple context-free grammars. *Theoretical Computer Science* 88(2):191–229.

Robert D. Van Valin, Jr. 2005. *Exploring the Syntax-Semantics Interface*. Cambridge University Press.

Robert D. Van Valin, Jr. and Randy LaPolla. 1997. *Syntax: Structure, meaning and function*. Cambridge University Press.

K. Vijay-Shanker, David J. Weir, and Aravind K. Joshi. 1987. Characterizing structural descriptions produced by various grammatical formalisms. In *Proceedings of ACL*. Stanford.

XTAG Research Group. 2001. A Lexicalized Tree Adjoining Grammar for English. Technical report, Institute for Research in Cognitive Science, Philadelphia.

Parsing with Dynamic Continuized CCG

Michael White and **Jordan Needle**
Department of Linguistics
The Ohio State University
Columbus, OH 43210
mwhite@ling.osu.edu
needle.6@osu.edu

Simon Charlow
Department of Linguistics
Rutgers University
New Brunswick, NJ 08901
simon.charlow@rutgers.edu

Dylan Bumford
Department of Linguistics
New York University
New York, NY 10003
dbumford@nyu.edu

Abstract

We present an implemented method of parsing with Combinatory Categorial Grammar (CCG) that for the first time derives the exceptional scope behavior of indefinites in a principled and plausibly practical way. The account implements Charlow's (2014) monadic approach to dynamic semantics, in which indefinites' exceptional scope taking follows from the way the *side effect* of introducing a discourse referent survives the process of delimiting the scope of true quantifiers in a continuized grammar. To efficiently parse with this system, we extend Barker and Shan's (2014) method of parsing with continuized grammars to only invoke monadic lifting and lowering where necessary, and define novel normal form constraints on lifting and lowering to avoid spurious ambiguities. We also integrate Steedman's (2000) CCG for deriving basic predicate-argument structure and enrich it with a method of lexicalizing scope island constraints. We argue that the resulting system improves upon Steedman's CCG in terms of theoretical perspicuity and empirical coverage while retaining many of its attractive computational properties.

1 Introduction

A long-standing puzzle in natural language semantics has been how to explain the exceptional scope behavior of indefinites. For example, (1a) has a reading where there's a specific relative (a steel magnate, say) such that if she dies, the speaker will be rich. By contrast, (1b) has no analogous reading where the universal takes wide scope: this sentence cannot mean that every rela-

tive is such that if that particular relative dies, I'll be rich.[1] If one takes the antecedent of a conditionals to be a *scope island* (as suggested by the $<\ldots>$ bracketing), then it's not surprising that the universal in (1b) is blocked from taking wide scope; what instead requires explanation is how the indefinite in (1a) can exceptionally take scope out of this island.

(1) a. If $<\underline{\text{a}}$ relative of mine dies$>$, I'll inherit a fortune. ($\exists >$ if)

   b. If $<\underline{\text{every}}$ relative of mine dies$>$, I'll inherit a fortune. (* $\forall >$ if)

Charlow (2014) has recently shown that the exceptional scope behavior of indefinites can be derived from their role of introducing discourse referents in a dynamic semantics. To do so, he showed that (1) a monadic approach to dynamic semantics can be seamlessly integrated with Barker and Shan's (2014) approach to scope taking in continuized grammars, and (2) once one does so, the exceptional scope of indefinites follows from the way the *side effect* of introducing a discourse referent survives the process of delimiting the scope of true quantifiers, such as those expressed with *each* and *every*.

To date, computationally implemented approaches to scope taking[2] have not distinguished indefinites from true quantifiers in a way that accounts for their exceptional scope taking. In Bos's (2003) implementation of Discourse Representation Theory (Kamp and Reyle, 1993, DRT), for example, scope taking is independent of how

---

[1]That is, (1b) cannot mean the same thing as *If any relative of mine dies, I'll inherit a fortune*; see Barker and Shan (2014) for a compatible treatment of negative polarity items such as *any*.

[2]See e.g. (Copestake et al., 2005; Koller et al., 2003; Gardent and Kallmeyer, 2003; Nesson and Shieber, 2006; Pogodalla and Pompigne, 2012), inter alia.

Proceedings of the 13th International Workshop on Tree Adjoining Grammars and Related Formalisms (TAG+13), pages 71–83,
Umeå, Sweden, September 4–6, 2017. © 2017 Association for Computational Linguistics

indefinites are treated. Although Steedman (2012) has developed an account of indefinites' exceptional scope taking in a non-standard static semantics for Combinatory Categorial Grammar (Steedman, 2000, CCG), this treatment has not been fully implemented (to our knowledge); moreover, as Barker and Shan point out, Steedman's theory appears to undergenerate by not allowing true quantifiers to take scope from medial positions.

Barker and Shan offer a brief sketch of how a parser for their continuized grammars can be implemented, including how lifting can be invoked lazily to ensure parsing terminates. In this paper, we show how their approach can be seamlessly combined with Steedman's CCG and extended to include Charlow's monadic dynamic semantics, thereby providing the **first computational implementation** of a system that accounts for the exceptional scope behavior of indefinites in a **principled** and **plausibly practical** way. To efficiently parse with this system, we devise rules to **only invoke monadic lifting and lowering where necessary**, and define novel **normal form constraints on lifting and lowering** to avoid spurious ambiguities. We also integrate a method of lexicalizing scope island constraints (Barker and Shan, 2006), as Charlow's account does not provide a practical and empirically satisfactory means of enforcing such constraints. We argue that the resulting system improves upon Steedman's CCG in terms of **theoretical perspicuity**—insofar as it builds upon an account of dynamic semantics that is independently necessary—and **empirical coverage**, in that it allows quantifiers to take scope from medial positions and from some subordinate clauses. At the same time, it also retains many of CCG's attractive computational properties; in particular, it respects Steedman's Principle of Adjacency, only combining overtly realized adjacent constituents, thereby making it easy to use with well-studied parsing algorithms. An open source prototype implementation, suitable for testing out grammatical analyses, is available online.[3]

2 Are Scope Islands Real?

Steedman (2012) observes that although the empirical status of scope islands remains unsettled in the linguistics literature (Farkas and Giannakidou, 1996; Reinhart, 1997; Ruys and Winter, 2011; Syrett and Lidz, 2011; Syrett, 2015), the possible scopings of true quantifiers appear to be much more limited than commonly assumed in computational approaches to scope taking, arguing therefore in favor of a surface-compositional approach that aims to capture all and only the attested readings; in particular, Steedman takes as his working hypothesis that scope inversion should be subject to syntactic island constraints. While we are sympathetic to Steedman's point of view, we are skeptical of his working hypothesis, as it appears to incorrectly predict that quantifiers should never be able to take scope from subjects of finite complement clauses. Acknowledging that universals sometime appear to do so, Steedman appeals to Fox & Sauerland's (1996) illusory scope analyis, where the quantificational force is argued to stem from a main clause generic. However, Farkas and Giannakidou (1996) provide numerous examples in English and Greek of episodic sentences such as (2) where the universal takes extra-wide scope.

(2) Yesterday, a guide made sure that $<$every tour to the Louvre was fun$>$. ($\forall > \exists$)

By contrast, a corpus analysis given in the appendix suggests that conditionals and relative clauses plausibly represent cases where scope islands should be treated as hard constraints. As such, in this paper we adopt the working hypothesis that scope island constraints can be given an accurate lexicalized treatment. Alternatively, one could pursue an approach based solely on soft constraints, where a probabilistic model simply makes scope taking beyond finite clause boundaries very unlikely. Even in this scenario, we contend that the approach to exceptionally scoping indefinites implemented here will greatly simplify the learning task, since the ability of indefinites to take exceptional scope would not need to be learned.

3 Continuized CCG

A continuized grammar is one where the meaning of expressions can be defined as a function on a portion of its surrounding context, or *continuation* (Barker, 2002; Shan and Barker, 2006; Barker and Shan, 2014). To make it easier to reason about continuized grammars, Barker & Shan devised the "tower" notation illustrated in Figure 1.[4] For example, *everyone* has a tower category with NP on

[4]Semantic types are suppressed in this and subsequent figures, except where essential for understanding.

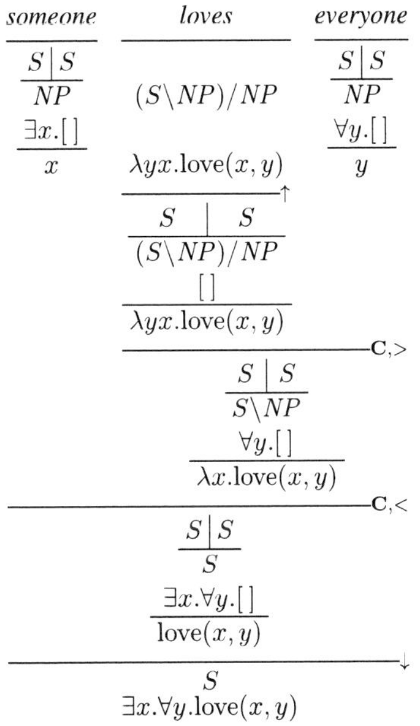

$$\frac{\begin{array}{ccc} someone & loves & everyone \end{array}}{}$$

(a) Surface Scope with Explicit Lifting

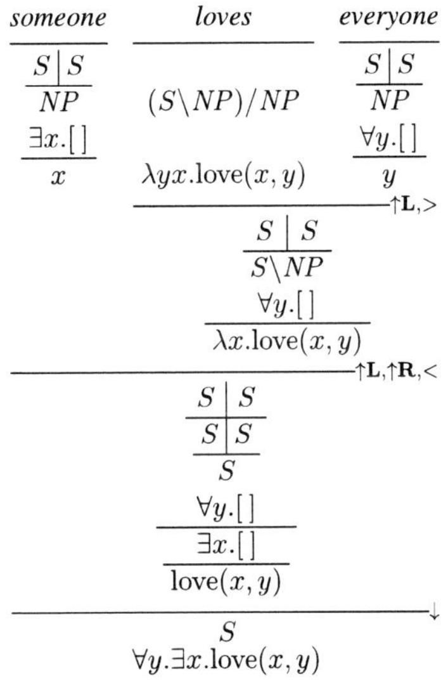

(b) Inverse Scope with Integrated Lifting

Figure 1: Continuized CCG Derivations

the bottom and two Ss on top; reading counterclockwise from the bottom, this category represents a constituent that acts locally as an NP, takes scope over an S, and returns an S. The semantics is $\lambda k.\forall y.ky$, a function from a continuation k of type $e \rightarrow t$ to a universally quantified expression of type t. A continuized meaning of this form can be abbreviated by representing the loca-

tion where the continuation argument applies with $[\,]$ and putting the argument to the continuation on the bottom of the tower, as shown.

In a continuized grammar, all expressions can potentially be given continuized meanings via the Lift ($\uparrow$) operation. This is illustrated in Figure 1a where the category for *loves* is lifted, taking on the semantics $\lambda k.k(\lambda yx.\text{love}(x,y))$. Lifting the category for *loves* allows it to combine with that of *everyone* using scopal combination. The way in which scopal combination works in the tower notation is shown in Figure 2b (left): on the tower top, the continuized functions $g[\,]$ and $h[\,]$ compose in surface order, yielding $g[h[\,]]$; meanwhile, recursing on the tower bottom, the expressions a and b combine as they normally would in CCG (using the combinators in Figure 2a), yielding c.[5] In the example, $[\,]$ and $\forall y.[\,]$ compose to again yield $\forall y.[\,]$ on the tower top, with $\lambda yx.\text{love}(x,y)$ applying to y and yielding $\lambda x.\text{love}(x,y)$ on the bottom.

As Barker & Shan observe, the explicit lifting step seen in Figure 1a can be integrated with the scopal combination step, as shown in the other recursively defined rules in Figure 2b, thereby avoiding an infinite regress when applying the lifting rule. Figure 1b shows how Lift Left ($\uparrow$**L**) and Lift Right ($\uparrow$**R**) can be applied in sequence—as part of a single parsing step combining adjacent signs—to create a three-level tower where *everyone* ends up taking inverse scope over the subject:[6] first, in applying Lift Left, the entire tower for *someone* is matched as A, while the bottom of the tower for *loves everyone*, $S\backslash NP$, is matched as B, and then the rules are reapplied with A and B as inputs; next, Lift Right is applied, with the bottom of the tower for *someone*, NP, matched as A, and $S\backslash NP$ again matched as B, and the rules are reapplied once more; this time, the categories can combine directly using Backward Application ($<$), ending the recursion; as the rules unwind, the three-level tower for *someone loves everyone* is constructed, with inverse scope semantics, as shown. The final representations are derived by collapsing the towers using the recursively defined Lower ($\downarrow$) operation in Figure 2c, which repeat-

---

[5] The combinator for combining two scopal terms m and n is $\lambda mnk.m(\lambda x.n(\lambda y.k(xy)))$, assuming forward application on the tower bottom. Formulating the rules recursively allows the base combinator to be factored out while also generalizing to multi-level towers.

[6] Though *everyone* is right peripheral in the example, nothing would prevent it from taking inverse scope from medial position, in contrast to Steedman's (2012) approach.

Forward
Application

$$\frac{X/Y \quad Y}{f : \alpha \to \beta \quad a : \alpha}{\frac{X}{fa : \beta}} >$$

Backward
Application

$$\frac{Y \quad X\backslash Y}{a : \alpha \quad f : \alpha \to \beta}{\frac{X}{fa : \beta}} <$$

Forward
Composition

$$\frac{X/Y \quad Y/Z}{f : \beta \to \gamma \quad g : \alpha \to \beta}{\frac{X}{\lambda x.f(gx) : \alpha \to \gamma}} \mathbf{>B}$$

Forward
Type Raising

$$\frac{\frac{NP}{a : e}}{\frac{S/(S\backslash NP)}{\lambda p.pa : (e \to t) \to t}} \mathbf{>T}$$

(a) Base CCG Combinators (not exhaustive)

Combine

$$\frac{\dfrac{D\,|\,E}{A}\ \dfrac{E\,|\,F}{B}}{\dfrac{g[\,]}{a}\ \dfrac{h[\,]}{b}}\ \mathbf{C}$$
$$\frac{D\,|\,F}{C}$$
$$\frac{g[h[\,]]}{c}$$

Lift Left

$$A\ \frac{\dfrac{E\,|\,F}{B}}{\dfrac{h[\,]}{b}}\ \uparrow\mathbf{L}$$
$$\frac{E\,|\,F}{C}$$
$$\frac{h[\,]}{c}$$

Lift Right

$$\frac{\dfrac{D\,|\,E}{A}}{\dfrac{g[\,]}{a}}\ B\ \uparrow\mathbf{R}$$
$$\frac{D\,|\,E}{C}$$
$$\frac{g[\,]}{c}$$

if $\dfrac{A : a \quad B : b}{C : c}$

(b) Combination with Lifting

Lower

$$\frac{\dfrac{S\,|\,S}{S}}{\dfrac{g[\,]}{a}}\ \downarrow \qquad \frac{\dfrac{S\,|\,S}{A}}{\dfrac{g[\,]}{a}}\ \downarrow$$
$$\frac{S}{g[a]} \qquad \frac{S}{g[c]}$$

if $\dfrac{A : a}{S : c}\downarrow$

(c) Lowering (base and recursive)

Figure 2: Continuized CCG

edly applies the continuized semantics to the identity continuation $\lambda k.k$.

4 Monadic Dynamic Semantics

Charlow's (2014) dynamic semantics makes use of the State.Set monad (Hutton and Meijer, 1996), which combines the State monad for handling side effects with the Set monad for non-determinism. The State monad pairs ordinary semantic values with a state, which is threaded through computations. The Set monad models non-deterministic choices as sets, facilitating a non-deterministic treatment of indefinites. For example, the dynamic meaning of *a linguist swims* appears in (3): here, the proposition that x swims, where x is some linguist, is paired with a state that augments the input state s with the discourse referent x.

(3) $\lambda s.\{\langle \mathrm{swim}(x), \widehat{sx} \rangle \mid \mathrm{linguist}(x)\}$

More formally, the State.Set monad is defined as in (4). For each type α, the corresponding monadic type $M\alpha$ is a function from states of type s to sets pairing items of type α with such states. The η function injects values into the monad, simply yielding a singleton set consisting of the input

item paired with the input state. The *bind* operation $\multimap$ sequences two monadic computations by sequencing the two computations pointwise, feeding each result of m applied to the input state s into π and unioning the results.[7] Less formally, the $\multimap$ operation can be thought of as "run m to determine v in π."

(4) State.Set Monad

$$\begin{aligned}
M\alpha &= s \to \alpha \times s \to t \\
a^\eta &= \lambda s.\{\langle a, s\rangle\} \\
m_v \multimap \pi &= \lambda s.\bigcup_{\langle a,s'\rangle \in ms} \pi[a/v]s'
\end{aligned}$$

Since the only operation on states that we will be concerned with in this paper is adding discourse referents, it suffices to leave the states implicit in the implementation, only explicitly representing the new discourse referents—much as in computational implementations of Discourse Representation Theory (Bos, 2003), where assignments are not explicitly represented in Discourse Representation Structures. Consequently, we will represent

---

[7]Note that the notation $m_v \multimap \pi$ is just syntactic sugar for $m \multimap \lambda v.\pi$, which may be more familiar.

(3) as (5), which can be translated to first-order logic in much the same way as with DRT.[8]

(5) $\{\langle \mathrm{swim}(x), x \rangle \mid \mathrm{linguist}(x)\}$
$\leadsto \exists x.\mathrm{linguist}(x) \land \mathrm{swim}(x)$

The definition of State.Set sequencing allows us to define a sequence reduction operation where the value of m is substituted into π for v and the discourse referents and conditions are combined. For example, the representation of *a linguist* can be sequenced with that of *swim* and simplified as in (6).

(6) $\{\langle x, x \rangle \mid \mathrm{linguist}(x)\}_y \multimap \{\langle \mathrm{swim}(y), \epsilon \rangle\}$
$\leadsto \{\langle \mathrm{swim}(x), x \rangle \mid \mathrm{linguist}(x)\}$

As in DRT, negation in Charlow's dynamic semantics is defined in a way that captures discourse referents, making them inaccessible for subsequent reference. Conditionals and universals are defined in terms of negation, thereby explaining their effects on discourse referent accessiblity; for representational simplicity, we will instead assume directly defined meanings for conditionals and universals, as in DRT.

5 Dynamic Combinatory Rules

The rules for combining signs in Dynamic Continuized CCG appear in Figures 3 and 4, augmenting those in Figure 2. We first give an overview of these rules and then illustrate with examples.[9]

As Charlow (2014) explains in detail, continuized grammars can be reconceptualized as operating over an underlying monad, where monadic lifting is identified with applying the underlying monad's sequencing operator ($\multimap$) and monadic lowering with applying the injection function (η). Accordingly, we include the rules for monadic lifting and lowering in Figure 3a-b. The lifting rule takes a category A with monadic value a of type $M\alpha$ and sequences it with a new continuation, yielding a function $\lambda k.a_v \multimap kv$ of type $(\alpha \to M\beta) \to M\beta$ for a tower category with A on the bottom. Monadic lowering is defined recursively, with the two base cases on the left and the two recursive cases on the right. The base cases apply η to the value a on the tower bottom before filling it in for the continuation; the second base case enables lowering to apply to the CCG categories S/NP and $S\backslash NP$ used in relative clauses. The recursive cases on the right again enable multi-level towers to be lowered in one fell swoop, with the second rule enabling towers with tower-result categories on the bottom to be fully lowered.

To implement scope islands, the rules in Figure 3c together with the unary type constructor $\langle \cdot \rangle$ enable categories to specify that their arguments must be scope delimited by undergoing a reset (i.e. lower then re-lift) before combination is permitted.[10] Figure 3d enables a double-continuation analysis of determiners by triggering a lowering when two categories combine to yield a category with a lowerable tower result. Finally, the rules in Figure 4 apply when the functor category expects a monadic value on the tower bottom; the rules in Figure 4a use η to coerce the input to the right type, while the ones in Figure 4b invoke lowering to do so.

An example illustrating exceptional scope for an indefinite appears in Figure 5a. Even though the category for *if* requires the category for its antecedent *someone complains* to be reset prior to combination, the side effect of discourse referent introduction survives the reset operation— enabling a wide-scope reading of the indefinite— irrespective of whether sequence reduction is carried out immediately, as in Figure 5c. (Figure 8 in the appendix shows how side effects are unaffected by reset in the general case, using the monadic identity and associativity laws.) Figure 5b shows how the narrow scope reading for the indefinite can be derived instead using monadic type–driven lowering. By contrast, Figure 6 shows why the narrow scope reading is the only one available for the universal in *if everyone complains*, since the reset operation closes off the scope of the universal, as illustrated in detail in Figure 6b. The appendix gives two further examples: Figure 10a illustrates result tower lowering in an inverse linking example—including the possibility of medial scoping, which is not possible with Steedman's CCG—while Figure 9 shows

---

[8]Explicitly representing the states could simplify the treatment of discourse referent accessibility; we leave investigating this alternative for future work.

[9]The side conditions for these rules (preceded by 'if') sometimes serve to define the rules recursively, as in the earlier Figure 2, and sometimes serve to specify sub-cases of interest. Rules for anaphora resolution are left for future work.

[10]The Delimit rules must apply first to ensure that entire towers are reset. This is accomplished using a cut in the Prolog implementation; alternatively, these rules could be defined at the level of signs rather than categories.

Lower

Lift

$$\frac{A}{a : M\alpha}\uparrow$$
$$\frac{S\,|\,S}{A}$$
$$a_v \multimap [\,] : M\beta$$
$$\overline{v : \alpha}$$

(a) Monadic Lifting

$$\frac{\dfrac{A\,|\,S}{S}}{\dfrac{g[\,]}{a}}\downarrow \quad \frac{A}{g[a^\eta]}$$

$$\frac{\dfrac{S\,|\,S}{A}}{\dfrac{g[\,]}{p}}\downarrow \quad \frac{A}{\lambda x.g[(px)^\eta]}$$

$$\frac{\dfrac{S\,|\,S}{A}}{\dfrac{g[\,]}{a}}\downarrow \quad \frac{C}{g[c]}$$

$$\frac{\dfrac{S\,|\,S}{A}}{\dfrac{g[\,]}{a}}\downarrow \quad \frac{C}{\lambda k.g[ck]}$$

, if A is

$$\frac{\dfrac{D\,|\,E}{F}\,\Big|\,S}{S}$$

if A is S/Y or $S\backslash Y$ \qquad if $\dfrac{A:a}{C:c}\downarrow$

(b) Monadic Lowering (base and recursive)

Delimit Right \qquad **Delimit Left**

$$\frac{\dfrac{\vdots\quad\vdots}{\dfrac{X/\langle Y\rangle\quad Y}{a\qquad b}}}{\dfrac{\vdots}{\dfrac{X}{c}}}\text{DR} \qquad \frac{\dfrac{\vdots\quad\vdots}{\dfrac{Y\quad X\backslash\langle Y\rangle}{b\qquad a}}}{\dfrac{\vdots}{\dfrac{X}{c}}}\text{DL}$$

if $\dfrac{\dfrac{\vdots}{Y}\,b}{\dfrac{\vdots}{Y}\,b'}\uparrow\downarrow$ by **Lower** then **Lift**,

and

$$\frac{\dfrac{\vdots\quad\vdots}{\dfrac{X/Y\quad Y}{a\qquad b'}}}{\dfrac{\vdots}{\dfrac{X}{c}}} \qquad \frac{\dfrac{\vdots\quad\vdots}{\dfrac{Y\quad X\backslash Y}{b'\qquad a}}}{\dfrac{\vdots}{\dfrac{X}{c}}}$$

(c) Delimiting Scope with Reset

Lower Result

$$\frac{A:a \quad B:b}{C:c}\downarrow\text{RS}$$

if

$$\frac{A:a \quad B:b}{\dfrac{\dfrac{D\,|\,E}{F}\,\Big|\,G}{H}} : d$$

and

$$\frac{\dfrac{\dfrac{D\,|\,E}{F}\,\Big|\,G}{H} : d}{C:c}\downarrow$$

(d) Result Lowering

Figure 3: Dynamic Continuized CCG: Monadic Lifting and Lowering

by contrast how universals are trapped in relative clause scope islands.

6 Prototype Implementation

Barker & Shan suggest that the rules in Figure 2 can form the basis of a practical parser. While the worst-case complexity of parsing with such rules has yet to be investigated, the way in which towers can grow to arbitrary heights is apt to at least limit the utility of dynamic programming in practice, potentially posing efficiency problems even when using aggressive statistical pruning (Clark and Curran, 2007). However, recent work on parsing with global neural network models has moved away from dynamic programming solutions, as the global models are incompatible with dynamic programming locality requirements. In particular, Lee et al. (2016) have shown that global neural models can be used with A* search to obtain a new state-of-the-art in CCG in parsing accuracy while maintaining impressive speed, even though the search space is exponential. As such, given that our approach respects Steedman's Principle of Adjacency, we suggest that it may be possible to extend CCG statistical parsing methods to the current setting, thereby resolving scope ambiguities the same way as other derivational ambiguities, rather than in a post-process as in earlier computational work on scope taking. While we are aware of no large-scale scope-annotated corpora at present, small-scale corpora do exist that would enable this conjecture to be tested in future work, such as the corpora used in work on CCG semantic parsing (Artzi and Zettlemoyer, 2013, inter alia).

Towards that end, we have implemented a prototype shift-reduce parser in Prolog that uses the unary and binary combination rules defined in Figure 2 together with additional rules defined in

$$\begin{array}{cc}
\textbf{Forward Application} & \textbf{Backward Application} \\
\textbf{with } \eta & \textbf{with } \eta
\end{array}$$

$$\frac{X/Y \quad\quad Y}{f : M\alpha \to \beta \quad a : \alpha} \quad\quad \frac{Y \quad\quad X\backslash Y}{a : \alpha \quad f : M\alpha \to \beta}$$

$$\frac{X}{fa^\eta : \beta}{>^\eta} \quad\quad \frac{X}{fa^\eta : \beta}{<^\eta}$$

(a) Base CCG Combinators with Monadic Type Coercion (not exhaustive)

$$\begin{array}{cc}
\textbf{Lower Right} & \textbf{Lower Left}
\end{array}$$

$$\frac{\overline{A} \quad\quad \overline{B}}{a : M\alpha \to \beta \quad b : \gamma}{\downarrow\mathbf{R}} \quad\quad \frac{\overline{B} \quad\quad \overline{A}}{b : \gamma \quad a : M\alpha \to \beta}{\downarrow\mathbf{L}}$$

$$\frac{\overline{C}}{c : \beta} \quad\quad\quad\quad \frac{\overline{C}}{c : \beta}$$

if

$$\frac{\overline{B}}{b : \gamma}$$
$$\frac{B'}{b' : M\alpha}{\downarrow}$$

and

$$\frac{\overline{A} \quad\quad B'}{a : M\alpha \to \beta \quad b' : M\alpha} \quad\quad \frac{B' \quad\quad \overline{A}}{b' : M\alpha \quad a : M\alpha \to \beta}$$

$$\frac{\overline{C}}{c : \beta} \quad\quad\quad\quad \frac{\overline{C}}{c : \beta}$$

(b) Monadic Type–Driven Lowering

Figure 4: Dynamic Continuized CCG: Monadic Arguments

Section 5 for implementing Charlow's monadic dynamic semantics.[11] When implementing the parser, we found it paid off to only invoke lowering where necessary, as discussed in Section 5, rather than simply invoking lowering whenever possible. Moreover, in Section 7, we will see how enforcing scope islands keeps tower heights under control, while also providing an opportunity to define normal form constraints that limit spurious ambiguity, another important practical consideration. To test the implementation, we developed an initial test suite of 40 examples of average length 6.7 words, roughly comparable in size and complexity to Baldridge's (2002) OpenCCG[12] test suite. With the normal form constraints, parsing time was 60ms per item on a laptop, similar to OpenCCG on the same hardware. By contrast, with the normal form constraints turned off, the parsing time increased to 4.6s per item, nearly two orders of magnitude slower.

7   Normal Form Constraints

A normal form parse is the simplest parse in an equivalence class of parses yielding the same interpretation. Normal form constraints can play an important role in practical CCG parsing by eliminating derivations leading to spurious ambiguities without requiring expensive pairwise equivalence checks on λ-terms (Eisner, 1996; Clark and Curran, 2007; Hockenmaier and Bisk, 2010; Lewis and Steedman, 2014). Continuized CCG can employ existing CCG normal form constraints at the base level. The main additional source of spurious ambiguity is illustrated in Figure 7.[13] In the figure, the two towers at the upper left are combined via ↑R and ↑L to yield a three-level tower, which potentially allows an operator to subsequently take scope between any scopal elements present in the left and right input signs. However, if this three-level tower is subsequently lowered without any operator taking intermediate scope, the derivation will yield an interpretation that is equivalent to the one yielded by the simpler derivation that just combines the two signs in their surface scope order (i.e., without yielding a three-level tower).[14] As such, the lowering operations triggered by scope islands or sentence boundaries provide an opportunity to recursively detect and eliminate such non–normal form derivations, as follows:

Trigger If a sign is created using a lower operation, check the input sign for a spurious ↑R, ↑L combination.

Base A sign constructed via $\ldots, ↑\mathbf{R}, ↑\mathbf{L}, \ldots$ has a spurious ↑R, ↑L combination.

Non-Scopal A sign that is derived from a non-scopal input sign—i.e., one whose category

---

[13]Spurious ambiguity can also arise from the inversion of two indefinites; we leave this issue for future work.

[14]As noted in Section 5, it remains for future work to add the lowering rules for multi-level towers that enable Charlow's treatment of selective exceptional scope; the normal form constraints will need to be augmented accordingly.

$$
\begin{array}{cccc}
\textit{if} & \textit{someone} & \textit{complains} & \textit{Vincent quits} \\[2pt]
\hline
 & \dfrac{S\mid S}{NP} & & \\[6pt]
S/\langle S\rangle/\langle S\rangle & & S\backslash NP & S \\[6pt]
\lambda xy.(x \to y)^{\eta} & \dfrac{\{\langle x,x\rangle\}_u \multimap [\,]}{u} & \lambda x.\mathrm{complain}(x) & \mathrm{quit(v)}
\end{array}
$$

$$
\cfrac{\cfrac{S\mid S}{S}}{\qquad\mathrm{complain}(u)}\ \{\langle x,x\rangle\}_u \multimap [\,] \qquad\uparrow\!\mathbf{R},<
$$

$$
\cfrac{\dfrac{S\mid S}{S}\quad \{\langle x,x\rangle\}_u \multimap [\,]}{\mathrm{complain}(u)}\ \mathbf{DR},\uparrow\!\mathbf{L},>^{\eta}
$$

$$
\cfrac{\dfrac{S\mid S}{S/\langle S\rangle}\quad \{\langle \mathrm{complain}(x), x\rangle\}_p \multimap [\,]}{\lambda y.(p^{\eta} \to y)^{\eta}}\ \mathbf{DR},\uparrow\!\mathbf{R},>^{\eta}
$$

$$
\cfrac{\dfrac{S\mid S}{S}\quad \{\langle \mathrm{complain}(x), x\rangle\}_p \multimap [\,]}{(p^{\eta} \to \mathrm{quit(v)}^{\eta})^{\eta}}\ \downarrow
$$

$$
\cfrac{S}{\{\langle \mathrm{complain}(x)^{\eta} \to \mathrm{quit(v)}^{\eta}, x\rangle\}}
$$

$$
\rightsquigarrow \exists x.(\mathrm{complain}(x) \to \mathrm{quit(v)})
$$

(a) Wide Scope Indefinite

$$
\begin{array}{ccc}
\textit{if} & \textit{someone complains} & \textit{Vincent quits} \\[2pt]
\hline
 & \dfrac{S\mid S}{S} & \\[6pt]
S/\langle S\rangle/\langle S\rangle & & S \\[6pt]
\lambda xy.(x \to y)^{\eta} & \dfrac{\{\langle x,x\rangle\}_u \multimap [\,]}{\mathrm{complain}(u)} & \mathrm{quit(v)} \\[6pt]
Mt \to Mt \to Mt & (t \to Mt) \to Mt & t
\end{array}
$$

$$
\cfrac{\cdots}{\dfrac{S/\langle S\rangle}{\lambda y.(\{\langle \mathrm{complain}(x), x\rangle\} \to y)^{\eta}}\ \ Mt \to Mt}\ \mathbf{DR},\downarrow\!\mathbf{R},>
$$

$$
\cfrac{\cdots}{\dfrac{S}{(\{\langle \mathrm{complain}(x), x\rangle\} \to \mathrm{quit(v)}^{\eta})^{\eta}}\ \ Mt}\ \mathbf{DR},>^{\eta}
$$

$$
\rightsquigarrow \forall x.(\mathrm{complain}(x) \to \mathrm{quit(v)})
$$

(b) Narrow Scope via Type-Driven Lowering

$$
\cfrac{\dfrac{\{\langle x,x\rangle\}_u \multimap [\,]}{\mathrm{complain}(u)}}{\{\langle x,x\rangle\}_u \multimap \{\langle \mathrm{complain}(u), \epsilon\rangle\}}\ \downarrow
$$

$$
\cfrac{\{\langle x,x\rangle\}_u \multimap \{\langle \mathrm{complain}(u), \epsilon\rangle\}}{\{\langle \mathrm{complain}(x), x\rangle\}}\ \equiv
$$

$$
\cfrac{\{\langle \mathrm{complain}(x), x\rangle\}}{\dfrac{\{\langle \mathrm{complain}(x), x\rangle\}_p \multimap [\,]}{p}}\ \uparrow
$$

(c) Resetting *someone complains*

Figure 5: Conditional with Indefinite Example

has no tower top—has a spurious $\uparrow\!\mathbf{R}, \uparrow\!\mathbf{L}$ combination if the other input sign has a spurious $\uparrow\!\mathbf{R}, \uparrow\!\mathbf{L}$ combination. This case is illustrated in Figure 7, where H is such a non-scopal input sign.

Inversion A sign that is derived by a $\uparrow\!\mathbf{L}, \uparrow\mathbf{R}$ inversion has a spurious $\uparrow\!\mathbf{R}, \uparrow\!\mathbf{L}$ combination if either input sign has a spurious $\uparrow\!\mathbf{R}, \uparrow\mathbf{L}$ combination.

Recurse Right A sign that is derived by a $\mathbf{C}, \uparrow\!\mathbf{L}$ has a spurious $\uparrow\!\mathbf{R}, \uparrow\!\mathbf{L}$ combination if the right input sign has a spurious $\uparrow\!\mathbf{R}, \uparrow\!\mathbf{L}$ combination. Note that $\uparrow\!\mathbf{L}, \mathbf{C}$ can derive intermediate scope for the left input sign.

Recurse Left A sign that is derived by a $\uparrow\!\mathbf{R}, \mathbf{C}$ has a spurious $\uparrow\!\mathbf{R}, \uparrow\!\mathbf{L}$ combination if the left input sign has a spurious $\uparrow\!\mathbf{R}, \uparrow\!\mathbf{L}$ combination. Note that $\mathbf{C}, \uparrow\!\mathbf{R}$ can derive intermediate scope for the right input sign.

These rules have been tested for safety in the reference implementation by ensuring that all six (3!) desired interpretations result from a ditransi-

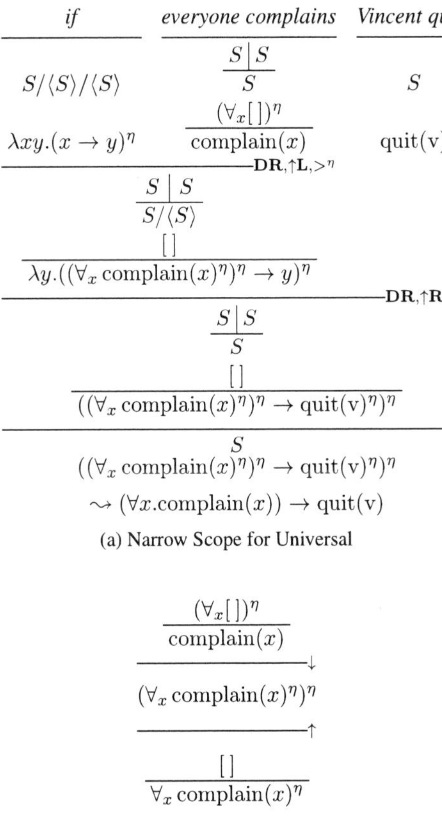

(a) Narrow Scope for Universal

(b) Resetting *everyone complains*

Figure 6: Conditional with Universal Example

Figure 7: Non–Normal Form Derivation

tive verb combined with three scopal arguments, and all 4! desired interpretations result from a 4-argument verb in combination with four scopal arguments. With the ditransitive verb, all spurious ambiguity is eliminated, reducing 78 derivations in an otherwise unambiguous sentence down to just the six normal form derivations. The rules are not quite complete though, as six spuriously equivalent derivations remain with the 4-argument verb, where 525 derivations are whittled down to 30; safely filtering the remaining six spuriously equivalent derivations would require more complex rules that track the level at which the $\uparrow\mathbf{R}, \uparrow\mathbf{L}$ operations apply in the base case, which may not be worth the added complexity in practice.[15]

8   Conclusion

We have presented a method of parsing with Dynamic Continuized CCG that for the first time derives the exceptional scope behavior of indefinites in a principled and plausibly practical way. Our approach (i) extends Barker and Shan's (2014) method of parsing with continuized grammars to only invoke Charlow's (2014) monadic lifting and lowering where necessary, (ii) integrates Steedman's (2000) CCG for deriving basic predicate-argument structure and enriches it with a practical method of lexicalizing scope island constraints, and (iii) takes advantage of the resulting scope islands in defining novel normal form constraints for efficient parsing. We have argued that the account (i) improves upon Steedman's (2012) approach to quantifier scope in terms of theoretical perspicuity by taking advantage of a dynamic semantics for indefinites independently needed for anaphora, and (ii) offers better empirical coverage by allowing quantifiers to take scope from medial positions and some subordinate clauses. At the same time, by respecting the Principle of Adjacency, only combining overtly realized adjacent constituents, our approach is easy to use with well-studied parsing algorithms, as with Steedman's CCG. Although the normal form constraints are quite effective in small-scale experiments, it remains for future work to verify quantitatively whether these constraints suffice for practical parsing in conjunction with statistical filtering techniques. It also remains for future work to computationally explore the novel analyses made possible by this framework, including order-sensitivity in negative polarity items (Barker and Shan, 2014) and selective exceptional scope for indefinites and focus alternatives (Charlow, 2014). Towards that end, we have made available online an open source prototype implementation suitable for testing out grammatical analyses.

---

[15]Normal form constraints need not be complete to be practically useful, as any remaining ambiguity can be handled by pairwise checks.

Acknowledgments

We thank Carl Pollard, Scott Martin, Mark Steedman, the OSU Clippers and Synners Groups, the Midwest Speech and Language Days 2016 audience and the anonymous reviewers for helpful comments and discussion. This work was supported in part by a Targeted Investment in Excellence Grant from OSU Arts & Sciences and by NSF grant IIS-1319318.

References

Yoav Artzi and Luke Zettlemoyer. 2013. Weakly supervised learning of semantic parsers for mapping instructions to actions. *Transactions of the Association for Computational Linguistics* 1(1):49–62.

Jason Baldridge. 2002. *Lexically Specified Derivational Control in Combinatory Categorial Grammar*. Ph.D. thesis, University of Edinburgh.

Chris Barker. 2002. Continuations and the nature of quantification. *Natural Language Semantics* 10(3):211–242.

Chris Barker and Chung-chieh Shan. 2006. Types as graphs: Continuations in type logical grammar. *Journal of Logic, Language and Information* 15:331–370.

Chris Barker and Chung-chieh Shan. 2014. *Continuations and Natural Language*. Oxford Studies in Theoretical Linguistics.

Johan Bos. 2003. Implementing the binding and accommodation theory for anaphora resolution and presupposition projection. *Computational Linguistics* 29(2):179–210. https://aclweb.org/anthology/J/J03/J03-2002.pdf.

Simon Charlow. 2014. *On the semantics of exceptional scope*. Ph.D. thesis, New York University.

Stephen Clark and James R. Curran. 2007. Wide-Coverage Efficient Statistical Parsing with CCG and Log-Linear Models. *Computational Linguistics* 33(4):493–552. https://aclweb.org/anthology/J/J07/.

Ann Copestake, Dan Flickinger, Carl Pollard, and Ivan Sag. 2005. Minimal recursion semantics: An introduction. *Research on Language and Computation* 3:281–332.

Jason Eisner. 1996. Efficient normal-form parsing for Combinatory Categorial Grammar. In *Proceedings of the 34th Annual Meeting of the Association for Computational Linguistics*. Association for Computational Linguistics, Santa Cruz, California, USA, pages 79–86. https://doi.org/10.3115/981863.981874.

Donka F. Farkas and Anastasia Giannakidou. 1996. How clause-bounded is the scope of universals? In *Proceedings of Semantics and Linguistic Theory*. Cornell University, volume 6, pages 35–52.

Danny Fox and Uli Sauerland. 1996. Illusive scope of universal quantifiers. In *Proceedings of the North Eastern Linguistic Society (NELS)*. volume 26, pages 71–86.

Claire Gardent and Laura Kallmeyer. 2003. Semantic construction in feature-based TAG. In *Proceedings of EACL-03*.

Julia Hockenmaier and Yonatan Bisk. 2010. Normal-form parsing for Combinatory Categorial Grammars with generalized composition and type-raising. In *Proceedings of the 23rd International Conference on Computational Linguistics (Coling 2010)*. Coling 2010 Organizing Committee, Beijing, China, pages 465–473. http://www.aclweb.org/anthology/C10-1053.

Graham Hutton and Erik Meijer. 1996. Monadic Parser Combinators. Technical Report NOTTCS-TR-96-4, Department of Computer Science, University of Nottingham.

Hans Kamp and Uwe Reyle. 1993. *From Discourse to Logic: An Introduction to Modeltheoretic Semantics of Natural Language, Formal Logic and DRT*. Kluwer, Dordrecht, The Netherlands.

Alexander Koller, Joachim Niehren, and Stefan Thater. 2003. Bridging the gap between underspecification formalisms: Hole semantics as dominance constraints. In *Proceedings of EACL-03*.

Richard Larson. 1985. Quantifying into NP. MIT Manuscript.

Kenton Lee, Mike Lewis, and Luke Zettlemoyer. 2016. Global neural CCG parsing with optimality guarantees. In *Proceedings of the 2016 Conference on Empirical Methods in Natural Language Processing*. Association for Computational Linguistics, Austin, Texas, pages 2366–2376. https://aclweb.org/anthology/D16-1262.

Roger Levy and Galen Andrew. 2006. Tregex and Tsurgeon: tools for querying and manipulating tree data structures. In *Proceedings of the Fifth International Conference on Language Resources and Evaluation (LREC'06)*. European Language Resources Association (ELRA). http://aclweb.org/anthology/L06-1311.

Mike Lewis and Mark Steedman. 2014. Improved CCG parsing with semi-supervised supertagging. *Transactions of the Association of Computational Linguistics* 2:327–338. http://aclweb.org/anthology/Q14-1026.

Rebecca Nesson and Stuart M. Shieber. 2006. Simpler TAG semantics through synchronization. In *Proceedings of the 11th Conference on Formal Grammar*.

Sylvain Pogodalla and Florent Pompigne. 2012. Controlling extraction in abstract categorial grammars. In *Formal Grammar*. Springer, pages 162–177.

Tanya Reinhart. 1997. Quantifier scope: How labor is divided between QR and choice functions. *Linguistics and philosophy* 20(4):335–397.

E.G. Ruys and Yoad Winter. 2011. Quantifier scope in formal linguistics. In *Handbook of philosophical logic*, Springer, pages 159–225.

Chung-chieh Shan and Chris Barker. 2006. Explaining crossover and superiority as left-to-right evaluation. *Linguistics and Philosophy* 29(1):91–134.

Mark Steedman. 2000. *The syntactic process.* MIT Press, Cambridge, MA, USA.

Mark Steedman. 2012. *Taking Scope: The Natural Semantics of Quantifiers.* MIT Press, Cambridge, MA, USA.

Kristen Syrett. 2015. Experimental support for inverse scope readings of finite-clause-embedded antecedent-contained-deletion sentences. *Linguistic Inquiry* .

Kristen Syrett and Jeffrey Lidz. 2011. Competence, performance, and the locality of quantifier raising: Evidence from 4-year-old children. *Linguistic Inquiry* 42(2):305–337.

$$\left(\frac{m_v \multimap [\,]}{f\,v}\right)^{\downarrow\uparrow} = (m_v \multimap (f\,v)^\eta)^\uparrow \qquad \downarrow$$

$$= \frac{(m_v \multimap (f\,v)^\eta)_u \multimap [\,]}{u} \qquad \uparrow$$

$$= \frac{m_v \multimap (f\,v)^\eta_u \multimap [\,]}{u} \qquad \text{Assoc}$$

$$= \frac{m_v \multimap [\,]}{f\,v} \qquad \text{LeftID}$$

Figure 8: Side Effects Not Affected By Reset (Charlow, 2014, Fact 4.1)

A Supplemental Material

A.1 Exceptional Scope in the Penn Treebank

As noted in Section 2, the empirical status of scope islands remains unsettled, with further corpus-based and experimental work necessary to adequately characterize the distribution of true quantifiers. Nevertheless, a search of the Penn Treebank reveals that if scope islands do not represent hard constraints, then violations are at least very rare. We used Tregex (Levy and Andrew, 2006) to search the Wall Street Journal portion of the Penn Treebank with the pattern

```
SBAR << /MD|VBD|VBP|VBZ/ << /^every|^each/
```

and found that only 385 finite subordinate clauses contain (a form of) *every* or *each*, including 80 relative clauses and just 9 conditionals, with none showing clear evidence of the universal scoping out of the finite clause. There were, however, a couple of potential counter-examples, such as 7, that appear amenable to an analysis involving functional readings, rather than exceptional scope; these deserve further study.

(7) Tandy said its experience during the shortage didn't merit the \$5 million to \$50 million investment$_i$ <U.S. Memories is seeking from each$_i$ investor>.

By contrast, exceptionally scoping indefinites are quite easy to find.

A.2 Side Effects and Reset

Figure 8 reproduces Charlow's (2014) proof that in the general case, side effects in an underlying monad are not affected by reset if the lift and lower

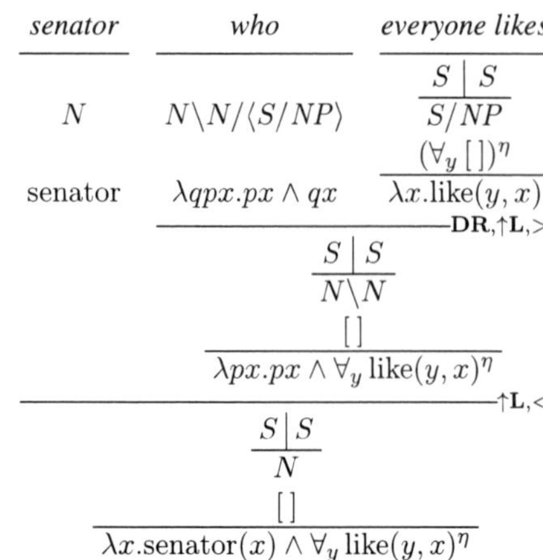

Figure 9: Relative Clause Example

operations in the continuized grammar are identified with the monad's sequencing ($\multimap$) and injection (η) operators.

A.3 Relative Clauses and Inverse Linking

Figure 9 gives an example of a relative clause scope island. The category for the relative pronoun requires its clausal argument to be delimited, triggering a reset via the Delimit Right (**DR**) rule, which closes off the semantic scope for *everyone*. Not shown is the derivation of the base category S/NP for *everyone likes*, which can be derived using standard CCG rules on the bottom without invoking empty string elements. The lowering rule for incomplete clauses is required in order for this base category to be lowerable.

By contrast, Figure 10 shows how inverse scope goes through for the nominal PP *in every state*, since the preposition category does not require its argument to be delimited. One-fell-swoop result lowering implements Larson's (1985) constraint barring interleaved inverse scope out of NPs while preserving the ability of the universal to bind subsequent pronouns. Although Steedman's (2012) account handles examples such as the one in Figure 10, where the inversely linked PP is right peripheral, his treatment—unlike the present one—cannot handle examples such as *few voters$_i$ [in every state] who$_i$ supported Trump participated in the protests* where the inversely linked PP is in medial position. (Note that the relative clause here must be interpreted restrictively, and thus is not tenable as an appositive, contra Steedman's suggested analysis of related examples.)

$$
\begin{array}{ccccc}
a & voter & in & every\ state & protests
\end{array}
$$

$$
\dfrac{\dfrac{\dfrac{S\,|\,S}{NP}\,\Big|\,S}{S/N}}{\dfrac{\lambda k.\{\langle x,x\rangle \mid [\,]\}_u \multimap ku}{\lambda p.px}}
\qquad
\dfrac{N}{voter}
\qquad
\dfrac{N\backslash N/NP}{\lambda yp x.px \wedge \mathrm{in}(x,y)}
\qquad
\dfrac{\dfrac{S\,|\,S}{NP}}{\dfrac{(\forall_y \mathrm{state}(y)^\eta\,[\,])^\eta}{y}}
\qquad
\dfrac{S\backslash NP}{protest}
$$

$$
\rule{6cm}{0.4pt}\ {\uparrow}\mathbf{L},{>}
$$

$$
\dfrac{\dfrac{S\,|\,S}{N\backslash N}}{\dfrac{(\forall_y \mathrm{state}(y)^\eta\,[\,])^\eta}{\lambda p x.p(x) \wedge \mathrm{in}(x,y)}}
$$

$$
\rule{7cm}{0.4pt}\ {\uparrow}\mathbf{L},{<}
$$

$$
\dfrac{\dfrac{S\,|\,S}{N}}{\dfrac{(\forall_y \mathrm{state}(y)^\eta\,[\,])^\eta}{\lambda x.\mathrm{voter}(x) \wedge \mathrm{in}(x,y)}}
$$

$$
\rule{8cm}{0.4pt}\ {\downarrow},{\uparrow}\mathbf{L},{\uparrow}\mathbf{R},{>}
$$

$$
\dfrac{\dfrac{S\,|\,S}{NP}}{\dfrac{(\forall_y \mathrm{state}(y)^\eta\,\{\langle x,x\rangle \mid \mathrm{voter}(x) \wedge \mathrm{in}(x,y)\}_u \multimap [\,])^\eta}{u}}
$$

$$
\rule{8cm}{0.4pt}\ {\uparrow}\mathbf{R},{<}
$$

$$
\dfrac{\dfrac{S\,|\,S}{S}}{\dfrac{(\forall_y \mathrm{state}(y)^\eta\,\{\langle x,x\rangle \mid \mathrm{voter}(x) \wedge \mathrm{in}(x,y)\}_u \multimap [\,])^\eta}{\mathrm{protest}(u)}}
$$

$$
\rule{9cm}{0.4pt}\ {\downarrow}
$$

$$
\dfrac{S}{(\forall_y \mathrm{state}(y)^\eta\,\{\langle \mathrm{protest}(x),x\rangle \mid \mathrm{voter}(x) \wedge \mathrm{in}(x,y)\})^\eta}
$$

$$
\leadsto\ \forall y.\mathrm{state}(y) \to \exists x.\mathrm{voter}(x) \wedge \mathrm{in}(x,y) \wedge \mathrm{protest}(x)
$$

(a) Wide Scope for Universal

$$
\dfrac{\dfrac{\dfrac{S \mid S}{\dfrac{S\,|\,S}{NP}}\,\Big|\,S}{S}}{\dfrac{(\forall_y \mathrm{state}(y)^\eta\,[\,])^\eta}{\dfrac{\lambda k.\{\langle x,x\rangle \mid [\,]\}_u \multimap ku}{\mathrm{voter}(x) \wedge \mathrm{in}(x,y)}}}
$$

$$
\rule{9cm}{0.4pt}\ {\downarrow}
$$

$$
\dfrac{\dfrac{S\,|\,S}{NP}}{\lambda k.(\forall_y \mathrm{state}(y)^\eta\,\{\langle x,x\rangle \mid (\mathrm{voter}(x) \wedge \mathrm{in}(x,y))^\eta\}_u \multimap ku)^\eta}
$$

(b) Lowering Result Tower

Figure 10: Inverse Linking Example

Multiword Expression-Aware A⋆ TAG Parsing Revisited

Jakub Waszczuk
LIFO
Université d'Orléans
6, rue Léonard de Vinci
45067 Orléans, France

Agata Savary
Laboratoire d'Informatique
Université François-Rabelais Tours
3, place Jean-Jaurès
41000 Blois, France

Yannick Parmentier
LIFO
Université d'Orléans
6, rue Léonard de Vinci
45067 Orléans, France

`firstname.lastname@univ-{orleans|tours}.fr`

Abstract

A⋆ algorithms enable efficient parsing within the context of large grammars and/or complex syntactic formalisms. Besides, it has been shown that promoting multiword expressions (MWEs) is a beneficial strategy in dealing with syntactic ambiguity. The state-of-the-art A⋆ heuristic for promoting MWEs in tree-adjoining grammar (TAG) parsing has certain drawbacks: it is not monotonic and it composes poorly with grammar compression techniques. In this work, we propose an enhanced version of this heuristic, which copes with these shortcomings.

1 Introduction

In the domain of syntactic parsing, a growing interest is dedicated to A⋆ parsing strategies (Klein and Manning, 2003) which allow to compute the most plausible parse tree(s) without having to generate the space of all the grammar-compliant solutions in advance. Such strategies enable efficient parsing within the context of large grammars and/or complex syntactic formalisms (Angelov and Ljunglöf, 2014). They were also shown to finely combine with probabilistic supertagging, which can be used to pre-score the individual solutions and, hence, guide the parser to quickly find the most probable one(s) (Lewis and Steedman, 2014). Once supertagging is correctly performed, determining the corresponding syntactic structure is greatly simplified (Bangalore and Joshi, 1999), and A⋆ parsing allows to backtrack and correct the possible misestimations of the supertagger.

Lewis and Steedman (2014) showed that it is possible to obtain a highly accurate and fast CCG parser by (i) adopting a simple probabilistic model factored on lexical category assign-

ments and (ii) using supertagging techniques to obtain relatively reliable probability estimations in a sentence-dependent manner. However, it seems that this proposal, even though quite generic, is not easy to extend to the context of a lexicalized grammar in which various categories of multiword expressions (MWEs) are represented as elementary grammar units, which is a standard approach to modeling MWEs in tree-adjoining grammars, TAGs (Abeillé and Schabes, 1989; Abeillé, 1995). While adapting the (Lewis and Steedman, 2014) approach to continuous MWEs, such as *all of a sudden* or *a hot dog*, could be achieved by using word lattices to represent ambiguous input segmentations (Constant et al., 2013), non-continuous MWEs (as in *he is making no good decisions*) seem harder to account for.

At the same time, Wehrli (2014) showed that promoting collocation-based derivations in syntactic parsing – MWEs often are statistical collocations – is potentially beneficial in that it helps to deal with syntactic ambiguity. MWEs account for up to 40% of words in a corpus (Gross and Senellart, 1998) and, due to their lexicalized nature, should be easy to spot before parsing, which suggests the usefulness of enriching A⋆ parsing strategies with MWE-dedicated mechanisms.

We previously proposed such a mechanism (Waszczuk et al., 2016b), extending the (Lewis and Steedman, 2014) heuristic to a variant allowing multi-anchored TAG elementary trees (ETs). We showed that considerable speed-up gains can be achieved by promoting MWE-based analyses with virtually no loss in syntactic parsing accuracy. This is in contrast to purely statistical approaches where the idiosyncratic properties of MWEs are hard to capture, and systematically promoting MWEs may decrease the parser's accuracy due to the lack of control of the underlying grammar which would certify the plausibility of the re-

Proceedings of the 13th International Workshop on Tree Adjoining Grammars and Related Formalisms (TAG+13), pages 84–93,
Umeå, Sweden, September 4–6, 2017. © 2017 Association for Computational Linguistics

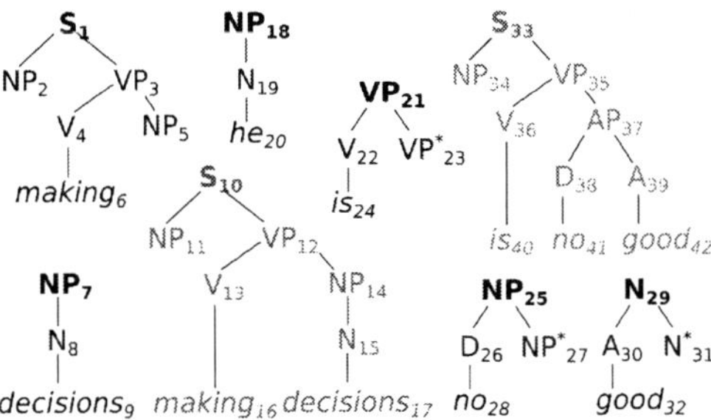

Figure 1: A toy TAG grammar

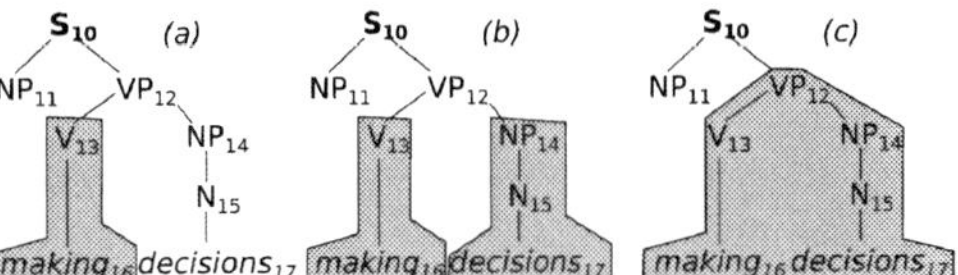

Figure 2: Traversal configurations

sulting derivations.

However, the MWE-based A* heuristic proposed in (Waszczuk et al., 2016b) has three important drawbacks. Firstly, it lacks the proof of correctness and, therefore, it is not clear whether the first derivation found by the parser is indeed the most probable one, a property normally assured by a well-defined A* heuristic. Secondly, it produces sub-optimal estimations – the bottom-up Early-style parser the heuristic relies on (Waszczuk et al., 2016a) performs predictions in order to identify the spans over which adjunction can be potentially performed, but the inside probabilities related to such spans are ignored. Finally, computing the values of the heuristic is relatively easy (it can be performed in close to constant time), but it composes badly with grammar compression. In a real-world context, different parsing speed-up optimizations should ideally combine to provide an optimal solution. In this work, we propose an enhanced version of this heuristic, which copes with the three drawbacks mentioned above.

We first describe the baseline parser and its heuristic, and give a motivating example demonstrating its drawbacks (Sec. 2). Then we formalize a compressed grammar representation (Sec. 3) and our new parser adapted to it (Sec. 4). We introduce the enhanced heuristic and sketch a proof of its monotonicity (Sec. 5). Finally we present some experimental results (Sec. 6), as well as conclusions and future work (Sec. 7).

2 Baseline heuristic

In this section, we shortly review the heuristic proposed in (Waszczuk et al., 2016b) and point out its shortcomings. We assume the toy TAG grammar from Fig. 1, where each node is marked with a unique ID. This grammar contains two ETs representing two possibly discontinuous verbal MWEs

(*making decisions* and *is no good*). We also assume an input sentence $s = s_1 \ldots s_n$ being a sequence of terminal symbols.

The parser in (Waszczuk et al., 2016b) is based on *deduction rules* (Shieber et al., 1995), which serve to infer *chart items*. Each chart item is a pair $\langle x, r \rangle$, where x is a *configuration* and r is a *span*. Each configuration x represents a position in the traversal of the corresponding ET t_x, and each span r represents a fragment of the input sentence. Informally, $\langle x, r \rangle$ asserts that the already traversed part of t_x can be matched against the words in r.

Fig. 2 shows three different configurations corresponding to the traversal of the ET rooted at S_{10}. For instance, Fig. 2 (a) stipulates that the parser has already matched the nodes VP_{13} and $making_{16}$, and that it still needs to match the remaining nodes in the ET. We will refer to the configurations by the nodes at which they are rooted – i.e., to Fig. 2 (a), (b), and (c) by $\{V_{13}\}$, $\{V_{13}, NP_{14}\}$, and $\{VP_{12}\}$, respectively. Any configuration x determines the split of the terminals present in t_x into two parts: (i) the terminals already scanned by the parser, and (ii) the remaining terminals, which the parser still needs to match against the input words. We denote by $inf(x)$ and $sup(x)$ the multiset of terminals (written $\{\}_{ms}$) in part (i) and (ii), respectively. For instance, $inf(\{V_{13}\}) = \{making\}_{ms}$, $sup(\{V_{13}\}) = \{decisions\}_{ms}$, $inf(\{AP_{37}\}) = \{no, good\}_{ms}$, $sup(\{AP_{37}\}) = \{is\}_{ms}$, etc.[1]

Let $pos(s) = \{0, \ldots, n\}$ be the set of positions between the words in s, before s_1 and after s_n. In TAGs, the yield of an ET can span two non-adjacent fragments of s, hence a span takes the form of a tuple $r = \langle i, j, k, l \rangle$, where $i, l \in pos(s)$ and $j, k \in pos(s) \cup \{-\}$. $\langle j, k \rangle$, when defined, represents the *gap* between the two non-adjacent fragments $\langle i, j \rangle$ and $\langle k, l \rangle$. For instance, in Fig. 3, $\langle 2, -, -, 6 \rangle$ corresponds to continuous *making no good decisions*, $\langle 2, 3, 5, 6 \rangle$ corresponds to discontinuous *making decisions* with

---

[1] We extend the standard set operations (sum, difference, etc.) to multisets.

85

the gap *no good*, etc. We will refer to spans of the form $\langle i, -, -, l\rangle$ as $\langle i, l\rangle$ for short. Each span r determines the split of the terminals present in the input sentence into: (i) the terminals in r, and (ii) the terminals outside r. We denote by $in(r)$ and $out(r)$ the multiset of terminals in part (i) and (ii), respectively. For instance, $in(\langle 2, 6\rangle) = \{making, no, good, decisions\}_{ms}$, $out(\langle 2, 6\rangle) = \{he, is\}_{ms}$, $in(\langle 2, 3, 5, 6\rangle) = \{making, decisions\}_{ms}$, $out(\langle 2, 3, 5, 6\rangle) = \{he, is, no, good\}_{ms}$, etc.

Given a deduced chart item $\langle x, r\rangle$, it holds that $inf(x) \subset in(r)$. Moreover, if $sup(x) \not\subset out(r)$, then the item is a dead-end – no final derivations (i.e. the derivations covering the entire input sentence) based on x can be created (the tokens remaining to parse do not contain all the terminals present in the remaining part of t_x's traversal).

To each derivation constructed via the deduction rules the parser assigns a *weight* which allows to discriminate the more probable (lighter) from the less probable (heavier) derivations. Given a chart item η, the goal of an A* heuristic $h(\eta)$ is to estimate $\alpha(\eta)$, the minimal outside derivation weight (roughly, the cost remaining to parse the entire input sentence). Formally, $\alpha(\eta) = \gamma(\eta) - \beta(\eta)$,[2] where $\gamma(\eta)$ is the minimal weight of a final derivation containing η, and $\beta(\eta)$ is the minimal weight of an inside derivation of η (roughly, the cost of the already parsed part of the sentence).

In (Waszczuk et al., 2016b) we assume a simple weighting scheme in which each ET t comes with its own weight $\omega_t \geq 0$ and the weight of a derivation is the sum of the weights of the participating ETs. Consider Fig. 3, where each ET has weight 1, and two items: $\eta_{gr} = \langle\{VP_{21}\}, \langle 1, 2, 6, 6\rangle\rangle$ corresponding to the derivation marked in green (solid line), and $\eta_{bl} = \langle\{VP_{12}\}, \langle 2, 6\rangle\rangle$ corresponding to the derivation marked in blue (dashed line). Then, $\beta(\eta_{gr}) = 1$ and $\beta(\eta_{bl}) = 2$.

A heuristic should be *admissible*, i.e., never overestimate $\alpha(\eta)$, and *monotonic*. Monotonicity means that, when a chart item η is inferred from another item μ contained in its lowest-weight derivation, $h(\eta) + \beta(\eta)$ should be at least as high as $h(\mu) + \beta(\mu)$ (Klein and Manning, 2002).

The A* heuristic presented in (Waszczuk et al., 2016b) is based on the observation that the weight of a particular TAG derivation tree can be refor-

---

[2] This equation holds provided that the weighting function is monotonic in the sense of (Huang and Chiang, 2005).

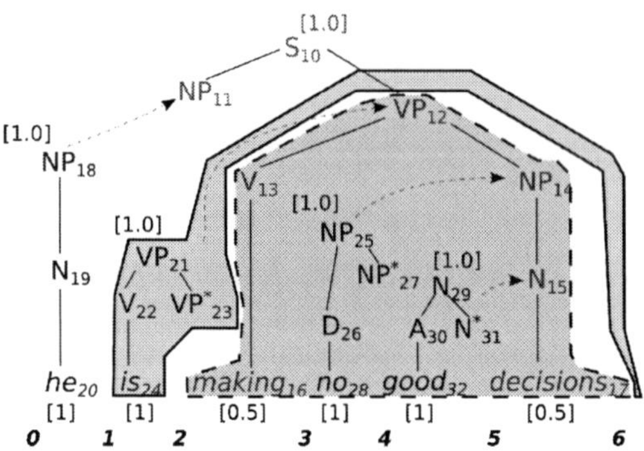

Figure 3: Projecting the weights of the ETs in a TAG derivation on the corresponding terminals. The weights of the ETs are shown, in square brackets, above their roots, while the projected weights are shown, also in square brackets, below the terminals.

mulated as follows. Firstly, the weights of the individual ETs are projected over the words in the input sentence to which they are attached. There are several possible ways of doing that, and the simplest one is to evenly distribute the weight of a given ET over its terminals, as shown in Fig. 3. Secondly, the weight of a derivation tree is redefined as the sum of the weights projected over the words in the sentence.

When the parser considers a particular item $\langle x, r\rangle$, the weights which can be projected over the words in r are known, but not the weights which can be projected over the words outside r. One can easily find the lower-bound estimates of the latter – i.e., assume that the minimum possible weight, denoted $minw(w)$ (e.g., $minw(\text{is}) = \frac{1}{3}$, $minw(\text{making}) = \frac{1}{2}$, etc.), will be projected over each word w outside r. Consequently, in (Waszczuk et al., 2016b) we define the baseline heuristic as:

$$h(\langle x, r\rangle) = \begin{cases} \mathcal{C}(out(r)), & \text{if } comp(x) \\ \infty, & \text{if } sup(x) \not\subset out(r) \\ \omega_{t_x} + \mathcal{C}(out(r) \setminus sup(x)), & \text{o/w,} \end{cases}$$

where $\mathcal{C}(m)$ is the globally minimal cost of scanning all the words in the multiset m (the sum of their $minw$ values) and $comp(x)$ is true iff the traversal represented by x is complete (all the nodes in t_x have been parsed). For instance:

$$h(\eta_{gr}) = \mathcal{C}(out(\langle 1, 2, 6, 6 \rangle))$$
$$= \mathcal{C}(\{he, making, no, good, decisions\}_{ms})$$
$$= 1 + \frac{1}{2} + \frac{1}{3} + \frac{1}{3} + \frac{1}{2} = 2 + \frac{2}{3},$$
$$h(\eta_{bl}) = 1 + \mathcal{C}(\{he, is\}_{ms}) = 2 + \frac{1}{3}.$$

The heuristic does not take the weight ω_{t_x} of the ET t_x being parsed into account if x is complete. This is because ω_{t_x} is already added to the weight of the inside derivation of $\langle x, r \rangle$ in this case. Moreover, $comp(x) \implies sup(x) = \emptyset_{ms}$.

This heuristic presents some important shortcomings, foremostly non-monotonicity. Given the predictive nature of the parser, an item $\langle x, \langle i, j, k, l \rangle \rangle$ such that $\langle j, k \rangle \neq \langle -, - \rangle$ is inferred iff an appropriate derivation, spanning $\langle j, k \rangle$, exists. In Fig. 3, η_{gr} thus relies on η_{bl} and when η_{gr} is inferred, the weights which can be projected over the words in $\langle 2, 6 \rangle$ are already known. Nevertheless, $h(\eta_{gr})$ assumes that the globally minimal weights will be projected over $\langle 2, 6 \rangle$, thus underestimating the weights projected over the words *no* and *good*. In Fig. 3, these projections are equal to 1, while $minw(no) = minw(good) = \frac{1}{3}$, since both words belong to the MWE *is no good*. As a result, $h(\eta_{gr}) + \beta(\eta_{gr}) = 2\frac{2}{3} + 1$ is smaller than $h(\eta_{bl}) + \beta(\eta_{bl}) = 2\frac{1}{3} + 2$, which shows that the heuristic is not monotonic.

A similar situation occurs in top-down CFG parsing with prediction when the weight of the premise item of the prediction rule is not transferred to the conclusion. Nederhof (2003) shows that a simplified version of the A* algorithm (the Knuth's algorithm, similar to the standard Dijkstra's shortest-path algorithm and relying on no heuristic) still correctly computes the derivations with the lowest weights in this case. While it can be stipulated that his proof applies to the algorithm used in (Waszczuk et al., 2016b), ignoring the weights of the items used for adjunction-related predictions not only makes the heuristic non-monotonic, it also means that the already computed inside weights, which could provide better estimations of $\alpha(x)$, are sometimes ignored.

3   Grammar representation

The complexity of TAG parsing is polynomial in the sentence length and linear in the grammar size ($\mathcal{O}(n^6 * |G|)$) (Gardent et al., 2014). With real-size grammars, especially those containing explicitly encoded MWEs, the latter factor can be prohibitive. Therefore – in order to speed up parsing – an A* algorithm should ideally be combined with grammar compression, as proposed below.

We assume a twofold representation of a TAG grammar. It is first transformed into an equivalent directed acyclic graph with ordered outgoing edges for each node (GDAG). Then, traversals of the ETs and their subtrees are represented as paths in finite-state automata (FSAs). This is a simplified variant of the grammar encoding applied in (Waszczuk et al., 2016a), where we showed that grammar compression alone can greatly speed-up TAG parsing, while using a variant of the standard, bottom-up Earley-style parser (Alonso et al., 1999).

Formally, we define a GDAG as a tuple $D = \langle V_D, E_D, \Sigma_D, N_D, S_D, \ell_D, foot_D \rangle$ such that V_D and E_D are the sets of DAG nodes and (ordered) edges, respectively, Σ_D and N_D are the sets of terminals and non-terminals, respectively, $S_D \in N_D$ is the start symbol, $\ell_D \colon V_D \to \Sigma_D \cup N_D$ is a function assigning non-terminals or terminals to D's nodes, and $foot_D \colon V_D \to \mathbb{B}$ tells whether a given node is a foot node. Also, $R_D, L_D \subset V_D$ are the sets of roots and leaves in D, respectively.

Fig. 1 is a straightforward encoding where each ET is represented by a separate tree. Fig. 4 compares two GDAG representations of three ETs from Fig. 1: (a) the straightforward encoding, and (b) the encoding with common subtrees shared among ETs. Both representations are equivalent, i.e., they entail the same TAG, which can be obtained by the traversals of the sub-DAGs rooted in the GDAG roots. For instance, the traversals starting from S_{10} in (a) and (b) entail the same ET.

We assume that a GDAG satisfies all the relevant, TAG-related well-formedness constraints – for example, that for each $r \in R_D$ there exists at most one $v \in V_D$ reachable from r such that $foot_D(v)$. Moreover, if such $v \in V_D$ exists, then $\ell_D(r) = \ell_D(v) \in N_D$, i.e., the root and the foot of an auxiliary tree must be labeled with the same non-terminal. Each $v \in V_D$ unambiguously determines the corresponding ET subtree (ES) *rooted at* v, denoted $es_D(v)$. Note that, by definition, each ET is also an ES.

Fig. 5 illustrates two possible FSA encodings, without and with prefix sharing, of the GDAG

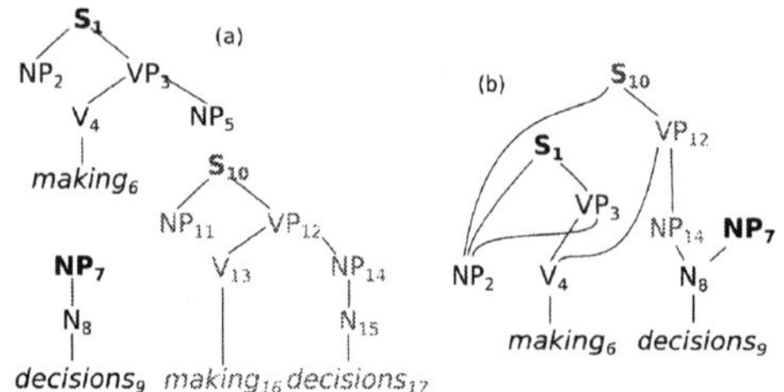

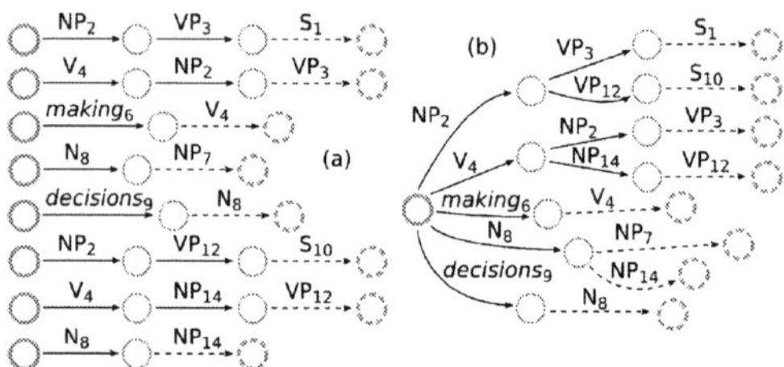

Figure 4: Two possible DAG encodings of three ETs from the grammar in Fig. 1. The values of ℓ_D are put in place of the corresponding nodes, and the node identifiers (the values of V_D) are placed in subscript on the right. All the edges are implicitly oriented downwards.

Figure 5: Two possible FSA encodings of the GDAG illustrated in Fig. 4 (b): (a) a simple FSA encoding in which each GDAG traversal is represented by a distinct path, and (b) a prefix-tree-like FSA encoding.

from Fig. 4 (b).[3] From the parsing perspective, each path in an FSA encoding represents the left-to-right traversal performed by the parser while matching, against the input words, a particular ES of height greater than 0.

Formally, we define an FSA encoding of a GDAG D as a tuple $M = \langle Q_M, \delta_M, S_M, heads_M \rangle$ such that Q_M is the set of FSA states, $\delta_M \colon Q_M \times V_D \rightarrow Q_M$ is the transition function consuming DAG nodes (V_D thus constitutes the set of the FSA alphabet symbols), $S_M \subset Q_M$ is the set of start states, and $heads_M \colon Q_M \rightarrow 2^{V_M}$ is a function which returns the final symbols outgoing from a given state. For convenience, we represent the particular states in the FSA encoding as dotted rules, e.g., $S_1 \rightarrow NP_2 \bullet VP_3$ corresponds to the state reached by following the symbol NP_2 on the path (NP_2, VP_3, S_1). Informally, $heads_M$ represent the left-hand-sides of such dotted rules.

Each $x \in V_D \cup Q_M$ represents a particular traversal configuration (cf. Sec. 2): $x \in V_D$ stipulates that the parser has matched $es_D(x)$, while $x \in Q_M$ stipulates that it has matched all the ESs on the path from one of the states in S_M to $x \in Q_M$. For instance, $VP_3 \rightarrow V_4 NP_2 \bullet$ stipulates that the parser has matched both $es_D(V_4)$ and $es_D(NP_2)$.

As mentioned in Sec. 2, when no grammar compression (i.e. no subtree or prefix sharing) occurs, each traversal configuration

corresponds to exactly one ET t_x. With grammar compression, however, there can be many ETs corresponding to a given $x \in V_D \cup Q_M$. We denote their set by T_x. For instance, in Fig. 4 (b) and 5 (b), $T_{V_4} = T_{VP_3 \rightarrow V_4 \bullet NP_2} = T_{VP_{12} \rightarrow V_4 \bullet NP_{14}} = \{es_D(S_1), es_D(S_{10})\}$, $T_{NP_7 \rightarrow \bullet N_8} = \{es_D(v) \colon v \in R_D\}$, etc.

This brings us to the second issue with the heuristic defined in Sec. 2. One of the first steps of computing the value of $h(\langle x, r \rangle)$ is to check whether $sup(x) \subset out(r)$. This step allows to obtain better estimations of $\alpha(\langle x, r \rangle)$ – namely, to exclude the dead-end chart items, which cannot possibly lead to final derivations. However, with grammar compression, sup depends not only on the configuration x, but also on the corresponding ET $t \in T_x$. Hence, we define a generalized version of sup as a two-argument function $sup(x, t)$ which determines the multiset of words remaining to parse on t's traversal starting from x.

When estimating $\alpha(\langle x, r \rangle)$, the parser needs to consider all the different ET traversals containing x, leading to different ETs, and with different multisets of the words remaining to complete the traversal. Assuming the prefix-tree grammar compression and that q_0 is the root of the prefix-tree FSA encoding, T_{q_0} is the set of all grammar ETs. Therefore, when grammar compression is used, computing h's values is $\mathcal{O}(N)$, where N is the number of ETs.

4 Enhancing the baseline A* TAG parser

In (Waszczuk et al., 2016b,a) we put forward a version of the bottom-up, Earley-like parser described in (Alonso et al., 1999) to test the idea of promoting MWEs in A* parsing. We now formalize an enhanced version of this parser, adapted to

---

[3]While a minimal FSA encoding, including both prefix and suffix sharing, might seem optimal, we empirically showed in (Waszczuk et al., 2016a) that it does not bring significant improvements over the prefix-tree encoding in TAG parsing.

AX (axiom):	$$\frac{}{(0,0):\langle q_0,\langle i,i\rangle\rangle_a}$$	$i\in pos(s)\setminus\{n\}$ $q_0\in S_M$
SC (scan):	$$\frac{(w,w'):\langle q,\langle i,j,k,l\rangle\rangle_a}{(w,w'):\langle\delta_M(q,v),\langle i,j,k,l+1\rangle\rangle_a}$$	$v\in L_D:\ell_D(v)=s_{l+1}$ $\delta_M(q,v)$ defined
DE (deactivate):	$$\frac{(w,w'):\langle q,\langle i,j,k,l\rangle\rangle_a}{(w+[\omega_{es_D(v)}|v\in R_D],w'):\langle v,\langle i,j,k,l\rangle\rangle_p}$$	$v\in heads_M(q)$
PS (pseudo-subst.):	$$\frac{(w_1,w_1'):\langle q,\langle i,j,k,l\rangle\rangle_a \quad (w_2,w_2'):\langle v,\langle l,j',k',l'\rangle\rangle_p}{(w_1+w_2,w_1'+w_2'):\langle\delta_M(q,v),\langle i,j\cup j',k\cup k',l'\rangle\rangle_a}$$	$\delta_M(q,v)$ defined
SU (substitution):	$$\frac{(w_1,w_1'):\langle q,\langle i,j,k,l\rangle\rangle_a \quad (w_2,0):\langle v,\langle l,l'\rangle\rangle_p}{(w_1+w_2,w_1'):\langle\delta_M(q,v'),\langle i,j,k,l'\rangle\rangle_a}$$	$v'\in L_D:\ell_D(v')=\ell_D(v)\wedge\neg foot_D(v')$ $\delta_M(q,v')$ defined $v\in R_D$
FA (foot-adjoin):	$$\frac{(w_1,0):\langle q,\langle i,l\rangle\rangle_a \quad (w_2,w_2'):\langle v,\langle l,j',k',l'\rangle\rangle_p}{(w_1,w_2+w_2'+[A(v)|v\notin R_D]):\langle\delta_M(q,v'),\langle i,l,l',l'\rangle\rangle_a}$$	$v'\in L_D:\ell_D(v')=\ell_D(v)\wedge foot_D(v')$ $\delta_M(q,v')$ defined $v\in R_D\implies(j',k')=(-,-)$
RA (root-adjoin):	$$\frac{(w_1,w_1'):\langle w,\langle i,j,k,l\rangle\rangle_p \quad (w_2,w_2'):\langle v,\langle j,j',k',k\rangle\rangle_p}{(w_1+w_2,w_2'):\langle v,\langle i,j',k',l\rangle\rangle_p}$$	$w\in R_D\wedge(j,k)\neq(-,-)$ $\ell_D(w)=\ell_D(v)$ $v\in R_D\implies(j',k')=(-,-)$

Table 1: Weighted inference rules of the Earley-style, bottom-up parser, where: (in PS) $i\cup j$ is equal to i if $j=-$ and j otherwise, and (in DE and FA) $[x|p]=x$ if p is true and $[x|p]=0$ otherwise.

the grammar representation introduced in Sec. 3, and to the new heuristic defined in Sec. 5.

We say that a chart item $\langle x,r\rangle$ is *active* if $x\in Q_M$, and that it is *passive* if $x\in V_D$. We also write $\langle q,r\rangle_a$ or $\langle v,r\rangle_p$ to refer to an active or a passive item, respectively.

Tab. 1 specifies the inference rules of the parser, using the weighted deductive framework (Shieber et al., 1995; Nederhof, 2003). Each of the inference rules takes zero, one or two chart items on input (*premises*, presented above the horizontal line) and yields a new item (*conclusion*, presented below the line) to be added to the chart if the conditions given on the right-hand side are met. Besides, to each item η in each rule a pair of weights (w,w'), given before the colon, is assigned, thus specifying how to compute the weights corresponding to the conclusion based on the weights corresponding to the premises. The meaning of w' and A (the latter used to compute w's values in the FA rule), both specific to the enhanced heuristic, will be detailed in Sec. 5. The value w, on the other hand, represents the weight of η's inside derivation. The idea of computing pairs of weights using inference rules comes from Nederhof (2003), who showed that such a solution can be used to overcome the non-monotonicity issue in top-down CFG parsing with prediction.

The way the inside weights are computed by the parser corresponds to the assumption that the probability of a derivation is the product of the probabilities of the participating ETs, hence the weight computed for the conclusion item is the sum of the weights of the premise items, with two exceptions. The DE inference rule, responsible for matching full ESs, adds the weight $es_D(v)$, provided that $es_D(v)$ is an ET. The FA rule, used to predict that adjunction over a particular span r is possible, does not transfer the weight of the premise item spanned over r. In the baseline parser, the same behavior was precisely the reason of the non-monotonicity in Fig. 3 discussed in Sec. 2. However, now this weight is accounted for in w', which preserves monotonicity, as shown below.

5 Enhanced heuristic

We now propose an enhanced version of the heuristic described in Sec. 2, with the goal of overcoming the issues related to non-monotonicity and grammar compression. However, for the sake of clarity, we start by assuming that no grammar compression is performed.

As mentioned before, w represents the weight of an *inside* derivation of the corresponding item η. The weight w', on the other hand, represents (roughly) the weight of η's *witness* derivation, i.e., the previously obtained derivation which can fill η's gap. Consider Fig. 6 (b) and three chart items: $\mu_{gr}=\langle S_8,\langle 1,2,4,5\rangle\rangle$, $\mu_{bl}=\langle S_3,\langle 2,2,3,4\rangle\rangle$, and $\mu_{rd}=\langle S_6,\langle 2,3\rangle\rangle$. Then, the derivation delimited by the green solid line is μ_{gr}'s inside derivation, while the derivation delimited by the blue dashed line is μ_{gr}'s witness derivation. Sim-

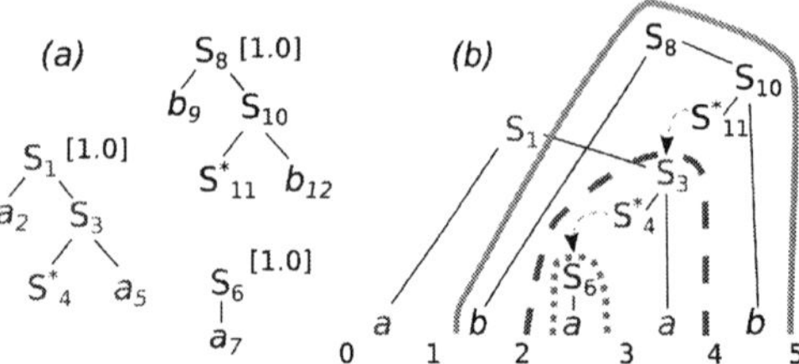

Figure 6: Copy language

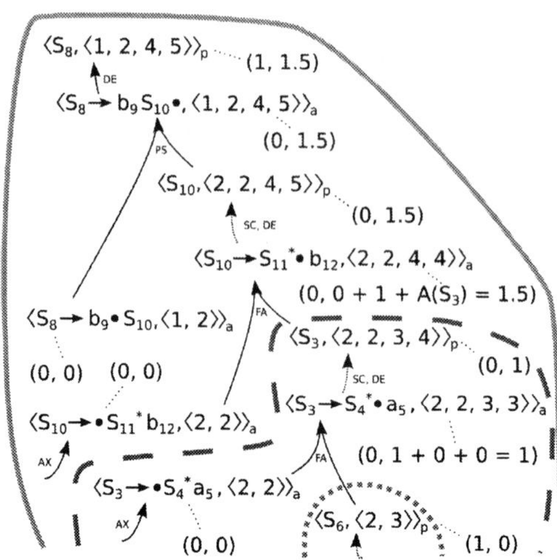

Figure 7: A fragment of an inside derivation of $\langle S_8, \langle 1, 2, 4, 5 \rangle \rangle_p$, represented as a hyperpath.

ilarly, the derivation delimited by the blue line is μ_{bl}'s inside derivation, while the derivation delimited by the red dotted line is μ_{bl}'s witness. Finally, the derivation delimited by the red line is μ_{rd}'s inside derivation, but μ_{rd} has no witness derivation, since it is not gapped. In general, for any non-gapped item η, $w' = 0$.

Given a configuration $x \in V_D \cup Q_M$, we define x's *amortized weight* as:

$$A(x) = \omega_{t_x} - C(sup(x)).$$

For instance, in Fig. 6 (a), $A(S_3) = A(S_{10}) = \frac{1}{2}$ (since $minw(a) = minw(b) = \frac{1}{2}$), and $A(S_6) = A(S_1) = 1$. $A(x)$ accounts for the weight of the ET t_x, and for the fact that t_x may still contain some terminals which need to be consumed (w.r.t. to the position of x in t_x's traversal). Thus, $A(x)$ can be intuitively understood as the weight of the already parsed part of t_x.

A version of h which performs no dead-end detection, i.e. never takes the ∞ value unlike h in Sec. 2, but, otherwise, provides identical estimations as h, can be defined in terms of A as:

$$h_{spl}(\langle x, r \rangle) = \begin{cases} C(out(r)), & \text{if } x \in R_D \\ A(x) + C(out(r)), & \text{o/w.} \end{cases}$$

We also define the *amortized weight* of a derivation δ as the sum of the amortized weights of the ESs (more precisely, their roots) present in δ. For instance, in Fig. 6 (b), the amortized weight of μ_{bl}'s inside derivation is $A(S_6) + A(S_3) = 1 + \frac{1}{2}$. The weight w', attached to each chart item η, is precisely the amortized weight of η's witness derivation (if η is gapped, otherwise $w' = 0$).

Then, given a chart item $\eta = \langle x, r \rangle$ such that $r = \langle i, j, k, l \rangle$ and the corresponding weight w', we define the enhanced A* heuristic as:

$$h_{adj}(\eta) = \begin{cases} C(rest(r)) + w', & \text{if } x \in R_D \\ A(x) + C(rest(r)) + w', & \text{o/w,} \end{cases}$$

where $rest(r) = out(r) \setminus in(\langle j, k \rangle)$, i.e. the multiset of words outside r but not in the gap, whose cost is already accounted for in w'. The advantage over the baseline heuristic is precisely that, instead of assuming that the lowest possible weights will be projected over all words in the gap, the weights of the existing derivations spanning the gap are considered. The disadvantage is that, by not checking that the remaining part of the sentence contains all the tokens required by t_x's traversal, h_{adj} does not detect the dead-end items, which is the price to pay for better integration with grammar compression techniques (see below).

Fig. 7 shows a fragment of the inference corresponding to μ_{gr}'s inside derivation in Fig. 6 (b). Each node in Fig. 7 represents a deduced chart item, and each hyperarc (which connects one target node with zero, one or two tail nodes) represents an application of an inference rule. Besides, to each item the corresponding pair of weights (w, w') is attached via an undirected dashed edge. In particular, the pair attached to $\langle S_8, \langle 1, 2, 4, 5 \rangle \rangle$ is $(1, 1.5)$, since the amortized weight of its witness derivation is 1.5. Note that the baseline heuristic would assume that the globally minimal weights $minw(a) = 0.5$ are projected over both a in the gap and, thus, underestimate the gap's parsing cost as 1.

The enhanced heuristic composes smoothly with grammar compression techniques. To recall, under compression, each configuration $x \in V_D \cup Q_M$ can belong to several ETs and, consequently, to several ET traversals. To ensure that the heuristic does not overestimate, it is sufficient to calculate the *minimal* amortized weight, i.e., assume that the least-weight traversal will be taken from any given $x \in V_D \cup Q_M$:

$$A(x) = \min\{\omega_t - \mathcal{C}(sup(x,t)) \colon t \in T_x\}. \quad (1)$$

The definition of h_{adj} remains unchanged. The values of A can be pre-computed on a per-grammar basis, just as the values of $\mathcal{C} \circ rest$[4] can be pre-computed on a per-sentence basis,[5] hence the robustness of h_{adj} w.r.t. grammar compression.

To show that h_{adj} is monotonic, it is sufficient to consider each inference rule from Tab. 1 separately and to show that the total weight $(w + h_{adj}(\eta))$ it computes for the conclusion item η is at least as high as the total weight of any of its premise items. As an example, we sketch below the proof of monotonicity of the PS rule.

Proposition 1. *Let $v \in V_D$ and $q \in Q_M$ such that $\delta_M(q,v)$ is defined. Then, $T_{\delta_M(q,v)} \subset T(q)$.*

Proof. Follows from the fact that any FSA path crossing $\delta_M(q,v)$ must also cross v. $\qquad\square$

Observation 1. *Let $v \in V_D$, $q \in Q_M$ such that $\delta_M(q,v)$ defined, and $t \in T_{\delta_M(q,v)}$. Then, $\mathcal{C}(sup(\delta_M(q,v),t)) = \mathcal{C}(sup(q,t)) - \mathcal{C}(inf(v))$.*

Proposition 2. *Let $v \in V_D$ and $q \in Q_M$ such that $\delta_M(q,v)$ defined. Then,*

$$A(\delta_M(q,v)) \geq A(q) + \mathcal{C}(inf(v)).$$

Proof. Follows from Pr. 1, Ob. 1, and Eq. 1. $\qquad\square$

Proposition 3. *Let $\eta = \langle x, r \rangle$ be a chart item such that $x \notin R_D$, $r = \langle i, j, k, l \rangle$, and (w, w') be the corresponding weights. Then,*

$$w + w' \geq \mathcal{C}(in(\langle i, l \rangle)) - \mathcal{C}(inf(x)).$$

Proof. The LHS is the total weight projected by η's inside derivation over $\langle i, l \rangle$, with the exception of the words in $inf(x)$. The RHS is, by definition, a lower-bound for the projected weight. $\qquad\square$

Observation 2. *In the PS rule, it holds that: $\mathcal{C}(rest(\langle i, l' \rangle)) = \mathcal{C}(rest(\langle i, l \rangle)) - \mathcal{C}(in(\langle l, l' \rangle)).$*

Proposition 4. *The PS rule is monotonic.*

---

[4]The symbol $\circ$ stands for function composition.

[5]In both cases dynamic programming techniques can be used to speed up the process.

Proof. Let η be the conclusion and μ be the active premise. Then:

$$
\begin{aligned}
&w_1 + w_2 + h_{adj}(\eta) - w_1 - h_{adj}(\mu) = && (h_{adj})\\
&w_2 + A(\delta_M(q,v)) + \mathcal{C}(rest(\langle i, l' \rangle)) + w_1' + w_2'\\
&\quad - A(q) - \mathcal{C}(rest(\langle i, l \rangle)) - w_1' = && (\text{Ob. 2})\\
&w_2 + A(\delta_M(q,v)) + w_2' - A(q)\\
&\quad - \mathcal{C}(in(\langle l, l' \rangle)) \geq && (\text{Prop. 2})\\
&w_2 + \mathcal{C}(inf(v)) + w_2'\\
&\quad - \mathcal{C}(in(\langle l, l' \rangle)) \geq 0. && (\text{Prop. 3})
\end{aligned}
$$

It can be shown that PS is monotonic w.r.t. its passive premise item in a similar fashion. $\qquad\square$

6 Experiments

We repeated the experimental evaluation proposed in (Waszczuk et al., 2016b) in order to compare the new heuristic (cf. Sec. 5) with the baseline (cf. Sec. 2). The experiment was based on the version of the Składnica treebank (Świdziński and Woliński, 2010) annotated with MWEs (Savary and Waszczuk, 2017). For each sentence in the corpus, the grammar was first reduced to only those ETs whose terminals occurred in the sentence, and compressed according to the methods described in Sec. 3. Then, the parser (specified in Sec. 4) was run and the search-space-size reductions stemming from promoting MWEs (a behavior obtained by assigning the weight 1 to each ET in the grammar) were measured. We also implemented runtime verification tests which empirically confirmed the monotonicity of (the implementation of) h_{adj}.

We observed only minor differences between the results obtained with both heuristics. On average (at most, respectively), h_{adj} led to search-space-size reductions of 16.8% (90.6%) vs. 18.1% (90.7%) reductions obtained with h, a drop in performance related to the lack of dead-end detection in h_{adj}. Recall, however, that calculating h's values can be costly (linear w.r.t. the number of ETs) when grammar compression is used, and can be thus infeasible in practical parsing applications. In our experiment, grammar compression alone decreased (on average) the search-space to less than $\frac{1}{3}$ of its original size.

7 Conclusions and future work

Our previous state-of-the-art A* heuristic for promoting MWEs in TAG parsing is not monotonic and it composes poorly with grammar compression methods. We have presented here an enhanced version of this heuristic, which improves the estimations of the outside derivation weights by making the predictions of the weights related to items' gaps more accurate. The new version is monotonic and combines with our grammar compression techniques with no significant computational overhead. The price to pay is the lack of detection of dead-end items, which partially explains the slight drop in search-space-size reductions in comparison with the baseline heuristic. To the best of our knowledge, this is the first approach explicitly addressing interactions between A* parsing and grammar compression.

For future work, we plan to repeat the experiment with a truly weighted grammar, i.e., with the weights corresponding to single-anchored ETs being estimated from a treebank. We believe that such an experiment will lead to more insightful conclusions as to the pros and cons of the new heuristic. We also plan to optimize the implementation of the parser, in order to verify that the search-space-size reductions transfer to proportional reductions in parsing time.

Acknowledgments

This work has been supported by the French Ministry of Higher Education and Research via a doctoral grant, by the French Centre-Val de Loire Region Council via the APR-AI 2015-1850 ODIL project, by the French National Research Agency (ANR) via the PARSEME-FR[6] project (ANR-14-CERA-0001), and by the European Framework Programme Horizon 2020 via the PARSEME[7] European COST Action (IC1207).

We are grateful to the anonymous reviewers for their insightful comments to the first version of this paper.

References

Anne Abeillé. 1995. The Flexibility of French Idioms: A Representation with Lexicalised Tree Adjoining Grammar. In M. Everaert, E-J. van der Linden, A. Schenk, and R Schreuder, editors, *Idioms: Structural and Psychological Perspectives*, Lawrence Erlbaum Associates, chapter 1.

Anne Abeillé and Yves Schabes. 1989. Parsing idioms in lexicalized tags. In *Proceedings of the Fourth Conference on European Chapter of the Association for Computational Linguistics*. Association for Computational Linguistics, Stroudsburg, PA, USA, EACL '89, pages 1–9. https://doi.org/10.3115/976815.976816.

Miguel Alonso, David Cabrero, Eric Villemonte de la Clergerie, and Manuel Vilares Ferro. 1999. Tabular algorithms for TAG parsing. In *EACL 1999*. pages 150–157. http://acl.ldc.upenn.edu/E/E99/E99-1020.pdf.

Krasimir Angelov and Peter Ljunglöf. 2014. Fast Statistical Parsing with Parallel Multiple Context-Free Grammars. In *EACL*. volume 14, pages 368–376.

Srinivas Bangalore and Aravind K. Joshi. 1999. Supertagging: An Approach to Almost Parsing. *Comput. Linguist.* 25(2):237–265. http://dl.acm.org/citation.cfm?id=973306.973310.

Matthieu Constant, Joseph Le Roux, and Anthony Sigogne. 2013. Combining compound recognition and PCFG-LA parsing with word lattices and conditional random fields. *ACM Trans. Speech Lang. Process.* 10(3):8:1–8:24. https://doi.org/10.1145/2483969.2483970.

Claire Gardent, Yannick Parmentier, Guy Perrier, and Sylvain Schmitz. 2014. Lexical Disambiguation in LTAG using Left Context. In Zygmunt Vetulani and Joseph Mariani, editors, *Human Language Technology. Challenges for Computer Science and Linguistics. 5th Language and Technology Conference, LTC 2011, Poznan, Poland, November 25-27, 2011, Revised Selected Papers*, Springer, volume 8387, pages 67–79. https://doi.org/10.1007/978-3-319-08958-4_6.

Maurice Gross and Jean Senellart. 1998. Nouvelles bases statistiques pour les mots du français. In *Proceedings of JADT'98, Nice 1998*. pages 335–349.

Liang Huang and David Chiang. 2005. *Proceedings of the Ninth International Workshop on Parsing Technology*, Association for Computational Linguistics, chapter Better k-best Parsing, pages 53–64. http://aclweb.org/anthology/W05-1506.

Dan Klein and Christopher D. Manning. 2002. A* Parsing: Fast Exact Viterbi Parse Selection. Technical Report dbpubs/2002-16, Stanford University.

Dan Klein and Christopher D. Manning. 2003. A* parsing: Fast exact viterbi parse selection. In *Proceedings of the 2003 Human Language Technology Conference of the North American Chapter of the Association for Computational Linguistics*. http://www.aclweb.org/anthology/N03-1016.

Mike Lewis and Mark Steedman. 2014. A* CCG Parsing with a Supertag-factored Model. In *Proceedings of the 2014 Conference on Empirical Methods in Natural Language Processing (EMNLP)*. Association for Computational Linguistics, pages 990–1000. http://aclweb.org/anthology/D14-1107.

---

[6]http://parsemefr.lif.univ-mrs.fr
[7]http://www.parseme.eu

Mark-Jan Nederhof. 2003. Weighted Deductive Parsing and Knuth's Algorithm. *Comput. Linguist.* 29(1):135–143. https://doi.org/10.1162/089120103321337467.

Agata Savary and Jakub Waszczuk. 2017. Projecting multiword expression resources on a polish treebank. In *Proceedings of the 6th Workshop on Balto-Slavic Natural Language Processing.* Association for Computational Linguistics, Valencia, Spain, pages 20–26. http://www.aclweb.org/anthology/W17-1404.

Stuart M Shieber, Yves Schabes, and Fernando CN Pereira. 1995. Principles and implementation of deductive parsing. *The Journal of logic programming* 24(1):3–36.

Jakub Waszczuk, Agata Savary, and Yannick Parmentier. 2016a. Enhancing practical TAG parsing efficiency by capturing redundancy. In *21st International Conference on Implementation and Application of Automata (CIAA 2016).* Séoul, South Korea, Proceedings of the 21st International Conference on Implementation and Application of Automata (CIAA 2016). https://hal.archives-ouvertes.fr/hal-01309598.

Jakub Waszczuk, Agata Savary, and Yannick Parmentier. 2016b. Promoting multiword expressions in a* tag parsing. In *Proceedings of COLING 2016, the 26th International Conference on Computational Linguistics: Technical Papers.* The COLING 2016 Organizing Committee, Osaka, Japan, pages 429–439. http://aclweb.org/anthology/C16-1042.

Eric Wehrli. 2014. The relevance of collocations for parsing. In *Proceedings of the 10th Workshop on Multiword Expressions (MWE).* Association for Computational Linguistics, Gothenburg, Sweden, pages 26–32. http://www.aclweb.org/anthology/W14-0804.

Marek Świdziński and Marcin Woliński. 2010. Towards a bank of constituent parse trees for Polish. In Petr Sojka, Aleš Horák, Ivan Kopeček, and Karel Pala, editors, *Text, Speech and Dialogue: 13th International Conference, TSD 2010, Brno, Czech Republic.* Springer-Verlag, Heidelberg, volume 6231 of *Lecture Notes in Artificial Intelligence*, pages 197–204.

Single-Rooted DAGs in Regular DAG Languages:
Parikh Image and Path Languages

Martin Berglund
Center for AI Research, CSIR
Dept. of Information Science
Stellenbosch University
pmberglund@sun.ac.za

Henrik Björklund
Dept. of Computing Science
Umeå University, Sweden
henrikb@cs.umu.se

Frank Drewes
Dept. of Computing Science
Umeå University, Sweden
drewes@cs.umu.se

Abstract

In a recent survey (Drewes, 2017) of results on DAG automata some open problems are formulated for the case where the DAG language accepted by a DAG automaton A is restricted to DAGs with a single root, denoted by $L(A)_u$. Here we consider each of those problems, demonstrating that: (i) the finiteness of $L(A)_u$ is decidable, (ii) the path languages of $L(A)_u$ can be characterized in terms of the string languages accepted by partially blind multicounter automata, and (iii) the Parikh image of $L(A)_u$ is semilinear.

1 Introduction

In many applications such as natural language processing (NLP) great value can be extracted from extending beyond the strings and trees which are most commonly offered by traditional language formalisms. In the other direction, however, moving to general graphs is a step too far for many NLP tasks, and directed acyclic graphs form a natural step between trees and general graphs, enforcing the hierarchical nature of sentences. For these reasons, the study of DAG automata, devices which accept a class of languages known as the regular DAG languages, have drawn some interest, see for example Blum and Drewes (2017); Chiang et al. (2016). (Here, we only consider the *ordered* case, but this makes no practical difference to the results we present, which apply equally to the unordered case.) In a recent survey (Drewes, 2017) the distinction between DAG automata which permit multiple roots (which is more natural in the way the formalism is defined) and ones restricted to a single root (which is natural from the perspective of many NLP applications) is considered at some length. The latter case is, somewhat surpris-

ingly, significantly stronger, and the survey states four open questions relating to it. We consider all these questions here, with the following outcomes:

Problem 1. Given a DAG automaton A as input, is the problem of deciding whether $L(A)_u$ is finite decidable? We demonstrate that it is.

Problem 2. Is there a natural characterization of the path languages of the regular DAG languages restricted to a single root? We relate, in both directions, this class of languages to the string languages accepted by partially blind multicounter automata (a formalism akin to a string-accepting Petri net). The only caveat preventing a full equivalence is that a single-rooted DAG automaton simulating a multicounter automaton will contain some extraneous strings, which are, however, clearly labeled by an additional alphabet symbol.

Problem 3. This is a variation on Problem 2, asking for a characterization of the path languages of regular DAG languages intersected with regular languages. Intersection with a suitably chosen regular language makes the language equivalence with multicounter automata direct. In fact, as noted above, an intersection with a language of the form Σ^* is already sufficient to achieve this.

Problem 4. Are the Parikh images (see e.g. (Parikh, 1961)) of $L(A)$ and $L(A)_u$ semilinear for all DAG automata A? We demonstrate that they are.

These results provide further theoretical evidence for the claim by Chiang et al. (2016) and Drewes (2017) that the regular DAG languages exhibit an appropriate level of complexity for the formalization of linguistically reasonable sets of Abstract Meaning Representations (Banarescu et al., 2013) and that it, in particular, is not advisable to consider languages of the form L_u instead. It was already known (Blum and Drewes,

Proceedings of the 13th International Workshop on Tree Adjoining Grammars and Related Formalisms (TAG+13), pages 94–101,
Umeå, Sweden, September 4–6, 2017. © 2017 Association for Computational Linguistics

2017; Chiang et al., 2016) that the path languages of regular DAG languages have the desired property of being regular. Thanks to the results of this paper, we now also know that their Parikh images are semilinear, which is another highly desirable property. Moreover, while it was concluded in the above-mentioned papers that the single-root restriction yields too powerful path languages, we can now precisely characterize how powerful they actually are.

2 Preliminaries

For $n \in \mathbb{N}$, we write $[n]$ for the set $\{1, \ldots, n\}$. For a vector $I \in \mathbb{N}^n$, we write I_i for the ith element of I. The empty string is denoted ε. If f is an is a function from set S to set T, we extend it to finite sequences in S^* by letting $f(s_1 s_2 \cdots s_n) = f(s_1)f(s_2) \cdots f(s_n)$. Given a string language $L \subseteq S^*$ (or a regular expression denoting such a language) we let L_ε denote $L \cup \{\varepsilon\}$.

Given two strings u and v over alphabet Σ, the *shuffle* of u and v, written $u \odot v$, is the set of all interleavings of u and v. We define the shuffle inductively. The base case is $\varepsilon \odot u = u \odot \varepsilon = \{u\}$, for every string $u \in \Sigma^*$. If $u = au'$ and $v = bv'$, with $a, b \in \Sigma$, then $u \odot v = a(u' \odot v) \cup b(u \odot v')$. For languages L_1 and L_2 we have $L_1 \odot L_2 = \{u \odot v \mid u \in L_1 \wedge v \in L_2\}$. The *shuffle closure* of a language L, written $L^{\odot}$, is the set of interleavings of zero or more strings from L, i.e., $L^{\odot} = \bigcup_{i=0}^{\infty} L^{\odot i}$, where $L^{\odot 0} = \{\varepsilon\}$ and $L^{\odot i+1} = L \odot L^{\odot i}$.

The graphs we are interested in here are directed, node-labeled, and ordered, in the sense that for each node, there is an order on the incoming and on the outgoing edges from the node. We formally define them as follows.

Definition 1. Let Σ be an alphabet. A *graph* over Σ is a tuple $G = (V, E, in, out, lab)$, where V and E are the sets of nodes and edges, respectively, $in : V \to E^*$ and $out : V \to E^*$ assign incoming and outgoing edges to the nodes, and $lab : V \to \Sigma$ assigns labels to the nodes. An edge goes from precisely one node to precisely one, that is, $|in^{-1}(e)| = |out^{-1}(e)| = 1$ for all $e \in E$.

A (directed) path in such a graph is a sequence $v_0 e_1 v_1 e_2 \cdots v_n$ such that, for each $i \in [n]$, e_i points from v_{i-1} to v_i, i.e., it occurs in both $out(v_{i-1})$ and $in(v_i)$. Such a path is a *cycle* if $v_0 = v_n$ and $n > 0$. A graph is a *DAG* (directed acyclic graph) if it has no cycles.

We next give the definition, taken from (Blum and Drewes, 2017; Chiang et al., 2016), of the automata on DAGs that interest us.

Definition 2. A *DAG-automaton* is a structure $A = (Q, \Sigma, R)$, where Q is a finite set of states, Σ is an alphabet, and R is a finite set of rules. Each rule in R has the form $\alpha \overset{\sigma}{\leftrightarrow} \beta$, where $\alpha, \beta \in Q^*$ and $\sigma \in \Sigma$.

For a DAG $G = (V, E, in, out, lab)$ over Σ a run of the automaton $A = (Q, \Sigma, R)$ on G is an assignment $\rho \colon E \to Q$ of states to the edges of G such that

$$\rho(in(v)) \overset{lab(v)}{\longleftrightarrow} \rho(out(v)) \in R$$

for every node $v \in V$. A DAG G is accepted by A if there is a run of A on G. The language consisting of all connected DAGs that are accepted (or recognized) by A is denoted $\mathcal{L}(A)$. A DAG language that can be recognized by a DAG automaton is called a regular DAG language.

Note that we include only connected DAGs in $L(A)$. Thus, in the following we implicitly assume that all DAGs we consider are connected. This is reasonable because a DAG is accepted by A if and only if all its connected components are; for details, see (Drewes, 2017).

A node in a DAG is a *root* if it has no incoming edges. Given a DAG language L, we write L_u for the set of all graphs in L that are single-rooted, i.e., that have exactly one root. A node is a *leaf* if it has no outgoing edges.

Definition 3. A *partially blind multicounter automaton* is a machined defined by a tuple $M = (Q, \Sigma, m, \delta, q_0, F)$ where, as in ordinary (non-deterministic) finite-state automata, Q is the finite set of states, Σ is the input alphabet, $q_0 \in Q$ is the initial state, and $F \subseteq Q$ is the set of final states. Furthermore, $m \in \mathbb{N}$ is the number of counters, and $\delta \subseteq (Q \times \Sigma_\varepsilon \times \mathbb{N}^m \times \mathbb{N}^m \times Q)$ is the transition relation.

The counters are numbered from 1 to m and take values from $\mathbb{N}$. The automaton starts reading a string in state q_0 and with all counters set to 0. When the automaton makes a transition (p, σ, D, I, q), the vector D is first subtracted from the counter values. If this results in some counter having a negative value, the transition and the computation fail (i.e. the transition cannot be taken). Otherwise, I is added to the counters, σ is read, and the automaton changes state to q.

The automaton accepts $w \in \Sigma^*$ if, after reading the string, it can reach a configuration with an accepting state and all counters set to 0. In this case, w belongs to the language $\mathcal{L}(M)$ accepted (or recognized) by M.

Note that there is no explicit zero-testing during the computation, only at the end. This is the "partial blindness". As a consequence, the automata, as opposed to 2-counter automata with zero tests, are not Turing complete. Instead, they can be seen as string-accepting vector addition systems with states (VASS) or Petri nets (Greibach, 1978). Among other things, this means that the emptiness problem is decidable for these machines (Kosaraju, 1982; Mayr, 1984).

Since we are only interested in partially blind multicounter automata here, we will simply refer to them as multicounter automata.

3 Semilinearity and finiteness

Let Σ be an alphabet and let $\sigma_1, \sigma_2, \ldots, \sigma_n$ be an (arbitrary) ordering of its elements. If s is a string over Σ, the *Parikh image* of s is a vector $\psi(s)$ such that $\psi(s)_i$ is the number of occurrences of σ_i in s for every $i \in [n]$. Similarly, for a DAG G, $\psi(G)_i$ is the number of occurrences of σ_i as the label of a node in G. For a language L, over strings or graphs, $\psi(L)$ is the set $\{\psi(s) \mid s \in L\}$.

A subset X of $\mathbb{N}^n$ is *linear* if there are vectors $v_0, v_1, \ldots, v_n$ such that

$$X = \{v_0 + i_1 v_1 + \cdots i_n v_n \mid i_1, \ldots, i_n \in \mathbb{N}\}.$$

A subset of $\mathbb{N}^n$ is *semilinear* if it is the union of a finite number of linear sets. In the following, we are going to use the fact that the semilinear sets are effectively closed under intersection and projection to a subset of their dimensions. The former fact was proved by Ginsburg and Spanier (1964). The latter is easily seen from the definition of linear and semilinear sets.

Theorem 1. *For every regular DAG language L, the set $\psi(L)$ is semilinear.*

Proof. Let $A = (Q, \Sigma, R)$ be a DAG automaton such that $\mathcal{L}(A) = L$. Let $G = (V, E, in, out, lab)$ be a DAG in L and let $\rho \colon E \to Q$ be a run of A on G. We describe a kind of linearization of such a run in the form of a string over the alphabet $\Gamma = \Sigma \cup Q \cup \overline{Q}$, where $\overline{Q} = \{\overline{q} \mid q \in Q\}$. Let the sequence $t = v_1, v_2, \ldots, v_n$ be a topological sorting of the nodes in G. For each node $v_i \in V$ we define $in_\rho(v_i)$ to be the sequence $\overline{\rho(in(v_i))}$, i.e., the sequence of states assigned to the incoming edges of v_i by ρ, but with each state replaced by its counterpart in $\overline{Q}$. Similarly, let $out_\rho(v_i)$ be the sequence $\rho(out(v_i))$, i.e., the sequence of states assigned to the outgoing edges from v_i by ρ. Then $lin_{G,\rho,t}$, the linearization of ρ on G (with respect to t) is given by $lin_{G,\rho,t} = w_1 \cdots w_n$ where

$$w_i = in_\rho(v_i)\, lab(v_i)\, out_\rho(v_i)$$

for all $i \in [n]$. For each rule $r = \alpha \overset{\sigma}{\leftrightarrow} \beta$, let $string(r) = \overline{\alpha}\sigma\beta$ and let $string(R) = \{string(r) \mid r \in R\}$. Then, for every DAG $G \in L$, topological sorting t of V_G, and run ρ of A on G, the string $lin_{G,\rho,t}$ belongs to the regular language $r_A = string(R)^*$.

Not every string in r_A is a linearization of a run of A on some DAG. We need to make sure that every state on an outgoing edge (represented by an element of Q) is matched by the same state on an incoming edge (represented by an element of $\overline{Q}$) and vice versa. For example, in the substring $in_\rho(v_1)\, lab(v_1)\, out_\rho(v_1)$ of $lin_{G,\rho,t}$, we must have that $in_\rho(v_1) = \varepsilon$, since v_1 must be a root of G and thus has no incoming edges. Let r_Q be the language $\{q\overline{q} \mid q \in Q\} \cup \Sigma$. Then $r_Q^{\odot}$ is the language over Γ such that for every $q \in Q$ and $w \in r_Q^{\odot}$, q and $\overline{q}$ appear the same number of times in w and every prefix of w contains at least as many instances of q as of $\overline{q}$.

We now argue that a string belongs to the language $r_A \cap r_Q^{\odot}$ if and only if it is a linearization of a run of A on some DAG. Consider a string $w = \alpha_1 \cdots \alpha_n \in \Gamma^*$. Let $O = \{i \in [n] \mid \alpha_i \in Q\}$ and $I = \{i \in [n] \mid \alpha_i \in \overline{Q}\}$. Then $w \in r_Q^{\odot}$ if and only if there exists a *matching*, i.e., a bijection $\mu \colon O \to I$ such that $\mu(i) > i$ and $\alpha_{\mu(i)} = \overline{\alpha_i}$ for all $i \in O$. This can be shown by a straightforward induction on n. With this in hand, for the "if" direction, a linearization will be in r_A by construction, and to demonstrate it is also in $r_Q^{\odot}$ a valid μ can be constructed along the edges of the DAG, as follows. By the definition of $lin_{G,\rho,t}$, if the topological sorting t of V is $v_1, \ldots, v_m$, then $w = w_1 \cdots w_m$ where $w_j = in_\rho(v_j)\, lab(v_j)\, out_\rho(v_j)$. Thus, every edge $e \in E$ leading from v_ℓ to $v_{\ell'}$ gives rise to an occurrence of $\rho(e)$ in w_ℓ and a corresponding occurrence of $\overline{\rho(e)}$ in $w_{\ell'}$. Let $i \in O$ and $i' \in I$ be the positions of these two occurrences in w, and define $\mu(i) = i'$. Since $\ell' > \ell$ we have $i' > i$, which means that μ is a matching because it is bijective by construction, and $\alpha_{\mu(i)} = \alpha_{i'} = \overline{\rho(e)} = \overline{\alpha_i}$.

For the "only if" direction one can similarly pick a matching μ (which exists as the string is in $r_Q^\odot$), and use the related positions as edges (each rule position forming one vertex), which produces a graph in L. More precisely, note first that $w = \alpha_1 \cdots \alpha_n \in r_A$ can uniquely be decomposed into $w = w_1 \cdots w_m$ such that $w_j \in string(R)$ for all $j \in [m]$. Define $V = \{v_1, \ldots, v_m\}$ and let $lab(v_j)$ be the label in w_j, for $j \in [m]$. To define the edges, assume in addition that $w \in r_Q^\odot$ and let $\mu\colon O \to I$ be a corresponding matching. Then we define $E = \{e_i \mid i \in O\}$. Moreover, if $w_j = p_1 \cdots p_r \sigma \overline{q}_1 \cdots \overline{q}_s$, $c = |w_1 \cdots w_{j-1}|$, and $d = |w_1 \cdots w_j|$, then

$$
\begin{aligned}
out(v_j) &= e_{d-s} \cdots e_{d-1} \\
in(v_j) &= e_{\mu^{-1}(c+1)} \cdots e_{\mu^{-1}(c+r)}.
\end{aligned}
$$

Since $\mu(i) > i$ for all $i \in O$, this defines a DAG, and by construction defining $\rho(e_i) = \alpha_i$ for all $i \in O$ yields a run of A on $G = (V, E, in, out, lab)$.

The next step is to note that $\psi(r_A \cap r_Q^\odot)$ is a semilinear set. We know that r_A is regular and thus that $\psi(r_A)$ is semilinear (Parikh, 1961). Also, r_Q^* is regular and $\psi(r_Q^\odot) = \psi(r_Q^*)$, which shows that $\psi(r_Q^\odot)$ is semilinear. This means that $\psi(r_A \cap r_Q^\odot)$ is semilinear since the semilinear sets are closed under intersection.

Finally, to complete the proof, since the semilinear sets are closed under projection to any subset of their dimensions, $\psi(L)$, which is the projection of $\psi(r_A \cap r_Q^\odot)$ onto the dimensions which correspond to Σ, is semilinear. $\qquad\square$

The following corollary is obtained by combining the above with an observation in (Drewes, 2017) that states that $\psi(L_u)$ is semilinear whenever $\psi(L)$ is.

Corollary 1. *For every regular DAG language L, the set $\psi(L_u)$ is semilinear.*

The semilinearity of the Parikh image also gives us the following decidability result.

Corollary 2. *Given a DAG automaton A, it is decidable whether $\mathcal{L}(A)_u$ is finite.*

Proof. Let $R_{\text{root}} = \{(\alpha \overset{\sigma}{\leftrightarrow} \beta) \in R \mid \alpha = \varepsilon\}$ and $R_{\text{non-root}} = R \setminus R_{\text{root}}$. By replacing the regular language r_A in the proof of Theorem 1 by $R_{\text{root}} R_{\text{non-root}}^*$ one ensures that only runs on DAGs with exactly one root are considered. Since both

intersection and projection are effective for semilinear sets, this gives us a way of effectively constructing the set $\psi(\mathcal{L}(A)_u)$. Since finiteness for semilinear sets is trivially decidable, the indicated result follows directly. $\qquad\square$

4 Path languages

As seen in the proof of Theorem 1 above, the single-rooted regular DAG languages are intimately connected with string languages of the form $L \cap K^\odot$, where L and K are regular. These, in turn, are closely connected to multicounter automata, as shown by the following result, essentially due to Gisher (1981), explicitly stated, e.g., in (Björklund and Bojańczyk, 2007).

Theorem 2. *The following language classes are equal, modulo morphisms.*

1. *Languages recognized by multicounter automata.*

2. *Languages of the form $L \cap K^\odot$, where L and K are regular.*

The statement remains valid if the language K is required to be finite.

To be precise, every language in class 2 also belongs to class 1 and every language in class 1 is the morphic image of a language in class 2. When representing the language of a multicounter automaton as a language from class 2, we sometimes need to include some bookkeeping that represents the counter configurations. This bookkeeping can then be erased by a morphism.

Example 1. Consider the multicounter automaton at the top of Figure 1. The automaton has two counters. When the symbol (is read, counter one is increased by one. When [is read, counter two is increased by one. Conversely, when the symbol) or] is read, the respective counter is decreased by one. If there were only one state, and only these transitions, the automaton would accept the shuffle of the Dyck language over (and) and the Dyck language over [and]. The final ϵ-transition, however, first decreases counter two by one and then increases it by one, in effect ensuring that its value is not zero. This means that the language accepted by the automaton is the shuffle of the two Dyck languages, but with the restriction that an open (can be closed by) only if at least one [is still open.

In order to form a language of class 2 that captures the same behavior, we introduce the four new

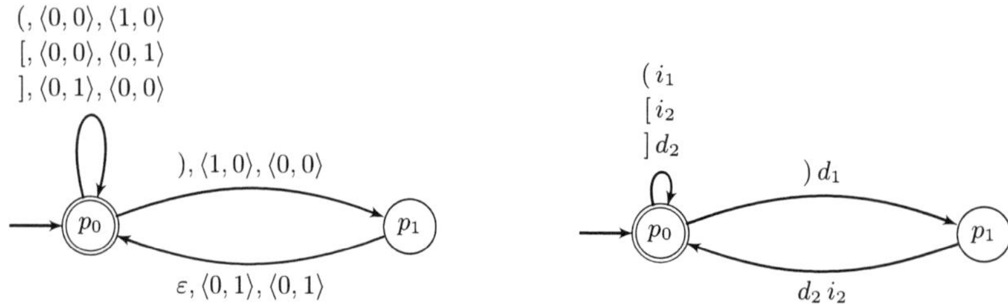

Figure 1: The multicounter automaton (with its counter operations indicated in brackets) and the corresponding finite automaton from Example 1.

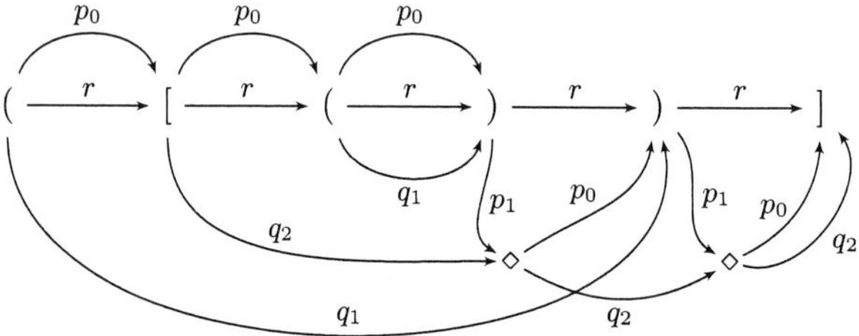

Figure 2: An example DAG of the form recognized by so-called special DAG automata. Its *main path*, consisting of the edges labeled with state r, corresponds to the input string processed by the multicounter automaton in Figure 1. The relationship will be formalized in Definition 4 and Lemma 2 (though for technical reasons we will require M to have dedicated initial and final states). Edges labeled with states q_1 and q_2 mimic counter actions. For example, an outgoing q_1 edge mimics incrementing counter 1 by 1, whereas an incoming q_1 edge decrements counter 1 by 1. The (off the main path) diamonds correspond to uses of the ε-transition from p_0 to p_1.

alphabet symbols i_1, i_2, d_1, d_2, representing increases and decreases to counters 1 and 2. The automaton to the right in Figure 1 reads an increase or decrease symbol each time it reads a parenthesis symbol. (Here, we let each transition read a string of symbols. The automaton can easily be transformed into a standard finite automaton by adding intermediate states.) Additionally, after reading a) with its corresponding d_1, it reads first a d_2 and then an i_2. Let L be the language accepted by this finite automaton, $K = \{(\,),[\,],i_1d_1,i_2d_2\}$, and h the morphism that is the identity on the four parenthesis symbols while simply erasing the increase and decrease symbols. Then $h(L \cap K^{\odot})$ is the language of the original multicounter automaton.

Let us now turn to the connection between path languages and multicounter automata. A path $v_0e_1v_1e_2\cdots v_n$ in a DAG is a *full path* if v_0 is a root and v_n is a leaf. The string corresponding to a path $v_0e_1v_1e_2\cdots v_n$ is $lab(v_0\cdots v_n)$. Given a DAG G and an alphabet Σ, we write $\pi_\Sigma(G)$ for the set of all strings in Σ^* corresponding to full paths in G. For a DAG language L, $\pi_\Sigma(L)$ is the set $\{\pi_\Sigma(G) \mid G \in L\}$.

As the main result of this section (stated formally in Theorem 3 below), we want to prove that the languages $\pi_\Sigma(\mathcal{L}(A)_u)$ for DAG automata A are exactly the languages $\mathcal{L}(M) \setminus \{\varepsilon\}$ accepted by multicounter automata M. For this, we show first that A can be brought into a special form which accepts only DAGs which contain a unique "main" path labeled with a string accepted by M, with nodes not on this path used for bookkeeping and corresponding to ε transitions in M. An example graph which is consistent with this form is previewed in Figure 2.

For the remainder of this section, fix an alphabet Σ, and let $\Sigma_\diamond = \Sigma \cup \{\diamond\}$ where $\diamond$ is a special symbol not in Σ. A DAG $G = (V, E, in, out, lab)$ over $\Sigma_\diamond$ is *special* if it has a unique full path with all node labels in Σ and all nodes not on this path are labeled $\diamond$. We call this path the *main path* of G. Consider a DAG automaton $A = (\{r\} \cup P \cup Q, \Sigma_\diamond, R)$, where $P \cap Q =$

$\{r\} \cap (P \cup Q) = \emptyset$. The DAG automaton A is *special* if all rules $\alpha \overset{\sigma}{\leftrightarrow} \beta$ are such that either $\alpha, \beta \in rPQ^* \cup \{\varepsilon\}$ and $\sigma \in \Sigma$ or $\alpha, \beta \in PQ^*$ and $\sigma = \diamond$. We call rules of the former kind *path-generating rules* and those of the latter kind *book-keeping rules*. Note that special DAG automata recognize languages of special DAGs. A run of such a DAG automaton assigns state r to the edges on the path whose nodes carry labels in Σ (the leftmost path) while all other nodes are labeled by $\diamond$.

Lemma 1. *Let $A = (Q, \Sigma, R)$ be a DAG automaton and $\Sigma_0 \subseteq \Sigma$. Then there is a special DAG automaton A' such that*

$$\pi_{\Sigma_0}(\mathcal{L}(A)_u) = \pi_{\Sigma}(\mathcal{L}(A')_u).$$

Proof. Let p, r be distinct states not in Q and define $P = \{p\}$. Let $h \colon \{r, p\} \cup Q \to Q$ be the homomorphism such that $h(q) = q$ for all $q \in Q$ and $h(r) = h(p) = \varepsilon$. Let R' be defined as follows: for every rule $\alpha \overset{\sigma}{\leftrightarrow} \beta$ in R, R' contains the bookkeeping rule $p\alpha \overset{\diamond}{\leftrightarrow} p\beta$. If $\sigma \in \Sigma_0$, then R' furthermore contains all path-generating rules $\alpha' \overset{\sigma}{\leftrightarrow} \beta'$ such that $h(\alpha') = \alpha$, and $h(\beta') = \beta$. If a bookkeeping rule obtained from $\alpha \overset{\sigma}{\leftrightarrow} \beta$ is applied in a run, we say that the label $\diamond$ of the corresponding node is a *hidden* σ.

By construction $A' = (\{r\} \cup P \cup Q, \Sigma_\diamond, R')$ is special. To see that $\pi_{\Sigma_0}(\mathcal{L}(A)_u) = \pi_{\Sigma}(\mathcal{L}(A')_u)$, we consider the two inclusions. Clearly, if ρ is a run of A' on a special DAG G' with $\pi_{\Sigma}(G') = \{w\}$, then $w \in \Sigma_0^*$ and by deleting all edges with states r or p and replacing every hidden σ by σ we obtain a run of A on a DAG G with $w \in \pi_{\Sigma_0}(G)$.

For the other direction, consider a DAG $G = (V, E, in, out, lab) \in \mathcal{L}(A)_u$ with an accepting run ρ and let $v_0 e_1 v_2 e_2 \cdots v_m$ be a full path with $lab(v_0 \cdots v_m) \in \Sigma_0^*$. Let $u_0, \ldots, u_n$ be a topological sorting of V such that $u_n = v_m$ (and $u_0 = v_0$ because v_0 is the unique root). We define a DAG G' by adding fresh edges $e_1, \ldots, e_n, e_1', \ldots, e_m'$ as follows:

- e_i ($i \in [n]$) is added as the first outgoing edge of u_{i-1} and the first incoming edge of u_i, and

- afterwards, e_j' ($j \in [m]$) is added as the first outgoing edge of v_{j-1} and the first incoming edge of v_j.

Finally, the labels of all nodes not in $\{v_0, \ldots, v_m\}$ are replaced by $\diamond$. Now ρ can be extended to a run ρ' on G' by defining $\rho'(e_i) = p$ and $\rho'(e_j') = r$ for all $i \in [n], j \in [m]$. $\qquad\square$

Next, we define the notion of *relatedness* between a (special) DAG automaton A with states in $\{r\} \cup P \cup Q$ and a multicounter automaton M with states in $P \cup \{q_0, q_f\}$. Each state in Q corresponds to a counter of M. Viewing a run of A as a top-down computation, the counter actions of m keep track of how many copies of each $q \in Q$ there are at the frontier of the computation. A path-generating rule $rpw \overset{\sigma}{\leftrightarrow} rp'w'$ of A relates to a transition of M that reads σ in state p and continues in state p'. The counter actions reflect how many times each state in Q occurs in w and w'. For example, the rule $rpq_1q_3q_1 \overset{\sigma}{\leftrightarrow} rp'q_1q_2$ would correspond to a transition from p to p' reading σ, with counter actions given by the vectors $(2, 0, 1)$ and $(1, 1, 0)$ (assuming that $Q = \{q_1, q_2, q_3\}$ and position i in the vectors corresponds to q_i). bookkeeping rules of A relate to ε-transitions of M in a similar way.

Definition 4. Let $A = (\{r\} \cup P \cup Q, \Sigma_\diamond, R)$ be a special DAG automaton and $M = (Q', \Sigma, m, \delta, q_0, \{q_f\})$ a multicounter automaton, where $Q = \{q_1, \ldots, q_m\}$ and $Q' = P \cup \{q_0, q_f\}$ with $q_0 \neq q_f$ and $\{q_0, q_f\} \cap P = \emptyset$.

Let ψ be the Parikh mapping associated with Q. A rule $\alpha \overset{\sigma}{\leftrightarrow} \beta$ in R and a transition (p, σ, D, I, p') in δ are *related* if the following hold:

If $\alpha \overset{\sigma}{\leftrightarrow} \beta$ is path-generating then $\sigma \in \Sigma$ and

- p is the unique state in P that occurs in α unless $\alpha = \varepsilon$ and $p = q_0$,

- p' is the unique state in P that occurs in β unless $\beta = \varepsilon$ and $p' = q_f$, and

- $D = \psi(h(\alpha))$ and $I = \psi(h(\beta))$.

If $\alpha \overset{\sigma}{\leftrightarrow} \beta$ is bookkeeping then $\sigma = \varepsilon$ and

- p and p' are the unique states in P that occur in α and β, respectively, and

- $D = \psi(h(\alpha))$ and $I = \psi(h(\beta))$.

A and M are related if for every rule in R there is a related transition in M and vice versa.

Note that relatedness between rules is injective in both directions. Thus, for every special DAG automaton A a related multicounter automaton M can be constructed, and the converse holds as well provided that the initial state of M has no incoming transitions, there is a single final state that has no outgoing transitions, and no initial or final transition is an ε-transition.

To simplify the technicalities of the proof of the next lemma, let us say that a *partial DAG* (pDAG, for short) is defined just like a DAG $G = (V, E, in, out, lab)$, except that $in^{-1}(e)$ may be empty for some edges $e \in E$, i.e., those edges are "dangling" without a target. A run of a DAG automaton on a pDAG is defined exactly as a run on a DAG. The notion of special DAGs carries over to the partial case in the obvious way.

Lemma 2. *If a special DAG automaton A and a multicounter automaton M are related, then $\mathcal{L}(M) = \pi_\Sigma(\mathcal{L}(A)_u)$.*

Proof. Let A, M, ψ, and h be as above. Note that each tuple in $\mathbb{N}^m$ can be seen as an assignment of values to the counters of M. Moreover, given a run ρ on a pDAG G and a subset $D = \{e_1, \dots, e_\ell\}$ of the set of edges of G, we let $\psi_\rho(D) = \psi(h(\rho(e_1) \cdots \rho(e_\ell)))$.

For the inclusion $\mathcal{L}(M) \subseteq \pi_\Sigma(\mathcal{L}(A)_u)$, let $t_1, \dots, t_{n+1} \in \delta$ be a sequence of transitions by which M accepts a string w. If $w = \sigma \in \Sigma$ then $t_1 = (q_0, \sigma, 0^m, 0^m, q_f)$ and R contains the path-generating rule $\varepsilon \overset{\sigma}{\leftrightarrow} \varepsilon$, thus accepting the DAG consisting of a single node labeled σ. Assume therefore that $n \geq 1$. We inductively construct runs $\rho_1, \dots, \rho_n$ on single-rooted pDAGs $G_1, \dots, G_n$ such that the following hold when M has executed transition t_ℓ ($\ell \in [n]$), where D_ℓ is the set of dangling edges of G_ℓ:

(i) D_ℓ contains exactly one edge with label r and exactly one edge e_ℓ with a label in P.

(ii) the counters of M store $\psi_{\rho_\ell}(D_\ell)$, and

(iii) the prefix v of w read by M so far labels the main path in G_ℓ, and $\rho_\ell(e_\ell)$ is the current state of M.

Transition t_1 is of the form $t_1 = (q_0, \sigma, 0^m, I, p)$, which means that R contains a path-generating rule $\varepsilon \overset{\sigma}{\leftrightarrow} rp\alpha$ with $\psi(\alpha) = I$. Choosing G_1 to be the single-node pDAG to which this rule applies, and defining ρ_1 accordingly, obviously satisfies (i)–(iii). For $\ell > 1$, assume that $G_{\ell-1}$ and $\rho_{\ell-1}$ have been constructed.

There are two cases. If $t_\ell = (p, \sigma, D, I, p')$ (with $p, p' \in P$) then it is related to a path-generating rule $rp\alpha \overset{\sigma}{\leftrightarrow} rp'\beta$ in R, and by the induction hypothesis $\psi_{\rho_{\ell-1}}(D_{\ell-1}) \geq D$. Hence we can construct G_ℓ from $G_{\ell-1}$ by taking any sequence $s \in D_{\ell-1}$ of pairwise distinct edges such

that $\rho_{\ell-1}(s) = rp\alpha$, and adding a fresh node v labeled σ with $in(v) = s$. Further, add $|\beta| + 2$ dangling outgoing edges to v, and let ρ_ℓ be the extension of $\rho_{\ell-1}$ obtained by setting $\rho_\ell(out(v)) = rp'\beta$. Clearly, this satisfies (i)–(iii) with e_ℓ being the second outgoing edge of v. The case where $t_\ell = (p, \varepsilon, D, I, p')$ is is similar, except that the rule in R to which it is related is a bookkeeping rule, and thus the label of v is $\diamond$ and it lacks incoming and outgoing edges whose state is r. Again, (i)–(iii) are clearly satisfied.

Thus we have shown that G_n satisfies (i)–(iii). We also know that $t_{n+1} = (p, \sigma, D, 0^m, q_f)$ and is thus related to a path-generating rule $rp\alpha \overset{\sigma}{\leftrightarrow} \varepsilon$. Constructing G_{n+1} similarly to the path-generating case above, but the outgoing dangling edge thus ensures that G_{n+1} contains a path labeled w from the root to the newly added node, which is a leaf. Note that G_{n+1} does not contain any dangling edges because M accepts only with all counters zero. Consequently, $G_{n+1} \in \mathcal{L}(A)_u$ and thus $w \in \pi_\Sigma(\mathcal{L}(A)_u)$.

For the other inclusion, note that every run ρ on a DAG G with $n+1$ nodes $v_1, \dots, v_{n+1}$ arranged in topological order can be decomposed into runs $\rho_1, \dots, \rho_{n+1}$ on pDAGs $G_1, \dots, G_{n+1}$ such that G_ℓ is the restriction of G to $v_1, \dots, v_\ell$ and their outgoing edges, and ρ_ℓ is the restriction of ρ to G_ℓ. Now, given a root-to-leaf path in G labeled w it should be clear how transitions $t_1, \dots, t_{n+1}$ related to the rules in R applied to $v_1, \dots, v_\ell$ can be chosen to mirror the arguments above, yielding a computation of M that accepts w. $\qquad \square$

Theorem 3. *A string language $L \subseteq \Sigma^* \setminus \{\varepsilon\}$ can be recognized by a multicounter automaton M if and only if $L = \pi_\Sigma(L_u)$ for a regular DAG language L.*

Proof. By Lemmas 1 and 2 it suffices to show that L can be recognized by a multicounter automaton M' which is related to some special DAG automaton, i.e., the initial state of M' has no incoming transitions, there is a single final state that has no outgoing transitions, and no initial or final transition is an ε-transition. The first two requirements are easily ensured by adding two new states, an initial and a final one. Making sure that the third requirement is met is also a straightforward matter since $\varepsilon \notin L$. $\qquad \square$

The relationship between multicounter automata and path languages of single-rooted regular DAG languages thus resembles that between multicounter automata and languages of the form $L \cap K^\odot$. Theorem 3 shows that for every DAG automaton A, the language $\pi(\mathcal{L}(A)_u)$ can be recognized by a multicounter automaton, the other direction needs some bookkeeping that must be removed by intersecting $\pi(\mathcal{L}(A)_u)$ with Σ^*. In this direction, we also have to exclude the empty string as full paths in DAGs are always nonempty.

An interesting consequence of Theorem 3 is that the path languages of single-rooted regular DAG languages are orthogonal to the Chomsky hierarchy. While multicounter automata can recognize all regular languages and some languages that are not context-free, such as, e.g., $\{a^n b^n c^n \mid n \in \mathbb{N}\}$, they cannot recognize all context-free languages. For instance, they can recognize the language $\{a^n b^n \mid n \in \mathbb{N}\}$, but not its Kleene closure, which is also context-free (Greibach, 1978). While the multicounter languages are closed under union, intersection, concatenation, and shuffle, they are thus not closed under Kleene star; for details, see, e.g., (Priese and Wimmel, 2008). Their Parikh images are semilinear, which for example follows from Theorem 3.

5   Conclusions

To summarize, each of the open problems given in (Drewes, 2017) (and recalled in the introduction) has been solved. Corollaries 1 and 2 close problems 4 and 1 respectively. Problem 3 is closed by Theorem 3, directly relating the languages captured by multicounter automata to the path languages in question. For problem 2 the characterization by multicounter automata very naturally models the computational power of the formalism itself, but the language equivalence involves projecting away some bookkeeping information by intersection with Σ^*.

References

Laura Banarescu, Claire Bonial, Shu Cai, Madalina Georgescu, Kira Griffitt, Ulf Hermjakob, Kevin Knight, Philipp Koehn, Martha Palmer, and Nathan Schneider. 2013. Abstract meaning representation for sembanking. In *Proc. 7th Linguistic Annotation Workshop, ACL 2013 Workshop*.

Henrik Björklund and Mikołaj Bojańczyk. 2007. Shuffle expressions and words with nested data. In *Mathematical Foundations of Computer Science (MFCS)*. pages 750–761.

Johannes Blum and Frank Drewes. 2017. Language theoretic properties of regular DAG languages. *Information and Computation* (to appear).

David Chiang, Frank Drewes, Daniel Gildea, Adam Lopez, and Giorgio Satta. 2016. Weighted DAG automata for semantic graphs. Unpublished manuscript.

Frank Drewes. 2017. On DAG languages and DAG transducers. *Bulletin of the EATCS* 121.

Seymour Ginsburg and Edwin H. Spanier. 1964. Bounded Algol-like languages. *Transactions of the American Mathematical Society* 113(2):333–368.

Jay Gisher. 1981. Shuffle languages, petri nets, and context-sensitive grammars. *Communications of the ACM* 24(9):597–605.

Sheila A. Greibach. 1978. Remarks on blind and partially blind one-way multicounter machines. *Theoretical Computer Science* 7:311–324.

S. Rao Kosaraju. 1982. Decidability of reachability in vector addition systems. In *ACM Symposium on Theory of Computing (STOC)*. pages 267–281.

Ernst W. Mayr. 1984. An algorithm for the general Petri net reachability problem. *SIAM Journal on Computing* 13(3):441–460.

Rohit J. Parikh. 1961. Language generating devices. Quarterly Progress Report 60, M.I.T.

Lutz Priese and Harro Wimmel. 2008. *Petri-Netze*, Springer, chapter Petri-Netz-Sprachen. 2nd edition.

Contextual Hyperedge Replacement Grammars for Abstract Meaning Representations

Frank Drewes
Umeå University
drewes@cs.umu.se

Anna Jonsson
Umeå University
aj@cs.umu.se

Abstract

We show how contextual hyperedge replacement grammars can be used to generate abstract meaning representations (AMRs), and argue that they are more suitable for this purpose than hyperedge replacement grammars. Contextual hyperedge replacement turns out to have two advantages over plain hyperedge replacement: it can completely cover the language of all AMRs over a given domain of concepts, and at the same time its grammars become both smaller and simpler.

1 Introduction

Natural language processing applications that receive sentences as input mainly make use of lexical and syntactic properties of the input sentences. Even though these properties are an important basis for the analysis of a sentence, one is usually more interested in the meaning of a sentence, i.e., its semantics. This is particularly true in the case of machine translation where a semantic error can cause far more bewilderment than a syntactic one.

Thus, a general-purpose formalism for modelling the semantics of sentences in a way that allows for efficient analysis would be widely useful in natural language processing. This study focuses on the generation of a semantic representation that was proposed some years ago, the abstract meaning representation (AMR) (Langkilde and Knight, 1998; Banarescu et al., 2013). An AMR[1] is a directed, rooted, acyclic, node- and edge-labelled graph that represents the se-

mantics of an English sentence[2]; the nodes and edges represent concepts and their relations, respectively. A corpus of AMRs over a limited domain can be found in (Braune et al., 2014). As in the case of syntax trees, where tree grammars and tree automata (Knight and Graehl, 2005) provide a model for distinguishing structurally correct trees from incorrect ones, the algorithmic processing of AMRs would benefit from the existence of appropriate formal models for their generation or recognition. Here, we focus on the generation of AMRs by graph grammars, which have previously been proposed as formal models for this very task (Chiang et al., 2013).

The usefulness of two types of hyperedge replacement grammar (HRG, see Habel (1992); Drewes et al. (1997)) for AMR generation was investigated by Jonsson (2016a) (see also (Jonsson, 2016b)), namely the predictive top-down (PTD) parsable grammar (Drewes et al., 2015) and the restricted directed acyclic graph (rDAG) grammar (Björklund et al., 2016). Both are of particular interest because their study was, among other possible application areas, motivated by AMR generation. A specific advantage of these special cases of HRGs is that their membership problem is solvable in polynomial time. However, Jonsson (2016a) concludes that neither of them is able to generate the complete set of AMRs over a given concept domain.

Unrestricted HRGs allow for better coverage at the expense of greater computational complexity. However, a general disadvantage of hyperedge replacement remains. The nonterminal items in an HRG are hyperedges – edges that may be attached to more (or fewer) than two nodes. Replacement of a hyperedge inserts a new subgraph in its place,

---

[1] We use the term AMR to refer not only to the concept of Abstract Meaning Representation as such (Langkilde and Knight, 1998; Banarescu et al., 2013), but also to its individual graphs.

[2] Although AMR is to some extent language independent, it is biased towards English (Banarescu et al., 2013), and therefore not truly an interlingua (Xue et al., 2014).

Proceedings of the 13th International Workshop on Tree Adjoining Grammars and Related Formalisms (TAG+13), pages 102–111,
Umeå, Sweden, September 4–6, 2017. © 2017 Association for Computational Linguistics

connecting it to the host graph via the nodes the replaced hyperedge was incident on. Intuitively, nonterminal hyperedges keep track of a number of potentially relevant nodes for the purpose of being able to attach new edges to them later on in the derivation. This process is well known (and easily seen) to generate graph languages of bounded treewidth. As shall be illustrated in Section 6 the ability of hyperedges to keep track of a bounded number of previously generated nodes can be used to ensure structural properties such as those caused by control verbs. However, it appears that other types of reentrancies, like those arising from the use of pronouns, are of a different nature. If, for example, several instances of the concept `boy` have been generated, any of them can in principle be referred to from anywhere else in the AMR. As a consequence, there is no reasonable a priori bound on the treewidth of the graph. Nonterminal hyperedges generating other parts of the AMR would have to keep track of all `boy` instances to accomplish full coverage. On the one hand, this is not possible in an HRG. On the other hand, it does not seem to be desirable either, because keeping track of every `boy` instance individually would enable a level of control far beyond what is needed.

Here we consider contextual hyperedge replacement grammars (CHRGs) (Drewes et al., 2012; Drewes and Hoffmann, 2015) to learn whether they can be used to overcome these disadvantages. CHRGs are also based on hyperedge replacement, but the left-hand side of a rule can contain so-called contextual nodes. This provides access to nodes other than those immediately controlled by the nonterminal hyperedge, thus enabling rules to establish connections of the type discussed in the previous paragraph. The additional ability is severely limited, far below true context-sensitivity in power, because nodes are terminal items and derivation steps cannot distinguish between contextual nodes with the same label. For instance, in the situation sketched above a rule application would just pick *any* occurrence of `boy` elsewhere in the host graph. As a consequence, however, the treewidth of generated graphs is not necessarily bounded anymore.

In the present paper we study and illustrate the advantages of CHRGs over HRGs for AMR generation by looking at an example concept domain in a theoretical case study. To this end, we build a CHRG that generates AMRs over a restricted domain and argue that it exhibits perfect coverage. The baseline domain is the one introduced by Braune et al. (2014), consisting of the concepts `boy`, `girl`, `want` and `believe` along with two basic relations (called `arg0` and `arg1`) that are used to bind the concepts together and correspond to the agent and patient of a `want` or `believe` event. We also consider the construction of CHRGs for more general AMRs to explore the advantages of the more generous rule format. Therefore we add a small set of possible modifiers, allow an arbitrary number of boys and girls to appear in an AMR,[3] and discuss how to handle control verbs.

The conclusion of our study is that contextual hyperedge replacement is indeed a promising formalism for describing sets of AMRs. On the one hand, AMRs contain the mentioned local structures that must satisfy certain well-formedness constraints, such as in the case of control verbs. This can be implemented like it would in an HRG, using a nonterminal hyperedge to keep track of the involved nodes. On the other hand, contextual nodes can be used to implement the kinds of coreferences which may occur anywhere without following strict local rules, such as those relating to the use of pronouns. As discussed above, the latter creates problems in HRGs because nonterminal hyperedges would have to keep track of potential antecedents, which seems inappropriate for various reasons: it is restricted by the rank of hyperedges, provides an unnecessarily detailed level of control (thus creating the risk of overfitting), and leads to a huge number of rules to account explicitly for all the possible nondeterministic choices arising from the (exponentially) many ways in which coreferences can be inserted.

The obvious downside of using CHRGs is that computational problems may potentially become more difficult. However, recent results on shift-reduce parsing for both HRGs and CHRGs (Drewes et al., 2017)[4] indicate that this may not be the case. In fact, as the rank of hyperedges and the number of rules are central parameters in the complexity of membership algorithms for both unrestricted HRGs and CHRGs, it may even pay off to turn to CHRGs since this leads to smaller ranks and much fewer rules, the latter

---

[3]Braune et al. (2014) only consider at most one boy and at most one girl.

[4]See `https://www.unibw.de/inf2/grappa/` for the extension to CHRGs.

because the use of contextual nodes removes the necessity to implement nondeterministic choices explicitly by creating a separate rule for each.

In Section 2, we lay the ground for the rest of the paper with some basic definitions. The CHRG is defined in Section 3, and the subset of AMR to be considered here is discussed in Section 4. The construction of a CHRG for this domain is described in Section 5. In Section 6, we indicate how to generalise it to larger domains, and in particular how control verbs can be added. Finally, the results are discussed in Section 7 followed by the conclusions and future work in Section 8.

Acknowledgement We thank the reviewers for useful comments that helped us clarify the line of argumentation (as we hope).

2 Preliminaries

For a set A, we write A^* to denote the set of finite sequences or strings over A, and $A^{\circledast}$ for the set of strings over A in which no element is repeated; ε denotes the empty sequence. Elements of A are identified with strings of length 1 over A, and thus subsets of A are string languages at the same time.

Furthermore, we let 2^A denote the power set of A, i.e., the set of all subsets of A. The extension of a function $f \colon A \to A'$ to sequences $a_1, \ldots, a_n$ where $a_i \in A$ for $0 \leq i \leq n$ is denoted $f^* \colon A^* \to A'^*$ and defined by $f^*(a_0, \ldots, a_n) = f(a_1) \cdots f(a_n)$. Concatenation of strings is denoted by simple juxtaposition, and element-wise concatenation of two string languages L, L' is denoted by $L \cdot L'$, i.e., $L \cdot L' = \{uv \mid u \in L, v \in L'\}$.

A *labelling alphabet* is a set Σ partitioned into three mutually disjoint sets Σ_V, Σ_E and Σ_N on which an *arity* function $arity \colon \Sigma_E \uplus \Sigma_N \to 2^{\Sigma_V^*}$ is defined. (See Section 5 for an example of an alphabet and its arity function.) The sets Σ_V, Σ_E and Σ_N are referred to as *node labels, (hyper)edge labels* and *nonterminal labels*, respectively.

A *hypergraph* is a generalisation of directed graphs by the usage of edges that can connect an arbitrary number of nodes. Here, we consider node- and edge-labelled hypergraphs.

Definition 1 (Hypergraph (Drewes et al., 2012)). *A labelled hypergraph (hypergraph, for short) over a labelling alphabet Σ is a tuple $G = (V, E, att, label_V, label_E)$ such that*

- *V is a finite set of* nodes.
- *E is a finite set of* hyperedges.
- *$att : E \to V^{\circledast}$ is the* attachment of hyperedges.
- *$label_V : V \to \Sigma_V$ is the* labelling of nodes.
- *$label_E : E \to \Sigma_E \cup \Sigma_N$ with $label_V^*(att(e)) \in arity(label_E(e))$ for all $e \in E$ is the* labelling of hyperedges.[5]

The *rank* of a hyperedge e is $|arity(label_E(e))|$. Hyperedges with labels in Σ_N are called *nonterminals*; $\mathcal{G}_\Sigma$ denotes the set of all hypergraphs over Σ. For a hypergraph G and a hyperedge $e \in E$, the hypergraph resulting from removing e from G is denoted by $G - e$. The empty hypergraph is denoted by $()$.

In illustrations, nodes and hyperedges are drawn as ellipses and squares, respectively, with inscribed labels. The attachment of a hyperedge is shown by lines, and the attachment order is depicted using numbers (these can be left out if the attachment order is clear from the context or irrelevant). If a hyperedge connects exactly two nodes (i.e., it is binary), it can be drawn as an arrow directed from the first node of the attachment to the second with its label next to it. See Section 5 for various examples of hypergraphs. Note that a hypergraph containing only binary hyperedges is equivalent to an ordinary directed graph; this is the case in e.g. Figure 1.

3 Contextual Hyperedge Replacement

Given a hypergraph containing nonterminals, rules can be applied to it in order to generate a new hypergraph. A set of such rules along with a fixed hypergraph to which they are to be applied forms a grammar. The grammar type considered here was proposed in (Drewes et al., 2012; Drewes and Hoffmann, 2015) and uses the following rule type.

Definition 2 (Contextual Rule). *A contextual hyperedge replacement rule (or contextual rule) is a pair (L, R) where L and R are hypergraphs over the labelling alphabet Σ such that*

- *L (the left-hand side) contains exactly one hyperedge e that must be a nonterminal, and*
- *R (the right-hand side) is an arbitrary supergraph of $L - e$.*

A contextual rule for which all nodes in the left-hand side are connected to e is called *context-free*. The nodes that are not connected to e are referred to as *contextual nodes*.

---

[5]The arity function used differs from the one in (Drewes et al., 2012), but the resulting hypergraph definition remains the same.

We denote a contextual rule by letting ::= separate the left- and right-hand sides. Moreover, we allow rules that share the same left-hand side to be drawn more compactly; in this case, the left-hand side is only drawn once, and a vertical line is used to separate the right-hand sides from each other. To save further space, we use rule schemata in which labels may be variables ranging over a specified subset of the set of all labels. As an example of a set of contextual rules, consider the rules in (iii) in Figure 4 of Section 5. Every choice of z, u, v and a_1, a_2 in the range specified beneath the rules yields three rules. Each has the nonterminal N_1 in its left-hand side, and the node labelled u is a contextual node. In addition, the third right-hand side contains a newly generated node labelled v.

A contextual rule (L, R) can be applied to a hypergraph G containing an isomorphic copy of L, i.e., a subgraph that is equal to L up to renaming of nodes and hyperedges. Suppose for simplicity that L is a subgraph of G. Then the application of the rule works in the following manner:

1. Remove e from G, yielding $G - e$.
2. Add R to $G - e$, disjointly.
3. Identify the nodes in $L - e$ with the corresponding nodes in R.

The resulting hypergraph is denoted by $G[R/e]$. Now, we can formally define the grammar type that makes use of contextual rules.

Definition 3 (Contextual Hyperedge Replacement). *A contextual hyperedge replacement grammar (CHRG) is a triple* $\Gamma = (\Sigma, \mathcal{R}, Z)$ *where*
- Σ *is a finite labelling alphabet,*
- $\mathcal{R}$ *is a finite set of contextual rules, and*
- $Z \in \mathcal{G}_\Sigma$ *is a start hypergraph.*

If $G' = G[R/e]$ for some contextual rule $(L, R) \in \mathcal{R}$, we say that G' is *derived* from G in Γ, and we write $G \Rightarrow_\mathcal{R} G'$. The language generated by Γ is $\mathcal{L}(\Gamma) = \{G \in \mathcal{G}_{\Sigma \setminus N} \mid Z \Rightarrow_\mathcal{R}^* G\}$ where $\Rightarrow^*$ is the reflective and transitive closure of $\Rightarrow$. Two CHRGs Γ_1 and Γ_2 are *equivalent* if $\mathcal{L}(\Gamma_1) = \mathcal{L}(\Gamma_2)$, i.e., if they generate the same language. If all of the rules of Γ are context-free, then Γ is a *hyperedge replacement grammar* (HRG). Thus, CHRG is a generalisation of HRG through the extension of context-free rules to contextual rules. Intuitively, the difference between the two is that CHRGs can nondeterministically pick a previously generated node with a specified label without that node being connected to the replaced nonterminal. HRGs do not have this ability.

The graph languages generated by CHRGs are in NP (Drewes and Hoffmann, 2015), and can thus be NP-complete, as this already holds for HRGs. Hence, unless P = NP there are CHRGs which do not admit a polynomial membership test. For HRGs, there exist polynomial membership algorithms for nontrivial special cases such as PTD parsable, shift-reduce parsable, and rDAG HRGs. The fact that membership testing is not harder for CHRG than for HRG (at least in theory) strengthens the hope that there are subclasses of CHRG with efficient membership tests. Indeed, this has partially been confirmed: the membership algorithms for PTD and shift-reduce parsable HRGs can be extended to CHRGs.[4]

4 Abstract Meaning Representation

Abstract meaning representation (AMR) (Langkilde and Knight, 1998; Banarescu et al., 2013) denotes sentence meaning as directed, rooted, acyclic graphs with node and edge labels. To the extent possible, AMR aims to provide a unique representation of semantics, i.e., while numerous sentences can express the same meaning, they should all map to the same AMR. The idea is that the nodes of the graph represent the concepts identifiable in the sentence, and the edges represent the relations between the concepts. Intuitively, the subgraph rooted at any one given node represents an event, a fact, or an entity. See Figure 1 for example AMRs that can be realised into the English sentences "The boy wants the girl to believe him" or "[...] to believe the other boy."

The previous example highlights that every event or entity represented in an AMR should occur once and only once. In fact, this is the major difference between AMRs and syntax trees, in which several subtrees may refer to the same semantic thing. In the second AMR in Figure 1, the fact that the wantee is not represented by the same node as the believee implies that these two are distinct. Representing the first sentence by the second AMR (or the second one by the first) is an error.

Thus, to achieve complete coverage, a grammar for generating AMRs over the given domain must generate both graphs in Figure 1. Figures 2 and 3 show another pair of AMRs, of which the former correctly represents the semantics of the sentence "The boy wants the girl to believe in herself and this is what the girl wants, too." The interpretation of the latter is less obvious. We do not endeav-

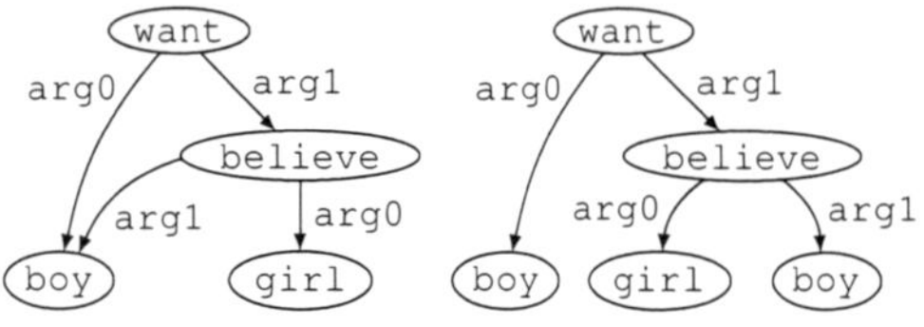

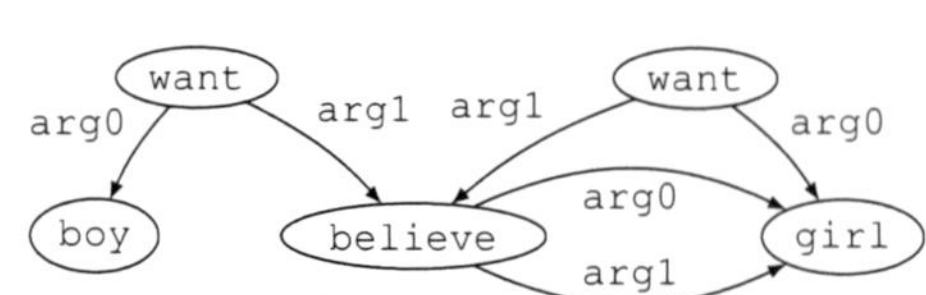

Figure 2: Another AMR.

Figure 1: AMRs representing an event want, where the wanter is a boy and the wantee is the event believe for which the believer is a girl and the believee is either the formerly mentioned boy (left) or a different one (right).

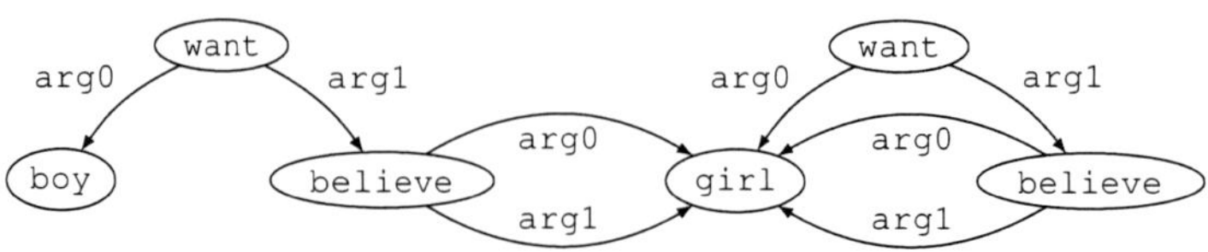

Figure 3: An AMR similar to the one in Figure 2, but with two distinct believe events.

our to discuss whether this AMR is meaningful at all, but it certainly seems to be less probable. Unfortunately, it turns out that structures such as the one in Figure 3 are easy to generate by a HRG and even by the aforementioned PTD parsable HRGs, whereas trying to include the more desirable one in Figure 2 meets severe difficulties. This is an instance of the problems mentioned in the introduction: a HRG generating structures like the one in Figure 2 (even one that is not PTD parsable) would have to generate the believe node early on and then keep track of it in its nonterminal hyperedges to establish the desired relations later on, when the two want nodes are generated.[6] The nondeterministic choices this creates seem to destroy PTD parsability. Further, even if PTD parsability is abandoned in favour of generative power, the desired effect can only be approximated: as the number of believe nodes grows, it eventually exceeds the number of nodes that the nonterminal hyperedges have been designed to keep track of.

4.1 The Boy-Girl AMR Corpus

The *boy-girl AMR corpus* is a set of 10 000 AMRs over a restricted domain that was presented in (Braune et al., 2014). Each AMR of this corpus fulfils the following conditions:

- The node label alphabet consists of the concept names boy, girl, want, and believe.

---

[6]This assumes for simplicity that a bottom-up generation strategy is employed. However, the difficulties arising depend only marginally on the choice of strategy.

- The edge label alphabet consists of the relation names arg0 and arg1.
- The node labels boy and girl occur at most once each, and label the leaves of the graph.
- For each want and believe node, the outgoing edges carry distinct labels and all incoming edges are labelled arg1.

The relation arg0 is used for marking the agent of an action expressed by a concept in the form of a verb, and the patient of the same action is given by the concept pointed to by arg1. The above restrictions simply give us the domain and tell us that a person cannot be used as a verb, and that verbs cannot be agents, but that an event (a subgraph with a verb concept as root) can act as a patient. The left AMR in Figure 1 is a boy-girl AMR, whereas the left one is not, as it contains two copies of boy.

To make things more interesting, we remove the restriction that there can only be one girl and one boy, and extend the concept domain by months, weekdays and the words happy and angry. Let Σ_V denote this extended domain. Finally, we add the relations manner, month and day, which together with arg0 and arg1 form Σ_E.

5 Construction of a Boy-Girl CHRG

Let us now discuss how to construct a CHRG that generates the complete language of boy-girl AMRs. The alphabet used is that of Section 4.1, enlarged by $\Sigma_N = \{S, N, N_1, M\}$ and with the arity function given as follows: for $A \in \Sigma_E$, $arity(A) = \{\texttt{want},\texttt{believe}\} \cdot TAR_A$ where

$$
\begin{aligned}
TAR_{\texttt{arg0}} &= \{\texttt{boy},\texttt{girl}\} \\
TAR_{\texttt{arg1}} &= \Sigma_V \setminus \{\texttt{happy},\texttt{angry}\} \\
TAR_{\texttt{manner}} &= \{\texttt{happy},\texttt{angry}\} \\
TAR_{\texttt{month}} &= \{\texttt{Jan},\ldots,\texttt{Dec}\} \\
TAR_{\texttt{day}} &= \{\texttt{Mon},\ldots,\texttt{Sun}\}.
\end{aligned}
$$

Furthermore, $arity(S) = arity(N) = \varepsilon$ and $arity(N_1) = arity(M) = \{\texttt{want},\texttt{believe}\}$. The start hypergraph Z consists of a single nonterminal labelled S. The rules of the boy-girl CHRG can be seen in Figure 4.

The initial rules of the grammar, the ones of schema (i), simply generate the first leaf of the graph. The rules of schema (ii) choose between terminating the derivation by generating the empty graph or continuing it by generating a non-leaf node. Schemata (iii) and (iv) connect the newly generated node with label z to at least one previously generated node. Moreover, these rules connect a nonterminal labelled M to the node, which makes it possible to add zero or more outgoing $\texttt{manner}$ edges from the node currently being handled to suitable (new) leaves. In addition, at most one $\texttt{month}$ and one $\texttt{day}$ edge can be generated, and the latter only in connection with the former. We note here that these restrictions are not intended to be semantically particularly meaningful. They only serve to illustrate that this type of "reg-

ular control" can be used to put together the combination of outgoing relations a node shall have.

To restart the cycle of either generating another $\texttt{want}$ or $\texttt{believe}$ node or terminating the derivation, (iii) and (iv) also create a new nonterminal labelled N.

We can see that each node must be given all of its outgoing $\texttt{arg0}$ and $\texttt{arg1}$ edges before another one is generated, making sure that the resulting AMR is acyclic (because $\texttt{manner}$, $\texttt{month}$, and $\texttt{day}$ edges only point to leaves). Every node generated by (iii), (iv), or (v) is immediately connected to an already existing node. Moreover, the new node generated by the second rule of (ii) is connected to a nonterminal labelled N_1 until that node, by (iii) or (iv), is connected to an older node. Using this, it follows by induction that only connected graphs are generated.

An example of a derivation using the boy-girl CHRG can be seen in Figure 5. The rule(s) used in every step are indicated above the derivation symbol ($\Rightarrow$) combined with the right-hand side index of the used rule (starting at 1). What variables are mapped to which labels throughout the derivation is shown implicitly. The resulting AMR is the previously discussed one in Figure 2.

It should be clear that this grammar generates the complete language of AMRs over our small domain: as we are only interested in generating acyclic graphs this is always possible by generat-

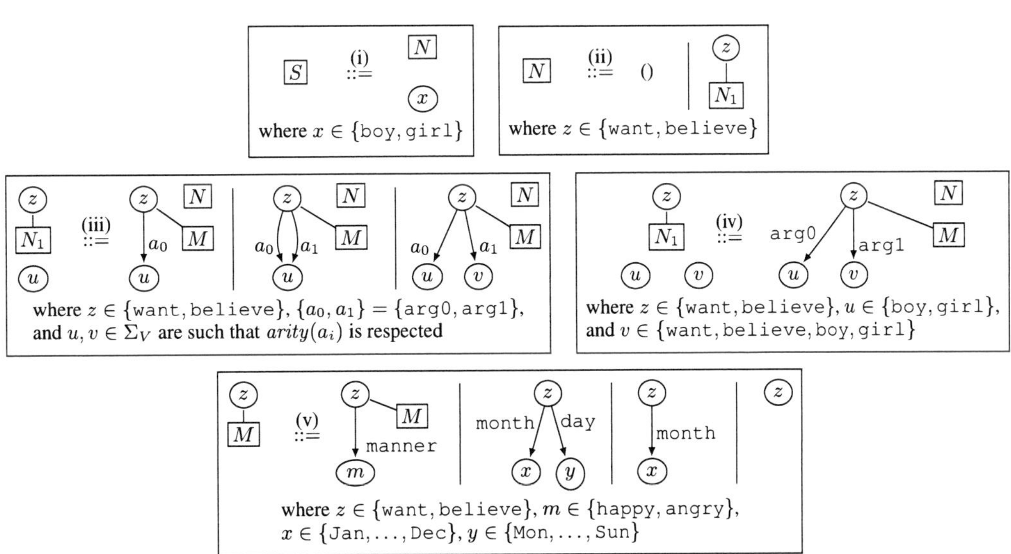

Figure 4: A boy-girl CHRG exemplifying general rule structures. Rules are named for later reference by a superscript on the operator '::='.

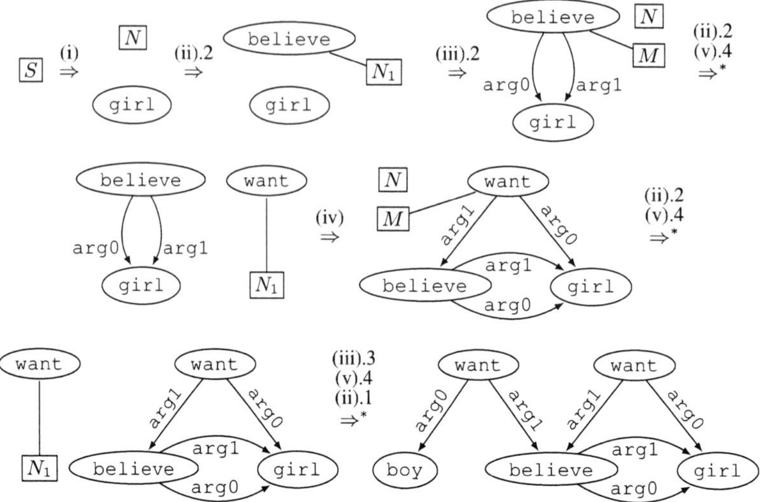

Figure 5: A derivation of an AMR using the boy-girl CHRG.

ing the nodes in reverse topological order. In other words, the CHRG constructed indeed generates the complete AMR language described above.

6 Generalisations

Let us now formulate some general rules about how to create a CHRG that generates AMRs over a given, finite domain of concepts and relations.

Let Σ_V contain the concept names of the domain and Σ_E its relations – these can be any sets as long as they are finite. Define the arity function of Σ as $arity(r) = \{c_i c_j \mid r$ is a valid relation from c_i to c_j for $c_i, c_j \in \Sigma_V\}$. The arity function is used to restrict which concepts can be connected using a particular relation. (For example, in the boy-girl case, we know that verbs cannot be agents and that persons cannot have agents. Thus, `want boy` and `want girl` are allowed in $arity(\text{arg0})$, but not `want believe` or `girl want`.)

As in the boy-girl CHRG, generation starts with the base case – a single leaf nondeterministically chosen from all the concept names that may appear as leaves. A nonterminal similar to N in the boy-girl case generates one new non-leaf node at a time. All of the outgoing edges to other non-leaf nodes are generated before returning to N. This guarantees acyclicity as it prevents nodes from being given outgoing edges to nodes generated posterior to them. As in the previous section, contextual rules are thus used to (1) enable the generation to refer back to previously generated nodes

by adding incoming relations and to (2) make sure that the AMRs are connected. Further leaves can only be generated along with the generation of an outgoing relation from another node.

We may also want for a CHRG to generate various combinations of outgoing relations from the latest non-leaf node (in the boy-girl grammar represented as z). This can be done similarly to the generation of `manner`, `month`, and `day` edges by M in Figure 4.

In view of the previous discussion the reader may wonder whether one will ever have the need to use nonterminal labels A with $|arity(A)| > 1$. It might seem that arguments can always be picked using contextual nodes. However, this selects targets exclusively based on their labels and is thus inappropriate if finer structural control is required. To illustrate this, let us add the object control verb `persuade` and the subject control verb `try` to our concept set (i.e., to Σ_V). We also need a new relation `arg2` to connect an occurrence of `persuade` to its indirect object, i.e., $arity(\text{arg2}) = \{\text{persuade}\} \cdot \Sigma_{\text{verb}}$ where $\Sigma_{\text{verb}} = \{\text{want}, \text{believe}, \text{persuade}, \text{try}\}$.

Recall that, whenever an `arg0` edge is created in one of the rules in Figure 4, the subsequent creation of further `want` and `believe` nodes is taken care of by a nonterminal N generated at the same time. To implement control, we use variants of these rules which, instead of N, use a nonterminal C with $arity(C) = \Sigma_{\text{verb}} \cdot \{\text{boy}, \text{girl}\}$. This nonterminal is attached to the two nodes of the `arg0` edge, thus remembering where the control should take place instead of floating freely.

Some of the new rules are illustrated in Figure 6. The rules in (vi) work like those in (iii), but create nonterminals labelled by C instead of N, in the way just described. A similar rule obtained from (iv) is left out to save space.

The remaining rules insert the control verbs: those in (vii) implement subject control by `try` whereas those in (viii) implement object control by `persuade`. Each of the rules corresponds to a succession of two rules in Figure 4, namely (iii).1 followed by rule (ii).2. The first of each pair of rules initiates another level of control whereas the second returns to the "uncontrolled" case. Note that we, for simplicity, drop the nonterminals M that should be attached to the control verbs to follow (iii).1 strictly. Also, there should be further rules corresponding to (iii).2, (iii).3, and (iv), which are omitted because they are constructed along the same lines as those shown in the figure.

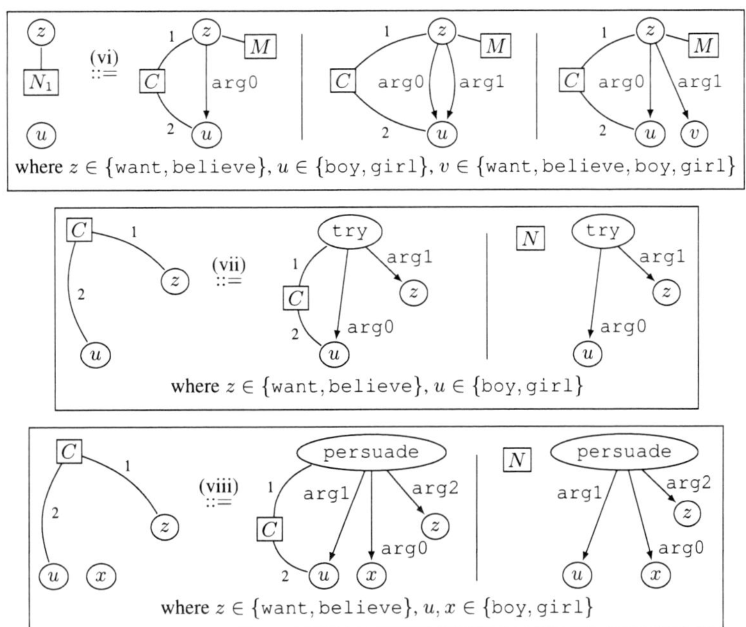

Figure 6: Rules implementing subject control (vii) and object control (viii).

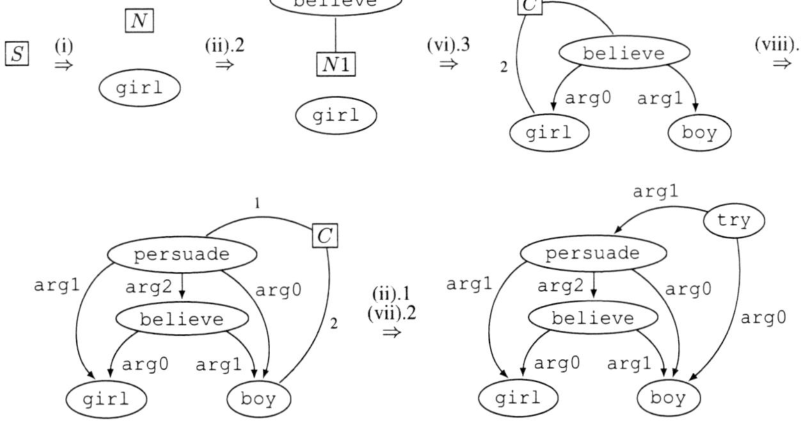

Figure 7: An example derivation using the rules in Figures 4 and 6.

Figure 7 shows an example derivation involving the new rules, the sentence being "The boy tries to persuade the girl to believe him." The reader may wish to add the remaining rules not shown in Figure 6, so that AMRs for sentences such as "The boy wants to persuade the girl to try to persuade the other girl to believe him" can be generated.

7 Discussion

Being able to generate complete AMR languages is a clear advantage of CHRGs compared to PTD parsable and rDAG grammars, and even over unrestricted HRGs. The latter can only generate graph languages of bounded treewidth, and despite the fact that real-world AMRs usually seem to be of small treewidth (Chiang et al., 2016) it does not seem to be justified to impose an a priori upper bound on their treewidth.

However, the advantage of CHRGs for modelling AMR languages exceeds the formal aspect of unlimited treewidth. In an HRG, nonterminal hyperedges have to keep track of all nodes to which edges shall (potentially) be attached later on in the process. This includes the implementation of non-local phenomena like anaphora, for which little if any structural control is required, thus resulting in an artificial increase not only in the rank of hyperedges but also in the number of rules. The latter may be significant, even exponential in the number of additional nodes to be kept track of, because in a right-hand side every nonterminal hyperedge would nondeterministically have to choose a subset of additional nodes to attach to. Even so, the number of nodes that can be kept track of is restricted by a constant depending on the rank of hyperedges. In contrast, CHRGs do not need to carry around such additional information at all as they can simply view antecedents as contextual nodes when it is time to insert a reference. The finer control provided by nonterminal hyperedges can be reserved for situations in which structural requirements must be met, such as implementing control verbs, quantifiers, and the like.

It remains to be seen whether the algorithmic properties of AMR-generating CHRGs are sufficiently good, especially when compared to HRGs. Since CHRGs generalise HRGs one may expect them to be algorithmically more demanding. However, the preceding discussion indicates that the converse may be true in practice. The efficiency of algorithms for analysing graphs with respect to a given (C)HRG depends most significantly on two things: the ranks of hyperedges and the number of rules (see in particular Chiang et al. (2013)). Thus, the greater algorithmic complexity of CHRGs may very well turn out to be outweighed by them requiring much smaller ranks and fewer rules, because the difference in size, as indicated above, will most likely be exponential in the desired number of potential antecedents.

The fact that CHRGs allow for structurally simpler rules may also make it possible to cast CHRGs like the one discussed here into a special form suitable for efficient analysis like shift-reduce parsing (Drewes et al., 2017) whereas the same may happen to be impossible for an HRG, even though the former has better coverage than the latter. Whether these possibilities can be realised is a question to be addressed by future work.

8 Conclusion

We have shown how CHRGs can generate complete AMR languages in cases where HRGs fail to do so because they do not provide appropriate means for the implementation of arbitrary coreferences. Whether CHRGs can generate complete AMR languages over arbitrary concept domains, including phenomena such as quantification while excluding structurally incorrect graphs, remains to be studied. In any case, the simplicity of the grammar discussed here seems to be promising. Future work, should investigate how efficiently problems such as the membership problem can be solved in practise for AMR-generating CHRGs. In this context, a better understanding of how quickly such CHRGs grow with the size of the input domain would also be valuable. If CHRGs indeed turn out to be a suitable device for AMR generation, a long-term goal should be to define a weighted version of CHRGs and to devise machine learning methods that make it possible to extract rule weights or even entire grammars from AMRbank.

Finally, it should be mentioned that there are other formalisms for defining languages of directed acyclic graphs that seem promising and should therefore be investigated for AMR modelling, e.g. DAG automata (Blum and Drewes, 2016, 2017; Chiang et al., 2016). In particular, it would be interesting to study the relative advantages and disadvantages of these options, and whether they can be combined in a fruitful way.

References

Laura Banarescu, Claire Bonial, Shu Cai, Madalina Georgescu, Kira Griffitt, Ulf Hermjakob, Kevin Knight, Philipp Koehn, Martha Palmer, and Nathan Schneider. 2013. Abstract meaning representation for sembanking. In *Proceedings of the 7th Linguistic Annotation Workshop and Interoperability with Discourse*. pages 178–186.

Henrik Björklund, Frank Drewes, and Petter Ericson. 2016. Between a rock and a hard place — parsing for hyperedge replacement DAG grammars. In *10th International Conference on Language and Automata Theory and Applications*.

Johannes Blum and Frank Drewes. 2016. Properties of regular dag languages. In *10th International Conference on Language and Automata Theory and Applications*.

Johannes Blum and Frank Drewes. 2017. Language theoretic properties of regular DAG languages. To appear.

Fabienne Braune, Daniel Bauer, and Kevin Knight. 2014. Mapping between English strings and reentrant semantic graphs. In *Proceedings of the Ninth International Conference on Language Resources and Evaluation*. pages 4493–4498.

David Chiang, Jacob Andreas, Daniel Bauer, Karl Moritz Hermann, Bevan Jones, and Kevin Knight. 2013. Parsing graphs with hyperedge replacement grammars. In *Proceedings of the 51st Annual Meeting of the Association for Computational Linguistics (Volume 1: Long Papers)*. pages 924–932.

David Chiang, Frank Drewes, Daniel Gildea, Adam Lopez, and Giorgio Satta. 2016. Weighted DAG automata for semantic graphs. Submitted.

Frank Drewes and Berthold Hoffmann. 2015. Contextual hyperedge replacement. *Acta Informatica* 52(6):497–524.

Frank Drewes, Berthold Hoffmann, and Mark Minas. 2012. *Applications of Graph Transformations with Industrial Relevance: 4th International Symposium, Revised Selected and Invited Papers*, chapter Contextual Hyperedge Replacement, pages 182–197.

Frank Drewes, Berthold Hoffmann, and Mark Minas. 2015. Predictive top-down parsing for hyperedge replacement grammars. In *Proceedings of the 8th International Conference on Graph Transformation*. pages 19–34.

Frank Drewes, Berthold Hoffmann, and Mark Minas. 2017. Predictive shift-reduce parsing for hyperedge replacement grammars. In *Proc. 10th Intl. Conf. on Graph Transformation (ICGT'17)*. Lecture Notes in Computer Science.

Frank Drewes, Hans-Jörg Krcowski, and Annegret Habel. 1997. Hyperedge replacement graph grammars. In *Handbook of Graph Grammars and Computing by Graph Transformation*, pages 95–162.

Annegret Habel. 1992. *Hyperedge replacement: grammars and languages*, volume 643. Springer Science & Business Media.

Anna Jonsson. 2016a. *Generation of Abstract Meaning Representations by Hyperedge Replacement Grammars – A Case Study*. Master's thesis.

Anna Jonsson. 2016b. On the generation of abstract meaning representations using polynomial-time parsable hyperedge replacement grammars. The Sixth Swedish Language Technology Conference.

Kevin Knight and Jonathan Graehl. 2005. An overview of probabilistic tree transducers for natural language processing. In *International Conference on Intelligent Text Processing and Computational Linguistics*. pages 1–24.

Irene Langkilde and Kevin Knight. 1998. Generation that exploits corpus-based statistical knowledge. In *Proceedings of the 36th Annual Meeting of the Association for Computational Linguistics and 17th International Conference on Computational Linguistics - Volume 1*. pages 704–710.

Nianwen Xue, Ondrej Bojar, Jan Hajic, Martha Palmer, Zdenka Uresova, and Xiuhong Zhang. 2014. Not an interlingua, but close: Comparison of English AMRs to Chinese and Czech. In *Proceedings of the Ninth International Conference on Language Resources and Evaluation*. pages 1765–1772.

Transforming Dependency Structures to LTAG Derivation Trees

Caio Corro   **Joseph Le Roux**

Laboratoire d'Informatique de Paris Nord,
Université Paris 13 – SPC, CNRS UMR 7030,
F-93430, Villetaneuse, France
`{corro,leroux}@lipn.fr`

Abstract

We propose a new algorithm for parsing Lexicalized Tree Adjoining Grammars (LTAGs) which uses pre-assigned bilexical dependency relations as a filter. That is, given a sentence and its corresponding well-formed dependency structure, the parser assigns elementary trees to words of the sentence and return attachment sites compatible with these elementary trees and predefined dependencies. Moreover, we prove that this algorithm has a linear-time complexity in the input length. This algorithm returns all compatible derivation trees as a packed forest. This result is of practical interest to the development of efficient weighted LTAG parsers based on derivation tree decoding.

1   Introduction

Lexicalized Tree Adjoining Grammars (LTAGs), that is TAGs where each elementary tree contains exactly one lexical anchor, have been proposed as an attractive formalism to model the phrase-structure construction in natural languages (Schabes et al., 1988; Abeille et al., 1990). An important property of lexicalized grammars is their ability to directly encode semantic information in combination operations. Borrowing the example provided by Eisner and Satta (2000), in the sentence "She deliberately walks the dog", the tree anchored with "dog" is combined to the tree anchored with "walks", see Figure 1a.[1] Thus, the object associated with a transitive realization "walks" can be restricted to a subset of allowed words, including "dog" but not "river".

Unfortunately, parsing with a LTAG is hardly tractable. Eisner and Satta (2000) proposed the best-known parsing strategy with a $\mathcal{O}(n^7)$ worst case time complexity and $\mathcal{O}(n^5)$ space complexity where n is the length of the input sentence. This is a major drawback for downstream applications where speed and low memory use is important. Moreover, by reducing boolean matrix multiplication to TAG parsing, Satta (1994) argued that obtaining a lower complexity bound for the latter problem is unlikely to be straightforward. Hence, parsing with weighted TAGs (Resnik, 1992) has received too little attention even though Chiang (2000) experimentally demonstrated their usefulness in the Penn Treebank parsing task. In order to bypass this major bottleneck, two main strategies have been explored. On the one hand, splittable grammars (Schabes and C. Waters, 1995; Carreras et al., 2008) are interesting because they have a lower asymptotic complexity than LTAGs. However, they cannot directly encode several properties that make TAGs linguistically plausible, such as cross-serial dependencies. In fact, they are restricted to context-free languages. On the other hand, a popular approach to speed up LTAG parsing is to include a preliminary step called supertagging: only a subset of tree fragments per word are retained as candidates, or exactly one in the most aggressive form (Chen and Bangalore, 1999). However, this pruning does not improve the asymptotic complexity of the parser.[2] Moreover, it is usually performed via local methods that can hardly take into account long distance relationships since lexical dependencies are unknown at this step. For instance, in the sentence "She deliberately walks, despite her hatred for quadruped mammals, the dog", capturing the transitive nature of the first verb is difficult without further analysis (Bonfante et al., 2009).

---

[1]We use a simplified grammar to ease the presentation.

[2]Intuitively, even when lexicon assigns only one elementary tree per word, a sentence can have several derivations which exhibit different tree structures.

Proceedings of the 13th International Workshop on Tree Adjoining Grammars and Related Formalisms (TAG+13), pages 112–121,
Umeå, Sweden, September 4–6, 2017. © 2017 Association for Computational Linguistics

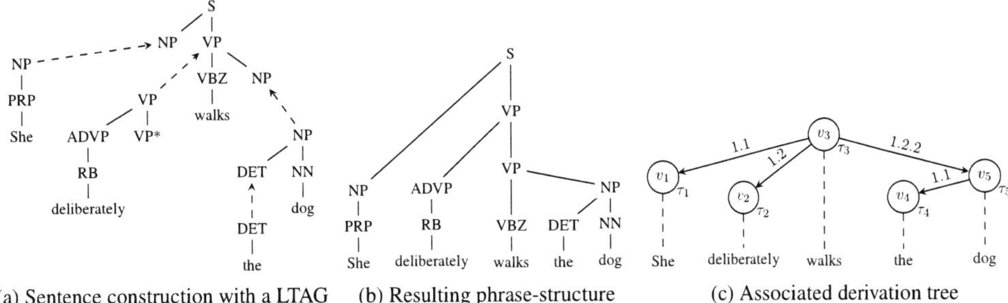

Figure 1: Phrase-structure of the sentence "She deliberately walks the dog", its construction thanks to a LTAG and the associated derivation tree. Dashed arrows in the left figure represent combination operations. Note that the derivation tree is a a labelled dependency structure.

In this work, we explore a component for a new alternative in fast and efficient LTAG parsing. Dependency structures can be interpreted as sets of derivation trees which share lexical composition operations. This property has already been investigated in order to propose efficient phrase-structure parsers under several formalisms (Section 2). The derivation tree induced by an LTAG analysis, as shown in Figure 1c, is a dependency structure exposing bilexical dependencies and labelled with elementary trees and operation sites (Section 3). As such, LTAG parsing can be seen as dependency parsing where both valid tree structures and valid labellings are constrained. Following the pipeline used in most labeled dependency parsers:

1. a parser starts by assigning a single head to each lexical item, without taking into account the grammar;

2. then, a parse labeler assigns elementary trees and operation sites.

Regarding the first step, seminal work of Bodirsky et al. (2005) showed that, ignoring labels, the derivation tree is an arborescence[3] that can be characterized thanks to two structural properties: 2-bounded block degree and well-nestedness. Gómez-Rodríguez et al. (2009) introduced an algorithm with a $\mathcal{O}(n^7)$ time complexity for decoding this type of structures. Still, this is a dependency parsing problem hardly tractable for sentences longer than $15 \sim 20$ words. More recently, Corro et al. (2016) proposed an experimentally fast alternative based on combinatorial optimization and the maximum spanning arborescence problem. Either way, this means that it is now possible to obtain dependency trees that are compatible with LTAG parsing.

Still, we are left with the second step: the parse labeler. Our contribution is a novel algorithm for this second step that can infer elementary trees and operation sites (Sections 4 and 5) as a postprocessing step to build all compatible derivation trees, from which derived trees are completely specified. The time complexity in the length of the sentence is linear (Section 6).

2   Related work

Syntactic content must not be confused with the type of representation, as clearly argued by Rambow (2010). As such, phrase structures can be encoded into dependency-like structures as long as the transformation is correctly formalized. One example of this fact is the correspondence between derivation trees constructed from lexicalized grammar and bilexical dependency relations. However, the equivalence with dependency-based linguistic theories may not be as straightforward as the similarity in the type of representation suggests (Rambow and Joshi, 1997; Kallmeyer and Kuhlmann, 2012). Following this line of thought, we reduce LTAG parsing to dependency parsing where unannotated bilexical dependencies represents abstract attachment operations and dependency labels specify the type of attachment and the site of the operation on the head elementary tree.

Historically, many syntactic dependency treebanks have been built by transforming phrase-structures using head-percolation tables (Collins, 2003; Yamada and Matsumoto, 2003), and thus one could learn a dependency parser from a

---

[3]In the rest of the paper, we use *tree* to denote the linguistic object and *arborescence* to denote the graph-theoretic object. The term *tree* may be confusing because in graph theory it refers to an undirected type of graph.

phrase-structure treebank. More Recently, following this observation, Fernández-González and Martins (2015) proposed to encode constituents as bilexical dependency labels without relying on a grammar, solving the two problems jointly. In this setting, constituent parse tree is recovered from a labeled dependency parse, which makes it possible to use tools developed for dependency parsing. This is appealing because dependency parsing has received a considerable amount of attention recently and is now well understood. Moreover, dependency parsing is usually less complex than phrase-structure parsing, at least in practice if not asymptotically. This technique has been showed to be experimentally efficient but it may be argued that the lack of an explicit grammar may result in non-interpretable structures. For instance, the valency of a verbal predicate may be incorrect.

Another line of work used predicted bilexical dependencies as a filter for a standard grammar parser. Recently, Kong et al. (2015) applied this technique to Context-Free Grammars with lexical projections, ie. head-projections are specified in right-hand sides of production rules (Collins, 2003). The resulting algorithm is certified to have quadratic worst time-complexity but, in practice, they observed a linear running-time with respect to the sentence length. Our method is very close but with one major difference. In an LTAG derivation each word is assigned a single elementary tree, while in CFGs with lexical projections a word can anchor several rules. This observation provides us with way to improve the worst-case time complexity of our algorithm from cubic to linear with regards to the input length. We believe that this observation could also be adapted to the framework of Kong et al. (2015). Also, we can interpret the low-order dependency parsing model explored by Carreras et al. (2008) as a similar filtering procedure. However, they did not study the theoretical complexity benefit of their approach. Note that both of these works only handle context-free languages whereas we focus on a mildly-context sensitive formalism.

Guided parsing has been studied for TAGs and related formalisms like RCGs (Barthélemy et al., 2001). Our approach differs because the predefined dependency tree cannot be considered as a guide, nor an oracle, since it is not required to be a superset of the set of possible derivations. Also, we could see our method as an algorithm to compute the intersection of the tree language defined by an LTAG and the tree language consisting of a single dependency tree. In this way our method can be seen as an instance of the framework defined in (Nederhof, 2009).

Finally, we follow the common idea that derivation trees should be built directly and that a derived tree is a by-product of a derivation tree. See for instance Debusmann et al. (2004) which introduced LTAG parsing as a constraint satisfaction problem.

3 Lexicalized Tree Adjoining Grammar

In this section, we describe notions related to LTAG parsing that we will use to expose the parsing algorithm in Section 4. We assume the reader is familiar with the TAG formalism (Joshi, 1987; Joshi and Schabes, 1992). We start by defining TAGs, then we introduce the structure of derivation trees and finally we give an overview of parsing with LTAGs.

3.1 Definition

We define a LTAG as a tuple $\langle N, T, \Gamma^I, \Gamma^A, \Gamma^S, f_{OA}, f_{SA}, f_{SS} \rangle$ where:

- N and T are disjoint finite sets of non-terminals (constituents) and terminals (words), respectively;

- Γ^I and Γ^A are the finite sets of initial and auxiliary trees, respectively, built upon N and T and we define the set of elementary trees as $\Gamma \triangleq \Gamma^I \cup \Gamma^A$;

- $\Gamma^S \subseteq \Gamma^I$ is the set of start trees.

We use Gorn addresses[4] to index nodes and $p \in \tau$ is true if and only if address p exists in tree τ. We use the term *site* to refer to both the Gorn address and the corresponding node.

Each node of the elementary tree $\tau \in \Gamma$ is labelled with a non-terminal except exactly one leaf labelled with the terminal whose address is denoted $lex(\tau)$, called the *lexical anchor*. For any auxiliary tree $\tau \in \Gamma^A$, the address of its mandatory foot node is written $foot(\tau)$. Without loss of generality, we restrict Γ to binary trees only.

In order to control combination operations over nodes in Γ, we use the following functions:

- $f_{OA} : \Gamma \times \mathbb{Z}^+ \to \mathbb{B}$ specifies whether adjunction is obligatory at a site in a tree or not;[5]

---

[4] A Gorn address for a node is a sequence of integers from $\mathbb{Z}^+$ indicating a path from the root to the addressed node.

[5] $\mathbb{B}$ is the set containing boolean values true and false.

- $f_{SA} : \Gamma \times \mathbb{Z}^+ \times \Gamma^A \to \mathbb{B}$ specifies the trees that can be adjoined at a site;

- $f_{SS} : \Gamma \times \mathbb{Z}^+ \times \Gamma^I \to \mathbb{B}$ is a similar function for substitution.

To simply notation, we also use function f_{SA} and f_{SS} in order to check if a site is an adjunction or substitution site, and thus assume these functions check if the given site is a leaf or not.

The derived tree is built by combining elementary trees thanks to combination operations: substitution and adjunction. In this paper, we have to distinguish three different types of adjunction. A *wrapping adjunction* is the attachment of a sub-analysis which has lexical anchors on both sides of the adjoined auxiliary tree's foot node. Similarly, *left adjunction* and *right adjunction* restrict lexical anchors to the left and right of the foot node, respectively. [6]

3.2 Derivation tree

Given a sentence $s = s_1 \ldots s_n$ and a LTAG, a derivation tree is a dependency structure representing a valid parse of the sentence by means of elementary trees and combination operations. It is a directed graph $G = (V, A)$ with $V = \{v_1 \ldots v_n\}$ the set of vertices, v_i corresponding to word s_i. The set of arcs $A \subset V \times V$ describes a spanning arborescence: A contains $n-1$ arcs with no circuit and each vertex has at most one incoming arc. The unique vertex v_r without incoming arc is called the root vertex. The set of children of a vertex is defined as $children(v_h) = \{v_m | v_h \to v_m \in A\}$. Moreover, vertices are labelled with elementary trees and arcs with Gorn addresses. Vertex labels indicate supertag assignment, while arc labels specify adjunction or substitution sites. The derivation tree contains all necessary information to construct the derived tree. See Figure 1b and 1c for an example. Different derivation trees can induce the same derived tree.

We borrow notation and definitions from Corro et al. (2016). The *predecessor* of a vertex $v_i \in V$ is v_{i-1}. We refer to the vertex with the smaller (resp. larger) index in a set as the *leftmost* (resp. *rightmost*) vertex. The *yield* of a vertex $v_k \in V$ is the set of vertices reachable from v_k with respect to A, including itself. We note $(v_k)_{\Leftarrow}$ and $(v_k)_{\Rightarrow}$ the leftmost and rightmost vertices in the yield of

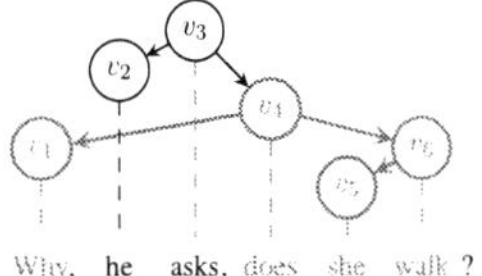

Notation	Value
$(v_4)_{\Leftarrow}$	v_1
$(v_4)_{\Rightarrow}$	v_6
$(v_4)_{\leftarrow}$	v_2
$(v_4)_{\rightarrow}$	v_3
$(v_4)_{\uparrow}$	v_3

Figure 2: Example of a 2-bounded block degree and well-nested dependency structure. The right table exposes notation we use for information we can extract about vertex v_4.

v_k respectively. The *span* of v_k corresponds to the set of vertices delimited by $(v_k)_{\Leftarrow}$ and $(v_k)_{\Rightarrow}$, possibly including vertices which are not in the yield of v_k. The *block degree* of a vertex set $W \subseteq V$ is the number of vertices of W without a predecessor inside W. The block degree of a vertex is the block degree of its yield and the block degree of an arborescence is the maximum block degree of its incident vertices.

Traditionally, dependency structures have been characterized as either projective (all vertices have a yield equal to their span) or non-projective (any arborescence). Previous work of Bodirsky et al. (2005) showed that the structure of G is highly constrained and can be characterized thanks to two finer-grained structural properties. First, G has a *2-bounded block degree*, meaning the block degree of G is less or equal to two. Given a vertex $v_k \in V$ with a block degree of 2, its *gap* is the vertex set of block degree 1 including a vertex with its predecessor and one with its successor in the yield of v_k. We note $(v_k)_{\leftarrow}$ and $(v_k)_{\rightarrow}$ the leftmost and rightmost nodes in the gap of v_k, respectively, $(v_k)_{\leftarrow} = (v_k)_{\rightarrow} = -$ if there is none (ie. v_k as a block degree of 1, thus its yield is equal to its span and contains no gap). An example is illustrated in Figure 2. Second, G is well-nested, that is two distinct sub-trees may not interleave. We will not explicitly use this property in the following and refer readers interested dependency structures characterization to Kuhlmann and Nivre (2006). However, we assume dependency structures to be well-nested. [7]

3.3 Parsing

So far we defined LTAGs and discussed the structure of derivation trees. We will now briefly focus

---

[6] These should not be confused with wrapping, left and right auxiliary trees which only describe the structure of auxiliary trees.

[7] More precisely, the algorithm proposed in Section 4 cannot parse ill-nested arborescences. Well-nestedness is a required property of the input.

on the parsing problem.

Given a sentence, this term may typically refer to three different but strongly related tasks via the notion of semi-ring parsing (Goodman, 1999). First, recognition: can this sentence be generated by a given grammar? Second, derivation forest parsing: decoding the set of all possible derivation trees. Third, weighted disambiguation: what is the best parse in the derivation forest given a scoring model? Our work was motivated by the weighted framework, but can generalize to others with some limitation.

Thus, a parser takes as input a grammar and a sentence. Because the LTAG chart-based parser has a high complexity, a standard approach is to use a pipeline system. First, a labeler assigns a single elementary tree to each lexical item. Then, the chart-based parser is run. This is merely a beam approach but it does not impact the assymptotic complexity of the second step. We propose to reverse this standard pipeline. In the first stage of the pipeline, which we consider already performed, a dependency parser assigns bilexical relations that we interpret as an abstract, ie. unlabelled, derivation tree. Contrary to the standard pipeline, this first step do not take into account the grammar, which lead to the development of an efficient parser based on combinatorial optimization (Corro et al., 2016). Next, the linear-time algorithm exposed in Section 4 can be used to assign elementary trees and operation sites.

4 Parsing with given bilexical relations

Not every labelled graph G describing an arborescence is a valid dependency tree. Indeed, many constraints must be satisfied in order to transform the derivation tree to into a derived tree. Since an arc $v_h \rightarrow v_m$ represents a combination operation of the tree of v_m into the tree of v_h, non-terminals at attachment sites must be equal and if the destination site is a leaf (resp. internal) node, the tree of v_m must be an initial (resp. auxiliary) tree, among others.

In this section, we propose a new algorithm for LTAG parsing with given bilexical relations in the form of a deduction system (Pereira and Warren, 1983). We formalize the algorithm as a recognizer: the **Goal** item can only be obtained if the input can be generated by the grammar. As usual, it can be implemented as a chart-based dynamic program with back-pointers in order to retrieve

every allowed derivation tree. Moreover, rules can be augmented with scores to build a weighted parser (Goodman, 1999).

Intuitively, our algorithm is an adaptation of the standard CYK variant for TAG parsing (Vijay-Shankar and K. Joshi, 1986; Vijay-Shanker and J. Weir, 1993), extended to handle constraints of lexicalized grammars. It is bottom-up in two ways. First, vertices of the dependency structure are traversed from leaves to root: a vertex is considered only after all its children. Second, given a vertex of the dependency structure, its corresponding elementary tree is visited in a similar fashion as in the CYK-like algorithm. The resulting algorithm has a linear time complexity. This is due to the fact that the maximum number of operations on a given elementary tree is bounded by its size. Thus, given a word, its maximum number of modifiers is not bounded by the sentence length but by the grammar, which leads to a tighter asymptotic complexity.

4.1 Item definition

Given a LTAG $\langle N, T, \Gamma^I, \Gamma^A, \Gamma^S, f_{OA}, f_{SA}, f_{SS} \rangle$, a sentence $s = s_1 \ldots s_n$ and the corresponding dependency structure $G = (V, A)$, items are 6-tuples of the form $[v_h, \tau, p, c, b_l, b_r]$ with:

1. **considered vertex** $v_h \in V$ in the dependency structure, corresponding to word s_h;

2. **elementary tree** $\tau \in \Gamma$, indicating the association of the anchor of τ with word s_h;

3. **Gorn address** $p \in \tau$ of a node in the elementary tree;

4. **combination flag** $c \in \{\bot, \top\}$ specifying if a combination operation has already been investigated $\top$ or not $\bot$ at node p;

5. **left boundary** $b_l \in V \cup \{l_h, g_h, \overleftarrow{g_h}, \overrightarrow{g_h}\}$ defines the left boundary of the yield of the item, which is discussed in more details below;

6. **right boundary** $b_r \in V \cup \{l_h, g_h, \overleftarrow{g_h}, \overrightarrow{g_h}\}$ defines its right boundary.

In most approaches, boundaries of the yield are given using integer indices. Instead, we use either vertices V or special values l_h, g_h, $\overleftarrow{g_h}$ and $\overrightarrow{g_h}$.[8]

---

[8] In the literature, the yield is often defined as a pair $\langle i, j \rangle$ meaning words s_{i+1} to s_j are covered. We do not follow this convention: a yield $\langle i, j \rangle$ indicates that words from s_i to s_j are covered.

If the left boundary of an item is node $v_m \in V$, the left (resp. right) boundary *position* is given by $(v_m)_{\Leftarrow}$ (resp. $(v_m)_{\Rightarrow}$). Special value l_h is used to indicate that the lexical anchor is used as a boundary, thus we define $(l_h)_{\Leftarrow} \triangleq h$ and $(l_h)_{\Rightarrow} \triangleq h$. The remaining values are used to indicate that the boundary is determined by the foot node span. The boundary is set to special value g_h if and only if the span of v_h has a gap, ie. $(v_h)_{\Leftarrow} \neq -$. Simply, we set $(g_h)_{\Leftarrow} \triangleq (v_h)_{\Leftarrow}$ and $(g_h)_{\Rightarrow} \triangleq (v_h)_{\rightarrow}$. Finally, note that vertices which do not have a gap in their span, can still be combined through left or right adjunction (see Figure 1c). Thus, we use $\overleftarrow{g_h}$ (resp. $\overrightarrow{g_h}$) in order to qualify the boundary of an sub-analysis which targets to be combined through a left (resp. right) adjunction. We set $(\overleftarrow{g_h})_{\Leftarrow} \triangleq (v_h)_{\Rightarrow} + 1$ and $(\overrightarrow{g_h})_{\Rightarrow} \triangleq (v_h)_{\Leftarrow} - 1$. Note that $(\overleftarrow{g_h})_{\Rightarrow}$ and $(\overrightarrow{g_h})_{\Leftarrow}$ are undefined, meaning that rules which use these values can not be applied.

Tree τ is a candidate for word represented by vertex v_h and its dependants if we can go up at its root node with boundaries equals to the span of v_h. In order to simplify notation, we use intermediate items to represent them. If the item has both boundaries defined, then:

Full:
$$\frac{[v_h, \tau, 1, \top, b_l, b_r]}{[v_h, \tau]} \quad \begin{array}{l}(b_l)_{\Leftarrow} = (v_h)_{\Leftarrow}, \\ (b_r)_{\Rightarrow} = (v_h)_{\Rightarrow}\end{array}$$

If $h \neq r$, this item will be a candidate to combination through substitution (resp. adjunction) if $\tau \in T^I$ (resp. $\tau \in T^A$), or similarly, if v_h has no gap (resp. has a gap). Two other intermediate items are used specifically to indicate that they are meaning to be combined through left and right adjunction:

Full left:
$$\frac{[v_h, \tau, 1, \top, b_l, \overleftarrow{g_h}]}{[v_h, \tau, \leftarrow]} \quad (b_l)_{\Leftarrow} = (v_h)_{\Leftarrow}$$

Full right:
$$\frac{[v_h, \tau, 1, \top, \overrightarrow{g_h}, b_r]}{[v_h, \tau, \rightarrow]} \quad (b_r)_{\Rightarrow} = (v_h)_{\Rightarrow}$$

A triplet item ending with the $\leftarrow$ (resp. $\rightarrow$) symbol is a candidate for left (resp. right) adjunction. Obviously, τ in the antecedent of both rules must be an auxiliary tree. This is constrained by the **Foot scan** rule introduced in the following subsection.

4.2 Axioms and goal

The first axiom is:

Lex scan:
$$\frac{}{[v_h, \tau, p, \top, l_h, l_h]} \quad \begin{array}{l}lex(\tau) = p, \\ \tau(p) = s_h\end{array}$$

meaning, for each vertex v_h and elementary tree τ, we instantiate items with compatible elementary trees, starting at the lexical anchor address. Moreover, we create items at the foot position of an auxiliary tree for vertices with a gap in their span:

Foot scan:
$$\frac{}{[v_h, \tau, p, \top, g_h, g_h]} \quad \begin{array}{l}\tau \in \Gamma^A, \\ foot(\tau) = p, \\ (v_h)_{\Leftarrow} \neq -\end{array}$$

Finally, the two last axioms are used to predict possible trees, on vertices without gap, that will be combined through left or right adjunction:

Foot scan left:
$$\frac{}{[v_h, \tau, p_{\top}, \overleftarrow{g}_h, \overleftarrow{g}_h]} \quad \begin{array}{l}\tau \in \Gamma^A, \\ foot(\tau) = p, \\ (v_h)_{\Leftarrow} = -\end{array}$$

Foot scan right:
$$\frac{}{[v_h, \tau, p_{\top}, \overrightarrow{g}_h, \overrightarrow{g}_h]} \quad \begin{array}{l}\tau \in \Gamma^A, \\ foot(\tau) = p, \\ (v_h)_{\Leftarrow} = -\end{array}$$

A proof completes if any tree $\tau \in S$ is a candidate for the root vertex v_r of the dependency structure:

Goal:
$$\frac{[v_r, \tau]}{} \quad \tau \in \tau^S$$

In the rest of this section, we describe rules governing allowed deductions.

4.3 Traversal rules

We start with tree traversal.[9] Obviously, the premise of any move operation is that we already checked any potential operation, marked by the $\top$ flag. Given address $p \cdot 1$ in tree τ, we consider two cases. First, if node $p \cdot 1$ do not have any sibling, ie. $p \cdot 2 \notin \tau$:

Move unary:
$$\frac{[v_h, \tau, p \cdot 1, \top, b_l, b_r]}{[v_h, \tau, p, \bot, b_l, b_r]} \quad (p \cdot 2) \notin \tau$$

Secondly, if $p \cdot 2$ exists, the siblings must share the same frontier:

---

[9]We assume binary elementary trees in the following presentation, but this can be generalized to other tree structures.

Move binary:

$$\frac{[v_h, \tau, p \cdot 1, \top, b_{l1}, b_{r1}] \quad [v_h, \tau, p \cdot 2, \top, b_{l2}, b_{r2}]}{[v_h, \tau, p, \bot, b_{l1}, b_{r2}]} \; (b_{r1})_{\Rightarrow} + 1 = (b_{l2})_{\Leftarrow}$$

4.4 Combination rules

Finally, let us concentrate on combination operations. The simplest, substitution, can only happen at substitution nodes and both attachment sites must be labelled with the same non-terminal. We assume that these conditions are checked by the f_{SS} function:

Substitute:

$$\frac{[v_m, \tau']}{[v_h, \tau, p, \top, v_m, v_m]} \; \begin{matrix} (v_m)_{\leftarrow} = -, \\ f_{SS}(\tau, p, \tau') \end{matrix}$$

The wrapping adjunction combines a modifier with a gap:

Wrapping adjoin:

$$\frac{[v_m, \tau'] \quad [v_h, \tau, p, \bot, b_l, b_r]}{[v_h, \tau, p, \top, v_m, v_m]} \; \begin{matrix} (v_m)_{\leftarrow} = (b_l)_{\Leftarrow}, \\ (v_m)_{\rightarrow} = (b_r)_{\Rightarrow}, \\ f_{SA}(\tau, p, \tau') \end{matrix}$$

Similarly, left and right adjunctions deal with vertices without gap:

Left adjoin:

$$\frac{[v_m, \tau', \leftarrow][v_h, \tau, p, \bot, b_l, b_r]}{[v_h, \tau, p, \top, v_m, b_r]} \; \begin{matrix} (v_m)_{\Rightarrow} = (b_l)_{\Leftarrow} - 1, \\ f_{SA}(\tau, p, \tau') \end{matrix}$$

Right adjoin:

$$\frac{[v_m, \tau', \rightarrow][v_h, \tau, p, \bot, b_l, b_r]}{[v_h, \tau, p, \top, b_l, v_m]} \; \begin{matrix} (b_r)_{\Rightarrow} = (v_m)_{\Leftarrow} - 1, \\ f_{SA}(\tau, p, \tau') \end{matrix}$$

Finally, adjunction may be skipped if this is allowed at the current site:

Null adjoin:

$$\frac{[v_h, \tau, p, \bot, b_l, b_r]}{[v_h, \tau, p, \top, b_l, b_r]} \; \neg f_{OA}(\tau, p)$$

5 Correctness

Since we use the deductive parsing framework, proving the correctness of the algorithm is straightforward from the notion of item invariant. Proving that every production rule maintains this invariant gives us soundness. Conversely, completeness can be proven by induction on items. In the following we explain our invariant.

An item $[v_h, \tau, p, c, b_l, b_r]$ can be deduced from the axioms through the application of deduction

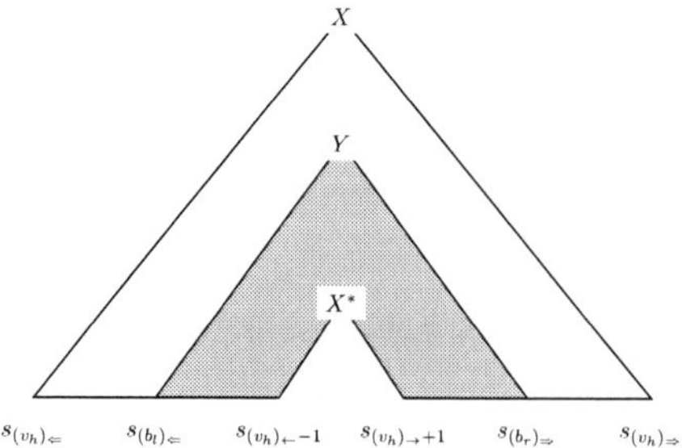

Figure 3: Invariant of an item $[v_h, \tau, p, c, b_l, b_r]$ when vertex v_h has a block degree of 2. X is the root node of τ, X^* its foot node and Y the node at address p. Only the gray area has been parsed.

rules if and only if, with respect to the input dependency parse, $\tau(p)$ can be derived to generate the subsequence of terminals and foot nodes:

- if address p in τ does not dominate a foot node, the subsequence is $s_{(b_l)_{\Leftarrow}} \cdots s_{(b_l)_{\Rightarrow}}$;

- if p in τ dominates a foot node and this is not a left nor a right adjunction $b_l, b_r \notin \{\overleftarrow{g_h}, \overrightarrow{g_h}\}$, the subsequence is $s_{(b_l)_{\Leftarrow}} \cdots s_{(v_h)_{\leftarrow}-1} X^* s_{(v_h)_{\rightarrow}+1} \cdots s_{(b_r)_{\Rightarrow}}$;

- if p in τ dominates a foot node and $b_l = \overleftarrow{g_h}$, the subsequence is $X^* s_{(v_h)_{\Leftarrow}} \cdots s_{(b_r)_{\Rightarrow}}$;

- if p in τ dominates a foot node and $b_r = \overrightarrow{g_h}$, the subsequence is $s_{(b_l)_{\Leftarrow}} \cdots s_{(v_h)_{\Rightarrow}} X^*$;

with X^* the foot node of τ. A visualization is provided on Figure 3.

6 Complexity

It is common practice to directly deduce space and time complexities from item structures and deduction rules, respectively. However, improving bounds in this setting may lead to algorithms difficult to understand. Thus, we decided to propose a rule-based algorithm that is simple to understand but which naively exposes a loose upper bound on its underlying complexity. In this section, we prove that the space and time complexities are linear.

In order to simplify the analysis, we suppose an agenda-based implementation (Kay, 1986). Each deduced item is placed in an agenda. While the agenda is not empty, the main loop pops out an item from it and add it to the chart. Then, the popped out item is tested as an antecedent, and all deduced consequents are pushed in the agenda if not already present in the chart. See Algorithm 1 for an outline of the algorithm.

Algorithm 1 Outline of the parsing algorithm. Lines 22-27 apply the **Binary move** rule.

```
 1:  A ← []                                    ▷ Empty Agenda
 2:  for 1 ≤ m ≤ n do                          ▷ Init
 3:     for τ ∈ Γ do                           ▷ Lex. scan
 4:        if τ(lex(τ)) = s_m then
 5:           A.push([τ, lex(τ), ⊤, l_m, l_m])
 6:        end if
 7:     end for
 8:     for τ ∈ Γ^A do                          ▷ Foot scan
 9:        if (v_m)_→ ≠ − then
10:           A.push([τ, foot(τ), ⊤, g_m, g_m])
11:        else
12:           A.push([τ, foot(τ), ⊤, ←g_m, ←g_m])
13:           A.push([τ, foot(τ), ⊤, →g_m, →g_m])
14:        end if
15:     end for
16:  end for
17:  C ← []                                     ▷ Empty Chart
18:  while |A| > 0 do
19:     [τ, p · 1, ⊤, b_l1, b_r1] ← A.pop()
20:     C.add([τ, p · 1, ⊤, b_l1, b_r1])
21:                                   ▷ apply Move binary
22:     Let b_l2 be the unique boundary with
            (b_r1)_⇒ + 1 = (b_l2)_⇐
23:        for [τ, p · 2, ⊤, b_l2, b_r2] ∈ C do
24:           if [τ, p, ⊤, b_l1, b_r2] ∉ C then
25:              A.push([τ, p, ⊤, b_l1, b_r2])
26:           end if
27:        end for
28:     ...Apply other rules...
29:  end while
```

Before analysing the algorithm complexity, we observe that the first value of an item, the current vertex, is redundant. Indeed, given the value of the left boundary (or right boundary), we can always retrieve the considered vertex in constant time. Obviously, when the boundary is given by a vertex v_m, we have $v_h = (v_m)_\uparrow$.[10] For special values allowed for boundaries, all indexed by a word position h, a similar operation is straightforward. For example, if a boundary is given by l_h then the considered vertex is v_h.

The algorithm has a maximum of two nested loops: the main while loop and for loops matching the second antecedent of binary rules. We first consider the while loop. An item is added to the agenda if only if it is not present in the chart. Thus, each item is considered exactly once by this loop. We note n the length of the input sentence, t the maximum number of nodes in an elementary tree $\tau \in \Gamma$ and $g \triangleq |\Gamma|$ the number of elementary trees.[11] Naively, the number of items is then bounded by $\mathcal{O}(n^2 tg)$. However, the number of combination operations which can be applied on an elementary tree is bounded by its number of nodes, provided we dismiss multiple adjunction sites. In this case, each node of an elementary tree may be adjoined or substituted on at most once. Thus, given an elementary tree and a left boundary, the number of values allowed as a right boundary is limited. This leads to a tighter bound on the number of items: $\mathcal{O}(\min(t, n)ntg)$.

We now investigate time complexity. **Move binary** is the only rule which has two free antecedents. Indeed, it is easy to see that, in the other binary rules, fixing the right antecedent always fixes the left one. For the **Move binary** rule, given the left antecedent, the number of candidates for the right one is naively bounded by $\mathcal{O}(n)$. However, we previously argued that, given a fixed left boundary, the maximum number of right boundary alternatives cannot exceed the number of sites on the current elementary tree. Thus, we can tighten the bound to $\mathcal{O}(\min(t, n))$.

In conclusion, the time complexity of the proposed algorithm is $\mathcal{O}(\min(t, n)^2 ntg)$, that is asymptotically linear with respect to the input sentence length.

7 Conclusion

We proposed an algorithm to compute LTAG derivations given a sentence and a dependency structure describing lexical attachments. We showed that under mild assumptions the worst-case complexity is linear in the length of the input.

This work fits in the more general project to interpret LTAG parsing as a dependency structure decoding problem. In this framework, it is common to label the graph structure in a post-processing step. Hence our approach relies on the availability of valid dependency structures for

---

[10] We assume that the data structure storing the dependency graph provides such function in constant time.

[11] Alternatively, g can be the number of elementary trees associated with the most ambiguous word of the vocabulary.

LTAGs, more precisely well-nested arborescences with 2-bounded block degree.

Experiments remain to be done in order to validate the practical interest of this approach. Moreover, one limitation of the pipeline system, as in all pipeline approaches, is the possibility of error cascades: the first step may decode a dependency structure that is not recognizable by the grammar while the sentence is grammatical.

We hope that this work will open new perspectives on parsing with lexicalized grammars. Exploring a similar technique, one may develop an efficient parsing algorithm for weighted Lexicalized Linear Context Free Rewriting System.

Acknowledgements

We thank the anonymous reviewers for their insightful comments. First author is supported by a public grant overseen by the French National Research Agency (ANR) as part of the Investissements d'Avenir program (ANR-10-LABX-0083). Second author, supported by a public grant overseen by the French ANR (ANR-16-CE33-0021), completed this work during a CNRS research leave at LIMSI, CNRS / Université Paris Saclay.

References

Anne Abeille, Kathleen Bishop, Sharon Cote, and Yves Schabes. 1990. A lexicalized tree adjoining grammar for english. Technical report, University of Pensylvania.

François Barthélemy, Pierre Boullier, Philippe Deschamp, and Éric Villemonte de la Clergerie. 2001. Guided parsing of range concatenation languages. In *Proceedings of 39th Annual Meeting of the Association for Computational Linguistics*. Association for Computational Linguistics, Toulouse, France, pages 42–49. https://doi.org/10.3115/1073012.1073019.

Manuel Bodirsky, Marco Kuhlmann, and Mathias Möohl. 2005. Well-nested drawings as models of syntactic structure. In *Proceedings of the 10th Conference on Formal Grammar (FG) and Ninth Meeting on Mathematics of Language (MOL)*. Edinburgh, UK, pages 195–203.

Guillaume Bonfante, Bruno Guillaume, and Mathieu Morey. 2009. *Proceedings of the 11th International Conference on Parsing Technologies (IWPT'09)*, Association for Computational Linguistics, chapter Dependency Constraints for Lexical Disambiguation, pages 242–253. http://aclweb.org/anthology/W09-3840.

Xavier Carreras, Michael Collins, and Terry Koo. 2008. *CoNLL 2008: Proceedings of the Twelfth Conference on Computational Natural Language Learning*, Coling 2008 Organizing Committee, chapter TAG, Dynamic Programming, and the Perceptron for Efficient, Feature-Rich Parsing, pages 9–16. http://aclweb.org/anthology/W08-2102.

John Chen and Srinivas Bangalore. 1999. New models for improving supertag disambiguation. In *Ninth Conference of the European Chapter of the Association for Computational Linguistics*. http://aclweb.org/anthology/E99-1025.

David Chiang. 2000. Statistical parsing with an automatically-extracted tree adjoining grammar. In *Proceedings of the 38th Annual Meeting of the Association for Computational Linguistics*. http://aclweb.org/anthology/P00-1058.

Michael Collins. 2003. Head-driven statistical models for natural language parsing. *Computational Linguistics, Volume 29, Number 4, December 2003* http://aclweb.org/anthology/J03-4003.

Caio Corro, Joseph Le Roux, Mathieu Lacroix, Antoine Rozenknop, and Roberto Wolfler Calvo. 2016. Dependency parsing with bounded block degree and well-nestedness via lagrangian relaxation and branch-and-bound. In *Proceedings of the 54th Annual Meeting of the Association for Computational Linguistics (Volume 1: Long Papers)*. Association for Computational Linguistics, pages 355–366. https://doi.org/10.18653/v1/P16-1034.

Ralph Debusmann, Denys Duchier, Marco Kuhlmann, and Stefan Thater. 2004. Tag parsing as model enumeration. In *Proceedings of the 7th International Workshop on Tree Adjoining Grammar and Related Formalisms*. Vancouver, Canada, pages 148–154. http://www.aclweb.org/anthology/W04-3320.

Jason Eisner and Giorgio Satta. 2000. A faster parsing algorithm for lexicalized tree-adjoining grammars. In *Proceedings of the Fifth International Workshop on Tree Adjoining Grammar and Related Frameworks (TAG+5)*. Université Paris 7, pages 79–84. http://www.aclweb.org/anthology/W00-2011.

Daniel Fernández-González and André F. T. Martins. 2015. Parsing as reduction. In *Proceedings of the 53rd Annual Meeting of the Association for Computational Linguistics and the 7th International Joint Conference on Natural Language Processing (Volume 1: Long Papers)*. Association for Computational Linguistics, pages 1523–1533. https://doi.org/10.3115/v1/P15-1147.

Carlos Gómez-Rodríguez, David Weir, and John Carroll. 2009. Parsing mildly non-projective dependency structures. In *Proceedings of the 12th Conference of the European Chapter of the ACL (EACL 2009)*. Association for Computational Linguistics, pages 291–299. http://aclweb.org/anthology/E09-1034.

Joshua Goodman. 1999. Semiring parsing. *Computational Linguistics, Volume 25, Number 4, December 1999* http://aclweb.org/anthology/J99-4004.

Aravind K Joshi. 1987. An introduction to tree adjoining grammars. *Mathematics of language* 1:87–115.

Aravind K Joshi and Yves Schabes. 1992. Tree-adjoining grammars and lexicalized grammars. *Tree Automata and Languages* .

Laura Kallmeyer and Marco Kuhlmann. 2012. A formal model for plausible dependencies in lexicalized tree adjoining grammar. In *Proceedings of the 11th International Workshop on Tree Adjoining Grammars and Related Formalisms (TAG+11)*. Paris, France, pages 108–116. http://www.aclweb.org/anthology/W12-4613.

Martin Kay. 1986. *Readings in Natural Language Processing*, Morgan Kaufmann Publishers Inc., San Francisco, CA, USA, chapter Algorithm Schemata and Data Structures in Syntactic Processing, pages 35–70. http://dl.acm.org/citation.cfm?id=21922.24327.

Lingpeng Kong, M. Alexander Rush, and A. Noah Smith. 2015. Transforming dependencies into phrase structures. In *Proceedings of the 2015 Conference of the North American Chapter of the Association for Computational Linguistics: Human Language Technologies*. Association for Computational Linguistics, pages 788–798. https://doi.org/10.3115/v1/N15-1080.

Marco Kuhlmann and Joakim Nivre. 2006. Mildly non-projective dependency structures. In *Proceedings of the COLING/ACL 2006 Main Conference Poster Sessions*. Association for Computational Linguistics, pages 507–514. http://aclweb.org/anthology/P06-2066.

Mark-Jan Nederhof. 2009. Weighted parsing of trees. In *Proceedings of the 11th International Conference on Parsing Technologies*. Association for Computational Linguistics, Stroudsburg, PA, USA, IWPT '09, pages 13–24. http://dl.acm.org/citation.cfm?id=1697236.1697239.

Fernando C. N. Pereira and David H. D. Warren. 1983. Parsing as deduction. In *21st Annual Meeting of the Association for Computational Linguistics*. http://aclweb.org/anthology/P83-1021.

Owen Rambow. 2010. The simple truth about dependency and phrase structure representations: An opinion piece. In *Human Language Technologies: The 2010 Annual Conference of the North American Chapter of the Association for Computational Linguistics*. Association for Computational Linguistics, pages 337–340. http://aclweb.org/anthology/N10-1049.

Owen Rambow and Aravind Joshi. 1997. A formal look at dependency grammars and phrase-structure grammars, with special consideration of word-order phenomena. *Recent trends in meaning-text theory* 39:167–190.

Philip Resnik. 1992. Probabilistic tree-adjoining grammar as a framework for statistical natural language processing. In *COLING 1992 Volume 2: The 15th International Conference on Computational Linguistics*. http://aclweb.org/anthology/C92-2065.

Giorgio Satta. 1994. Tree-adjoining grammar parsing and boolean matrix multiplication. *Computational Linguistics, Volume 20, Number 2, June 1994* http://aclweb.org/anthology/J94-2002.

Yves Schabes, Anne Abeille, and Aravind K. Joshi. 1988. Parsing strategies with 'lexicalized' grammars: Application to tree adjoining grammars. In *Coling Budapest 1988 Volume 2: International Conference on Computational Linguistics*. http://aclweb.org/anthology/C88-2121.

Yves Schabes and Richard C. Waters. 1995. Tree insertion grammar: A cubic-time, parsable formalism that lexicalizes context-free grammar without changing the trees produced. *Computational Linguistics, Volume 21, Number 4, December 1995* http://aclweb.org/anthology/J95-4002.

K. Vijay-Shankar and Aravind K. Joshi. 1986. Some computational properties of tree adjoining grammars. In *Strategic Computing - Natural Language Workshop: Proceedings of a Workshop Held at Marina del Rey, California, May 1-2, 1986*. http://aclweb.org/anthology/H86-1020.

K. Vijay-Shanker and David J. Weir. 1993. Parsing some constrained grammar formalisms. *Computational Linguistics, Volume 19, Number 4, December 1993* http://aclweb.org/anthology/J93-4002.

Hiroyasu Yamada and Yuji Matsumoto. 2003. Statistical dependency analysis with support vector machines. In *Proceedings of the IWPT (Volume 3)*.

Linguistically Rich Vector Representations of Supertags for TAG Parsing

Dan Friedman[*1]   **Jungo Kasai**[*1]   **R. Thomas McCoy**[*1]

Robert Frank[1]   **Forrest Davis**[2]   **Owen Rambow**[3]

[1]Department of Linguistics, Yale University

[2] Columbia University

[3] DSI, Columbia University

{dan.friedman,jungo.kasai,richard.mccoy,robert.frank}@yale.edu

fld2111@columbia.edu

rambow@ccls.columbia.edu

Abstract

In this paper, we explore several techniques for producing vector representations of TAG supertags that can be used as inputs to a neural network-based TAG parser. In the simplest case, the supertag is encoded as a 1-hot vector that is projected to a dense vector. Secondly, we use a tree-recursive neural network that is given as input the structure of the elementary tree. Thirdly, we use hand-crafted feature vectors that describe the syntactic features of each supertag, and project these to a dense vector. These three representations are learned during the training of a neural network TAG parser with a layer that embeds supertags in a low-dimensional space. Finally, we consider an embedding that is trained only on patterns of linear co-occurrence among supertags. By testing the resulting vector representations on the task of completing syntactic analogies, we show that these vector representations capture syntactically relevant information. While our linguistically-informed embeddings outperform atomic embeddings on the syntactic analogy task, we find that the same embeddings lead to only a slight improvement on the task of TAG parsing, indicating that the neural parser is able to induce useful representations of supertags from the data alone.

1 Introduction

In a Tree Adjoining Grammar (TAG), the set of elementary trees can be thought of as the possible lexical grammatical category assignments, much like the part of speech tags in a Context Free Grammar (CFG). However, the number of elementary trees is considerably larger than the category set typically found in other formalisms. In the TAG that is extracted from the Penn Treebank by Chen (2001), there are more than 4,700 distinct elementary trees, as compared to the 48 POS tags found in the Penn Treebank or even the 1,286 categories found in the Combinatory Categorial Grammar (CCG) bank (Hockenmaier and Steedman, 2007). While this is indeed a large number, the set of elementary trees in a linguistically adequate TAG is finely structured, with systematic relationships holding between elementary trees. Past work on grammar development in TAG has explored a variety of methods for capturing the relationships among and within so-called tree families (Vijay-Shanker and Schabes, 1992; Evans et al., 1995; XTAG Research Group, 1998; Becker, 2000), where all members of a tree family have the same basic argument structure (or have the same value for some other syntactic dimension) but differ from each other based on transformations such as passivization or *wh*-movement.

Under the approach suggested by Bangalore and Joshi (1999), the first step of TAG parsing, called supertagging, involves the assignment of elementary trees to lexical items. Given the high degree of supertag ambiguity and the fact that state-of-the-art TAG supertagging accuracy is only around 90% (using the bi-LISTM supertagger reported in Kasai et al. (2017)) as compared to 95% for CCG supertagging (Lewis et al., 2016), it is useful indeed if the parser can be made sensitive to the relationships between elementary trees. Certain errors in the supertagger might then not prove fatal to a parser if a single supertag can be interpreted as related to other elementary trees, providing potentially useful derivational options. Furthermore, if relations among supertags are encoded, problems of data sparsity during training

---

*Equal Contribution.

Proceedings of the 13th International Workshop on Tree Adjoining Grammars and Related Formalisms (TAG+13), pages 122–131,
Umeå, Sweden, September 4–6, 2017. © 2017 Association for Computational Linguistics

might be overcome; nearly half of the supertags present in the PTB WSJ Sections 1-22 appear only once, but they may be related to other supertags that occur more frequently.

Previous work by Chung et al. (2016) has proposed a way of exploiting relationships among supertags in a transition-based parser, by adding a series of hand-coded linguistic features that characterize properties of the elementary trees in the grammar. Such features had a beneficial effect on parser performance when used in conjunction with lexical identity, supertag identity, and POS tag.

In this paper, we demonstrate how the use of a neural network TAG parsing model, proposed by Kasai et al. (2017), facilitates the representation of similarity among supertags. The input to this parser is a sequence of 1-best supertags output by a bidirectional LSTM supertagger. As the first step in computation, the parsing network maps each supertag into a vector via an embedding matrix. Given a set of supertag vectors, we can study the similarity relations among them using methods similar to those that have been applied to lexical vectors by Mikolov et al. (2013a,b). For example, we can consider analogies between elementary trees that correspond to an operation of detransitivization, by asking whether an elementary tree representing a clause headed by a transitive verb (t27) stands in the same relationship to an elementary tree headed by an intransitive verb (t81) that a subject relative clause elementary tree headed by a transitive verb (t99) stands in to a subject relative headed by an intransitive verb (t109). By interpreting these elementary trees as vectors, we can express this analogy by $t27 - t81 + t109 \approx t99$. As we will demonstrate below, this formalization allows us to study the degree to which a representational scheme successfully captures a wide range of linguistic relationships among elementary trees.

Our discussion will compare four alternatives for constructing supertag embeddings. Three of these are trained in conjunction with parser, and differ only in the representation of the supertag input to the parser: atomic encodings of supertag identity, recursive encoding of the structure of the elementary tree, and the hand-coded linguistic features from Chung et al. (2016). The fourth derives embeddings via a GloVe-type model of distributional similarity (Pennington et al., 2014).

Recent work by McMahan and Stone (2016) has proposed a method to embed TAG supertags in the context of natural langauge generation. They utilize structural information of elementary trees through convolutional neural networks. Our recursive encoding is similar to their approach in that the embedding procedure respects tree structure of supertags. It should be noted, however, that our induction process runs in the opposite direction from that in McMahan and Stone (2016). In their application to natural language generation, the objective is surface realization from (unlabeled) dependency trees, whereas the problem of interest in this paper is derivation of dependency trees from surface realization.

In the next section, we briefly describe the parsing model that is the foundation of our experiments, along with our four methods for constructing supertag embeddings. Section 3 lays out our experimental set-up and Section 4 explains how we perform evaluation for supertag similarity and for parsing. Section 5 reports the results and discusses their implications.

2 Parsing Model and Embedding Construction

2.1 Neural Network TAG Parser

In our experiments, we make use of the neural network TAG parser from Kasai et al. (2017). This is an arc-eager shift-reduce parser that uses a feedforward neural network as an oracle. At each time step, the oracle takes as input the configuration of the parser, which consists of a fixed number of cells from the top of the stack and the front of the buffer, each containing a supertag. The parser's task is to construct a derivation tree from the individual supertags. This derivation is constructed in the usual way for transition-based parsers, namely through a series of actions (shift, reduce, left-arc, and right-arc). Left-arc and right-arc create links in the derivation tree, and these operations are further specified by the type of operation (substitution and adjoining) as well as the node within the elementary tree to which the operation applies (specified for substitution as 0-4, encodings of the deep grammatical role of the substitution site). The output of the network is a softmax layer, whose activations can be interpreted as a probability distribution over actions and labels. The parser is unlexicalized; the only information that the parser uses to determine its action is the supertags in the relevant cells of the stack and buffer. For the current work, we make use of the bi-LSTM supertagger discussed in Kasai et al. (2017), which is pre-trained on the WSJ Penn Treebank and does not vary across the experiments reported here. This supertagger provides as output a distribution over possible supertags for each word in a sentence.

Our focus in this paper is the first layer of the neural network, which maps each supertag in a parser configuration to a vector in a low-dimensional space. The input to the subsequent feed-forward layer is the concatenation of the dense vectors associated with the relevant cells in the stack and buffer. In our experiments, we vary the representation of the supertag that is provided as input to the parser, and retrain. Our hypothesis is that using a more linguistically informed embedding function will produce linguistically interpretable vector representations and improve parsing accuracy.

2.2 Atomic Embedding

The first type of embedding function we consider is the one from Chen and Manning (2014) (POS tags), Lewis et al. (2016); Xu (2016) (CCG supertags), and Kasai et al. (2017) (TAG supertags): here, each supertag in a parse configuration is represented as a one-hot column vector in $\mathbb{R}^{|V|}$, where $|V|$ is the total number of supertags. That is, each supertag is represented as a vector in which all entries are 0 except for a single entry, which is 1, corresponding to the integer ID of the supertag. The supertags are then projected into a lower-dimensional space by multiplying the one-hot vectors with an embedding matrix $L \in M_{d \times |V|}$. Thus each supertag t is associated with a distinct vector $x_t \in \mathbb{R}^d$, corresponding to a column in the embedding matrix L. The embeddings are then concatenated and passed to the feed-forward network. The embedding matrix L is trained jointly with the parser via the back-propagation algorithm to optimize the negative log-likelihood of outputting the correct parser actions. As a result, although the 1-hot encoding does not convey any information about relationships between supertags, the optimization process may favor an embedding matrix where the vector encoding of the supertag does convey such information to the degree to which similar supertags are best treated similarly by the parser.

2.3 Recursive Tree-Based Embedding

There are several theoretical drawbacks to using an atomic representation of supertags for parsing.

First, the parser makes no use of the linguistic meaning of supertags. Each supertag is considered to be a distinct entity, and the only way for the parser to associate similar supertags is to learn associations in the process of optimizing the training objective. Second, supertag data is sparse: of the 4,724 supertags in the TAG-annotated version of the Penn Treebank, 2,165 occur only once (Chen, 2001; Kasai et al., 2017). Because each supertag is considered to be distinct in the input layer, the parser will learn little information about nearly half of all supertags.

For these reasons we next consider a tree-recursive embedding layer that associates each supertag with a low-dimensional vector by passing the corresponding elementary tree through a recursive neural network. A recursive neural network (RNN)[1] in a bottom-up fashion, by using a neural network layer to combine the hidden states of the node's constituents (Goller and Kuchler, 1996; Socher et al., 2011). This recursive model has the advantage of both encoding linguistic information about supertags and also making efficient use of sparse data: even if a supertag appears infrequently in the corpus, the parser learns the parameters for embedding that supertag from encountering other, structurally similar supertags.

We use a syntactically untied RNN, similar to the model described in Socher et al. (2014). First, for each leaf node j in an elementary tree, the hidden state h_j is obtained by taking the jth column of an embedding matrix $E \in M_{d \times |L|}(\mathbb{R})$, where $|L|$ is the size of the vocabulary of labels used in TAG trees. Then, for each non-terminal node i, let $C(i)$ denote the set of children of node i and let $\mathrm{rel}(i, j)$ denote the relation between node i and its child j, defined by the label of i and the left-to-right position of j. For example, if i is a VP node and j is its leftmost child, then $\mathrm{rel}(i, j)$ is VP_0. The hidden state of node i is then

$$h_i = f\left(\sum_{j \in C(i)} W_{\mathrm{rel}(i,j)} h_j \right),$$

where f is a nonlinear activation function. We use tanh as the activation function in all of our experiments. $W_{\mathrm{rel}(i,j)}$ is a square matrix in $M_{d \times d}(\mathbb{R})$, so the resulting h_i is a vector in $\mathbb{R}^d$.

---

[1] Note that throughout this paper we use the abbreviation RNN to refer to recursive neural networks, not *recurrent* neural networks.

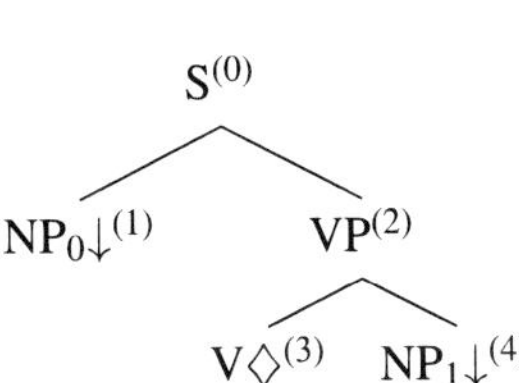

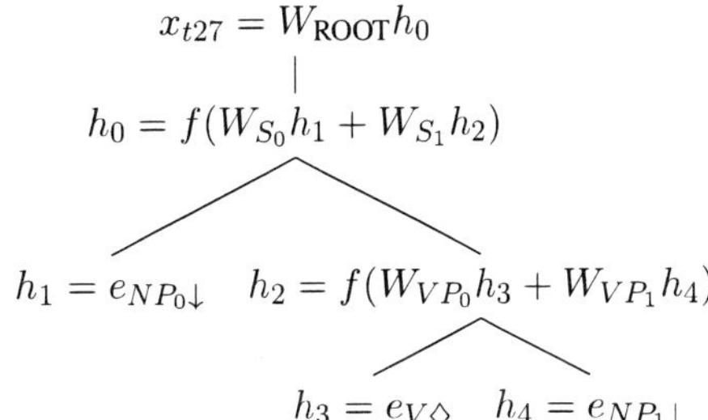

(a) The elementary tree for t27, a transitive verb. Nodes are indexed by their position in the breadth-first traversal of the tree.

(b) The recursive activation states for t27. e_l is the column in the embedding matrix E corresponding to label l.

Figure 1: Example of an RNN structure for generating a vector for a supertag.

Once the hidden state for each node in the tree has been computed, we obtain the final vector representation of the supertag by multiplying the hidden state of the root node by a special weight matrix $W_{\text{ROOT}} \in M_{d \times d}(\mathbb{R})$ and applying the activation function. Figure 1 gives an example of how the RNN is used to generate a vector representation for a transitive verb.

As with the Atomic Embeddings, the weight matrices W's and E can be learned during training of the parser via backpropogation.

2.4 Feature-based Embeddings

Our third representation of supertags and corresponding embedding derives from the hand-selected features associated with elementary trees in the grammar used in MICA (Bangalore et al., 2009). Each elementary tree is associated with a set of dimensions describing phrase structure, interpretation (e.g., subcategorization frame), and linguistic transformations (e.g., dative shift). The features include binary- and ternary-valued dimensions, whose values can be "yes", "no", or "NA," as well as dimensions whose values are a part of speech tag or a list of part of speech tags. See Chung et al. (2016) for the complete list of features.

To feed these feature vectors to a neural network, and to allow us to compare the vectors directly with our recursive embeddings, we convert each feature vector into a d-dimensional real-valued vector. We use two approaches to encoding features. First, we encode binary- and ternary-valued features as one-hot vectors. Since the other fields take on a much larger range of possible values, we choose to embed those features in a low-dimensional space. Specifically, we randomly initialize an embedding matrix $E \in M_{k \times |L|}(\mathbb{R})$,

where $|L|$ is the number of part of speech labels, and associate each part of speech label with a column in the matrix. We set k equal to 8. For fields with list values–for example, the list of adjunction nodes–we pad the list with zeros to ensure a fixed width representation. We concatenate the one-hot vectors and the label embeddings to obtain an n-dimensional feature representation of the supertag. In order to compare these vectors more directly with our d-dimensional recursive embeddings, we then multiply each vector by a weight matrix $W \in M_{n \times d}(\mathbb{R})$ to obtain a final, d-dimensional vector for each supertag. Once again, these embedding matrices are trained in conjunction with training of the parser.

2.5 GloVe Model

As a final point of comparison, we generate vector representations of supertags by training a GloVe model on our training corpus of supertags. The GloVe model is a widely used method for generating dense representations of words from corpus co-occurrence counts (Pennington et al., 2014). A GloVe model is trained on a co-occurrence table $X \in M_{|V| \times |V|}(\mathbb{R})$, where X_{ij} is the number of times word i appears in the context of word j. Context is determined by a hyperparameter c: an occurrence of word i is in the context of an occurrence of word j if that occurrence of i appears within the window of c words on either side of that occurrence of j. The cost function is

$$J = \sum_{i,j=1}^{|V|} f(X_{ij})(w_i^T \tilde{w}_j + b_i + \tilde{b}_j - \log W_{ij})^2.$$

f is a weighting function defined $f(x) = \min(1, (x/x_{max})^\alpha)$, where x_{max} and α are hyperparameters to be tuned. w_i and $\tilde{w}_j$ are the word vector and the context vector for words i and j, respectively. Similarly, b_i and $\tilde{b}_j$ are word and context biases for words i and j. Intuitively, the GloVe model attempts to learn a dense representation of words that will allow it to estimate the likelihood that any pair of words co-occur.

We train a GloVe model to convergence on the training portion of the TAG-annotated PTB training corpus, from which we were able to extract a co-occurrence table for supertags. We then use the resulting vectors to initialize an embedding matrix for the parser.

3 Experimental Setups

The experiments we conducted employ the same experimental setups as Kasai et al. (2017). Specifically, we follow the protocol from Chung et al. (2016) and Bangalore et al. (2009), and use the grammar and the TAG-annotated WSJ Penn Tree Bank extracted by Chen (2001). We use Sections 01-22 as the training set, Section 00 as the development set, and Section 23 as the test set. The training, development, and test sets comprise 39832, 1921, and 2415 sentences, respectively.

We use a publicly available string representation of supertags to associate each supertag with an elementary tree.[2] We consider the label of a node in an elementary tree to consist of the part of speech tag as well as the deep argument position and the node type, if relevant. For example, an NP node marked for substitution with a deep argument position of 0 will be labeled "NP0s" and will be considered distinct from, for example, an NP foot node ("NPf"). The relation between a node i and a child j ($\mathrm{rel}(i, j)$) is then considered to be the label of i subscripted by the index of j in the ordered list of children of i.

We implement the recursive neural network in TensorFlow and TensorFlow Fold, a library for creating TensorFlow models that take dynamically sized, structure inputs, like trees (Looks et al., 2017).[3] For the sake of comparison with the results in Kasai et al. (2017), we use an embedding size of 50 in all of our experiments and set all of the hyperparameters of the parser to be the same as the best performing ones. Specifically, we use two fully-connected layers with 200 hidden units each, dropout rates of 0.2 for the input and 0.3 for

the hidden layer, and 3 for the stack and buffer scope. We train stochastically using the Adam optimization algorithm and minibatches of size 100.

We use a publicly available TensorFlow implementation of the GloVe model (available at `https://github.com/GradySimon/tensorflow-glove`) training for 50 iterations. The hyperparameters are the same as those reported in Pennington et al. (2014). We use a context size of 5, which we found performed better than larger context windows.

4 Methods of Evaluation

4.1 Supertag Similarity and the Analogy Task

In the literature on word embeddings (e.g., Mikolov et al. (2013a) and Pennington et al. (2014)), word analogies are often used to evaluate whether the word embeddings have captured relevant semantic relationships between words. Similarly, we use syntactic analogies to evaluate whether our supertag embeddings have captured relevant syntactic relationships between supertags. To create our test set, we considered 9 different syntactic transformations that can relate two supertags either within or across tree families. These transformations are (i) subject relativization, (ii) object relativization, (iii) subject *wh*-movement, (iv) object *wh*-movement, (v) transitivization, (vi) infinitivization,[4] (vii) passivization with a *by* phrase, (viii) passivization without a *by* phrase, and (ix) dative shift.

For each of these transformations, we identified all pairs of supertags $(tag1, tag2)$ such that applying the transformation to $tag1$ yields $tag2$. For example, if the transformation in question is subject relativization, an example of such a pair would be $t27$ (the supertag for the verb heading a transitive clause, such as *found* in *the boy found the treasure*) and $t99$ (the supertag for the verb heading a transitive subject relative clause, such as *found* in *the boy who found the treasure*). We then generated syntactic analogies by matching up two such pairs that were both generated based on the same transformation; for example, the pairs $(t27, t99)$ and $(t81, t109)$ were both generated based on subject relativization, so combining these pairs gives

---

[2] The grammar is available here: `http://mica.lif.univ-mrs.fr`

[3] `https://github.com/tensorflow/fold`

[4] Infinitivization is the process of turning a verbal tree with a substitution node in subject position into a tree with an empty category in its subject position. It is called infinitivization because typically trees with empty subjects are anchored on infinitival verbs.

the analogy "$t27$ is to $t99$ as $t81$ is to $t109$", since conducting subject relativization on $t27$ generates $t99$ and conducting subject relativization on $t81$ generates $t109$. These trees are shown in Figure 2.

We wish to test if the linear relationships between our supertag embeddings properly express the syntactic relationships between the elementary trees these embeddings represent. To test if this is the case, we represent each of our analogies in the form of an equation; for example, the analogy "$t27$ is to $t99$ as $t81$ is to $t109$" would be written as $t27 - t99 \approx t81 - t109$. We then rearrange the equation so that there is only one term on the right-hand side to get $t27 - t99 + t109 \approx t81$. Each such equation becomes one test in the test set, and to test the equation we perform the arithmetic on the left hand side (here, $t27 - t99 + t109$) using the embeddings we have generated and evaluate how similar the resulting vector is to the desired right hand side (here $t81$).

We use two basic metrics for evaluating performance. The first metric (*% correct* in Table 1) is the proportion of analogies in the test set for which the most similar vector to the result of the computation is the desired one as measured by cosine distance. The second metric (*Avg. position* in Table 1) is the average rank of the correct answer within the ranked list of the embeddings that have the smallest cosine distance from the result of the computation.

In addition, it may be the case that the embeddings we generate are better for more frequent supertags due to a larger number of training examples on which to train the embedding. In order to ascertain the effects of frequency, we also compute both of the aforementioned metrics upon various restricted test sets consisting of only those analogies for which all four supertags in the analogy are among the n most common supertags in the training set for some value n, and where the ranked list of nearest neighbors is filtered to only include the n most common supertags. These metrics are listed as *% correct (top n)* and *Avg. position (top n)* in Table 1.

4.2 Parsing

We also present parsing results for models trained using each embedding scheme. We use the same neural TAG parser in each experiment, varying only the embedding layer. In all cases the parameters for the embedding layer are trained jointly with the parser. We give labeled and unlabeled attachment scores given gold supertags and predicted supertags from the supertagger in Kasai et al. (2017), using first a greedy decoding strategy and then beam search with a beam size of 16.

5   Results and Discussion

5.1   Analogy Task

Our results for the analogy task are given in Table 1. The GloVe vectors perform significantly worse than any other embedding, suggesting that co-occurrence information alone in the absence of information about grammatical structure is not enough to learn the kind of syntactic information tested in the analogy task.

The atomic embeddings trained with the parser learn a surprising amount of syntactic information about supertags. Despite initially having no information about the underlying syntactic meaning of supertags, the parser is able to discover syntactic features in the process of optimizing parsing performance on the training set. As we would expect, however, the performance of the atomic embeddings degrades quickly as n increases. The atomic embeddings get around two thirds of the analogy tests correct when the tests and answers are restricted to the top 300 supertags, but the embeddings perform considerably worse with larger values of n; the embeddings get only 4.62% accuracy on analogy tests drawn from the full set of supertags. This is consistent with what we would expect: the atomic embedding scheme treats each supertag as distinct from the others, and the majority of supertags are very sparse in the training data, so the parser has scarce information with which to learn better representations for rare supertags.

In contrast, both the recursive embeddings and the feature-based embeddings achieve very high accuracy on the analogy tests, with hardly any degradation with larger values of n. Of particular note is average position of the correct supertag in the ranked list of possible answers. For both the recursive and the feature-based embeddings, the target supertag is, on average, within the top 2 supertags most similar to the result of the analogy tests, even using tests drawn from the full set of supertags. This is not surprising given that both embedding schemes encode syntactic information about supertags by construction, so, unlike atomic embeddings, they produce meaningful representations of supertags even when the su-

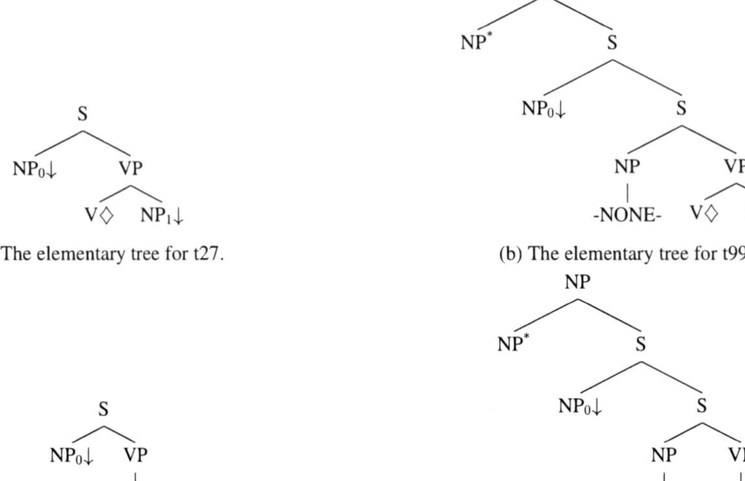

(a) The elementary tree for t27.

(b) The elementary tree for t99.

(c) The elementary tree for t81.

(d) The elementary tree for t109.

Figure 2: The supertags involved in the subject-relativization-based analogy $t27 - t99 + t109 \approx t81$.

Embedding	n	# equations	% correct	% correct (top n)	Avg. position	Avg. position (top n)
GloVe	300	246	0.00	0.00	71.21	101.30
Atomic	300	246	50.40	67.07	7.98	2.36
RNN	300	246	83.33	93.50	1.83	1.08
Features	300	246	**97.56**	**100**	**1.02**	**1.00**
GloVe	500	776	0.13	0.13	128.04	158.16
Atomic	500	776	36.47	41.62	22.15	5.67
RNN	500	776	82.09	91.36	1.68	1.15
Features	500	776	**95.62**	**99.87**	**1.05**	**1.00**
GloVe	4724	57220	0.02	–	2086.35	–
Atomic	4724	57220	4.62	–	289.48	–
RNN	4724	57220	83.34	–	1.61	–
Features	4724	57220	**94.14**	–	**1.10**	–

Table 1: Analogy task results.

pertags appear infrequently in the training data. The feature-based vectors in particular directly encode many of the dimensions we inspect with the analogy tests since several of the transformations used in the analogy tests, such as dative shift and passivization, are among the features derived from Chung et al. (2016) that we used.

The feature-based embeddings outperform the recursive embeddings. In particular, the feature-based embeddings seem to be even more robust with larger values of n. The recursive embeddings achieve above 90% accuracy when the space of possible answers is limited to the n most common supertags, but accuracy decreases by around 10% when we are allowed to consider all possible supertags. Using feature-based embeddings, how-

ever, accuracy remains above 94% for all tests, and is 100% for low values of n. One reason for this disparity might be that the recursive neural network, like the atomic embedding matrix, contains parameters that might be updated rarely; the RNN includes a weight matrix W for each parent-child relation, and some relations (e.g., VP_6) appear in only a few rare elementary trees. By contrast, the parameters trained to produce the feature-based embeddings are shared across all elementary trees, so the information learned by the parser generalizes better to rare or even unseen supertags.

Figures 3 and 4 provide a visual representation of certain atomic embeddings by plotting their first two principal components. They show how even the comparatively syntactically uninformed

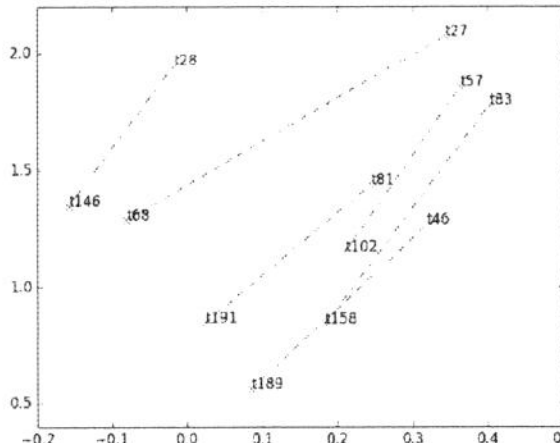

Figure 3: Graph of the first two principal components of the atomic embeddings for supertag pairs related by infinitivization.

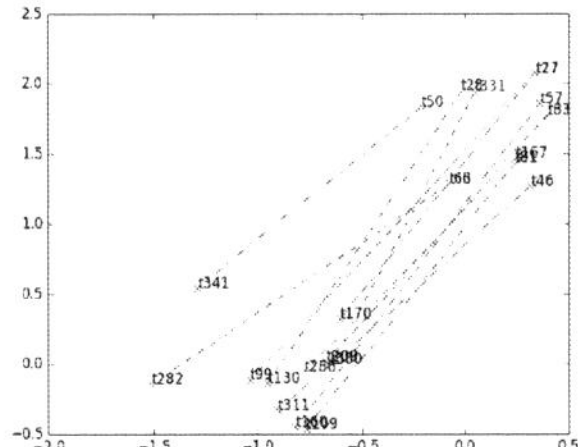

Figure 4: Graph of the first two principal components of the atomic embeddings for supertag pairs related by subject relativization.

method of using atomic embeddings still creates relatively consistent linear structure between pairs of vectors related by the same syntactic transformations.

5.2 Parsing

The parsing results are in Table 2. Although both of our linguistically informed representations of supertags (the RNN embeddings and the feature-based embeddings) significantly outperform the atomic embeddings at the analogy task, these large increases in performance do not carry over to the task of parsing. When parsing with gold supertags, the atomic embeddings outperform both the RNN embeddings and the feature-based embeddings. With predicted supertags, the feature-based embeddings do slightly overtake the atomic embeddings, but the increase in performance is quite small, while the RNN embeddings continue to achieve lower scores than the atomic embeddings.[5]

The fact that the parser achieves state-of-the-art performance even with the atomic embeddings suggests that the parser may be able to induce meaningful linguistic relationships from the data alone. If this is the case, it could explain why the linguistically informed embeddings do not make much of a difference in parsing: If the parser can learn the syntactic relationships between supertags that are most relevant to parsing solely from the data, then it does not require the additional linguistic information that the RNN-based and feature-based embeddings provide.

The fact remains that the linguistically informed embeddings do perform much better at the analogy task than the atomic embeddings. This may be because the analogies contain some syntactic constructions (such as relativization of an indirect object) that are relatively uncommon. Since these constructions are uncommon, it may be possible to attain high parsing performance without being able to properly handle such constructions. Thus, the atomic embeddings are able to yield high parsing performance despite having poorer analogy task performance. It would be interesting to parse only those sentences containing uncommon syntactic constructions to see if the linguistically informed embeddings outperform the atomic embeddings in such cases, since we would expect that the greatest improvements in performance from linguistically informed embeddings would come with the parsing of infrequent supertags, since the parser would not have much training data with which to learn representations of these supertags.

6 Conclusions and Future Work

We presented two techniques for computing real-valued vector representations of TAG supertags and applied these vector representations to the shift-reduce parsing system. We showed that the vectors produced by all but the non-syntactic GloVe embeddings performed reasonably well on the syntactic analogy task. The two representations which were built on the basis of explicitly represented linguistic structure, namely recursive tree-based embedding and feature-based embedding, on average produced the correct answer to an analogy question as one of its top two guesses, thereby outperforming both the distribution-based embeddings trained using the GloVe method and the atomic embeddings. On the parsing task, our two linguistically-rich embedding methods per-

---

[5]To see if the two types of linguistically informed embeddings are complementary, we also trained a model combining both RNN embeddings and feature-based embeddings, but there was no significant improvement over either of the models with only one form of embedding.

Parsing Model	Beam size	Dev Results				Test Results			
		Gold Stags		Predicted Stags		Gold Stags		Predicted Stags	
		UAS	LAS	UAS	LAS	UAS	LAS	UAS	LAS
bi-LSTM Stagger + MICA Parser	–	97.60	97.30	90.05	88.32	96.97	96.59	90.20	88.66
GloVe	1	93.01	91.97	88.35	86.46	–	–	–	–
Atomic	1	**96.82**	**96.45**	89.48	88.00	–	–	–	–
RNN	1	95.53	95.21	89.55	88.05	–	–	–	–
Features	1	94.90	94.74	**89.63**	**88.19**	–	–	–	–
GloVe	16	93.91	92.96	89.14	87.32	94.10	93.16	88.83	87.15
Atomic	16	**97.67**	**97.45**	90.23	88.77	**97.87**	**97.64**	90.25	88.90
RNN	16	96.39	96.10	90.30	88.81	96.73	96.46	90.24	88.85
Features	16	95.78	95.62	**90.36**	**88.91**	96.42	96.21	**90.31**	**88.96**

Table 2: Parsing results on the development and test sets. In each cell, shown is the mean of 5 trials with different initialization; the standard deviation for these values ranges from 0.01 to 0.26.

formed comparably with the atomic embedding method; the fact that the linguistically informed embeddings did not significantly improve performance compared to the atomic embeddings is an interesting indication that the parser can learn most relevant syntactic information purely from its training data. In the future, we will explore the application of these linguistically-rich embeddings in different systems of parsing such as the graph-based parsing system that has recently been successful in dependency grammar parsing.

Acknowledgments

We thank the anonymous reviewers for their helpful suggestions on this work.

References

Srinivas Bangalore, Pierre Boullier, Alexis Nasr, Owen Rambow, and Benoît Sagot. 2009. MICA: A Probabilistic Dependency Parser Based on Tree Insertion Grammars. In *NAACL HLT 2009 (Short Papers)*.

Srinivas Bangalore and Aravind K. Joshi. 1999. Supertagging: An Approach to Almost Parsing. *Computational Linguistics* 25:237–266.

Tilman Becker. 2000. Patterns in metarules for TAG. In *Tree Adjoining Grammars*, page 331342.

Danqi Chen and Christopher Manning. 2014. A fast and accurate dependency parser using neural networks. In *Proceedings of the 2014 Conference on Empirical Methods in Natural Language Processing (EMNLP)*. Association for Computational Linguistics, Doha, Qatar, pages 740–750. http://www.aclweb.org/anthology/D14-1082.

John Chen. 2001. *Towards efficient statistical parsing using lexicalized grammatical information*. Ph.D. thesis, Ph. D. thesis, University of Delaware.

Wonchang Chung, Suhas Siddhesh Mhatre, Alexis Nasr, Owen Rambow, and Srinivas Bangalore. 2016. Revisiting supertagging and parsing: How to use supertags in transition-based parsing. In *Proceedings of the 12th International Workshop on Tree Adjoining Grammars and Related Formalisms (TAG+12)*. pages 85–92.

Roger Evans, Gerald Gazdar, and David Weir. 1995. Encoding lexicalized tree adjoining grammars with a nonmonotonic inheritance hierarchy. In *Proceedings of the 33rd Annual Meeting of the Association for Computational Linguistics*. pages 77–84.

Christoph Goller and Andreas Kuchler. 1996. Learning task-dependent distributed representations by back-propagation through structure. In *IEEE International Conference on Neural Networks*. volume 1, pages 347–352.

Julia Hockenmaier and Mark Steedman. 2007. CCGbank: a corpus of CCG derivations and dependency structures extracted from the penn treebank. *Computational Linguistics* 33(3):355–396.

Jungo Kasai, Robert Frank, R. Thomas McCoy, Owen Rambow, and Alexis Nasr. 2017. TAG Parsing with Neural Networks and Vector Representations of Supertags. In *Proceedings of EMNLP*.

Mike Lewis, Kenton Lee, and Luke Zettlemoyer. 2016. Lstm ccg parsing. In *Proceedings of the 2016 Conference of the North American Chapter of the Association for Computational Linguistics: Human Language Technologies*. Association for Computational Linguistics, San Diego, California, pages 221–231. http://www.aclweb.org/anthology/N16-1026.

Moshe Looks, Marcello Herreshoff, DeLesley Hutchins, and Peter Norvig. 2017. Deep learning with dynamic computation graphs. *Proceedings of the International Conference on Learning Representations* https://openreview.net/pdf?id=ryrGawqex.

Brian McMahan and Matthew Stone. 2016. Syntactic realization with data-driven neural tree grammars. In *Proceedings of COLING 2016, the 26th In-*

ternational Conference on Computational Linguistics: Technical Papers. The COLING 2016 Organizing Committee, Osaka, Japan, pages 224–235. http://aclweb.org/anthology/C16-1022.

Tomas Mikolov, Ilya Sutskever, Kai Chen, Greg S Corrado, and Jeff Dean. 2013a. Distributed Representations of Words and Phrases and their Compositionality. In C. J. C. Burges, L. Bottou, M. Welling, Z. Ghahramani, and K. Q. Weinberger, editors, *Advances in Neural Information Processing Systems 26*, Curran Associates, Inc., pages 3111–3119. http://papers.nips.cc/paper/5021-distributed-representations-of-words-and-phrases-and-their-compositionality.pdf.

Tomas Mikolov, Wen tau Yih, and Geoffrey Zweig. 2013b. Linguistic regularities in continuous space word representations. In *Proceedings of the 2013 Conference of the North American Chapter of the Association for Computational Linguistics: Human Language Technologies (NAACL HLT 2013)*. Atlanta, page 746751.

Jeffrey Pennington, Richard Socher, and Christopher D Manning. 2014. Glove: Global vectors for word representation. In *Proceedings of the 2014 Conference on Empirical Methods in Natural Language Processing (EMNLP)*. pages 1532–1543.

Richard Socher, Andrej Karpathy, Quoc V Le, Christopher D Manning, and Andrew Y Ng. 2014. Grounded compositional semantics for finding and describing images with sentences. *Transactions of the Association for Computational Linguistics* 2:207–218.

Richard Socher, Cliff C Lin, Chris Manning, and Andrew Y Ng. 2011. Parsing natural scenes and natural language with recursive neural networks. In *Proceedings of the 28th International Conference on Machine Learning (ICML-11)*. pages 129–136.

K Vijay-Shanker and Yves Schabes. 1992. Structure sharing in lexicalized tree-adjoining grammars. In *Proceedings of the 14th conference on Computational linguistics*. Association for Computational Linguistics, volume 1, pages 205–211.

XTAG Research Group. 1998. A lexicalized tree adjoining grammar for English. Technical report, Department of Computer and Information Sciences, University of Pennsylvania.

Wenduan Xu. 2016. LSTM shift-reduce CCG parsing. In *Proceedings of the 2016 Conference on Empirical Methods in Natural Language Processing*. Association for Computational Linguistics, Austin, Texas, pages 1754–1764. https://aclweb.org/anthology/D16-1181.

TAG Parser Evaluation using Textual Entailments

Pauli Xu[1], **Robert Frank**[1], **Jungo Kasai**[1], and **Owen Rambow**[2]

[1]Yale University ({pauli.xu, bob.frank, jungo.kasai}@yale.edu)
[2]Columbia University (rambow@ccls.columbia.edu)

Abstract

Parser Evaluation using Textual Entailments (PETE, Yuret et al. (2013)) is a restricted textual entailment task designed to evaluate in a uniform manner parsers that produce different representations of syntactic structure. In PETE, entailments can be resolved using syntactic relations alone, and do not implicate lexical semantics or world knowledge. We evaluate TAG parsers on the PETE task, and compare our results to the state-of-the-art. Our TAG parser combined with structural transformations to compute entailments outperforms the CCG-based results on the development set, though it falls behind these results on the test set. The CCG parser makes use of a number of heuristics for entailment comparison, however. Adding such heuristics to our best TAG parser yields state-of-the-art results on the test set when using accuracy as a metric. This sensitivity to heuristics suggests that the PETE task may suffer from an unrepresentative development set, and that we need to improve upon formalism-independent parsing evaluation methods.

1 Introduction

There has been a flurry of recent work, involving neural network architectures, on parsing that has improved performance across a variety of frameworks that make different assumptions about the target output for the parsing process: Dependency grammar (Chen and Manning, 2014; Dyer et al., 2015; Andor et al., 2016; Kuncoro et al., 2017; Dozat and Manning, 2017), Combinatory Categorial Grammar (CCG) (Xu et al., 2015; Ambati et al., 2016; Lewis et al., 2016), Tree Adjoining

Grammar (TAG) (Kasai et al., 2017), Constituent structure (Dyer et al., 2017; Kuncoro et al., 2017)). However, it is as yet unknown the degree to which these improvements in parsing scores contribute to downstream NLP tasks. Moreover, since the different frameworks make different representational assumptions about the target of the parsing process, these results are not directly comparable.

Parser Evaluation using Textual Entailments (PETE) is a shared task from the SemEval-2010 Exercises on Semantic Evaluation (Yuret et al., 2013). The task was intended to evaluate syntactic parsers across different formalisms, focusing on entailments that could be determined entirely on the basis of the syntactic representations of the sentences that are involved, without recourse to lexical semantics logical reasoning or world knowledge. For instance, syntactic knowledge alone tells us that the sentence *Peter, who loves Mary, left the room* entails *Peter left the room* and *Peter loves Mary* but not, for example, that *Peter knows Mary* or that *Peter was no longer in the room*.

In this paper, we apply a number of TAG parsers to the PETE task. In the next section, we discuss the PETE task in further detail. Then in Section 3 we describe how we apply TAG parses to this task. Doing so requires a means of determining whether one TAG derivation entails another syntactically. We do this through a set of task-independent, linguistically-motivated transformations. After reviewing the TAG supertaggers and parsers we evaluate in Sections 4 and 5, we discuss our results in Section 6. We demonstrate that improvements in TAG parsing and supertagging do indeed contribute to improvements in the extrinsic PETE task, reaching state-of-the-art results in accuracy and near state-of-the-art in f-measure. In particular, we compare our results to the top-scoring systems of SemEval-2010, Cam-

Proceedings of the 13th International Workshop on Tree Adjoining Grammars and Related Formalisms (TAG+13), pages 132–141,
Umeå, Sweden, September 4–6, 2017. © 2017 Association for Computational Linguistics

bridge (Rimell and Clark, 2010) and SCHWA (Ng et al., 2010), both based on the Clark and Curran (2007) CCG parser, as well as a later system based on an HPSG-Minimal Recursion Semantics parser (Lien, 2014). We also conduct an error analysis and discuss limitations of TAG parsing in the context of this task.

2 The PETE Task

PETE (Yuret et al., 2013) is a restricted instance of the recognizing textual entailment (RTE) task, aimed at evaluating syntactic parsers. As in other RTE tasks, the task includes a set of *Text-Hypothesis* pairs, for which a system must determine whether or not the content of the Text entails the content of the Hypothesis. For PETE, the texts are individual sentences that were drawn from one of three sources: the Unbounded Dependency Corpus (Rimell et al., 2009), the Brown section of the Penn Treebank, and a list of sentences in the Penn Treebank on which the Charniak parser (Charniak and Johnson, 2005) performed poorly. A sentence S from these sources were selected as a candidate Text if S was misparsed by at least one phrase structure or dependency parsers that was state-of-the-art in 2009.

Given a candidate Text T, an associated Hypothesis H was constructed by identifying a pair of content words in T whose syntactic relationship is implicated in the difference between the gold parse and the incorrect parse. These words were then used to form a minimal sentence. If such a sentence involved a verb that required additional arguments, these could be filled in with indefinite expressions (*somebody*, *someone*, and *something*) or the verb could be passivized. Similarly, in the case of a head and modifier, a copular sentence, or one involving existential *there*, could be constructed. The resulting T-H pair would then be assigned the label 'YES' if the content words in H stand in a relation that is also present in the gold parse of T, and is otherwise assigned the label 'NO'. Each of the resulting T-H pairs were then given to five untrained annotators on Amazon Mechanical Turk and was retained in the dataset if three of them agreed on the presence or absence of the entailment. This left a dataset containing 367 T-H pairs (of which 51.83% were labeled 'YES'). These were then randomly divided into a development set containing 66 sentences and a test set containing 301 sentences. For more details on the construction process, see Yuret et al. (2013).

3 Applying TAG Parsing to PETE

Our TAG-based PETE system determines the entailment status of a T-H pair through the following four steps:

1. T and H are tokenized using the NLTK tokenizer (Bird et al., 2009).

2. T and H are supertagged and parsed, yielding derivation trees D_T and D_H.

3. Structural transformations are applied to D_T to yield a modified derivation graph D'_T.

4. Return 'YES' if D_H is a subderivation of D'_T.

In the following subsection, we describe the properties of the TAG grammar we use for supertagging and parsing and the derivation trees which result from the parser. We then describe the set of structural transformations that are applied to the Text's derivation tree, and define how we determine the subderivation property.

3.1 The TAG Grammar and Derivation Trees

Our experiments make use of the TAG grammar extracted from the Penn Treebank by Chen (2001), and used by the MICA parser (Bangalore et al., 2009). This grammar makes use of the representations developed for TAG starting with the XTAG project (XTAG Research Group, 2001). Positions for a lexical anchor's arguments are labeled with numbers that represent the argument's deep syntactic role. Deep subjects are labeled 0, direct objects and objects of prepositions are labeled 1 and indirect objects are labeled 2. These numbers remain constant across elementary trees that differ with respect to grammatical operations such as passivization and dative shift. In the elementary tree associated with the verb *played* in the passive sentence *The piano was played by Fred*, *the piano* will be labeled as role 1, while *Fred* will be labeled as role 0, just as in the active counterpart *Fred played the piano*.

In the derivation trees that result from a parse with this grammar, the arcs deriving from substitution are labeled by the deep role of substituted argument. Distinct labels in the derivation tree are used for the insertion of co-heads and of adjoining (which are not distinguished by locus of adjoining). Nodes in the derivation tree are associated with a token in the sentence and its corresponding elementary tree. A derivation tree can be thought of as a set of parent-child-relation triples.

Because of the use of deep labels in the grammar, the derivation trees of active and passive sentences will be structurally identical, apart from the identity of the elementary trees. As a result, the most common kind of mismatch between T and H in the PETE task, namely passivization, is handled directly by the parser without any further addition.[1]

3.2 Transformations on the Derivation Tree

As we noted earlier in the description of the PETE task, the sentences comprising T and H may differ in certain syntactically defined ways, giving rise to distinct TAG derivations. As a result, we apply a set of transformations to these derivations to make them more comparable. These were motivated by well-understood properties of TAG derivations as well as by divergences found in the T-H pairs in the development set. The phenomena dealt with by these transformations include NP modification, relative clauses, clausal complementation by predicative auxiliaries, predicative clauses, and coordination.

Modification in a TAG derivation is dealt with via adjoining. In the derivation tree, this will result in the modifier being a child of the head it modifies, with the arc labeled as adjunction. However, there are entailments where we will want to consider a different relationship between these words. For example, in the sentence *I reached into that funny little pocket* (from the PETE development set), the NP modifier *funny* is adjoined to *pocket*. However on a hypothesis like *The pocket is funny*, a predicative sentence, *pocket* is a 0-argument (i.e., subject) of *funny*. To deal with this mismatch, when we find a adjoining dependency between an N-headed tree and an auxiliary tree headed by an adjective, preposition or noun, we add a triple to the derivation tree in the reverse direction with the arc label 0, signifying that the head is a subject argument of the predicate (as it would be in a predicative sentence. This is depicted in the top line of Figure 1.

---

[1]Note however that the grammar does not retain argument labels across alternations like the causative-inchoative. In *The vase broke*, *the vase* will be argument 0, while in *I broke the vase*, it will be argument 1. Consequently, the entailment from the latter to the former would not follow directly from the parse. We would need PropBank-style argument labeling to recognize such cases.

When the elementary tree that is adjoined to the noun is a relative clause, we do something similar but slightly more complex. In order to determine the role that the reverse dependency should have, we must consult the properties of the relative clause elementary tree. For a subject relative, we add a 0-labeled arc, for an object relative, we add a 1-labeled arc, etc. This is shown on the second line of Figure 1. For adjectival passives that are adjoined to a noun (e.g., *the thrown ball*), we add a 1-labeled arc between the head noun and the verbal head, yielding the inference that *the ball was thrown*.

Sentential complementation in TAG derivations can be analyzed via either adjoining the higher clause into the embedded clause (necessarily so in cases of long-distance extraction from the embedded clause) or substituting the embedded clause in the higher clause. For example, on the third line of Figure 1, we see the derivation tree for *want to watch*, where *want* adjoins into *watch*. In order to normalize this divergence, for adjunction links involving a predicative auxiliary tree, we add a reverse link involving the 1 relation (i.e., that involving sentential complements).

For predicative clauses, like *trading is something we want to watch*, we want to allow for entailments like *we want to watch trading*. Given the transformations we have considered thus far, we will only derive that *we want to watch something* (via the relative clause and predicative auxiliary transformations). However, for auxiliary trees involving nominal predication (*A is B*), we add a derivational link that asserts that A stands in the same relation to predicates which have B as their argument. Thus, since *something* in our example is a 1-argument of *watch*, this rule will assert that *trading* is such an argument as well.

The final structural transformation involves coordination. Under the TAG analysis, VP coordination involves a VP-recursive auxiliary tree headed by the coordinator that includes a VP substitution node (for the second conjunct). We see part of the resulting derivation for the sentence *My host went over and stared out the window* in the top line of Figure 2. In order to allow the first clause's subject argument (as well as modal verbs and negations) to be shared by the second verb, we add the relevant relations to the second verb.[2]

---

[2]There is some indeterminacy concerning the label of the argument that should be added to the second verb, since this VP tree does not encode what role its subject would be, at

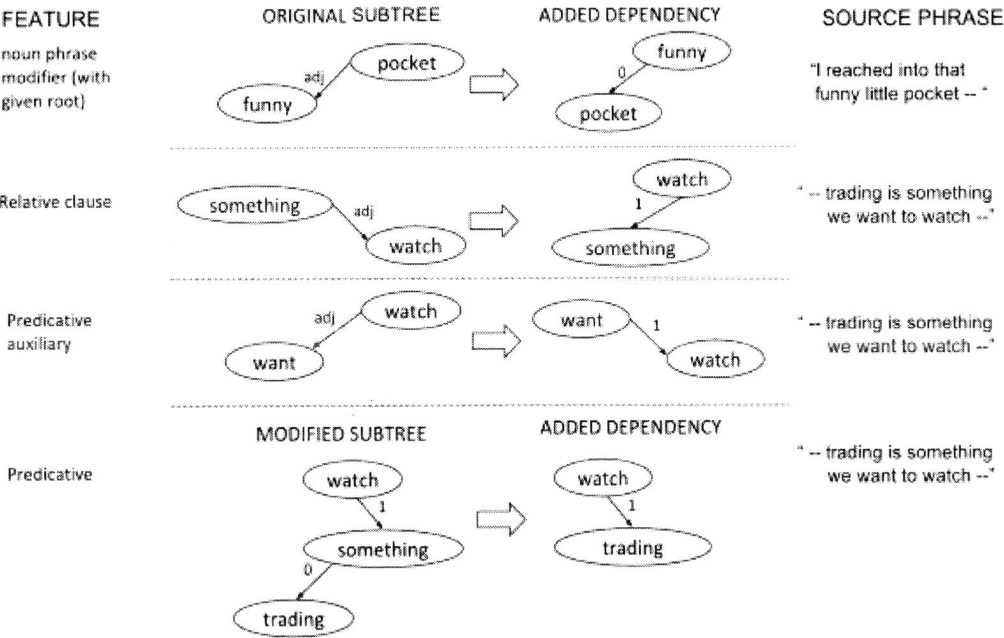

Figure 1: Structural transformations for features NP modifier, relative clause, predicative auxiliary, and predicative clauses

In the case of conjuncts that are the argument of some other predicate, seen in the bottom line of Figure 2 for the sentence *I like John and Mary*, the second conjunct (*Mary* in this example) will inherit any numbered parents of the first conjoined word.

This set of structural transformations is applied in the order in which we have presented it, so that the output of previous transformations can feed subsequent ones.

3.3 Recognizing Entailment

Having applied this series of transformations to the Text's derivation, we determine the presence or absence of an entailment essentially by asking whether the derivation of the Hypothesis is a subset of the derivation of the Text. This cannot however be done in the simplest fashion, because of possible superficial divergences between the derivations, concerning upper and lower case, the location of punctuation and the derivational

root, contraction, and the presence of extra functional material (auxiliary verbs or determiners). We therefore ignore these differences when we consider whether D_H is a subderivation of D'_T. We say that D_1 *is a subderivation of* D_2 iff for every $(w_1, w_2, Rel) \in D_1$

1. (Subset) there is a triple $(w'_1, w'_2, Rel) \in D_2$ such that $w_1 \approx w'_1$ and $w_2 \approx w'_2$; or

2. (Ignore root, punctuation and some function words) w_1 or w_2 is ROOT, a punctuation symbol or is lemmatized as one of *be, have* or *the* and is adjoined to its parent; or

3. (wildcard indefinites) $w_1 \in \{somebody, something, someone\}$ and there is a triple $(w'_1, w_2, Rel) \in D_2$ where w'_1 is a noun.

This definition depends on a near equality relation $\approx$ between holding between words a and b when

1. (lowercase) lowercase(a) = lowercase(b); or

2. (contraction) $a =$ ''s' and $b =$ 'is' or $a =$ 'n't' and $b =$ 'not' (or vice versa)

---

least not in the current grammar. As a result, we follow the heuristic of adding the subject with the same argument label that it has in the first conjunct, unless the second verb already has that argument, in which case we do not add anything. Neither do we add modals or negations if the second verb already has them.

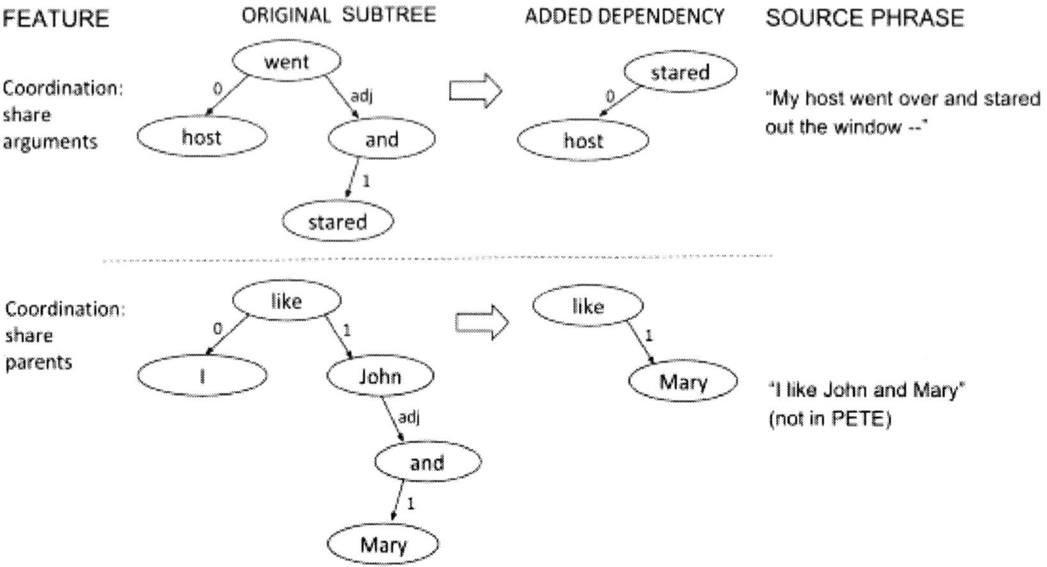

Figure 2: Structural transformations for coordination.

In Section 6.2, we report our main results based on the transformations and this notion of sub-derivation above, and compare those results to other systems. It is interesting to observe that the Cambridge system (Rimell and Clark, 2010) made use of the following heuristic procedure to determine whether the result of one CCG derivations (converted into a dependency structure) entails another:

1. Lowercase and lemmatize all tokens

2. From D_H, discard dependencies involving tokens not present in D_T.

3. Let core(D_H) be the dependencies with subject and object relations in D_H. Answer YES if $core(D_H) \subset core(D_T)$ and $D_H \cap D_T = \emptyset$, NO otherwise.

We see little a priori motivation for the whole-sale elimination of tokens in H not present in T, or for the restriction to subject and object relations. Nonetheless, for comparability, we also include separate results where we apply our structural transformations, but rather than using our notion of subderivation, instead follow the heuristic procedure adopted in the Cambridge system.

4 Supertagging Models

In the experiments reported below, we compare performance with two different supertaggers.

4.1 bi-LSTM Supertagger

The current state-of-the-art in TAG supertagging is reported in (Kasai et al., 2017), a model based on a bidirectional LSTM that get as input word sequences and predicted part of speech tags, and produces as output a probability distributions over the TAG supertags at the last softmax layer. This supertagger is trained on Section 1-22 in the TAG-annotated WSJ Penn Tree Bank extracted by Chen (2001). Its supertagging accuracy on Section 0 is 89.32%. For more details, see Kasai et al. (2017).

4.2 MICA Supertagger

The MICA supertagger is a maxent model, which uses lexical and part-of-speech attributes of words in a 3-word window on either side of the target word in a one-versus-all classification task. (The tagger does not use tagging history.) It achieves 88.52% accuracy on Section 0.

5 Parsing Models

We compare two parsing models here, one a neural network-based transition based parser, and another a chart parser.

5.1 Shift-Reduce Neural Network TAG Parser

The currently best performing TAG parser is reported in Kasai et al. (2017). This is an arc-eager shift-reduce parser that uses a feed-forward neural network as an oracle. At each time step, the oracle takes as input the configuration of the parser, which consists of a fixed number of cells from the top of the stack and the front of the buffer, each containing a 1-best supertag from the supertagger. The parser's task is to construct a derivation tree from the individual supertags. This derivation is constructed in the usual way for transition-based parsers, namely through a series of actions (shift, reduce, left-arc, and right-arc). Left-arc and right-arc create links in the derivation tree, and these operations are further specified by the type of operation (substitution and adjoining) as well as the node within the elementary tree to which the operation applies (specified for substitution as 0-4, encodings of the deep grammatical role of the substitution site). The output of the network is a softmax layer, whose activations can be interpreted as a probability distribution over actions and labels. It should be noted that the parser is unlexicalized; the only information that the parser uses to determine its action is the supertags in the relevant cells of the stack and buffer. We train this parser on WSJ Sections 1-22 similarly to the bi-LSTM supertagger. For more details, see Kasai et al. (2017).

5.2 MICA Parser

The MICA parser (Bangalore et al., 2009) is based on the SYNTAX system (Boullier, 2003), a full Earley parser with additional performance optimizations to deal with large grammars. The TAG grammar is transformed into a variant of a probabilistic CFG which allows Kleene stars on righthand side nonterminals to model adjunction. MICA produces a full parse forest and can output n-best parses, but in these experiments we only consider the 1-best parse.

5.3 Intrinsic task results

Table 1 shows that the NN parser outperforms the MICA parser on both the development set (Section 0) and the test set (Section 23).

6 Results and Discussions

The results of PETE are provided using both accuracy and f-measure for finding the entailment cases (which represent around 52% of the cases in the test set). Both metrics are reasonable metrics for the task, and the choice of primary metric depends on exactly why one wants to perform this extrinsic textual entailment task. The fact that both metrics are reasonable ways of assessing performance makes it more difficult to rank the systems, and we comment on both accuracy and f-measure.

6.1 Previous Results

The top part of Table 2 shows the previous results from the best performing systems in the 2010 SEMEVAL PETE task. All of these involve systems which make use of grammatical formalisms that provide rich linguistic description: the CCG-based Cambridge and SCHWA systems, and the HPSG/MRS-based system from Lien (2014). The Cambridge system does best by accuracy, the SCHWA system by f-measure. We note that the MRS system, which uses a grammar to derive a deeper semantics from the parse than we are using in our approach, gets the highest precision among these systems, but at the cost of a lower recall, as is often the case with grammar-based systems.

6.2 Performance

The middle part of Table 2 shows results using structural transformations and our notion of sub-derivation. We evaluate our system with three combinations of MICA and neural network supertaggers and parsers. In general, the more neural networks, the better. We note a large discrepancy between our results for development and test set (accuracies 78.8% v.s 68.4% for bi-LSTM+NN system). We note that all of our transformations and subderivation notion *increase* the number of yes-answers (by enlarging T or reducing H). Yet, our high precision and low recall values show that we miss a significant amount of 'yes'-answers. Thus, we evidently did not devise enough transformations; or perhaps our formulation of the criterion for entailment was not applicable to the test set.

6.3 Cambridge Heuristics

Because of the drop off when using our subderivation notion, we also explored the use of the Cambridge heuristics. The bottom part of Table 2

Parsing Model	Beam size	Dev Results				Test Results			
		Gold Stags		Predicted Stags		Gold Stags		Predicted Stags	
		UAS	LAS	UAS	LAS	UAS	LAS	UAS	LAS
MICA Stagger + MICA Parser	–	97.60	97.30	87.91	86.14	96.97	96.59	86.66	84.90
bi-LSTM Stagger + MICA Parser	–			90.05	88.32			90.20	88.66
bi-LSTM Stagger + NN Parser	1	96.82	96.45	89.48	88.00	–	–	–	–
bi-LSTM Stagger + NN Parser	16	**97.67**	**97.45**	**90.23**	**88.77**	**97.87**	**97.64**	**90.25**	**88.91**

Table 1: Intrinsic task parsing results on the development and test sets.

Supertagger	Parser	Entailment Identification	Dev Results				Test Results			
			%A	%P	%R	%F1	%A	%P	%R	%F1
Cambridge	Cambridge	Cambridge	66.7	78.6	57.9	66.7	**72.4**	79.6	62.8	70.2
SCHWA	SCHWA	SCHWA	78.8	84.2	**80.0**	**82.0**	70.4	68.3	**80.1**	**73.7**
MRS	MRS	MRS	77.3	92.6	65.8	76.9	70.7	88.6	50.0	63.9
bi-LSTM	Feed-Forward NN	Subderivation	**78.8**	**92.9**	68.4	78.8	68.4	90.7	43.6	58.9
bi-LSTM	MICA	Subderivation	74.2	92.0	60.5	73.0	66.1	**90.9**	38.5	54.1
MICA	MICA	Subderivation	68.2	90.5	50.0	64.4	63.8	87.3	35.3	50.2
bi-LSTM	Feed-Forward NN	Cambridge	66.7	73.5	65.8	69.4	72.4	85.4	56.4	68
bi-LSTM	MICA	Cambridge	69.7	75	71.1	73	**75.7**	88.1	61.5	72.5

Table 2: PETE task previous system scores and TAG system scores on dev and test sets, using structural transformations together with either our notion of subderivation or Cambridge's heuristics. Accuracy (A) gives the percentage of correct answers for both YES and NO. Precision (P), recall (R) and F1 are calculated for YES.

shows results using our structural transformations together with Cambridge heuristics for entailment identification.

Surprisingly, the system comprised of the neural supertagger and MICA parser is the best performing of our systems now, based on both accuracy and f-measure. In fact, it has the best result on accuracy compared to all systems, and is beat only by SCHWA in f-measure. We note that the development set results with the Cambridge heuristics are much lower than with our subderivation notion. This shows that the heuristics are crucial in this evaluation, and that they apply differently for the development and test sets.

6.4 Discussion

We note a disconnect from parser performances when we use the Cambridge heuristic. We can compare these results to the intrinsic evaluation results of Table 1. The bi-LSTM+NN model performs better on the intrinsic parsing evaluation metrics UAS and LAS (unlabeled and labeled attachment scores) than the bi-LSTM+MICA model. This is reflected in the results using structural transformations and our subderivation notion. However, this performance difference is inverted with structural transformations and Cambridge heuristics.

These results also document that the heuristics are crucial in this evaluation; the Cambridge heuristics do not appear to be motivated by general linguistic considerations. It appears to be important to understand the specific data chosen for the evaluation in order to derive good heuristics. As noted in Section 2, the T sentences were manually selected and transformed by the workshop organizers, in order to maximize the presence of certain syntactic phenomena known to be difficult. The entailment sentences (H) were constructed by hand using certain types of transformations, which are not completely specified in the task description. So there is a certain human idea (that of the workshop organizers) of "entailment" operating here which we are trying to reverse engineer. As we created our heuristics based only on the development set and kept to linguistically well-grounded notions, we ended up with low recall on the test set. Consequently, a good understanding of the data creation process will probably benefit performance. This is not to say PETE is not an interesting evaluation exercise, but it is (necessarily) limited in what it shows because of the data creation process.

6.5 Error analysis

6.5.1 Sources of Errors

In order to better understand the nature of the data set as well as what kinds of cases are causing problems for the neural network TAG parser, we inspected the examples from the development set that led to errors. A number of these were parsing errors without any simple diagnosis. However a number of the others were more intriguing.

One case in the development set was misparsed because of an attachment ambiguity: *It is the last of the three tests of manhood which the women impose* is supposed to entail that *the women impose tests*. The NN parser mistakenly attaches the relative clause headed by *impose* to the noun *manhood* instead of to *tests*. Such examples inevitably pose difficulties for our TAG-based parsers, since they are unlexicalized and therefore cannot make use of lexical information to make attachment decisions.

Another case in the test set involves the resolution of an anaphoric dependency: *Mary said 'I have seen'* is supposed to entail *Mary has seen something*. It is not clear to us that such cases should be treated as syntactically governed (or even if the entailment is correct – she could be mistaken or lying). If the verb is changed from *said* to *heard*, the entailment no longer goes through, suggesting that the lexical semantics of the embedding predicate, not to mention the indexical, is at issue.[3]

The fine-grained character of TAG derivations gives rise to derivational ambiguities that do not exist in other frameworks, but which can prevent the recognition of entailments. The development set contains the phrase *Japan hadn't come up with specific changes*. For reasons that are not clear to us at present, the phrasal verb is parsed correctly in H, with both *up* and *with* treated as co-heads to the verb *come*. However in the parse of T, which also contains this phrasal verb, only *up* is treated as a co-head, while *with* is treated as the head of a PP modifying the VP. One of the major differences between the Cambridge heuristics and our subderivation notion is the former's exclusive focus on "core arguments". This would allow misparses of this sort to be ignored, though it might pose problems for other cases.

Finally, we note a surprising parsing error arising from an error in Part of Speech tagging that is input to our supertagger. For the Hypothesis *Many bear resemblances to movie personalities*, both our bi-LSTM supertagger and the Stanford PCFG Parser (Manning et al., 2014) tag *many bear resemblances* as an adjective, noun, and verb (as in

---

[3]Rimell and Clark (2010) also cite the example discussed earlier, *trading is something we want to watch*, as anaphoric. However, we believe that a syntactic treatment can be given if predicative sentences are correctly recognized.

red bear runs), instead of the correct sequence determiner, verb, and noun. In the pre-trained Parsey McParseface model (Andor et al., 2016), *many bear resemblances* is tagged as an adjective, noun, and noun, a sequence that is locally possible, but not compatible with the sentence as a whole. This is surprising, given that POS tagging is often regarded as a largely solved task. This sentence is short and contains no unbounded dependencies, nor are its lexical items unusual.

6.5.2 Differences between Subderivation Condition and Cambridge Heuristics

To compare our subderivation condition to the Cambridge heuristics, we compared their respective test set results under the bi-LSTM+NN model: out of 301 entailment hypotheses, there are 20 cases that are correctly recognized by Cambridge heuristics but not our heuristics, and eight cases for which the opposite is true.

All of the 20 cases that Cambridge heuristics succeed in are True entailments that our heuristics mislabeled as False. Eight cases involve parser errors: either one of two coheads was mislabeled as an adjunction, a relative clause was misattached due to an attachment ambiguity, the grammatical function of the relative clause head is misidentified, or quotation marks are misparsed. Eight cases stemmed from the fact that our subderivation condition does not involve lemmatization of non-auxiliary verbs; hence it will fail on cases where a non-auxiliary verb is in different forms in the hypothesis and entailment, for example *Something includes* vs. *Examples include*. One further failure involved ellipsis, whose underlying structure our TAG parse does not allow us to recover: with the text *Consider the ingredients, not the name*, our parse attaches *not* to *name*, whereas with the hypothesis *Do not consider the name*, our parse attaches *not* to *consider*. Another case involved a difference in choice of determiner between the hypothesis and text, i.e., *the* vs. *an*. A final case involved what we take to be a contestable gold label, where the text *he would have a place to hang* is granted the hypothesis *he would hang* as a True entailment.

For these cases, the Cambridge heuristics succeed by lemmatizing all tokens (8 cases), by considering only the core arguments (11 cases), and by skipping an unseen token (1 case).

In contrast, the eight cases where Cambridge heuristics fail but where the subderivation condition succeeds are all instances of False entailments that Cambridge heuristics mislabels as True. Here, we see that the Cambridge heuristics lose relevant grammatical distinctions as a result of ignoring non-core arguments (6 cases) or skipping unseen tokens (2). For example, with the text *that is exactly what I'm hoping for* and hypothesis *I'm hoping exactly*, it is the non-core adjunction relation between *exactly* and *hoping* that makes the hypothesis False. Or, with the text *to live like Christians* and hypothesis *someone likes Christians*, it is the unseen token *someone* with the tokens *like* or *likes* that make the hypothesis False.

As observed in Table 2, precision is higher but accuracy is lower for our subderivation condition than for Cambridge heuristics under the bi-LSTM+NN model. Based on the inspection above, Cambridge heuristics result in gains and losses in entailment prediction as a result of their coarse-grained nature. Our subderivation condition fails to predict certain entailments because of its lack of verb lemmatization and its lack of robustness to "minor" parse failures.[4] However, its success is more directly tied to parser performance in a more linguistically rigorous way.

7 Conclusions and Future Work

In this paper, we have presented results for the PETE task using three systems for TAG parsing. Our results confirm previous exploration of this task in which parsers that provide rich linguistic descriptions fare best. Using linguistically motivated structural transformations and a subderivation criterion for detecting entailments, we have shown that TAG parsers can outperform the state-of-the-art on the development sets. However, on the test set, our results decrease sharply. In contrast, when we instead apply the heuristics used by the (previously) best performing CCG-based system (Cambridge) to detect entailment, we obtain accuracy results that surpass the state-of-the-art on this task. These results demonstrate that heuristics greatly affect task performance.

Since the development set is small, and we inferred structural transformations by observing the linguistic changes in the development set, there may be linguistic features that TAG parses do provide, but which we did not think to make use of. This reflects a common challenge for rule-based systems. More rules could be derived by observing the Penn Treebank and our particular grammar. We intend to analyze which cases the Cambridge heuristics perform better on than our subderivation-based heuristics; in so doing, we will treat the test set as an expanded development set, but we feel the provided development set is too small to truly understand this problem. We hope it will be possible to create a new test set in the future if there is sufficient community interest.

Finally, because our structural transformations are based on general properties of TAG derivations and are task-independent, this suggests that the utility of the current work may extend to other extrinsic tasks, such as semantic role labeling and textual entailment tasks that involve lexical semantics, world knowledge and logical reasoning. We leave such explorations for the future.

---

[4]Note that if we add lemmatization of main verbs to our subderivation condition, we gain 8 additional correct predictions (the aforementioned lemmatization failures), but lose no other cases. This would yield the following performance scores: accuracy 71.1, precision 91.6, recall 48.7, and F1 63.6.

References

Bharat Ram Ambati, Tejaswini Deoskar, and Mark Steedman. 2016. Shift-Reduce CCG Parsing using Neural Network Models. In *Proceedings of NAACL-HLT 2016*. pages 447–453.

Daniel Andor, Chris Alberti, David Weiss, Aliaksei Severyn, Alessandro Presta, Kuzman Ganchev, Slav Petrov, and Michael Collins. 2016. Globally Normalized Transition-Based Neural Networks. In *Proceedings of the 54th Annual Meeting of the Association for Computational Linguistics*. pages 2442–2452.

Srinivas Bangalore, Pierre Boullier, Alexis Nasr, Owen Rambow, and Benoît Sagot. 2009. MICA: A Probabilistic Dependency Parser Based on Tree Insertion Grammars. In *NAACL HLT 2009 (Short Papers)*.

Steven Bird, Ewan Klein, and Edward Loper. 2009. *Natural Language Processing with Python*. OReilly Media.

Pierre Boullier. 2003. Guided Earley parsing. In *Proceedings of the 8th International Workshop on Parsing Technologies (IWPT03)*. Nancy, France, pages 43–54.

Eugene Charniak and Mark Johnson. 2005. Coarse-to-fine n-best parsing and maxent discriminative reranking. In *Proceedings of the 43rd Annual Meeting on Association for Computational Linguistics*. pages 173–180.

Danqi Chen and Christopher D Manning. 2014. A Fast and Accurate Dependency Parser using Neural Networks. In *Proceedings of the 2014 Conference on Empirical Methods in Natural Language Processing (EMNLP)*.

John Chen. 2001. *Towards efficient statistical parsing using lexicalized grammatical information*. Ph.D. thesis, University of Delaware.

Stephen Clark and James R. Curran. 2007. Wide-coverage efficient statistical parsing with CCG and log-linear models. *Computational Linguistics* 33(4).

Timothy Dozat and Christopher D. Manning. 2017. Deep biaffine attention for neural dependency parsing. In *Proceedings of ICLR*. http://arxiv.org/abs/1611.01734.

Chris Dyer, Miguel Ballesteros, Wang Ling, Austin Matthews, and Noah A Smith. 2015. Transition-based Dependency Parsing with Stack Long Short-term Memory. In *Proceedings of the conference on Empirical Methods in Natural Language Processing (EMNLP)*. pages 334–343.

Chris Dyer, Adhiguna Kuncoro, Miguel Ballesteros, and Noah A. Smith. 2017. Recurrent Neural Network Grammars. In *Proceedings of NAACL*. pages 1249–1258.

Jungo Kasai, Robert Frank, R. Thomas McCoy, Owen Rambow, and Alexis Nasr. 2017. Tag parsing with neural networks and vector representations of supertags. In *Proceedings of EMNLP*. Association for Computational Linguistics.

Adhiguna Kuncoro, Miguel Ballesteros, Lingpeng Kong, Chris Dyer, Graham Neubig, and Noah A. Smith. 2017. What Do Recurrent Neural Network Grammars Learn About Syntax? In *Proceedings of the 15th Conference of the European Chapter of the Association for Computational Linguistics (EACL)*. pages 1249–1258.

Mike Lewis, Kenton Lee, and Luke Zettlemoyer. 2016. LSTM CCG Parsing. In *Proceedings of NAACL-HLT 2016*. pages 221–231.

Elisabeth Lien. 2014. Using minimal recursion semantics for entailment recognition. In *Proceedings of the Student Research Workshop at the 14th Conference of the European Chapter of the Association for Computational Linguistics*. Gothenburg, Sweden, page 7684.

Christopher D. Manning, Mihai Surdeanu, John Bauer, Jenny Finkel, Steven J. Bethard, and David McClosky. 2014. The Stanford CoreNLP natural language processing toolkit. In *Association for Computational Linguistics (ACL) System Demonstrations*. pages 55–60. http://www.aclweb.org/anthology/P/P14/P14-5010.

Dominick Ng, James W.D. Constable, Matthew Honnibal, and James R. Curran. 2010. SCHWA: PETE using CCG dependencies with the C&C parser. In *Proceedings of the 5th International Workshop on Semantic Evaluation*. page 313316.

Laura Rimell and Stephen Clark. 2010. Cambridge: Parser evaluation using textual entailment by grammatical relation comparison. In *Proceedings of the 5th International Workshop on Semantic Evaluation*. pages 268–271.

Laura Rimell, Stephen Clark, and Mark Steedman. 2009. Unbounded dependency recovery for parser evaluation. In *Proceedings of the 2009 Conference on Empirical Methods in Natural Language Processing*. Singapore, page 813821.

XTAG Research Group. 2001. A lexicalized tree adjoining grammar for English. Technical Report IRCS-01-03, Institute for Research in Cognitive Science, University of Pennsylvania.

Wenduan Xu, Michael Auli, and Stephen Clark. 2015. CCG supertagging with a recurrent neural network. In *Proceedings of the 53rd Annual Meeting of the Association for Computational Linguistics and the 7th International Joint Conference on Natural Language Processing (Short Papers)*. pages 250–255.

Deniz Yuret, Laura Rimell, and Aydin Han. 2013. Parser Evaluation Using Textual Entailments. *Language Resources and Evaluation* 47(3):639–659.

Author Index

Aggazzotti, Cristina, 31

Berglund, Martin, 94
Björklund, Henrik, 94
Bumford, Dylan, 71
Burkhardt, Benjamin, 21

Charlow, Simon, 71
Corro, Caio, 112

Davis, Forrest, 122
Drewes, Frank, 94, 102

Fowlie, Meaghan, 11
Frank, Robert, 122, 132
Friedman, Dan, 122

Han, Chung-hye, 43

Jonsson, Anna, 102

Kallmeyer, Laura, 21, 61
Kasai, Jungo, 122, 132
Koller, Alexander, 1, 11

Le Roux, Joseph, 112
Lichte, Timm, 21

McCoy, R. Thomas, 122

Needle, Jordan, 71

Osswald, Rainer, 61

Parmentier, Yannick, 84

Rambow, Owen, 122, 132

Sarkar, Anoop, 43
Savary, Agata, 84
Shieber, Stuart M., 31
Storoshenko, Dennis Ryan, 53

Waszczuk, Jakub, 84
White, Michael, 71

Xu, Pauli, 132

Association for Computational Linguistics
209 N. Eighth Street
Stroudsburg, Pennsylvania 18360

ISBN 978-1-5108-4757-6